W9-BBT-357

Trudeau

GEORGE RADWANSKI

Taplinger Publishing Company

New York

First published in the United States in 1978 by
Taplinger Publishing Co., Inc., New York, New York

Library of Congress Cataloging in Publication Data

Radwanski, George.
  Trudeau.

  Bibliography: p.
  Includes index.
  1. Trudeau, Pierre Elliott. 2. Prime ministers—Canada—Biography.
3. Canada—Politics and government—1945-   I. Title.
F1034.3.T7R32 1978b   971.06'44'0924 [B]
ISBN 0-8008-7897-3   78-67827

Contents

Author's Note

I HAVE long known that I wanted to attempt an in-depth study of Pierre Trudeau, who is at once one of the most intriguing and least understood leaders on the public scene. The only real question was whether to proceed now, or to await the end of his prime-ministerial career. Writing about a leader who is still in power has the obvious drawback that there is no way of telling how his story will end, and that consequently a certain number of judgments must be either tentative or conditional. The advantage, on the other hand, is that any insights such a study provides can assist in understanding and judging contemporary events; they can thereby have a usefulness beyond merely satisfying historical interest or curiosity.

This prime minister is now playing a central role in shaping the outcome of one of the most crucial moments in Canadian history. And yet, despite the fact that he has been in power for a full decade, serious gaps have continued to exist — even among those of us who must professionally report and assess his actions — in the knowledge of the man and his motivations. Because of this state of affairs, I have felt that there was more merit in proceeding than in waiting.

Partly to overcome some of the difficulties of writing about an unfinished career, and even more because it struck me as the area most in need of exploration, I have focussed this book rather on the man himself — his formative influences, his personality, his approach to the tasks of leadership, his political theory — than on the course of events. This is more a book about Pierre Trudeau than about "The Trudeau Years". The duration and outcome of the

Trudeau years are still uncertain, but the nature of the man and his motivations are unlikely to change substantially no matter what turn events may take. Even if Trudeau were to be defeated or to retire by the time this book is being read or re-read, all that would really be required, I believe, is a mental change to the past tense.

A few words about the preparation of this book are in order. In the spring of 1976, I submitted to Pierre Trudeau a written request for extensive interview access to him and to the key people around him, on a no-strings-attached basis. In the autumn of 1976, the request was accepted. In the intervening months, there had been no negotiation or even discussion as to the contents of the proposed book; the only question discussed was how much of the prime minister's time the project would require.

Trudeau agreed to give me a total of eight hours of interview time, and those interviews were conducted in eight one-hour sessions in the winter and spring of 1977. The interviews all took place in the prime minister's office in the Centre Block of the House of Commons. He and I were the only ones present in the room on each occasion, and I tape-recorded each session. The atmosphere was generally relaxed and informal, and our meetings took the form of free-flowing conversations rather than rigidly structured interviews.

Although I was alert to the possibility that a politician involved in this sort of project might try to limit himself to self-serving or manipulative answers, I instead found Trudeau remarkably candid and introspective throughout. He did not refuse to answer any of my questions, nor did he attempt to steer the conversations into advantageous subject areas of his own choosing. There were only a few instances in which he asked that his answers be off the record, and in each instance it was because the remarks were either critical of, or might cause embarrassment to, a third party; on each occasion, he permitted me to use the information, provided that I did not quote him directly. As far as I can determine, his co-operation was motivated simply by a desire to be understood more clearly — for better or worse — as the sort of individual and leader he really is; as several of his aides remarked to me, he was gambling that an accurate portrait of him would work to his advantage.

In addition to the time he himself spent with me, Trudeau also encouraged his aides, his key ministers, and even his sister to accede to my interview requests and to be candid in their replies to my questions. Some of these sources allowed me to quote them by name, others insisted on anonymity. I did not limit myself, of course, to interviews arranged through the prime minister's co-operation; to ensure a balanced view, my research extended to a variety of other sources, many of them hostile to Trudeau. I also supplemented my interviews with extensive study of the written record, particularly Trudeau's own writings and the transcripts of the interviews he has given since 1968.

It is important to stress that this is not an "authorized biog-raphy", in the sense of any outside editorial control or influence. Neither Trudeau nor anyone associated with him has seen a word of my manuscript prior to publication, and there has been no dis-cussion of any kind with him or his associates as to its contents.

A word about footnotes: Since this is not intended to be an academic work and since footnotes tend to be distracting for the general reader, I have tried to hold them to the inescapable mini-mum. I have used footnotes only to indicate the origin of substan-tively important quotations drawn from sources other than my own interviews. Where a substantive quotation is not otherwise identi-fied in a footnote or in the text, the reader may infer that it was made directly to me. In a few instances, I have spliced quotations from Trudeau's interviews with me together with related remarks he has made on other occasions; in those instances, I use footnotes to distinguish what was said to me from what originated elsewhere.

I am indebted to a great many people who have contributed to making this project possible. The prime minister and his associates were generous with their time and candour. Richard O'Hagan, Trudeau's senior advisor on communications, was the official liaison in arranging the access and information I requested. Jim McDonald, of the Prime Minister's Office, was most helpful in opening doors that might otherwise have remained closed to me. Bob Murdoch, the keeper of the prime minister's schedule, understood the time pressures under which I was operating and did what he could to schedule my interviews with Trudeau accordingly. A number of other people in the political system provided exceptionally valuable help for which, politics being what it is, I can best express my appreciation by not mentioning their names here.

David Tafler and Donald Carlson, respectively the editor and the publisher of the *Financial Times*, gave me a generous gift of time in which to write this book, and encouraged me throughout the project. Colleague and friend John Gray, of the Ottawa *Citizen*, read the manuscript and offered many helpful comments. Louise Stuart provided valued secretarial assistance. Doug Gibson, my editor at Macmillan, was a pleasure to work with.

Of an entirely different order of magnitude is my indebtedness to my wife, Julie. She typed interview transcripts, contributed invaluable insights and suggestions, debated my ideas with me until they were honed and refined, provided unceasing moral support during a project that was often as wearying as it was fascinating, and proved herself once again to be my best editor. Without her help, this book quite literally would not be.

Ottawa, January 1978

CHAPTER ONE

A Day in the Life

AT 9.07 on a typical Tuesday morning, the huge silver limousine — five sleek tons of special glass and armour-plating so thick it could withstand the blast of a grenade, with CAN 001 on its Ontario licence plates and with a small Canadian flag fluttering on its right front fender — glides through the stone gates and slips into the stream of traffic on Ottawa's Sussex Drive. With a single unmarked RCMP car following discreetly behind, it makes its way at a leisurely pace toward Parliament Hill, drawing only the most casual glances from civil servants on their way to work.

Inside, while retired army sergeant Dave Dempster expertly pilots the massive vehicle, Canada's fifteenth prime minister is still working at fully waking up. Pierre Trudeau is a slow starter in the morning; he resists getting up before eight whenever possible, and admits that he isn't at his best "until I have my coffee in my blood-stream". Leaning back against the comfortable grey velour uphol-stery, he glances casually at the front page of a newspaper in the few minutes it takes to travel from his residence to his office.

At 9.16, the limousine pulls up at the porticoed west entrance of Parliament's Centre Block. Trudeau steps out, and bounds up the two flights of stairs to his office with the lithe movements of an athlete. Meanwhile, in the third-floor prime-ministerial suite, Cécile Viau, his personal secretary since his days as justice minister, hears the slam of a car door and looks out the window to check. "Here he comes, Bob," she calls back over her shoulder.

Bob Murdoch, the affable young Vancouver lawyer who is Trudeau's executive assistant and keeper of his schedule, goes to the door of the suite to meet him. "Good morning, sir. Would you like me to call the staff?" A curt "Yes". The question is a daily ritual, the first of several fixed elements in the prime minister's schedule. His first appointment of the day, unless he has an earlier breakfast meeting, is always a brief session with his four key staff advisors. Some mornings he wants them summoned as soon as he arrives; on others, he wants a little time first to read briefing documents he hasn't gotten around to studying at home the night before.

On this July morning Murdoch is a little surprised by his boss's affirmative answer, because Trudeau was busy the previous evening hosting a dinner for visiting German Chancellor Helmut Schmidt. He asks the prime minister if he has had time to read his briefing papers. "More or less." Briefing papers are the mainstay of Trudeau's operation, and he must read some 1,000 pages of documents every week. He hates going into any discussion unprepared, and there is no way he could keep track by himself of the swirl of issues, proposals, and problems around him, so he relies on his staff to keep him informed. For each substantive meeting with a minister, an MP, or an outsider, he is given a concise memo outlining what is to be discussed, its background and implications, and either a suggested approach for him to take or a choice of options. For cabinet discussions, he receives the same cabinet document on each issue as all other ministers, plus an independent briefing memo from the Privy Council Office and sometimes a note from his political advisors.

Murdoch returns to his small cubbyhole of an office adjacent to Trudeau's, taps a button on his intercom, and tells his secretary to summon the four advisors. Trudeau, meanwhile, goes into his own office, his fingers automatically moving to open his shirt collar and loosen his necktie the moment he steps through the door; dress shirts and ties are an inevitable concession to the dignity of his post, but the concession is still made a little grudgingly.

As soon as he is settled behind his desk, Cécile Viau comes in to deliver a last-minute document for the meeting of the cabinet committee on priorities and planning later that morning. Only rush documents are sent through her; the rest are routed via admini-

strative assistant Mary Macdonald directly to his residence for
overnight attention.

Then Murdoch steps into the office, with a notepad on which he
has a list of a half-dozen items — mostly matters of scheduling —
he needs to discuss. Since Trudeau must have time to read the
newly arrived material, Murdoch mentions only the most urgent
items. Does the prime minister want to juggle his schedule slightly
to accompany Chancellor Schmidt to the airport and finish up any
left-over business with him en route in the limousine? "No, there's
no need. We said good-bye last night." Murdoch tells him that he
has tentative appointments with two MPs after the afternoon question period in the Commons, and that he may have to place a call
to President Carter some time in the afternoon. Then, for the time
it takes the four advisors to come from the Langevin Block, where
most of the staff of the Prime Minister's Office and the Privy
Council Office are based, across busy Wellington Street and the
broad lawn of Parliament Hill for the daily meeting, Trudeau is left
alone in the office to study his papers.

The prime minister's office, redecorated in 1973 by Arthur
Erickson, one of Canada's leading architects, is a spacious room
that conveys power through its air of serene elegance. Everything
in it is simple, clean-lined; everything in it is luxurious and expensive, the finest quality money can buy. The room is a large square
set on its point, and you enter at one of the corners. Along the
walls to the right and left of the door are sofas covered in rich,
yellowish-tan suede; a third and smaller sofa stands under the
window along the next wall on the right. In front of the sofa to the
right of the entrance is a low white marble table, on which stands
a pot of bright yellow chrysanthemums. Near the sofa on the left
is a similar-sized table, this one of chrome and glass, with another
splash of fresh yellow flowers. Chairs covered in the same yellowish-tan suede are arranged near the sofas.

The walls are panelled in handsomely carved, light honey-
coloured oak. They are unadorned except for an Eskimo tapestry
over one sofa, and a jutting wood carving of a black loon — a gift
Trudeau received on a visit somewhere and found so evocative of
the wilderness he loves that he had it mounted on his wall. At two

corners, there are little alcoves with built-in bookshelves. One carries mostly law-books and a few volumes of parliamentary debate; the other holds a scattering of general reference books, a large globe, framed pictures of Trudeau's family, and a small coloured statuette of a Mountie on horseback.

Directly opposite the entrance, across a broad expanse of thick beige carpet, is the huge, spindle-legged desk that was once Sir Wilfrid Laurier's. It is set diagonally across the corner of the square facing the door, and that corner is squared off by a built-in cabinet whose panelling conceals a water cooler, a small safe — and, usually, a box of chocolates to appease Trudeau's sweet tooth. The top of the light-coloured desk has been covered with the same suede as the furniture, and the large desk-chair is of the same material. The suede is used, too, in most of the furnishings atop the desk: a suede-edged desk blotter; a small stand-up frame that holds Trudeau's neatly typed schedule for the day; an 8½" x 11" looseleaf binder containing his tentative schedule for the week; and the "in" and "out" baskets. Also atop the desk are pictures of Trudeau's three children in a simple silver frame, and a marble pen-holder with a built-in clock. Built into the underside of the desk are little buttons for unobtrusively summoning either his secretary or a messenger. Behind it is a sophisticated telephone-intercom console which enables him to reach any of his key aides at the touch of a single button, and any other official in the PMO-PCO complex by tapping out a two-digit combination. Also near the desk — but out of sight — is another telephone, with a gold circle instead of a dial, which is the hot-line to Washington.

A large window to the left of the desk looks out on the front lawn of Parliament, and the United States Embassy and the exclusive Rideau Club on Wellington Street. Through the window to the right of the desk Trudeau can see the Gatineau River and Hull, Quebec, on the other side. Near the left window is a large Canadian flag on a pole crested with a gold maple leaf. Beside the other window, on a small marble table, stands a personally signed photo of Laurier in a gold oval frame.

While Trudeau works his way through the briefing document, Murdoch calls Ivan Head, the prime minister's foreign-policy advisor, on the intercom to discuss the planned call to President Carter. They confer briefly, then Murdoch telephones Carter's personal secretary, Susan Clough, at the White House. He tells her that Trudeau promised to call Carter this week, and says the prime minister can place the call any time between 2.45 and 5 p.m. today. She suggests 4.15. Murdoch calls Head back and tells him Trudeau will want him to come over at 4 o'clock to confer before the call. By now it is 9.30, and the four advisors start arriving, one by one, for the staff meeting. At 9.42, Trudeau buzzes Murdoch to indicate that he is ready. The foursome goes into his office, and the daily meeting starts.

These four men — Michael Pitfield, Jim Coutts, Dick O'Hagan, and de Montigny Marchand — are there by virtue of the positions they occupy, but the meeting itself gives them a power quite apart from their other functions. It gives each of them, every normal day that Parliament is in session, guaranteed access to the prime minister's ear to raise whatever problems or make whatever recommendations he thinks appropriate.

Pitfield, as clerk of the Privy Council and secretary to the cabinet, is Trudeau's "deputy minister" and chief policy advisor. A tall, bespectacled, slow-talking forty-year-old, whose short hair-style and conservative narrow-lapelled suits — and, sometimes, vocabulary — are vaguely reminiscent of the 1950s, Pitfield is the clearing-centre for the most important business of government, with a key role in everything from preparing cabinet agendas to deciding how to achieve policy objectives by means that are politically feasible and administratively efficient. He is also Canada's mandarin-in-chief, responsible for ensuring the smooth functioning of the vast federal bureaucracy.

(Intellectually brilliant, Pitfield tends toward conservatism and caution in the advice he offers, and he is very much a "systems man" in the emphasis he puts on organizational structures.) His influence is enormous, not only because of his position but also because of the personal confidence Trudeau has in him; he has been something of a Trudeau protégé since they met in the early 1960s, and his appointment to the cabinet secretary post — after extensive public-service experience — at the end of 1974 was widely criticized as the elevation of a friend. But Trudeau says of him: "I wouldn't say he's a friend in the sense that Gérard Pelletier is a friend. I mean, he's not of the same generation, the same age, the same background, we didn't grow up together; but he's a man that I relate to very well intellectually, and who has a lot of human qualities. I just admire the quality of the man's mind and his extraordinary discipline, his agility and quickness of mind, and his ability to work fast and give advice which on balance I find good."

Jim Coutts, as principal secretary, is Trudeau's top political advisor and his chief of staff in the Prime Minister's Office. A short, deceptively cherubic-looking thirty-nine-year-old, Coutts is in fact a tough and wily political manipulator. His roots are with the Liberal Party rather than with Trudeau personally. He was president of the Young Liberal Federation of Canada in 1961, an unsuccessful Liberal candidate in his native Alberta in the 1962 federal election, and appointments secretary to Prime Minister Pearson from 1963 to 1966. After a few years away from the action, during which he obtained an MBA from Harvard and worked as a high-priced management consultant, he was recruited to the Trudeau team by another alumnus of the Pearson years, Keith Davey. Senator Davey, who was managing the 1974 election campaign for the Liberals, assigned Coutts to remain at Trudeau's side throughout the campaign as on-the-spot political advisor; in the summer of 1975, he became principal secretary.

Coutts's main concern is politics rather than policy. Stated in its bluntest terms, his preoccupation is with keeping the prime minister out of political trouble and ensuring that he wins the next election. Trudeau also values him for his extensive nation-wide contacts and his skills as an evaluator and recruiter of personnel for various prime-ministerial appointments.

O'Hagan is Trudeau's senior advisor on communications — in other words, the prime minister's PR man. He is not exactly the press secretary; a lesser luminary holds that title and the day-to-day chores of dealing with the press. O'Hagan's job, rather, is to supervise all aspects of the prime minister's communications — the press office, the handling of major announcements, relations with top media executives — and to advise him on how best to get his message across and maintain a favourable image. Another retread from the Pearson years, he was Pearson's press secretary and special assistant until 1966, when he was rewarded with a plum posting as minister-counsellor (information) at the Canadian Embassy in Washington. On Coutts's advice, Trudeau brought him back from Washington in the fall of 1975 to direct the communications campaign to sell price and income controls, and then made him press secretary. A former executive at Toronto's MacLaren Advertising, he still displays many of the characteristics of a stereotypical ad man: he is gregarious, determinedly trendy in attire, pragmatic, uptight, and cautiously self-protective.

The fourth member of the daily morning meeting is de Montigny Marchand, deputy secretary to the cabinet for operations. A suavely charming, outgoing Montrealer with a background in university administration, Marchand is a key member of Pitfield's Privy Council Office team. His job, as its title implies, is to supervise and keep track of the government's decision-making operations; he must keep the prime minister informed of upcoming decisions and problems to be confronted, and channel and follow policy proposals through the various stages of the decision-making process.

When there is an immediate decision to be made or a specific major problem to be handled, Trudeau's morning meeting with these four advisors becomes a planning session in which each offers advice from his particular perspective and area of expertise. But on this July morning, Parliament is moving slowly toward a summer recess and there is no single outstanding matter to discuss. The atmosphere is relaxed but businesslike. Trudeau sits behind his desk, while the others draw up a semicircle of chairs in front of him. There is the occasional wisecrack, but the demands on Trudeau's time are too many to allow anything but a brisk pace.

Pitfield starts by raising the prospective appointment of a new deputy minister for the solicitor general's department. Trudeau slips on a pair of reading glasses with heavy black frames and follows along in the relevant briefing memo while Pitfield goes over the proposed terms of the appointment: since the appointee is a judge coming over from the bench, there are a number of intricacies involving pension arrangements, salary, and timing. They go through these items one by one, with the prime minister asking a number of questions, then he says, "Okay, let's get this done as quickly as possible."

Marchand mentions that the Quebec government is about to reintroduce its Bill One language legislation in modified form, and that the prime minister will need to have a position on it and be prepared to answer questions. Trudeau agrees. He says he wants Privy Council Office officials to examine it quickly, establish what's in the new bill, and develop a recommended position for him to take. "And I also want to know what position the opposition parties in Quebec are taking. I noticed a headline in the paper that said something about the Quebec Liberals and language, but I haven't had a chance to read it. And the Union Nationale — I want to know their position, too."

By now the reading glasses are off and he is toying with them, opening and closing them and nudging them across the suede-covered surface of the desk. In any conversation, Trudeau's hands are never still. When he isn't gesturing or running his fingers through his thinning hair, he's playing absently with something on the desk: a pencil, a paper clip, a rubber band, anything that comes to hand.

Marchand also brings to Trudeau's attention that the Canadian Radio-Television Commission's report on its inquiry into charges of separatist bias in the Canadian Broadcasting Corporation is to come out the following week. It isn't known yet what's in it, he says, but the assumption is that it will recommend a royal commission. (This assumption later proves unfounded; the CRTC says a royal commission would be too disruptive.) Marchand isn't offering Trudeau any advice, however. He is just reminding him of an upcoming development. O'Hagan interjects that he ran into CRTC Chairman Harry Boyle at a reception the other day, and Boyle was concerned about reports that his relationship with Communications Minister Jeanne Sauvé had been strained and wanted Trudeau to know that this wasn't his feeling.

O'Hagan then moves on to an item of his own: Maxwell Cohen, the Canadian chairman of the International Joint Commission has asked him whether it is necessary to send the IJC's report on the Garrison Dam diversion project in the United States to Parliament in both official languages. Trudeau replies, with mild impatience, that the law requires reports submitted to Parliament to be in both French and English. Even though he concedes that it can be argued that the Garrison project is far removed from socio-linguistic matters, he wants the IJC to conform to the law.

Coutts reports that former Quebec minister Claude Castonguay has declined an invitation to be the Quebec member on the national unity commission co-chaired by John Robarts and Jean-Luc Pépin. Trudeau wants to know why. After Coutts has outlined the reasons — having mostly to do with the demands of a new job Castonguay has just taken on — Trudeau says, "Well, he would have been good," then asks about other prospects. Coutts mentions several names, and Pitfield and Marchand comment on each. Pitfield says the choice should be somebody whose visibility is fairly high, though not particularly identified with any school of thought. It would be advantageous, he argues, to find someone well known.

Trudeau is sceptical about whether that really matters. "Was Richard Cashin [the Newfoundland member of the commission] very known and visible outside his own province?" he counters. He says Pépin and Robarts are widely known; what matters for the rest is that they be federalist and well qualified, and that they take their responsibilities seriously. He asks Coutts to come forward soon with a new list of names for serious consideration, and stresses the importance of filling the vacancy as quickly as possible.

Coutts reports next on a minor problem Trudeau had referred to him: the question of a subcontractor with a grievance. The man had accosted the prime minister in the hallway of Parliament, stated his problem, appealed for help, and handed Trudeau a sheaf of documents. Few individual problems reach Trudeau's personal attention, but when one does, he is meticulous about insisting that it be thoroughly investigated. Trudeau had passed the documents on to Coutts and asked him to find out what it was all about.

It turns out, Coutts says, that the man is a subcontractor on a federal building project and he is caught in the middle of a dispute between the contractor and the federal department of public works. Because of the dispute, he can't get his payments, and he is being squeezed by creditors. The man has a legitimate complaint, Coutts says, and the department has now agreed to give his case some special attention. "Well, if they think his case is justified, make sure they hurry up and settle it," Trudeau says.

Trudeau has one item of his own to mention. He is concerned about some alterations that are being made by the public works department to the prime-ministerial cottage at Harrington Lake, something to do with altering the doors. If not altogether unnecessary, the work strikes him at least as too expensive, and he asks Pitfield to see what can be done to reduce the cost.

At 10.10 the meeting ends. Trudeau pauses at the door of his suite to chat privately for a minute with Coutts, and then walks down the hall to the cabinet room to chair the weekly meeting of the cabinet committee on priorities and planning.

The priorities and planning committee — or "P and P", as it is known within the government — is the closest thing Trudeau has to an "inner cabinet". P and P and its Siamese twin, the committee on federal-provincial relations — in practice they are the same body, with the same membership and the same meeting time, functioning some weeks in one capacity and some in the other — are the only two of the eight standing committees of cabinet that Trudeau chairs himself. P and P is the main forum for discussion of the government's over-all direction and priorities. In its federal-provincial-relations capacity, it is the forum for discussion of the subject that Trudeau values above all others: national unity.

P and P, like all the other cabinet committees, cannot make irrevocable decisions. But, unlike the committees in Lester Pearson's day, all the committees in Trudeau's system do make provisional decisions rather than merely recommendations to the full cabinet. These decisions are listed in an annex to the agenda for the next full cabinet meeting. Any minister can give notice before the meeting that he wants to have any given committee decision discussed in cabinet; he can then make his arguments, and the issue is debated and decided by the cabinet. But if no such notice is given, committee items listed in the annex are deemed to have been approved by cabinet, and they automatically become its own decisions and government policy without further discussion.

P and P is the main co-ordinating committee of the cabinet. It functions as a sort of seminar in which the government's broad objectives are debated and tentatively set. The priorities it establishes serve as guidelines for Treasury Board in the actual allocation of funds; it is in P and P that the most extensive discussion takes place as to what should be the government's most important goals, how these goals should rank in terms of the spending and effort allocated to each, and which areas of government action should be emphasized more or which less. P and P also deals with specific policy decisions, if they are particularly important or have long-range implications.

The eight ministers who sit on P and P are invariably the most powerful members of cabinet — partly because of the very fact that they sit on this key committee, and partly because the ministers Trudeau names to the body are naturally those in whom he already has the most confidence. The membership of cabinet committees — traditionally kept secret — changes somewhat with every shuffle, but on this July morning in 1977 the ministers sitting around the large oval table with Trudeau are: Privy Council President Allan MacEachen; Industry, Trade and Commerce Minister Jean Chrétien; Finance Minister Donald Macdonald; Justice Minister Ron Basford; External Affairs Minister Don Jamieson; Treasury Board President Robert Andras; Transport Minister Otto Lang; Health and Welfare Minister Marc Lalonde; Public Works Minister Judd Buchanan; and Fisheries and Environment Minister Roméo LeBlanc.

On the meeting's agenda are two related questions: a review of possible changes in bilingualism policy for the federal public service, and the problem of whether bilingual federal employees should be paid extra for having this additional language skill.

The discussion entails a lot of soul-searching and philosophizing. It is an issue on which few of the ministers have sharply defined positions or departmental decisions to defend, so the talk ranges widely over the implications of various options — how different courses of action would be received by the public service and the public, what they would cost, how they would affect other aspects of the government's language policy.

Trudeau functions much like a seminar leader. He gives the ministers wide latitude to express their views, but he keeps a tight rein on the proceedings, and moves in quickly whenever a digression threatens to stray too far from the issues at hand. His approach is more Socratic than dogmatic; rather than dominating the discussion by stating his own views first, he draws out the opinions of the others, and then probes them with questions: "Why couldn't we . . . ? What would happen if . . . ? But how would you deal with . . . ? What are your figures on . . . ?" Occasionally, but very rarely, he will nip a line of argument in the bud by saying flatly: "Well, we can't do that."

The discussion goes right through lunch hour, and a light meal — juice, a cold roast-beef plate, salad, and coffee — is brought in from the Parliamentary Restaurant; the ministers munch away as the debate continues. In the end, the committee agrees on what changes are to be made in the implementation of public-service bilingualism and it agrees in principle that bilingual employees should be paid a bonus. But it remains bogged down in uncertainty as to how this bonus should be handled. Should it be a flat percentage of extra pay right through the public service, or should the size of the bilingualism bonus vary from job to job? The committee decides, finally, to send the question back to Treasury Board for some more thought by officials.

At 1.25 the meeting ends. Marc Lalonde, who is Trudeau's chief minister for Quebec in addition to his duties as health and welfare minister, walks back to the prime minister's office with him to discuss a Quebec-related matter of strategy. He stays for twenty minutes; then Murdoch comes in to remind Trudeau that it's time to prepare for the Commons. Lalonde leaves, and Joyce Fairbairn, Trudeau's legislative assistant, enters to brief him for the two-o'clock question period.

Joyce Fairbairn, a former reporter with a good instinct for the human side of politics, is the prime minister's link with Parliament — and, in a sense, with what's happening in the outside world as well. Except when he must vote or make a speech,

Trudeau is seldom in the House of Commons for more than an hour a day. But, as head of the executive, he is accountable to Parliament for everything his government does, and that hour in the House is his most important daily forum for public exposure. It is up to his legislative assistant to try to ensure that he is never caught unprepared. That includes anticipating the questions he is likely to be asked and providing him with suggested answers; serving as his liaison with the government's House leader; keeping him informed of the progress of legislation through Parliament; and telling him of any important developments.

In addition, since Trudeau seldom reads a newspaper in detail or listens to the news, she keeps him abreast of developments in Canada and abroad by means of a daily digest. This includes a summary of major news events, plus a selection of clippings she thinks he should see; these range from editorials and political commentaries to cartoons and non-political human-interest stories that strike her as particularly interesting or amusing.

On this day, since it's already 1.47 and Trudeau must leave his office for the House of Commons a few minutes before two o'clock, there isn't time to supplement his written briefing with a verbal one. She simply comes in, gives him the memo she has prepared for the day's question period, and leaves him alone to study it. The ten-page memo anticipates questions on unemployment figures which have been released that day, and on the Schmidt visit, particularly with regard to future uranium sales to Germany. It also mentions the shooting death of an Ottawa policeman and the possible effects it may have on a gun-control bill that is before Parliament, and it draws to his attention a television interview Jean-Luc Pépin has given on the weekend in which he speculates on the chances of saving Confederation.

At three minutes before two, Murdoch opens the office door and asks: "Are you ready for the House, sir?" Trudeau closes his shirt collar and tightens his tie, and with Murdoch at his side to fend off any buttonholers, he trots down one flight of stairs and takes his place in the House of Commons.

Seated at his desk in the centre of the front row of government benches, Trudeau is oblivious to the daily ritual that precedes question period. While Opposition members pop to their feet with "matters of urgent and pressing necessity" which require unanimous consent to be debated, and which are routinely denied that consent, the prime minister is absorbed in working his way through a two-inch-thick stack of documents he has brought into the chamber in a leather binder; he periodically pauses to underline a phrase and write a comment in the margin with his gold fountain pen.

Then the question period begins, and the first question is for the prime minister. His desk-mate, House leader Allan MacEachen, touches him on the arm to draw his attention. The question, as predicted, is on unemployment.

In his response, Trudeau is quiet-spoken and forthcoming, almost professorial. Standing between two desks, his hands toying with the earpiece that is connected to the amplification and simultaneous-translation system, he concedes nothing, but his answer is long and detailed. "I must remind the honourable member that an increase of one-tenth of one per cent this month is in contrast with a decrease of four-tenths of one per cent in the previous month and that it is impossible to ascertain a trend from these contradictory figures. . . . Unemployment is, of course, something about which we do care a great deal. That is why in the budget we brought in substantial tax cuts for consumers and the corporations. We are still hopeful that the long-run trend will be in line with what happened last month. . . ."

On this day, Trudeau is giving quiet-spoken, detailed answers. On another day, he might have handled the same question with a curt, one-sentence reply; shown snappish irritation; been fiercely partisan in accusing the Opposition of some inconsistency; offered only a sarcastic wisecrack; or droned on and on in a barely audible monotone. Coutts, his principal secretary, is convinced that these fluctuations in Trudeau's performance are deliberate and have little to do with his mood: "He's the best actor I've ever seen. He's got more moves than Bobby Orr. You know, in the House one day he's baiting the Opposition, the next he's doing the mumbling number so you can hardly hear him, another he's doing the professor and giving a lecture. He does it to keep everybody off balance. The greatest weapon in a prime minister's arsenal is surprise."

A few more routine questions about unemployment, a few more similar Trudeau answers. Then New Democratic Party leader Ed Broadbent rises with a question for the prime minister, and this one takes an unexpected tack: "In the prime minister's reply to Premier Schreyer's request for a first ministers' conference to deal with unemployment, he said that federal job-creation plans are almost complete. This is new to Premier Schreyer and it is new to the people of Canada, that the federal government has some new job-creation programs. If these plans are near completion, I should like to ask the prime minister when we can expect an announcement about them."

This question, unlike the earlier ones, is dangerous. It seeks to trap Trudeau into either prematurely confirming the existence of a new program before the government is ready to announce it, or admitting that he has misled a premier. Trudeau responds with the verbal equivalent of a seasoned boxer's reaction to an unexpected onslaught: he keeps his distance, covers up, plays for time to find a weakness in his opponent's attack. His answer is bland to the point of meaninglessness: "Mr. Speaker, the minister of manpower and immigration has repeatedly indicated to the House what new funds were put into job-creation programs such as Canada Works and other areas."

Broadbent persists, referring again to the prime minister's letter to Schreyer and demanding to know if there is indeed a new plan in the works. Trudeau senses a possible opening now, and tries a tentative jab: "Mr. Speaker, I do not remember having tabled that letter to Premier Schreyer, nor the date of it. If it was referring to plans that the minister of manpower and immigration has already announced, then my first answer is correct. If it is a very recent letter, then it has to do with the plans that the minister is working on now. I repeat, however, I cannot recall having tabled that letter or made it public."

Broadbent lunges ahead, saying that the Manitoba premier had referred to the contents of Trudeau's letter in a press statement, and repeats again his original question. Trudeau sets him up for a haymaker: "The honourable leader of the NDP has not indicated the date of the letter." Broadbent gives it — "June 22" — and that's all Trudeau needs: "In that case, I was taking Premier

Schreyer into my confidence, and I am surprised that he has taken the honourable member into his confidence." A technical knock-out! Broadbent gives up the fight. The issue has been diverted from whether the Liberals are preparing a new employment pro-gram to whether an NDP premier has improperly leaked a prime-ministerial letter to the federal NDP leader.

There are a few more perfunctory questions from other MPs about unemployment, then the questions move on, other ministers find themselves in the spotlight, and Trudeau is left alone. He returns to his paperwork, pausing several times to chat briefly with Liberal MPs who come up to him to ask a question or discuss a problem.

At 3.21, after question period has ended and a few questions of privilege have been resolved, Trudeau leaves the chamber and hands his folder of documents to Murdoch, who is waiting in the lobby. The prime minister is grinning broadly. "Schreyer struck out again," he says. "It was hilarious. Wait till you see the tran-scripts." It later turns out that he is referring to Broadbent, not Schreyer; Trudeau has a curious memory — he can remember minor details of conversations many months later, but he is forever calling people by the wrong names, even to their faces.

In the hallway of Parliament outside the Commons chamber, a group of some twenty visitors from a Liberal MP's riding are wait-ing to meet the prime minister. This is an almost daily occurrence; Liberals with visiting constituents make arrangements with Mur-doch, and he delivers Trudeau for a quick round of handshakes in the corridor. The visitors on this day, all in late middle age, are delighted to meet Trudeau. They cluster around him excitedly, shaking hands, posing with him while other members of the group click away with their Instamatic cameras. Trudeau is very adept at scenes like this: he focusses his attention on one person at a time, however briefly, and seems raptly interested in whatever is being said. A few quips, a few more flashes from the cameras, and Murdoch is at his elbow to move him on. The whole encounter has taken exactly three minutes.

Upstairs, outside Trudeau's office, another group is waiting. This one is made up of teen-aged girls, half of them from Alberta, half from a Quebec minister's riding, together on an exchange program. Trudeau chats jovially with them, teasing, wisecracking, making a game of trying to guess which are from Alberta and which from Quebec. He guesses wrong, and quips: "Just goes to show you, all Canadians are the same." The girls giggle happily, and more cameras click. At 3.28 Trudeau wishes them luck and moves on into his office. Seven minutes have elapsed since he left the House of Commons; thirty-two people will long remember and recount their "personal" chats with the prime minister of Canada.

While a Liberal MP waits in the anteroom for his appointment, Joyce Fairbairn goes into the prime minister's office to talk for a moment about the question period. She always sees him both before and after the session. They agree that the fielding of the unemployment questions went relatively well, and speculate on the fall-out from Trudeau's Schreyer gambit. Then she brings up a less weighty matter: she has recently seen a revue of Noel Coward songs at an Ottawa supper club and found it terrific. She thinks he'd enjoy it. Would he like her to make arrangements for him to go one evening? He asks a few questions about the show, then says yes.

She leaves, and Murdoch invites the MP to enter. By now, Trudeau's collar and tie are open again, his jacket is off, and his shirt-sleeves are rolled up. He comes out from behind the desk, and he and the MP sit down on a couple of the suede-upholstered chairs near one of the little tables.

Since Parliament is moving toward its summer recess and there is talk of a fall election, this veteran MP has come to solicit Trudeau's advice on whether he should run again; he is, in fact, fishing for the promise of a cabinet post. Trudeau is friendly but non-committal. He balks at any form of pressure, and he doesn't believe — out of both pride and principle — in asking people to stay in government. He has lost ministers and advisors far more important to him than this MP because he wouldn't say, "Please stay, I need your help." He believes that every man must determine his own destiny and that it would be wrong for him to apply pressure — and he also believes such a request would limit his own freedom by making him beholden to the man persuaded. Instead, he spends the allotted half-hour chatting amiably with this MP. He discusses the man's accomplishments and frustrations with him at some length, and tells him that his contribution has been valuable and appreciated, but that he must decide for himself whether he can accomplish more by continuing as an MP or by entering some other sphere of activity.

At four o'clock, Murdoch comes in to say that Ivan Head has arrived for his appointment. The MP leaves three minutes later, and Head takes his place.

A forty-seven-year-old former professor of constitutional law, whose face — bland, even features combined with an edge of hardness — and trim, athletic build somehow suggest a senior policeman more than an academic, Head is one of Trudeau's closest and longest-serving aides. Their relationship dates back to 1967, when the then justice minister recruited Head as a special advisor on the constitution. When Trudeau became prime minister, Head became his legislative assistant, speechwriter, and general advisor. But Head's particular interest was foreign policy, and his role in that field gradually expanded until it became his sole official area of responsibility in 1970. He is Trudeau's personal advisor on foreign policy, and often functions as his emissary in dealings with other heads of government.

Their relationship is something more than employer-employee, something less than friendship in any social sense. There is a great deal of mutual empathy and respect, and when Trudeau goes skiing on a trip abroad or slips in a few days of adventurous sightseeing, it is Head who is most likely to accompany him. But there is also an element of competitiveness between them, in matters intellectual as well as athletic.

Though they often have long, relaxed conversations, there is no time for that in the few minutes available before the scheduled 4.15 call to President Carter. Head is there for a quick discussion of the points to be made to the president, and to remain at hand throughout the conversation. The call is being made at the request of Carter, who had telephoned Trudeau in Vancouver the previous week and asked to hear from him again after the Schmidt visit.

The German chancellor is going on from Ottawa to Washington, and Carter wants to prepare himself by hearing what impressions Trudeau gathered from his talks with Schmidt. A second purpose of the call is to brief Carter on some comments about the state of Soviet-United States relations that Head has heard on a recent visit to Moscow.

The call is placed at 4.16, and Jimmy Carter is on the line four minutes later. The conversation lasts twenty-five minutes. When it ends, there is no time for Trudeau and Head to discuss the talk immediately, because the French ambassador is waiting outside. "Let's talk tomorrow," Trudeau tells Head, hurrying meanwhile to button his collar, tighten his tie, and slip into his suit jacket. As Head goes to the door, the prime minister calls to him, "Tell Bob two minutes." He takes those minutes for a memory-refreshing glance at his briefing memo for the ambassador's visit, and then Murdoch opens the door to ask if he is now ready.

At 4.50, the ambassador is ushered into Trudeau's office. The visit is a courtesy call to say good-bye, because the ambassador is leaving after five years to take up a new posting. Trudeau chats in French with him for half an hour about his experiences in Canada, the general state of Canadian-French relations, his successor, and his plans for the future.

When the ambassador leaves, Trudeau moves almost at once to his last appointment of the day, which is with another Liberal MP. This one is a newcomer, recently elected in a by-election, and the meeting is part of the getting-acquainted process. He has a few specific riding problems to discuss, but apart from that, the conversation is mostly an informal discussion of their respective expectations and approaches to government.

The MP leaves at 5.55, and Cécile Viau comes in, as she always does at day's end. She brings two telephone messages, a few documents that require the prime minister's signature, and a personal letter for Trudeau's approval. She handles much of his private correspondence with the far-flung network of friends and intellectuals with whom he periodically exchanges ideas; in those instances, he tells her what he roughly wants the letter to say, and she drafts it for his approval.

Trudeau spends ten minutes going over the documents and the letter, then buzzes for Murdoch. The executive assistant is always the last to see him at the end of each day, to go over any outstanding problems of scheduling. Now Murdoch points out that Trudeau has a choice between two tentatively arranged working lunches tomorrow: he can meet with an outgoing senior official, or with members of his staff for a planning session. He opts for the official. And he is scheduled to have dinner with a group of business leaders tomorrow evening; does he want to have it at 24 Sussex Drive, or in a downtown hotel? Sussex Drive. Murdoch instructs his secretary to make the necessary arrangements, then at 6.16, he and the prime minister go downstairs to the waiting limousine.

Murdoch usually rides home with Trudeau in the limousine and is dropped off at his house near Sussex Drive. He uses the travel time to discuss anything he didn't get a chance to mention during the day, as well as longer-range questions of scheduling. For Murdoch, that ends the day. For Trudeau, there is still work remaining.

After dinner, some time with his children, and a swim in the indoor pool or a jog around the governor general's estate across the road, he faces his nightly average of some two hours of paperwork on briefing memos and cabinet documents.

No two days are exactly alike, but this Tuesday in July is typical of Trudeau's activities as chief of the executive, leader of his party, and public figure. In an average month, he works about 250 hours. Roughly 90 of them, or 36 per cent of his working time, are spent on government business, including cabinet and its committees, the House of Commons, the governor general and other government officials, foreign visitors and ambassadors, outside groups, and foreign travel. Political activities involving ministers, MPs, senators, or Liberal Party officials account for 50 hours, or 20 per cent of his time. He spends 12.5 hours, or 5 per cent, in press conferences or other forms of contact with the news media; 30 hours, or 12 per cent, with staff in the Prime Minister's Office and Privy Council Office; and 67.5 hours, or 27 per cent of his time, on paperwork, correspondence, and telephone calls.

(On this typical day, his activities as prime minister have spanned 11 hours. But he has been publicly visible for only 88 minutes, and it is on those 88 minutes that most perceptions of him will be based. That, coupled with a personality that in very few respects is what it superficially seems, goes a long way toward explaining why Pierre Trudeau remains so remarkably little known or understood after a decade in power.)

CHAPTER TWO

"Will the real Mr. Trudeau please stand up?"

PIERRE ELLIOTT TRUDEAU's decade as prime minister makes him the senior elected leader in the Western world. His term in office reaches across four U.S. presidencies: Lyndon Johnson's last months, the Nixon years, the brief tenure of Gerald Ford, and now the Carter mandate. Germany's chancellor has changed twice since 1968, from Kiesinger to Brandt to Schmidt. Three men — de Gaulle, Pompidou, and now Giscard — have occupied France's Elysée Palace. The prime-ministry of Britain has passed from Wilson to Heath, back to Wilson, and then on to Callaghan.

Not only has Trudeau outlasted all his political contemporaries, but he has managed to do so in one of the most turbulent and rapidly changing periods in North America's post-war history. On the eve of the Liberal convention which elected Trudeau leader, Martin Luther King was shot in Memphis. Two weeks before the federal election which confirmed him as prime minister, Robert Kennedy was assassinated. The big issues of the 1960s, spilling over the border or vicariously experienced by Canadians, were the Vietnam war, civil rights, and the swelling tide of student protests. Canada was a nation simultaneously aglow with a post-Expo 67 flush of optimism and wracked with worry over its future as a country: terrorist bombs were exploding periodically in Montreal, a separatist party with the avowed purpose of taking Quebec out of Confederation was being founded by René Lévesque, and the eve of the 1968 federal election exploded into a bloody battle between separatist rioters and Montreal police.

Now, in a much-changed world, energy crises and economic malaise have replaced faraway war in the hierarchy of troubles. The "Great Society" of LBJ and the "Just Society" of Pierre Trudeau have given way to cautious societies groping for new directions in an unfamiliar setting of slow growth and dwindling resources. Student radicalism has yielded to a new wave of cynicism and apathy, and the trend now is to look back in fond delusion on the 1950s rather than to stride ambitiously toward the 1980s. In our politics, the daily cries and alarms of the Diefenbaker and Pearson years have suddenly been replaced by a single dominant crisis: the possibility that Quebec's separatist government may succeed in rending the fabric of our nationhood.

Through it all, in an era when public impatience with the failures of government has combined with an insatiable thirst for novelty to topple leaders and heroes everywhere, Trudeau has succeeded in retaining power. He has accomplished this largely through a remarkable ability to keep presenting himself in new guises. Like a kaleidoscope whose pieces are constantly rearranged into ever-changing patterns, Trudeau is able to reach into his complex personality and summon hitherto-unseen aspects to the fore. The dashing, banister-sliding Trudeau of 1968 bears scant resemblance to the droning, professorial campaigner of 1972 or the aroused, gut-fighting politician of 1974. Says Mitchell Sharp, a now-retired senior minister in both the Pearson and the Trudeau governments: "This is one of the most intelligent people I have ever encountered. His intellectual prowess is enormous. And as more limited people have a limited range, Trudeau seems to have an unlimited range. He just calls up another part in himself, and it's quite simple for him."

Voters in other countries, bored and disillusioned with their leaders, switch their support to some new prospect; in Canada, they have been given the opportunity in each recent election to "change leaders" by voting for a new Trudeau. He has been assisted in this, too, by a certain political — if not always personal — luck which has made his changing life-style the very embodiment of the changing times. In 1968, when the New Morality was all the rage and open sexuality was a new adventure, there was

Trudeau the swinging bachelor, dating a dazzling succession of beautiful young women and trading kisses with nubile teen-aged fans. By the early 1970s, the times were settling down, and so was Trudeau; now he was the stable family man, with an adoring young wife and charming little children. And if there has been a social phenomenon which characterizes the closing years of this decade, it has been the erosion of marriage as an institution. Virtually everyone knows someone whose marriage has collapsed, and scarcely a week passes without yet another article in some newspaper or magazine about the problems of the single parent — and there, in 1977, was Trudeau the single father, abandoned by a flighty wife and coping bravely with the demands of his job and three small children.

If the changing face he presents to the world has helped him survive politically, the interplay of facets in his personality has also made him exceptionally difficult to perceive accurately. Like the three proverbial blind men who clutched respectively at an elephant's leg, its trunk, and its tail and reported in turn that an elephant resembles a tree, a snake, and a rope, different observers have focussed on different aspects of Trudeau's personality and thinking, and have reached wildly disparate conclusions about the nature of the man. In 1968, the star Tory candidate in Quebec, financier Marcel Faribault, described him as "a socialist of the worst kind — a doctrinaire socialist". NDP leader Tommy Douglas, at about the same time, found him to be an orthodox conservative in the mould of R. B. Bennett. Seven years later, the confusion still had not been dispelled: When Trudeau spoke vaguely in a 1975 year-end interview about the failures of the free-market economy, labour leaders saw in his words a right-wing threat to union freedom, while businessmen smelled a socialist plot.

It is possible, on any given day, to hear him described by two equally reasonable persons as a ruthless, cold-blooded autocrat and as a man so soft-hearted that he cannot bring himself to get tough with inept ministers; as a dabbler in issues and as a man who insists with excessive tenacity on finishing anything he starts; as an arrogant, remote patrician and as a person of exceptional charm and sensitivity; as the only leader who can put Quebec in its place, and as a Quebecer who values the welfare of his own province above all else. As a Liberal insider once put it: "Somebody is going to say some day, 'Will the real Mr. Trudeau please stand up,' and about fifty-eight people will rise."

Little understood though he may be, few would dispute the impact — for better or worse — of Trudeau's intellect and personality. In Canada, he has come to tower unrivalled over the landscape of federal politics; abroad, he stands as a major figure in the international community of leaders, respected for the quality of his mind and his skills as a political survivor. Observers as disparate in time, place, and outlook as French editor and politician Jean-Jacques Servan-Schreiber in 1968 and U.S. political columnist Joseph Kraft in 1976 have singled him out as outstanding among the world's leaders. Servan-Schreiber described him as "the first truly modern political figure in the West", and Kraft, nearly a decade later, judged him to be "perhaps the world's most gifted leader".

Trudeau's relationship with the Canadian public has been as complicated as his own personality. He entered the political arena with qualities and flaws which seemingly suited him better to behind-the-scenes government than to electoral politics; instead, those characteristics have plunged him onto a roller-coaster ride of great peaks of popularity followed by nearly unprecedented troughs of public hostility. The Canadian public seems incapable of a calm, balanced relationship with this prime minister; scarcely understanding him, it sees only the positive aspects of his leadership one day, and only the negative the next, bouncing him between the apex and the nadir of its esteem. And he, too, is erratic in approach, alternating between apparent carelessness about his popularity and dazzlingly effective attempts to restore it; twice now, he has allowed himself to slip to the brink of political disaster, and twice he has struggled his way back up to a commanding position.

Says a top civil servant who has long been closely associated with Trudeau: "He's almost a textbook prime minister, in that he's what you expect a prime minister to be — but what I think prime ministers never are: Very intelligent, not only in terms of common sense but of expertise in a wide variety of fields. A pretty good businessman, who managed his own inheritance very well before he became PM and increased it quite considerably. A very honest man in his dealings with people — and prime ministers rarely are. A very secure person. An extremely logical person. . . . It's all very well to have a brilliant prime minister, but it's a lot to ask a country to put up with. When it chose to make him PM, the country bought an extremely able and gifted decision-maker. Whether the country is going to be prepared to continue maintaining that decision-maker over a politician remains to be seen."

But barring yet another change in his political fortunes, it is Trudeau who will carry federalist hopes in the tug-of-war between Quebec's separatist government and the rest of Canada over the fate of Confederation. All the more reason to strip away the mythologies, to cease seeing Trudeau in fragments distorted by the funhouse mirror of politics, and both to understand and to judge the man as he really is.

Pierre Trudeau is in very few respects what he seems from a distance. But what he is, and how he governs, is not so much unfathomable as previously unexplored.

CHAPTER THREE

The Passionate Rationalist

"Dispassionately, let us be intelligent."
PIERRE TRUDEAU, 1950

IF THERE is any prevailing image of Trudeau, it is that of a brilliant but cold man, a kind of intellectual automaton lacking in passion, sensitivity, or empathy for the feelings of others. To the extent that this is the face he so often chooses to show the world, the image and its occasionally damaging political consequences are deserved. Confronted with an adversary — or even with a neutral participant in a professional encounter — he can be ruthless in debate, abrupt in manner, and remote and indifferent in personal relations to the point of insult. But that is only one facet of the man. The reality is infinitely more complex. At his core, Pierre Trudeau is not a passionless man, but one with so much emotion that he has rigorously walled it in; not arrogant and thick-skinned, but rather so vulnerable that he has erected a barrier of remoteness that only a trusted few can penetrate; not inflated with confidence and a sense of his own power, but quite unassuming and even, in certain situations, curiously unsure of himself. If all this is hidden from public view, it is neither by accident nor by play-acting: The impression that emerges from conversations with Trudeau and people who know him well is that from earliest childhood he consciously set out to mould himself into the sort of person he chose to be, and this moulding process involved suppressing the traits he considered flaws. The key elements of his personality are self-discipline, sensitivity, and an almost obsessive sense of independence or freedom — and all three can be traced back to his childhood.

His self-discipline was originally rooted in insecurity. He grew up believing that he was physically and even intellectually weaker than other children, and that he had to apply himself extra hard if he was to avoid being left behind.

He was, in fact, not robust as a young child. His sister Suzette, a year and a half older, recalls that he was slight for his age and several times had illnesses that worried their parents; on one occasion, meningitis was suspected, but it ultimately proved to be something less serious. He himself recalls: "I remember being made aware rather early that I was of somewhat frail health and that I'd probably have to be more careful than others if I wanted to grow up healthy. These are the kind of things you tell a boy — you know, 'eat your spinach and you'll get muscles' — but the remembrance I have of it is something more vivid than that. I was starting, as it were, with two strikes against me, and if I wanted to be reasonably strong physically I'd have to discipline myself."

That discipline, beginning at the age of about six, initially involved a rigorous program of exercises. "I remember very early doing what I suppose today we'd call 5BX or involving myself in those kinds of exercises, which requires discipline in a child, every night for whatever it was, ten to fifteen minutes. I can remember myself going out on the back balcony in the fresh air because you had to do it where it was cold, in the fresh air so that your lungs would grow strong and so on. I needed physical discipline if I was going to grow up as healthy as the boy next door. And from that, I think, developed my interest in sport, and perhaps from there physical prowess. Wanting to learn how to box — being weak I'd have to be able to defend myself more than the next guy. Or learning how to wrestle or being good at tumbling. . . . And I think it was at that age mainly physical discipline, but I suppose it develops the will in a sense."

It didn't take long, in fact, for the physical discipline to become not just a matter of fitness, but a kind of self-imposed test of the will: "When we were kids, in the country, I'd sort of vow that every day that we were in the country I'd swim. Which is easy most of the time, but when it's a very, very cold, rainy day, people would say, 'You're crazy! What are you going swimming for?' 'Oh, well, you know, it does me good.' And I can see that after fifty years of that kind of thing, it develops something or other, probably a very obdurate, inner-determined, inner-directed guy."

On the intellectual side, too, his early discipline was born of suspicions of inferiority. "There is an age in your life, in the teens, when you discover what genius is. You might be reading Rimbaud or you might be reading Balzac. You discover that there is such a thing as genius. And, maybe a year or two later, you discover that you haven't got it and that it's not going to come like the grace of God, that you have to work bloody hard to be as good as a genius. . . . I remember being very much influenced by a phrase by Buffon, one of the pioneers of modern science. He said, 'Le génie n'est qu'une grande aptitude à la patience.' ('Genius is nothing but a great aptitude for patience.') This sort of consolation: gee, maybe I wasn't a genius, but genius is nothing else but patience or dedicated application." That quote may have provided a rationale for diligence in school when he was in his teens, but the pattern was set much earlier. Recalls his sister: "The youngest brother and myself, we had facility in studying and we did what we had to do, but not too much more, whereas Pierre always worked much harder than we did. At the time, I thought he had a harder time learning, but now I realize that it's because he always did things very thoroughly. That's since his first years at school." The real spur, it seems, was insecurity about his own capacity. As Trudeau puts it: "I had to work harder not to be left behind, and having worked harder, I found myself surging to the front. I suppose there was an element of competitiveness in this. But I don't know if it's true of all competitiveness, but mine was probably born of a fear of being left behind rather than from a desire to surge ahead."

The development of Trudeau's discipline was helped along, too, by a father who pressed him to do things that don't come easily to a youngster. "When I was seven or eight in primary school, seven, I guess, I was in my first grade, but some of my friends on the same street were in second grade, and I wasn't learning much in first grade and I didn't see why I shouldn't be in second grade. And I spoke to my dad, and he says: 'Well, go talk to the director.' I said, 'Me?' You know, when you're seven years old, to go talk to the director and ask him to jump a grade. . . . My heart was just pounding in my chest, but I went to talk to him and I skipped a grade."

Similarly, the summer Trudeau was thirteen, his whole family toured Europe by car, and he recalls being pressed into assuming an adult's responsibilities. "I remember, for instance, one particular place in Germany, but it happened in other places too. My father would sort of say, 'Well, Pierre, you go into this hotel and see if they have rooms for us and book us rooms.' And here I was — I was thirteen — I'd sort of say, 'Who, me?' and he'd say, 'Yeah, go here.' So I'd go, and with whatever little German and English I could command, I'd go up to the front desk and say, 'Well, look, haben Sie drei Zimmer frei?' and whatever it would be. And, you know, I suppose the clerks would look down at me, for all I knew they might have seen this big car drive up outside, I don't know. But my father would make me do these things, and book rooms for the whole family and haggle over the price or whatever it was, and was service included or not."

If the roots of Trudeau's self-discipline can be traced to early childhood, so too can the sensitivity he so carefully shields behind a wall of remoteness. "I was a very sensitive child and the least word of blame, or indeed the least word of praise, moved me to tears, and I guess that was basic insecurity as a child. You know, I can remember incidents going back to very early school age, I would say when I was eight or nine, when I was finding myself in fistfights with kids who would be bigger than myself, but suddenly discovering that I could not only defend myself, but I could get the better of bullies who were bigger than me. And I remember one incident where this happened, and when I got back into the classroom I was terribly afraid that I would get hell for fighting during recreation. And the teacher, on the contrary, said, 'Gee, I see that you got the better of that bully, congratulations' — and I just burst into tears. I wasn't sure quite what mixture of blame and of support there was in there, but at least there was some of both, and probably more support than blame, and I just . . . I don't know how you analyse that, but I do remember being that way, and that would seem to communicate that at a very early age I was very dependent on outside criticism or outside support, because it caused deep emotions in me. And it may have been a defence mechanism of sort of saying, well, obviously in the world we live in I'm not only going to get support, I'm going to get a lot of blame, therefore I had better train myself to do without it."

He also learned at an early age that such visible displays of emotion can leave one open to ridicule, and the lesson was never forgotten. "A neighbour of ours who was in my class said after such an incident when I cried, 'You made a show of yourself,' and that really, coming from him, made it look as if I had been pretty weak if I cried in class. So I kind of resolved never to make a show of myself. All those things influence you . . . I was a very sensitive child. And I guess when you are that way, you have to develop a strong suit of armour to be sure that you are not buffeted by every frown and elated at every smile. And I think that's a very known and visible part of my makeup, that access to my inner self is not very easy for anybody. And when people say, 'He doesn't have too many friends,' or 'People really don't know him,' it's not a de- liberate secrecy or hiding, but I am sure it's the expression of a long-developed character of being cautious in opening the gates to my inner self. I know I can be as hurt as anyone, and therefore I don't, I never did, let just anybody in."

Another aspect of Trudeau's sensitivity — and one of his most attractive qualities — is his remarkable zest for life. Hidden behind the cold façade is a man who hasn't lost his sense of wonder and who is easily exhilarated — by beauty, new experiences, fresh ideas, interesting people, unexplored places. There is about him a constant determination to savour life's experiences to the full, try everything, and see everything, and this aliveness may well be the main reason he so often seems younger than his years.

This compelling curiosity began manifesting itself in Trudeau's earliest school days. "I would never be able to skip a chapter in a book, even though the teacher would say, 'Well, you can skip this chapter, it's not important.' I didn't want to miss it." Later, it led him to experiment with a broad range of activities, even such seem- ingly unlikely ones for him as studying ballet and the violin, just to see what they were like. It manifested itself, too, in his globetrotting travels, not only prompting him to try to explore the most remote corners of the world, but also determining his approach to the places he visited: "My friends would say, 'Sit down and let's just have an apéritif.' And they'd sit down at five and just watch the world go by, whether they'd be in Paris or Seville or whatever. And it was just wasting time; it's not that I didn't like to drink. It's just, you know: 'We haven't done this or seen this part of town yet.' If I'm in Seville or in Barcelona or in Zagreb, 'Let's forget about eating — we only have seven hours before the train or the bus leaves; let's walk around the town on foot.' Not to save the taxi fare, but so we can swoop into back alleys and so on."

That zest is still very much a part of him. "I have never felt bored," he says. "There's so many books I still want to read, so many records I want to listen to, so many people I want to see, so many things to hear, do, find, see . . ." And when he leaves public life, he adds, he will want to go live in the country. Why? "Because I know virtually all the streets of Montreal. I don't know all the trees, all the rocks, all the wild flowers, or even all the stars."[1]

Trudeau's inherent sensitivity is also apparent, finally, in the remarkable rapport he has with children. He is very close to his own three young sons now, but even in his bachelor days he derived special enjoyment from the company of youngsters. Says his sister Suzette: "He's always been interested in children. He was still living at mother's when he was perhaps thirty because he was also travelling, but the kids next door who were perhaps ten, twelve, fourteen would come and ring the doorbell and ask him to go out and play, because he'd make them play games or play baseball or whatever was going, and he was always interested in seeing youngsters, the way they functioned and developed." Trudeau explains his feeling about children this way, speaking of his own boys: "Creation is a constant marvel and I guess the best thing for me is that I'm laughing all the time when I see these human beings develop. I'm just amazed, you know — mankind is always attracted by beauty or truth, a beautiful sunset, a beautiful woman, a beautiful symphony, and here you see these human beings, they're right there and they're doing beautiful things. It just makes you feel great. It's seeing beauty and it's seeing reality, in the making."[2]

The third key element of Trudeau's personality — and perhaps largely a product of the other two — is his fierce sense of personal freedom and independence, a trait that predisposes him to be a loner. "I remember very young hearing someone recite one of Cyrano's famous 'tirades', the conclusion of which is, 'Ne pas monter bien haut peut-être, mais tout seul.' ('To climb not very high, perhaps, but all alone.') And I don't think that determined me, but I think suddenly I found there an expression of who I was and what I wanted to be: I don't care if I don't make it, providing I don't need anyone else's help, providing what I do make I make alone, you know, without begging for favours."

Trudeau was by no means friendless as a child, but his sister recalls that the role of his friends was carefully compartmentalized: "He had friends. I don't know whether he was popular, but he was always disciplined and had a certain time for his friends and then when that time was over, well, they had to go."

It was in his teens, however, that his individualism burst into full, and sometimes eccentric, flower. "Being this way, and deciding to be my own man, and seek for approval in myself, I suddenly began to take a kind of a perverse pleasure at being what in those days we used to call 'un original' — in dress, in manner of speaking, in my readings, in artistic taste. And I rather went out of my way to make it appear that it was my discipline, and if you read the school paper from those days, you will see I had articles against fashion, submitting to the slavery of fashion, or of custom, or of accepted truths and values."

The assertion of individuality quickly became a major priority in both his life-style and his philosophy. The important thing, he decided, was not to compete against others or to seek outside approval, but to constantly test and improve himself: "I guess I was competing against myself all the time, which contains an element of immaturity. Just look at sports. When I was in college, there were no other sports but team sports. I played them, hockey and lacrosse, but as soon as I was out of college, I didn't stay in team sports. I went into solitary things like skiing or cycling or skindiving or canoeing or things that you do alone or with very few people. You're testing yourself."

In philosophical terms, too, his main preoccupation during his student days was the concept of freedom: "How can man be free, you know, with all the behaviourists and heredity, and are you actually free? And the problem of God and freedom. If God created us, can he really have created us free?" He found an answer, to his delight, in the philosophy of Thomas Aquinas, which resolved for him the conundrum of wanting to be independent and yet feeling a need to obey the moral code of the Catholic Church and the priests who were his teachers. "I discovered that Thomas had reconciled it in a very beautiful way, making a distinction between the morals of a slave and the morals of a free man. And suddenly I found that I could be a free man and yet accept certain moral codes and certain precepts. Hence, I guess, my love for saying that if I was disciplined it was self-discipline, it wasn't because the teachers or the peer groups were imposing anything on me. I was imposing it on myself.

"And in order to prove that it was my choice, I went out of my way in a regular fashion to disobey the imposed discipline. I was one of those troublesome children who was expelled many times from class, but a few times from school, which is very serious to a teen-ager. You don't have anywhere else to go, and your parents have told you, 'If you ever get expelled, that's the end.' I guess I was trying to do rebellious things from time to time just to prove a point: I was I, I was me."

His rebelliousness at the élite, Jesuit-run Collège Jean de Brébeuf in Montreal, which he attended from the age of twelve to the age of twenty, was both physical and intellectual. On the physical side, he was quick with his fists, on one occasion abruptly knocking down a classmate who had persisted in calling him "Toto" immediately after Trudeau had announced that he no longer wanted the nickname to be used. In intellectual matters, one of his favourite tricks for riling teachers and classmates was to launch himself into deliberate collisions with the school's Quebec nationalist mood. He was thoroughly disinterested in politics at that stage, he says, but "since they were nearly all nationalists, I would say I wasn't. And when, during history class, they used to applaud the victories of the French armies, I, on the contrary, would applaud the victories of the English armies. I was always taking the opposite stand from people, from my teachers, and this used to get them quite annoyed, but it wasn't really serious."[3] During one political economy class, he suddenly stood up and announced: "I've had enough of this. If you all agree, we'll sing 'O Canada' and get out of here."

Even his name was, in a sense, the product of perversity. Because there was another Pierre Trudeau in his class at Brébeuf, he originally began using one of his middle names — he was christened Joseph Philippe Pierre Yves Elliott Trudeau — to become known as Pierre-Philippe. Then, in his later teens, he switched to styling himself Pierre Elliott — his mother's Scottish surname — in another gesture apparently designed to taunt the French nationalists around him.

The rebelliousness, Trudeau himself concedes, was something more complicated than youthful hijinks: "If anyone wanted to psychoanalyse me, through my works or my acts, I think they'd find some hostility that I have towards authority which makes me love freedom so much." Even in his youngest childhood, he was somewhat rebellious toward the authority of his father, who was a loving but strict disciplinarian. His father's death when Trudeau was only fifteen — a loss that hurt him so deeply that he still cannot talk about it without visible emotion — may well have transformed a youngster's normal assertions of independence into a nearly lifelong resistance against authority. It is a subject about which Trudeau doesn't like to speculate publicly, but he did in a 1975 television interview with Britain's Lord Chalfont: "Probably I lost the object of my revolt in the family and didn't have to fight my father, so I went out and fought other people like my teachers, or the church, or politicians, or whatever happened to be established."

As Trudeau moved into his later teens and young adulthood, the basic elements of his personality found new and changing forms of expression.

The self-discipline took the form of a never-ending series of stern, self-imposed tests. For a while, associates of the period recall, these included deliberately provoking fistfights so that he could try out his courage and considerable prowess on unsuspecting opponents. Then the tests became more private: arduous canoe trips into the wilds, travels into exotic parts of the world on a shoestring and without proper documents, deliberate manoeuvrings to get into political hotspots — Shanghai, Palestine, Burma, Vietnam — at the most dangerous moments possible. The one common thread was self-imposed peril and hardship: "I used to deliberately put myself into some pretty tricky situations just to see how I would handle them."

Even in more mundane matters, Trudeau could not resist setting himself compulsive little challenges to test his self-discipline. When he was articling in a Montreal law firm in the early 1940s, for instance, he resolved to eat lunch in a different restaurant every day — and he kept up the vow for a full year, exploring obscure back streets in search of new greasy-spoons and beaneries. In everyday life, the reflection of his discipline was, and remains, a meticulousness about every form of activity; he structures his time carefully, and whatever he happens to be doing, be it work or play, commands his total involvement and must be done as thoroughly as he is capable of doing it.

His rebellion against authority and his sense of independence also went through a process of evolution, beginning with vulgarity and culminating in a set of intellectual conclusions that eventually contributed to his becoming prime minister. The vulgarity came during the Second World War, when Trudeau — who is recalled as an avid prankster and tease — and a few friends amused themselves by roaming the Quebec countryside dressed up as German invaders or deserters, frightening inhabitants and then taunting the police who came to investigate. In this, too, there was an element of self-testing in addition to the obvious desire to be shocking. One of Trudeau's companions in these escapades has said: "It was funny once or twice, but I got bored and asked him why all the fuss. He said he found it a good way to develop confidence in himself and to learn to control the circumstances around him."[4] His dislike of authority also manifested itself, for years after this, in a kind of compulsion to go out of his way to thumb his nose at police in Canada and abroad.

At another level, Trudeau's notion of freedom led him for most of his adult life to avoid any professional or personal commitments that would tie him down to inescapable responsibilities and restrict his options. He worked hard at whatever he happened to be doing, but he refused to do anything he couldn't give up at a moment's notice if his inclinations changed. The philosophical side of his freedom-loving individualism found expression, meanwhile, in the evolution of his theories on the role of the state and the importance of rowing against the tide by creating counterweights.

In religious matters, he has reconciled freedom and duty in accordance with the Thomistic philosophy that delighted him as a teen-ager. He is a devout Catholic who attends Mass most Sundays, but he puts more emphasis on conscience than on legalistic religious rules. "Yes, God exists for me," he says. "I encounter Him everywhere; I also look for Him in church, but rather elsewhere. I believe in eternal life, hence in God."[5] But his concept of sin, as he himself says, is rather more Protestant than Catholic. "The notion of sin is not a term I like to use. . . . The only really basic sin is to hurt others. I say with Tom Paine, 'my religion is to do good'."[6]

As Trudeau matured, meanwhile, his reaction against his sensitivity was twofold. Intellectually, his flight from emotionalism led him to embrace rationality in all matters. Socially, he became a young man with a great many acquaintances, but only a relatively few, carefully picked friends; apart from those few to whom he allowed "access to my inner self", as he puts it, his companions found that they could spend great amounts of time with him and still come away not really knowing him. His genuine friendships seemed to develop primarily not from social contact, but from professional or intellectual interaction: he would work with someone on a project or exchange ideas over a period of time, and then — presumably as the person proved himself trustworthy — Trudeau would gradually lower the barriers.

Those he did choose as his friends, however, have found that he has the gift of true, loyal friendship. His closest friends are those he made years ago, in his twenties, and though he may not see them often, there is little he wouldn't do to help if any of them were in difficulty. Says one of them: "He's the sort of man who won't pick up your check in a restaurant, because he feels that would somehow hurt the dignity of the relationship. But if you're in trouble, he can be very, very generous."

What is particularly striking about the evolution of Trudeau's personality in childhood and early youth is the force of will that he consistently displayed. Frail, he made himself into a superbly conditioned athlete. Painfully sensitive, he deliberately insulated his emotions behind a barrier impenetrable to all but a chosen few. Attracted by the idea of autonomy, he braved the opinion of his peers to make himself the most individualistic of youths. These changes didn't just happen; they were wrought by a calculating exercise of will that is perhaps best captured by Trudeau's description of his decision to switch abruptly from Québécois joual to classical French pronunciation:

"I guess it was a matter of logic. I was in classical studies, probably around fourteen or fifteen, and I liked poetry and reading a great deal, and I suddenly began to realize that I wasn't reading the way I was speaking. Because in those days I was beginning to read Racine and Corneille and God knows who, and Molière, and the words I was speaking weren't really the words that were written. And I said, 'Something is wrong here; either I start reading something else, or I start speaking a bit more the way it's supposed to be done.' In that sense, I remember a turning point, almost overnight, or perhaps during the summer break. I decided that, and I remember being rather penalized for it, because when you're fifteen and you suddenly begin to say 'le gateau' rather than 'le gaaaateau', people begin poking fun at you. Not only in school, but in the neighbourhood, and even some of my relatives: 'Oh, look, he's putting on airs.' "

Marc Lalonde, a close associate who has known Trudeau for years — as his intellectual comrade-in-arms in the early sixties, as his constitutional advisor when Trudeau was justice minister, as his principal secretary when he became prime minister, and currently as a senior minister — is struck by this self-created quality of the man: "He's an austere man, a very disciplined man, who built himself up by sheer will and intellect. My impression is very much of a solitary man who through reading and reflection built himself up."

This self-building process, together with the force of will involved, goes a long way toward explaining Trudeau's ability, in public life, to present himself in different guises by accentuating different aspects of his personality. As an architect who built a house can change its appearance more easily and gracefully than an outsider, so too a man like Trudeau, who has spent so much of his life designing his own persona, can more easily work additional subtle changes in its presentation than people whose original evolution was less consciously guided.

Trudeau has not been able, of course, to depart totally from the self he began with as a child.

Physically, the rather frail youngster has been replaced by an athletic man who carries about 160 lean, powerfully muscled pounds on his 5' 10" frame, who excels at such demanding sports as skiing, water-skiing, judo, parachute-skiing, canoeing, and scuba diving, and who can leave most men twenty years his junior panting in his wake at most forms of physical endeavour. But a reminder of the original frailty remains in his relatively low over-all stamina. He tires quite easily, and needs to average eight hours' sleep a night; he can get by on five hours a night for periods of time when necessary, but then he has to compensate with a period of sleeping twelve or thirteen hours. Says a close associate and advisor: "When he doesn't let himself tire quickly, for instance during a crisis or an election campaign, at the end he is absolutely exhausted. The only thing to do is get him away so he can sleep and rest for a couple of days."

Similarly, the original sensitivity has not been banished, just buried deeper and hidden from most people's view. He doesn't particularly like compliments, for instance, and most forms of praise or criticism float past him with minimal impact; but sincere praise from people he particularly respects still has an effect not that far removed from his childhood reactions. Recalls an aide who has never heard Trudeau's reminiscences about his tendency to cry over compliments when he was small: "The PM gave a speech in Toronto, and afterwards Eugene Forsey came up to him and said:

'That was just a first-rate speech, it was really excellent.' And Trudeau just sort of stepped back as if he'd been hit, and I swear that for a moment he looked like he was going to burst into tears."

Marc Lalonde also notes Trudeau's continuing sensitivity. "He's a man with a lot of heart, a very sensitive man — contrary to what a lot of people think. I've seen the man cry, at the funeral of a friend. At the funeral of [Liberal MP] Albanie Morin. And he cried at the funeral of an old friend of both of us. He's moved by children easily. He projects an image of being a heart of stone — he's not. You find that quite often among fundamentally shy people, that they project a very stony image. They don't know how to handle one-to-one situations."

But an image that is projected almost constantly acquires a reality of its own. Lalonde's perception of Trudeau is shared by virtually everyone who knows him well. But very few people, even among his own ministers and staff, are allowed to know him well, and what most others see is quite different: an impressive but hard loner sealed in an impenetrable shell, socially ungenerous in his reluctance to give anything of himself, unwilling to be touched except on his own terms. It's not the real core of the man, but that core is so carefully hidden that for the majority of people who must deal with him it scarcely matters.

Some basic elements of Trudeau's character have evolved and perhaps softened with the passage of years. Discipline is now pursued a little less single-mindedly, he seems a shade more willing to leave himself emotionally vulnerable, and his assertions of independence are acted out less crudely. But those three elements — discipline, and the expectation of finding it in others; sensitivity, and the effort to camouflage it; and the determination to be always his own man — remain paramount. Together with his upbringing and other formative influences, they are an indispensable key to understanding his personality and his actions.

CHAPTER FOUR

The Formative Years I: Home Environment

TRUDEAU's home environment, like the man it eventually produced, was a complex mix of French and English, visceral Québécois feeling and cosmopolitanism, discipline and freedom, urban sophistication and rustic adventure.

On his father's side, his ancestry was entirely French Canadian, traceable back ten generations to one Etienne Truteau, a tall, sturdy carpenter from La Rochelle on the Atlantic coast of France, who emigrated to New France at the age of seventeen in 1659. He lived for a time in Ville Marie, later to become Montreal, before settling down to farm at Longueuil across the St. Lawrence River from the city. Until recently, when the building to which it was affixed was demolished, a small plaque on the corner of Montreal's La Gauchetière and St. André streets recorded one of his adventures: "Here Truteau, Roulier, and Langevin-Lacroix resisted 50 Iroquois, May 6, 1662." Such confrontations with hostile natives were only one of the hazards of life in New France in those days, but Truteau survived at least long enough to father fourteen children and become the progenitor of all the Trudeaus now living in Canada and the United States.

Trudeau's paternal grandfather, like generations before him, was a well-to-do farmer at St. Michel de Napierville, about twenty miles south of Montreal. Joseph Trudeau, a short, easy-going man with a huge waxed moustache, died in 1919 when Trudeau was only two months old, but the prime minister recalls hearing him described as a man of prodigious physical strength. He was a simple man who didn't even learn to sign his name until middle age, but — largely at the urging of his wife Malvina, the ambitious, strong-willed daughter of the local mayor — he sent his sons to the best schools: Collège Ste. Marie, Loyola, and the University of Montreal.

Trudeau's father, Charles — known as Charlie to all his friends — was a wiry little extrovert of a man, with dark hair, intense eyes, a thin toothbrush moustache, and quick, nervous movements and speech. After graduating from the University of Montreal, he practised law for a time, then went into business for himself in 1921 by founding the Automobile Owners' Association. Despite its name, the association was a commercial enterprise: For ten dollars a year, members got free around-the-clock breakdown service within a twenty-five-mile radius of Montreal, a road map, and reduced rates on gas and oil at Trudeau service stations; Trudeau also managed to get permission from the Quebec government to issue provincial licence plates at two of his outlets. The enterprise proved immensely profitable. It started with two service stations, one in the east of the city and one in the west; by the time Trudeau sold it to an agent for Imperial Oil in the fall of 1932 for $1.4 million, it comprised fifteen thousand members and thirty filling stations.

In the two and a half remaining years of his life, he proceeded to double his money through a series of shrewd investments; these included such rapidly rising stocks of the day as Hollinger and Algoma Steel, as well as extensive real estate holdings in Montreal and the Laurentian mountains north of the city. He also bought a large share in a Montreal amusement park, the twenty-six-acre Belmont Park on the banks of the Rivière des Prairies. And, mostly for the fun of it, he invested fifteen thousand dollars to become vice-president and principal shareholder of the Montreal Royals baseball team.

Work was only a small part of Charlie Trudeau's life. Hugely gregarious, he would bring swarms of friends home to dinner on weekend evenings, or arrive at the family's country place in the summer with carloads of guests. He was an inveterate poker player who would indulge in the game several nights a week at the Club St. Denis — a popular hangout of rich young businessmen, where he was a director — for stakes that easily ran to $1,000 or $1,500 an evening. He also loved sports and the company of athletes; in addition to buying the Montreal Royals, he involved himself in such ways as backing a lightweight boxer and giving hockey star Phil Watson his first job, in one of the service stations. Politically, Trudeau was a life-long Conservative and a close friend and financial backer of Camillien Houde, the colourful and controversial mayor who presided over one of the most wide-open and corruption-ridden eras in Montreal's history.

Amid his varying interests and hectic social life, Charlie Trudeau always made the time to be a dedicated and involved father. Like many of today's parents, he believed that it wasn't the quantity but the quality of the time set aside for children that counted. Promptly at 5.15 every day, he would drop whatever he was doing at work and go home to spend at least an hour giving his three children — Suzette, Pierre, and Charles, the youngest — his undivided attention. Then he would usually go out and spend the evening with friends.

Suzette, a friendly, intelligent, but somewhat shy woman with a striking facial resemblance to her brother, is married to Montreal dentist Pierre Rouleau and lives a few blocks from their childhood home in the fashionable Outremont section of the city. Charles was a successful architect whose projects included designing Ottawa's city hall, but he retired early and lives in semi-seclusion in the Laurentians.

Suzette Rouleau remembers her father as "a very strong-charactered man. He was a small man — smaller than Pierre physically — but wiry and very lively. He had lots of friends. He was interested in our friends. During his vacation, he'd always be interested in our games. He wasn't with us an awful lot, but when he was there he was very much present. . . . He was very interested in our schooling. He'd come home for the night meal and then he'd leave afterwards, but he always had to see our homework and see what kind of marks we were getting.

"He was very strict, and on the other hand he was very open-minded. He was very strict if he forbade us to do something — that was it, and we got a licking if we didn't listen. But, on the other hand, he wanted us to see a lot of things, and I remember if we were travelling — I was twelve, fourteen, fifteen — he'd bring me to nightclubs, which was something my friends' parents didn't do. But he wouldn't have me playing bridge with friends, for instance, because he thought that was not for me."

Though he was severe when disobeyed, Charlie Trudeau preferred to encourage his children with incentives. In the summers, for instance, when his three kids were in the country with playmates their own age, he would offer to give a quarter to whoever could jump the highest or run the fastest or hang by his legs the longest, or he would promise to buy a canoe when his children could swim a certain distance.

Recalls Trudeau: "He was basically a very good father, because he didn't punish very often; he rewarded much more than he punished. When I was doing my 5BX exercises, he would reward me: 'Have you done them this week, and if so, I'll give you a dime.'" Even in intellectual matters, he favoured material incentives. "He urged me to read, and he'd say, 'If you can tell me the story, I'll give you a reward.'"

Trudeau grew up adoring his father, and being a little dazzled by him:

"He was a man I admired very much, you know, for everything, because at least in the eyes of the world I lived in, he was a successful man. He had a lot of friends, the house was always full of friends. And he was big in my eyes, but he was obviously big in the eyes of his friends, too. He was a leader, he had wit, he was a physically . . . I don't know, I always think he was physically strong, but I am sure my sons think I am physically strong, too. He wielded some authority; that made me respect him and, during the last years of his life, probably also challenge him from time to time, as adolescents do. But he died before I ever got into any open conflict with him. I remember that he had demanding standards, which didn't consist of saying, 'You must be more like me,' but did consist of saying, 'You must do whatever you are doing properly.'

"He would teach me boxing, he would teach me tricks in wrestling, he would teach me how to shoot a gun, how to make a bow and arrow. It's amazing, because he didn't spend all that much time with me; he worked very hard. He would come home at the end of the day and spend an hour with me, but that was an hour which was full of everything. . . . I can't think of anything I really hated or despised or doubted my father about, so in that sense he was a rather ideal father figure.[1]

"He gave me a taste for life; he was much more exuberant than I and I wanted to imitate him. But he was stern. He had principles: when we were fooling, we were fooling; but when it was serious, it was very serious."[2]

When Trudeau speaks of his father his eyes light up and his gestures become more animated, and the listener gets the impression of a child who may have been unknowingly overawed by an exceptionally dynamic father, perhaps in ways that contributed to his childhood sensitivity, insecurity, and later self-testing and rebelliousness. In most conversations, he denies this, saying, for instance: "I wouldn't say he was formidable, because I'm afraid you'd try to read into it that I was really a dominated child and I felt that I was awestruck in front of him. I don't have that feeling."

But in one recent interview on French television, he appeared to acknowledge that there might be at least an element of this: "Perhaps, by a mechanism which the psychologists could explain, because I felt so inferior to him in all respects — a man of spirit who played, had friends, was strong physically, etc. . . . But he gave me the means to be like him: He taught me boxing, to shoot a rifle, he taught me to talk, to read. . . ."[3]

While Trudeau's father represented verve, discipline, and a French Canadian environment, his mother gave their household serenity, freedom, and an element of English reserve. Though her mother was French Canadian and she herself was fluently bilingual and had many French-speaking friends, Grace Elliott Trudeau was essentially English in upbringing and manner, and was descended from United Empire Loyalist stock. The daughter of a businessman of Scottish ancestry, she was educated at Dunham Ladies' College in Quebec's Eastern Townships near the Vermont border.

She was a small, delicate-looking woman with an air of quiet refinement, a cultured *grande dame* who frequently visited museums and attended concerts and who is remembered as both intelligent and charming. Though quiet, she was an adventurous woman who enjoyed taking her small children on canoe trips, loved foreign travel, and thought nothing of roaring across Paris with young Pierre on his motorcycle when he was a student there. Even when she was crowding seventy, she would cheerfully stand on Trudeau's shoulders at the beach to demonstrate acrobatics to his nieces and nephews.

Says Suzette: "She was quiet. My father was very outgoing, mother was not. She had many friends — old friends, new friends. She had a good sense of humour. And I think she understood everybody. Perhaps that's why she had so many friends: she didn't criticize. I never heard her criticize anybody or say somebody should have done something some other way, whether it was the help or whether it was relatives or friends."

Trudeau is much more matter-of-fact about her than about his father, and conversations about her lead before very long to some reminiscence which steers him back to talking about his father. Asked to describe her, his first response is: "Well, a mother is a mother. She was a good mother, spent a lot of time with us." At one point, he observes: "I suppose until you're ten or twelve, you think that nobody can be better than your father, whether it's the way he tells jokes or teaches you to box or whatever it is. So, in a sense, all the period I was with him was much less a period of criticism than with my mother. So during the time he was there, he was probably a stronger influence."

But then he quickly corrects himself: "No, I don't think that's fair. I think there was a good, balanced influence. He was a very vital person, full of laughter and strength and wit and friends all around him. And during that whole period, I suppose my mother was more discreet and withdrawn, didn't loom so large. But in terms of love and presence, of course, she was always there.

"Since my earliest childhood, I remember spending a lot of time with her. I remember her as being rather less severe than my father, but able to punish us good and hard when we did something wrong. But it was always a surprise when my mother punished me, whereas when my father punished us, it was more expected. She loved liberty perhaps more than my father did.

"She never gave me the impression of an overly protective

mother, didn't go around saying, 'Don't do that, it's dangerous,' or 'Don't do that, you'll fall and hurt yourself.' I can always remember rather an encouragement to whatever I was doing — it could be hanging upside down from a tree or learning acrobatics or going off on hikes or, much later in life, taking canoe trips into the wilderness.[4]

"If I was going off to James Bay, for example, she would say, 'So long. Have a nice trip, and don't get drowned.' She never said, 'Why don't you work or study instead?' She just said, 'I'll expect you back when I see you.' She wasn't always off to parties, didn't break down and weep, never took things too tragically, never imposed her wishes on us. She left her children free. What I most admire about her was her lack of possessiveness: I never felt held back in any way."[5]

The differing approaches of his two parents complemented, and almost certainly accentuated, the inherent tendencies toward both discipline and freedom in Trudeau's personality. His childhood sensitivity made him particularly susceptible to parental influences, and the sense of discipline stressed by his father provided a solid base from which Trudeau could exercise his pursuit of freedom without totally losing his perspective.

The two other family players in the cast of Trudeau's childhood were his maternal grandfather and his paternal grandmother, both of whose spouses had died too early for him to know them. Though their influence was limited, he has vivid memories of both.

His mother's father represented travel, adventure, and sophistication. "He was an old Scot, rather short, I think; quite powerfully built; a very mobile face, quite pockmarked. Very lively. He was an all-round man. He spoke English, French; he had travelled; he wore magnificent watch-chains. He'd show us his collection of swords and sabres, his collection of clocks, his collection of coins, his collection of stamps. It seemed he had been everywhere, had souvenirs of everywhere.

"And he was a man who knew how to do everything, and who taught us — who helped us in the country to find nails, who had us climb up on the roof to help him lay shingles, who taught us how to saw. . . . To me, he embodied universal wisdom."[6]

If his maternal grandfather represented English-Canadian in-

fluences and world travel, his paternal grandmother was the opposite: French, and of the countryside. "She was always dressed in
black, it seemed to me, with her hair pulled back and gathered
behind her head — a rather austere look. But she was a fine old
woman. A very lined face. Very religious, very strict in that sense.
She was a country woman who came to the city in her last years to
be closer to her children. She was a fine old woman who told us
stories, who taught us our prayers. It's with her that I most associate the learning of French; she didn't speak English, obviously, so
with her we spoke only French. And I associated her with life in
the country."[7]

Trudeau's first childhood home was on Durocher Street in
Montreal's Outremont area. It was a middle-class neighbourhood
of row houses and small gardens, with a cosmopolitan cultural mix
that his sister remembers as being somewhat more English than
French. Later, when Trudeau was eleven, his father bought a house
at 84 McCulloch Avenue, just a few blocks up the hill in the same
parish, but in a much more prosperous section. A large but un-
imposing structure of brownish brick with an old-fashioned front
porch, situated on a narrow lot and less ornate than the neighbour-
ing houses, it remained Trudeau's home base until he became prime
minister, and it was his mother's home until her death in 1973.

His first playmates on Durocher Street were the Jewish children
of his next-door neighbours. He recalls their mother as being a
rather cultivated, avant-garde woman, and he and these children
used to exchange books; they gave him the first Jack London book
he read as a young child, and he reciprocated by lending them
books in French. The neighbours two doors down were French
Canadian, and the household next to theirs was Irish. Playing on
the sidewalks and laneways of Durocher Street meant switching
constantly and naturally between French and English, and young
Pierre even picked up a smattering of Yiddish as well.

At home, the Trudeau children usually spoke English to both
parents — to their mother because it was her first language, and to
their father because he wanted to practise and polish his command
of it. But to their grandmother and other relatives on their father's

side, and to the household servants — usually a country girl who had come to the city to work as maid for a few years, and a handyman-cum-driver named Grenier who was with the family for some forty years — they spoke French. The elementary school they attended had both French and English classes; they were enrolled on the English side for the first few grades, and then transferred to the French.

The result of these various influences was that Trudeau spent all his formative years with one foot in each of Quebec's two major linguistic and cultural groups, differing from most of the children of his generation in his lack of total identification with either side. At first, in fact, he wasn't even entirely sure of the distinctions between the two languages, combining them in single sentences such as "We'll go down to the bord de l'eau," or "On va marcher sur le boardwalk." Later, in school, he switched cultural allegiances back and forth without difficulty: "I was first with the English, when I was in English classes, and I gladly fought against the French Canadians. Then when I changed to the French side, it was the opposite. But these were gangs based more on the need boys feel to be active, to organize themselves, to go around making noise, than on any serious divisions."[8]

Trudeau enjoyed elementary school from the outset and his insecurity about his abilities made him intensely competitive, but he says it wasn't really intellectual curiosity that motivated him most in those days. "I remember that I won a lot of prizes, but at that stage it wasn't a love of knowledge, a love of learning. It was rather a matter of excelling at a game called 'reading and writing', just as in recreation period you'd try to excel at basketball or something."[9]

While winters were an urban experience on Montreal's Durocher Street, summers in Trudeau's early childhood meant adventure in the northern wilderness. In late June, just after St. Jean Baptiste Day on the twenty-fourth, Charlie Trudeau would take his children to the barbershop for haircuts short enough to last the whole summer; then the family would pile into the car for a three- or four-hour drive over bad roads to Lac Tremblant, an area of the Laurentians more frequented in those days by lumberjacks than by vacationers. The children and their mother, usually accompanied by a few cousins or other playmates their own age, would spend two and a half months at the lake, while Charlie worked in the city and drove up on Friday nights.

"Summers meant being amid nature," Trudeau recalls. "They meant the joys of the forest, the lake, canoeing, swimming, running, climbing mountains. They were very physical vacations — the discovery of nature, of wild animals, hearing the howling of wolves for the first time, or catching fireflies to light up your little room. . . . And then on Friday afternoons, at the end of the day, we'd hear a faraway rumbling from the other side of the lake, and it was cars arriving from the city, it was my father arriving with his friends. And that meant candies, and games, and new faces. He brought all sorts of people. I remember especially the athletes; one weekend he brought Leo Roy, who was world lightweight boxing champion — he had a beautiful golden belt — and who gave us lessons. Other times, he'd bring businessmen, lawyers, judges, notaries, and the weekends were always very lively."[10]

Later, when Trudeau was seven or eight, the family began dividing its summers between Lac Tremblant and the seashore at Ocean Park, Maine, and later at Old Orchard Beach.

In addition to Lac Tremblant and the seashore, there was also another non-urban element in Trudeau's upbringing — the farm country of Napierville, south of Montreal, which was home to his father's side of the family. "We'd visit our cousins and relatives, and those were very happy times, because in the country you can do everything: you can harness horses, ride in a wagon, go sleighing, skate on the river, explore the cannery. . . . Mont Tremblant was wild nature, with the wolves and such, and the Richelieu Valley was civilized, a whole new range of experiences. My cousins were very strong, they played hockey very well; I was a rather puny city kid, I had a lot to learn."[11]

It was in the farm country of Napierville, too, that Trudeau was most exposed to the family life-style and traditions of the working-class Québécois. "At Christmas or New Year's, there was the big meal in the kitchen near the stove. My aunt would serve the goodies. My uncle would carve the turkey, in his shirtsleeves, his brow dripping wet, and serve it to the sort of huge brood of kids you only find in the country. . . . And there were the games we played. And the prison in the village, the cells, the men: the village idiot, the village drunk, all those characters you don't see in the city, but who in the country are well known, perhaps better known to kids than the parish priest or the mayor or the doctor."[12]

At the age of twelve, Trudeau began the most formative phase of his intellectual life when he became a student at the élite, Jesuit-run Collège Jean de Brébeuf. The cluster of big cream-coloured buildings about a mile from Trudeau's home housed one of the finest academic institutions in the country, a classical college that combined the high school and university levels in a program for boys from twelve to twenty. Trudeau's intellectual curiosity and the decision he had already made, however vaguely, to counteract his sensitivity by emphasizing reason over emotion, were factors that made him particularly receptive to the Jesuit approach to education.

Then, as now, it was an approach that emphasized leadership training and the development of each student's individuality. It laid heavy stress on rationality, on careful Cartesian logic, on the ability to argue and debate cogently. And, in true classical style, it sought to broaden the horizons of the students by encouraging their interest not only in practical academic subjects, but in the arts, in philosophy, and in politics.

Classmates from Brébeuf remember Trudeau as a brilliant student who was always at or near the head of his class. But he was not, by most accounts, a lovable personality. He was already intent, by the time he entered Brébeuf, on asserting his individuality through an aggressive combination of mischief, rebelliousness, eccentricity, and pugnacity. Aloof, arrogant and sharp-tongued toward most fellow students, he was the de facto leader of a small clique of similarly bright, rich Outremont kids evocatively known as Les Snobs.

But Trudeau's obnoxiousness had certain limits. Though his father's successful business insulated the family from the hardships that working-class Montrealers were experiencing because of the Depression, for instance, young Pierre never flaunted his comfortable affluence — in part, at least, because he had no real sense of being privileged: "My parents were very strict about money, so I never had any more than people who were suffering because of the depression."[13] And, unlike most youngsters of that age, he never liked to brag about any special experiences he might have had outside school. Even the trip to Europe at the age of thirteen went unmentioned at Brébeuf, either out of modesty or out of the beginnings of the deep sense of privacy Trudeau has displayed in later life. Says a classmate: "It didn't happen very often at that time that someone in the class would go to Europe, but we didn't know anything about Pierre's going. He would never boast about anything in his personal or family life."

That trip to Europe, in the summer of 1933, added yet another unusual element to Trudeau's upbringing, giving him the sort of taste of the outside world that was available to very few contemporaries in the rather insular Quebec of that time. It also lit the spark of the wanderlust that later dominated his twenties and thirties. And, at least indirectly, it contributed to the development of his views on nationalism. A thirteen-year-old doesn't see the world in political terms, but some impressions of Nazi Germany and Fascist Italy were etched deeply into his memory: "All I noticed at the time were the fanfares and the soldiers and the motorcycles and all that. I obviously didn't see the political significance at all. But when I went back after the war and saw the consequences, I began to look for the causes. I found them in economic crises and in nationalism, which I have always detested."[14]

Two years later, in April of 1935, Trudeau's world was suddenly transformed by the death of his father. Charlie Trudeau had gone to Orlando, Florida, over the Easter holiday to watch the spring training of his baseball team. He caught a virus which turned into pneumonia, which in turn resulted in heart failure, all within three days; he died at the age of forty-six. Trudeau recognizes his father's death as a major turning point in his development, but he cannot define precisely how it changed him. "It was traumatic, very traumatic," he says. "I still can't go to a funeral without crying. . . ."

In his home life, the death had the effect of arresting his natural teen-ager's tendency to rebel against parental authority. Trudeau had become mildly rebellious toward his father's discipline, but it had not reached the stage of any real conflict. Had he then transferred this rebellion to his mother, his strength of will and propensity toward mischief would have made it almost impossible for her to control him. Instead, at home, he accepted her authority — or rather, in a sense, imposed a discipline of obedience on himself. Says Suzette: "I remember my mother's first words when we heard that my father was dead, because we were flying down to Florida when he was ill. And the first thing she said was, 'I'll never be able to bring the boys up alone.' Which meant, you know, that she relied very much on my father for discipline and schooling. But I don't remember anything striking me that Pierre was different after my father died. He didn't shock or disturb us or react in a way that I would think was because my father was gone. . . . Perhaps he took on a certain responsibility. I remember later, when I was still at the house — I suppose Pierre wasn't very old, maybe seventeen or eighteen — and my father was no longer there to discuss things with me or help me make decisions, I remember feeling that I could speak with Pierre. He was younger than I was, but I felt I could ask his opinion — so perhaps he did take on certain responsibilities that I didn't really realize at the time."

If his father's death sobered Trudeau at home, it had precisely the opposite effect in school. It was followed by the period in which he was at his most rebellious, and the transfer of hostilities from the domestic to the public arenas may well — as he himself suggests — have helped freeze him into an almost lifelong posture of resisting authority.

Charlie Trudeau's demise had the effect, too, of changing the whole cultural atmosphere of the household. Though the language of communication had been English, the father's dominant personality had made the over-all ambience distinctly Gallic: hearty, demonstrative, boisterous with the laughter and discussion of countless guests. After his death, it was Grace Trudeau's English reserve that set the tone. Recalls Trudeau: "When my father was around, there was a great deal of effusiveness and laughter and kissing and hugging. But after he died, it was a little bit more the

English mores which took over, and we used to even joke about, or laugh at, some of our cousins or neighbours or friends — French Canadians — who'd always be very effusive within the family and towards their mother and so on."

By this time, however, Trudeau was spending relatively little of his waking life at home. Brébeuf was taking up most of his time, with classes six days a week and Mass on Sundays, plus long afternoons and evenings of discussion with classmates or teachers. And it was at Brébeuf, a year after his father's death, that he encountered the teacher whom he regards as the greatest intellectual influence in his years as a student.

Father Jean Bernier was twenty-five at the time, in only his second year of teaching, a French Canadian Manitoban whose father was a lawyer and a long-time member of the Manitoba legislature. "Father Bernier was the most highly cultivated man I had met," Trudeau has said, "and he confirms what I am always saying — that you can be a damned good French Canadian outside Quebec. Bernier was the man who talked politics to me. He was my teacher of letters, of French literature. He really taught me to like beautiful things, poetry or books or art; he really set standards of appreciation which have never left me."[15]

Father Bernier himself, in a 1969 interview with Edith Iglauer of the New Yorker magazine, explained his approach this way: "We were very close, the boys and I. Part of the teaching was the idea of meeting a man, of getting to know him deeply. We passed books back and forth. Literature, philosophy, music, painting — all went together. We lamented the lack of museums in Montreal, but we got acquainted with Cézanne, Renoir, Degas, Gauguin, Manet, van Gogh, and the ultimate, Picasso — and even the sculptor Maillol — through reproductions in books. In architecture, we bought the books of Le Corbusier. Great music was beginning to be heard in Montreal, with Wilfrid Pelletier conducting there. We wouldn't miss any concerts if we could help it, especially if they included our favourites — Fauré, Debussy, Stravinsky. And, of course, there were records. All this was a bit cut off from the atmosphere of daily life, but these were the sons of bourgeois and didn't have money troubles, so they could throw themselves into art and beauty. It was an atmosphere of elation, where everything was beautiful.

"In addition, I taught them French, Greek and Latin literature, and although this was a typical modern French culture, it was open to other streams of thought, like Tagore, the Indian poet, and outside of class we would read and discuss, in English, Hemingway, Faulkner, Henry James, Hawthorne, and Thoreau, particularly what Thoreau said about the wilderness, which was very appealing to Canadians. We could enter easily into the mind of Locke, de Tocqueville, Acton, Jefferson. Our little life gave the boys respect for the rational, an instinctive repulsion against the rising Fascism and Nazism. I insisted on a respect for man-made beauty. They had to understand that our real men are not destroyers but builders — of society, of poetry, and of beauty — and that all these things are linked together. I used to give the boys Plato as a model of intellectual courage — the man who by himself caused the Greeks to pass from a mythical to a rational mode of knowledge. You could feel that Pierre had this kind of courage; even as a boy, he would say what he thought any place."

It was Father Bernier who provided Trudeau's first serious exposure to politics and history, and the themes he stressed were later to find a strong echo in his pupil's writings and theories: "I insisted not only on facts and dates, but on thoughts: the importance of the democratic spirit and the idea of federalism as a way of having political unity and cultural differences in the same country — a pluralistic society, with a sense of the universal and a love of differences for themselves, where outside all the differences of nation, religion, sex, colour, and so on, a man is a man and is respected as such."[16]

The years at Brébeuf were decisive, too, in determining the balance between French and English in Trudeau's life. His earlier upbringing, which had made him neither entirely French nor entirely English, shaped his development at Brébeuf by keeping him at a sceptical distance from the Quebec nationalism of his classmates and thereby providing the first major channel for his urge to swim against the prevailing currents of thought. But it was Brébeuf, in turn, which determined that Pierre Trudeau would be essentially a French Canadian who speaks impeccable English, rather than a French-speaking anglophone.

Trudeau is a man who compartmentalizes areas of experience, and the eight years at Brébeuf — the period that laid the foundations of his intellectual development — ensured that he would classify his intellectual life in the "French" category. Like most people who are fluently bilingual, he says he thinks in whichever language he happens to be speaking — and, indeed, he can switch from speaking one to the other in mid-sentence without skipping a beat. But when he is writing in private, it is usually in French. It was in French that he wrote virtually all his political articles in the 1950s, and associates say he feels he can express himself with greater precision in that language. When he is tired, it is usually his English that suffers first; at such times, he will occasionally grope for the right word in English or offer its French equivalent, but the reverse when he is speaking French happens much more rarely. It is significant, too, that nearly all his closest personal friends are primarily French-speaking. But English was compart-mentalized in his experience as the language of the home, and it may be not entirely coincidental that when he finally married late in life, it was to an English-speaking woman.

After graduating from Brébeuf with a BA in 1940, Trudeau had to make a major decision about his future. "One fork in the road was law, and another was all the area of the mind — I'm thinking of psychology, philosophy, and so on.[17] What interested me was to know what makes a society tick, what it was that produced either order or disorder . . . either in the mind through psycho-logical derangement . . . or in society itself by legal or monetary troubles.[18] Naturally, in my family there were people who talked to me about the law; my father had always said, 'Study law, get that under your belt, and then you can do other things as I did.' But 'other things' might have meant just as easily business, in his mind and in mine. In fact, what I liked about the law was that it prepared for an understanding of society."[19]

Trudeau's resolution of the choice between law and psychology was dictated as much by circumstance as by preference. The Uni-versity of Montreal didn't teach psychology in those days, and though his student status allowed him to stay out of the army, he couldn't leave the country to study abroad because of the war. But the study of law also dovetailed neatly with his own inclinations: "I have always loved justice. I have always loved a sense of balance. . . . I wanted to know my rights in order to be able to push them to the limit. I didn't like authority. Consequently, I liked to be able to contradict people who said I didn't have a right to do such and such a thing."[20]

He studied law less as a preparation for practice than as a social science: "I studied it much as one would study economics or political science, to understand how a society works, how it governs itself, how it controls itself — just like you study fiscal policy to know how you control the economy." His sister's recollection is that "he hated studying law, and he just finished because he had started, I think. He didn't like his classes." But he himself says: "My delight with the law developed a couple of years after I'd begun, after I began to realize that here was an instrument of social control, and it was an extraordinary creation of society. I wasn't interested in the lawmakers as much as I was interested in the whole process."

During his years at the University of Montreal, and even earlier, young Trudeau's appetite for outdoor adventure, whetted in those childhood days at Lac Tremblant, led him to make long, arduous, and potentially dangerous canoeing expeditions deep into the northern wilderness. On these trips, as on later world travels, he exhibited a characteristic combination of daring and prudence. "He liked to take chances," says one companion, "but only after he made sure the odds were strongly in his favour." The expeditions, which he would propose with studied casualness, were hazardous by their very nature: isolation in remote forests with scant hope of rescue if something went wrong, churning rapids, freezing waters. But Trudeau never took uncalculated risks, and he would prepare for each outing with an attention to detail that was the very antithesis of recklessness. His long-time friend Gérard Pelletier points out, significantly, that in all his risky exploits Trudeau has suffered serious injury only once — a broken collarbone in a motorcycle accident: "He projects the image of a breakneck type, but he is actually very careful. He is physically very courageous, but in a very calculated way."[21]

Though he pursued other forms of adventure, including roaring off on long trips on his big Harley-Davidson motorcycle or going on 100-mile hiking expeditions through the woods, canoeing has always held a special place in Trudeau's affections. In a revealing 1944 essay entitled "Exhaustion and Fulfilment: The Ascetic in a Canoe", he described it in almost mystical terms:

"What is essential at the beginning is the resolve to reach the saturation point. Ideally, the trip should end only when the members are making no further progress within themselves. They should not be fooled, though, by a period of boredom, weariness or disgust; that is not the end, but the last obstacle before it. Let saturation be serene! . . . It is a condition of such a trip that you entrust yourself, stripped of your worldly goods, to nature. Canoe and paddle, blanket and knife, salt pork and flour, fishing rod and rifle; that is about the extent of your wealth. To remove all the useless material baggage from a man's heritage is, at the same time, to free his mind from petty preoccupations, calculations and memories. On the other hand, what fabulous and undeveloped mines are to be found in nature, friendship and oneself! The paddler has no choice but to draw everything from them. . . . I know a man whose school could never teach him patriotism, but who acquired that virtue when he felt in his bones the vastness of his land, and the greatness of those who founded it."[22]

This was also the period of Trudeau the obnoxious prankster, with such escapades as his impersonations of a stray German soldier in the Quebec countryside. On another occasion, after losing a public debate on the subject of "Gallantry" at the University of Montreal, he suddenly produced a pistol, pointed it at the prominent Montrealer who had acted as judge, and fired with a loud bang and a puff of smoke. It was a blank, of course, and Trudeau coolly told the badly startled judge: "That will put some stuffing into your head." Such pranks, performed not by a child but by a highly intelligent young man in his early twenties, reveal a streak of cruelty, a willingness to amuse himself by frightening others. The same tendency occasionally shows up in his fondness, then as now, for teasing people, testing them by verbally prodding in some sensitive spot. Says his sister: "He used to tease a lot, tease me and my younger brother. He'd like to tease, see how far we could stand being teased before we broke out." A prime-ministerial staffer describes the inclination in much the same terms: "He likes to give you a good shot now and again, just to see how you'll react."

In this same period at the University of Montreal, Trudeau would also regularly put aside the roles of irrepressible student and northern adventurer, and slip into the guise of Outremont aristocrat; in this capacity, it was the taste for culture instilled first by his mother and later by Father Bernier that predominated. The war had made cultural events scarce in Montreal, so Pierre and Charles would invite their friends — forty or fifty at a time — for Sunday night soirées of recorded classical music from the family's large collection. Guests sat in the basement playroom where the record player was located, all the way up the basement stairs, and on the ground floor, where extra speakers had been installed. The program was always eclectic, anything from Bach to Stravinsky, and the evenings were really concerts rather than parties, with the guests listening seriously in silence.

His years at the University of Montreal also laid the foundations for Trudeau's later flirtation with socialism in the 1950s: "It per-haps came precisely from a feeling of repugnance at the injustice of the fact that I had been more favoured in life than some of my friends and that I had been able to complete my studies without hardship. . . . I saw certain friends at university who had to prepare their exams on the kitchen table with a dozen brothers and sisters around, whereas I could work quietly in a room at home. I found it was unjust. I have always sought remedies for things like that in society. . . . In looking for these remedies, I found them first of all in the study of socialist thought. . . . But I became aware later that the systems that these people had elaborated, whether it be called socialism or something else, were designed for a certain country or a certain period, and that we would be wrong to try to apply them to another country and another period."[23]

For all his diverse interests, what did not command very much of Trudeau's attention was the major preoccupation of the time — the Second World War. "I scarcely paid any attention to the news of the world conflict at that time," he has said. "It bothered me to be in the present. I said to myself that if you want to understand societies, you have to begin with the great thinkers. I had applied myself to read almost everything that had been written in political philosophy from antiquity until the present time. Towards the end of this work, I arrived at Hitler, Mussolini, Lenin, and so on, but it was really abstracted from the present."[24]

His student status allowed him to sidestep regular military service, undergoing training instead in the Canadian Officers Training Corps. Even here, however, he was so rebellious against authority that he was, in his own words, eventually "kicked out for lack of discipline" and transferred near the end of the war to the much tougher Fusiliers Mont-Royal. By the time his student exemption ran out, the need for soldiers had abated enough to keep him from being called up. His decision not to fight in the war was not that unusual for the time and place, since a great many of his Quebec contemporaries felt the same way. But it is something that he doesn't like to talk about, and he usually falls back on the explanation he gave at a Toronto press conference when he was contesting the Liberal leadership in 1968: "Like most Quebecers, I had been taught to keep away from imperialistic wars. The error was on the part of the politicians who promised in the 1930s that there would be no conscription and, if there was, it would be over their dead bodies." The reference to what he had been "taught" isn't an entirely convincing explanation, given Trudeau's inclination in those days to question anything he was taught, and especially anything that smacked of nationalism; if his decision wasn't simply a matter of having no urge to take chances he couldn't control and risk getting killed, it probably reflected a sense of betrayal over the conscription issue.

In the spring of 1939, Prime Minister Mackenzie King, mindful of the crisis the same issue had produced in the First World War, had pledged there would be no conscription for overseas service in the event of war. By 1940, a shortage of soldiers prompted

Parliament to legislate a measure of conscription, but only for duty at home. Then, after Japan had entered the war, the government decided to hold a plebiscite in April 1942, seeking release from its pledge not to conscript for service overseas; the result was a majority vote for release everywhere except in the Province of Quebec, where the shift in government policy had produced a widespread feeling of betrayal. Trudeau was sufficiently angered — or mischievous — to suspend his disinterest in politics and to plunge head-long into the anti-conscription battle in a federal by-election in Outremont.

The King government had brought a distinguished soldier, Major-General Léo LaFlèche, into the cabinet as associate minister of national war services, and then sought to get him into Parliament via the Outremont seat in late fall of 1942. LaFlèche was stridently opposed by the anti-conscriptionist forces of the Bloc Populaire, with a young lawyer named Jean Drapeau — later to become Montreal's mayor — as their candidate. *Le Devoir* quoted young Trudeau, enthusiastically strewing hyperboles at a pro-Drapeau rally, as saying:

"There is at present a government which wants to apply conscription and a people which will never accept it. So the government has recourse to ruses such as the plebiscite and the elevation of the general to the cabinet. This is all sickeningly dishonest. . . . If we are no longer in a democracy, let us begin the revolution without delay. The people is being asked to commit suicide. Citizens of Quebec, do not be content to gripe. Long live the flag of freedom. Enough patchwork solutions, now is the time for cataclysms."

Drapeau was soundly defeated, and Trudeau, whatever his feelings at the time, has subsequently dismissed his own involvement as something of a lark, just another attack on authority: "Outremont was perhaps the only time I plunged into current politics, and I fear my motives were not the most noble. I think it was sort of to bug the government."[25]

CHAPTER FIVE

The Formative Years II: Around the Globe, Home to Quebec

"**M**Y LIFE," Trudeau once told an interviewer, "is one long curve, full of turning points."[1] But if there was one moment when that curve became a sharp veer, it came about a year after he had graduated from the University of Montreal with a law degree in 1943. After graduation, he had slipped tentatively into the traditional pattern, joining a Montreal law firm and beginning the practice of his chosen profession. But he found the limited scope of a neophyte lawyer's activities desperately confining, and the restlessness that was to dominate much of his adult life quickly took command: "I practised one year, and I found it just terrible. A client would come in, and I'd be tempted to say, 'Well, you know, I'm not really interested in your case, sir or madam.' And that's the problem when you have an office. People come to you with their problems."

By then it was 1944, the war was ending, and he was free to travel abroad, so he decided to leave both Montreal and the practice of law, and further satisfy his curiosity about what makes societies tick. From that departure until he entered politics in 1965, Trudeau lived the life of a hummingbird, hovering over what interested him without ever quite alighting, extracting as much as he could from it, and then abruptly flitting on to something else.

His first stop was Harvard, for a two-year master's degree in political economy. "I went to Harvard because I wanted to know more about the organization of society. I wanted to know the laws of the economy, of monetary systems and banks, and to study political science. I wanted to find out how governments work. I took political economy because I wondered how the Depression had come about and where money went when suddenly there was no more of it. I wanted to know why societies are poor or rich. It was a taste for knowledge — knowledge of the human being, but also knowledge of the social order."[2]

The two years at Harvard convinced him of the inadequacy of his education in Quebec, and impelled him toward further study. "The majors in political science at Harvard had read more about Roman law and Montesquieu than I had as a lawyer. I realized then that we were being taught law as a trade in Quebec and not as a discipline."[3] To try to fill those gaps while seeing some more of the world, he moved on to Paris in the 1946-47 academic year for courses at both the Ecole des Sciences politiques and the law faculty of the Sorbonne. But he found the classes uninteresting — "I had just left Harvard and, in all modesty, I knew more about these subjects than most of my professors"[4] — and spent most of that year studying on his own, having discussions with colleagues, indulging in the odd practical joke, and travelling around Europe on his motorcycle.

It was also during that year in post-war Paris that he really got to know Gérard Pelletier, who was to become probably his closest friend and the key partner in all his later ventures into political proselytizing and action. A small, quietly humorous, slightly stooped man with the gnomish look of a medieval alchemist and an aristocratic air despite humble origins, Pelletier had a great deal in common with Trudeau — except for the advantages of affluence. He, like Trudeau, had lost his father at an early age: Achille Pelletier, an intelligent, self-educated railway station agent in Victoriaville in Quebec's Eastern Townships, died of cancer when Gérard was nine, leaving him to be brought up by a strong-willed mother and older sisters. Like Trudeau, he is considered exceptionally warm and sensitive by close friends, but is so shy that he generally gives the opposite impression: "Some call me cold and arrogant," he admits. "I feel it is my greatest fault that it takes me so long to relate to people."[5] And, also like Trudeau, young Pelletier had an inquiring mind and the sharp pen of a social critic. But, unlike him, Pelletier had no money to support a prolonged student existence and had to plunge much earlier into earning his keep.

The two first met when Trudeau was still at Brébeuf and Pelletier, of the same age but enrolled in a less élite school, was editor of an intercollegiate youth-movement newspaper. Pelletier wrote an article challenging other student editors to define their roles and become more socially committed, and Trudeau, who was then editor of Brébeuf's student paper, published a witty, sarcastic reply. "I thought it was so good that I wanted to discover who wrote it," Pelletier says. "We met and I liked him, though his flippancy disconcerted me a little. But he was obviously so intelligent."[6] They remained in touch at the University of Montreal, but it wasn't until Trudeau's year in Paris that their mutual wariness dropped and they became close friends. Pelletier was based in Geneva, working full time for a student relief organization distributing aid in war-shattered Europe, and the two frequently sought out each other's company.

"I sensed in Pierre an intellectual capacity that attracted me very much," Pelletier says. "I think he envied me a certain gift for action. I was more involved, because I had to earn a living and was working in an international student relief agency. He was studying, and I picked his brains as much as I could, since I had no formal training in economics and politics."[7] Trudeau introduced Pelletier to the major works of political philosophy and they would discuss theories for hours on end. But his own thinking was beginning to move from the general to the particular, and to focus on Canadian problems. He would organize discussions on such subjects as the Canadian constitution and, Pelletier recalls, "he was already a fund of knowledge on Canada at that time. He could reel off the history of the railways in Canada or quote from any given speech by Sir John A. Macdonald."[8] It was during the Paris year, too, in conversations between Trudeau, Pelletier, and a few other friends, that the first vague ideas for what was to become *Cité*

Libre — the influential political journal that served as Trudeau's principal forum until he entered politics — were germinated.

After Paris, in 1947, Pelletier returned to Canada and became a journalist, while Trudeau went on to another year of study at the London School of Economics. By the end of that year, he had spent a total of eight years at various universities. Then, as an antidote to academe and an alternative to any form of commitment, he embarked on a year-long trip around the world.

That much-chronicled trip, remarkable both for the austere conditions he imposed on himself despite his wealth and for the number of trouble-spots he sought out, was the beginning of a long string of travels that extended right through the 1950s. A pattern quickly established itself: he would work for a time in Canada, then abruptly depart for some exotic destination. In late 1951, he left for some six months of travelling around Africa, followed by a visit to the Soviet Union to attend a world economic congress in Moscow; in 1955, he attended a Commonwealth relations conference in Lahore, Pakistan, and took several extra months to travel through parts of the Middle East he had not yet seen; in 1956, he lived in London and Paris for six months while editing a book, *La Grève de l'Amiante*; in 1957, he went to a World University Service seminar in Nigeria and travelled around Africa some more; in 1959, his destination was Japan and Vietnam; and in 1960, with publisher Jacques Hébert and three others, he made the six-week tour of China that led to the book *Two Innocents in Red China*, co-authored by Trudeau and Hébert. In the years when he didn't have a major journey, Trudeau almost invariably spent at least several weeks in Europe.

In his year-long trip in 1948, Trudeau dressed like a rag-picker, carried only what few belongings he could cram into a packsack, and lived so frugally that the whole enterprise cost him only $800. He crossed borders without proper documents, and generally courted trouble at every turn. "Those travels were alternative ways of accumulating knowledge on the one hand, and I guess testing myself on another," he says. "I'd gone through the schools and universities and I'd proved to myself to a certain extent that I could do well there, but what about the real world? Could I do well there? You know, how would I handle myself in the middle of China, not knowing the language and being absolutely alone and having nobody to rely on but myself?" Not content with the risks normally inherent in such an undertaking, he deliberately raised the odds: "I tempted fate. I used to deliberately put myself into some pretty tricky situations just to see how I would handle them[9]. . . . I scrounged around everywhere, and when I found some unsavoury-looking types, I tagged along with them."[10]

His risk-taking was almost certainly related, to some extent, to his earlier decision to abstain from action during the war. In a single one-year trip, he contrived to come into contact with at least five war situations — the Arab-Israeli conflict in the Middle East, a civil war in Burma, the chaos of post-partition Pakistan and India, the war against France in Vietnam, and the Chinese revolution. He admits a connection only obliquely: "Having missed the big war — not by thoughtlessness as much as by inadvertance — I wanted to see other battles."[11] But the impression that comes across is that of a man repeatedly thrusting himself into dangerous battle conditions to prove to himself that his earlier avoidance of war hadn't been due to cowardice.

The over-all record of his travels in the 1950s also suggests a fundamental rootlessness, which he does not entirely deny. "I guess I was like Herman Melville's hero: after being back for a while, I felt that I had to take to the sea again, otherwise I'd get down in the streets and knock people's hats off. I don't know . . . I suppose you could get some psychologist to analyse it, but I've never really attempted to. The early trips one can have a rationale for, in particular after I'd just finished my studies in Europe. I had, like many post-graduate students, the idea that I'd write a thesis, and the thesis was going to be on the interface of Communism and western Christian democracy in the countries of the Third World. And I was honest at it. I took a lot of notes and wrote a fair amount of articles. But it was also a good way to get to see the local political leader or local editor or the local missionary or the local wise man, and talk about his country.

"But what did the wanderlust correspond to? Was it a basic loneliness? Or a basic desire to . . . I think the best answer would be that I was really completing the pedagogy of Pierre Trudeau, the growing up of Pierre Trudeau. As for the later travels, I suppose it was my reward to myself for having worked reasonably hard, as I used to in those days. And I had friends in Europe, too, and I used to go back to see them, whether it would be literary friends or artists or girl friends."

The impression of a certain rootlessness is also conveyed by the fact that, for most of his life, he never seems to have needed a real full-time home. He kept a room in his mother's house and also had a small bachelor apartment in downtown Montreal, but both were totally functional arrangements containing a bed, a great many books, and little else — places to work and sleep, but not his own homes in any deeper sense. From his election in 1965 until he moved into 24 Sussex Drive three years later, he lived in a simple, even mildly tatty room in Ottawa's Château Laurier. "I always liked living in hotels," he says. "I guess I had to, because I never had a house of my own for so many years. I still don't — I mean, when I lose this job as prime minister, I have nowhere to move my goods and chattels to. But I liked living in hotels. People had flats and everything else, and I'd try to choose one and I just couldn't see myself coming home and making the bed and changing the linen; to me, living in a hotel was a great luxury. Living in a flat was sort of having to look after yourself."

Trudeau's travels on a shoestring also revealed an asceticism that still remains an element of his personality. Its origins appear to have been a need to prove to himself, over and over, that he could make it on his own, without his father's money. His essay "The Ascetic in a Canoe" leaves no doubt that this was one of the major things he loved about canoeing: ". . . You entrust yourself, *stripped of your worldly goods*, to nature. . . . Canoe and paddle, blanket and knife . . . *that is about the extent of your wealth. . . . To remove all the useless material baggage from a man's heritage* is, at the same time, to free his mind . . ."[12] Of his frugality abroad he says: "In my first trip around the world, I guess I was doing what so many young people do when they go and write a book, 'around the world on $100' or whatever. I was trying to prove to those friends who didn't come along because they said, 'Jeez, we just can't afford it,' I was trying to show that you could do it on a shoestring, and get a great kick out of it. . . . There may have been some penny-pinching to it, too. But I doubt it, because when I went to the Commonwealth relations conference in Lahore, my ticket was paid by the Canadian Institute of International Affairs, but rather than fly there, I took the harder route of taking the train ride from Karachi to Lahore. I guess it was a couple of days' train ride through the dusts of the desert."

What was originally a matter of self-proving eventually became a habit, leaving Trudeau a sort of part-time ascetic. Although the perks of prime-ministerial life have given him a much greater taste for luxury than he had before 1968, he is still a man who doesn't amass many possessions, who likes to travel light, and who prefers rugged simplicity to luxury. But he likes fast, costly sports cars, his clothes are invariably expensive, and when he does make a purchase or order work done — as when he had the prime-ministerial office and 24 Sussex Drive redecorated — he wants the best. His attitude is typified by his account of the time he spent in Paris working on *La Grève de l'Amiante* in 1956:

"I had bought myself a Jaguar in London. I took it over to France and I was living in a very little hotel on the Left Bank, one of the most beautifully situated hotels but a very small one, one where I had stayed in 1946 as a student. And once or twice I'd have some friends visit me, and they couldn't get over it: There was this Jaguar, which was quite a car in those days, in this very, very shabby part of Paris. It caused some puzzlement, and I'd say, 'What the hell, I'm just sleeping here. If I've got a lot of dough, I'd rather spend it on buying beautiful shirts or having a dîner gastronomique or buying good cars.' "

Trudeau's self-imposed hardships in his early travels make his perceptions different from those of a typical millionaire who has never known poverty; few people could feel poorer than a youth alone in the midst of the Orient or the Middle East, without sufficient money, proper documentation, or an understanding of the local language. But it doesn't follow that his perceptions of poverty are better, or even necessarily as good, because self-imposed hardship can be a distorting mirror of reality. Experiencing a form of poverty by choice as a temporary adventure is quite different from being lastingly impoverished with no choice in the matter, but it could make it difficult to understand why the genuinely deprived — even though they lack the same options, outstanding intelligence and training — can't handle their troubles with similar ingenuity.

When Trudeau came home from his world travels in April of 1949, he was just in time to involve himself in the bitter Asbestos strike which was to become one of the watersheds in Quebec's political history. The strike, begun in February of that year by the 5,000 miners at Asbestos and Thetford Mines, was in the first instance a battle for higher pay, improved working conditions, and a say for the union in such matters as hiring, firing, promotions, seniority, and the treatment of grievances. But, more fundamentally, it was a collision between illusion and reality in a rapidly evolving Quebec. The illusion, fostered by the provincial government of Maurice Duplessis and the hierarchy of the Catholic Church, was that Quebec remained a rural, agrarian society whose survival depended on inward-looking nationalism and unquestioning deference to established authority, and in which there was no room for militant unions or any other groups working for social change. The reality was that the Quebec of 1949 was already overwhelmingly urbanized and industrialized, a society in which 67 per cent of the population lived in cities and towns, in which agriculture accounted for only 10.5 per cent of the total dollar value of commodities produced — and in which corresponding social changes could be prevented only by the most Draconian repression.

Such repression was what Duplessis attempted against the asbestos strikers by sending in the Quebec Provincial Police to beat and harass the miners, protect strike-breakers, and make arbitrary arrests. But the excesses backfired, hardening the resolve of the strikers and eventually turning public opinion overwhelmingly in their favour. When the strike finally ended in July, the arbitrated settlement gave the miners far less than they had set out to obtain, but forces had been set in motion which would gradually lead to profound social change. The long-standing alliance between the government and the Church had been permanently damaged when the Archbishop of Montreal, Msgr. Joseph Charbonneau, and other leading clergymen had felt compelled to publicly take the side of the strikers because, as Msgr. Charbonneau put it in a sermon on May 1, "The working class is a victim of a conspiracy which seeks to crush it, and when there is a conspiracy to crush the working class, the Church has a duty to intervene."[13] And, no less importantly, the long, bitter dispute had served as a rallying point for all progressive elements in the province, simultaneously underlining both the anti-democratic nature of the Duplessis régime and its vulnerability to concerted resistance. It took another decade for these developments to have fully visible results, but the asbestos strike began the psychological preparation of Quebec society for abrupt and belated entry into the twentieth century.

When Trudeau returned from abroad in April, however, the strike was only at its mid-point, feelings were running high, and resolution was nowhere in sight. His friend Gérard Pelletier, meanwhile, had become a reporter for Le Devoir and was deeply involved in covering the dispute, so Trudeau — eager as usual to be where the action was — asked to accompany him to Asbestos. He had barely set foot in the town when he was introduced to the brutality of the situation: He and Pelletier were stopped by the provincial police, their car was stripped and searched, and they were taken to the makeshift police headquarters and ordered — unsucessfully — to leave town.

After that rough initiation, Pelletier introduced him to Jean Marchand, who, as secretary-general of the Confédération des Travailleurs Catholiques du Canada, was the top labour leader involved in the strike. Marchand, a year older than Trudeau and Pelletier, was later to become the third member of their triumvirate, but he was radically different from the other two. A small, peppery man with an unruly shock of hair and a dapper moustache, Marchand operates not on detached intellect but on passions: he is volatile, thin-skinned, emotional, and fiercely proud. But he was also a relentlessly tough gutfighter, a brilliant political organizer and tactician, and a superb orator with a deep understanding of working-class Quebecers — just the sort of political operator, in short, to balance the more cerebral skills of the Trudeau-Pelletier team.

Marchand invited Trudeau to address the miners on the legal aspects of the strike. The burly strikers were sceptical at first, joking about his rather eccentric, scruffy attire and calling him "St. Joseph" because of the long beard he had grown in his travels. But they listened spellbound as Trudeau, still smarting from his encounter with the provincial police, ridiculed policemen by recounting the derogatory terms used to describe them in the various countries he had visited and then went on to speak simply and eloquently about justice, democracy, freedom, and their right to fight for their cause. Says Jacques Hébert, who was also at Asbestos as a journalist: "It was quite a thing to see this young man go out and speak to 5,000 miners. It was profoundly moving. I remember him standing in the big hall talking about democracy and liberty in a way they understood right off. He spoke their language."[14]

But Marchand was not so much moved as worried. As in his anti-conscription speeches of 1942, Trudeau did not err on the side of moderation in his attacks against authority. "Miners are not schoolchildren, you know," Marchand has said, recalling the incident, "and while students might steal pencils, the miners steal dynamite. I had managed to defuse two or three cute little plots by the boys which would have blown up the mine manager and most of his staff. So you can imagine that when Trudeau urged physical resistance by the strikers, I got a little worried."[15]

The performance nevertheless made such a favourable impression on both the union leader and the miners that Marchand subsequently asked him to join the CTCC as a full-time legal advisor; but Trudeau wasn't ready for that sort of commitment. Unlike the anti-conscription effort in Outremont, however, Asbestos wasn't just a lark for Trudeau. He spent a great deal of time in the strike area, including the most brutal phase in May when the provincial police improperly invoked the riot act and indiscriminately made mass arrests, and he later worked — without pay — on the union's $25,000 damage action against the police for brutality. He took the Asbestos experience seriously enough, too, to edit a book on it seven years later, contributing a lengthy introductory chapter and a conclusion. Throughout the 1950s, he remained deeply involved in the labour movement, acting as an unpaid legal advisor to Marchand's union confederation from time to time, negotiating for the unions in several contract disputes, and travelling the province to give workers lectures in rudimentary political theory; he was involved, in one way or another, in most of the big labour confrontations of the decade.

The most important effect of the Asbestos strike on Trudeau, however, was that it focussed his interest on the battle for democracy in Quebec, a battle that was to become the basis of his rise to prominence in the 1950s. "We decided then, at Asbestos, that something should be done about Quebec," Pelletier has said. "And out of this came *Cité Libre*, in which we hoped to develop our ideas. Pierre, more easily than any of the rest of us, could have escaped and had a brilliant career any place as a writer or teacher. We were the first generation to say, 'God damn it, we'll stay home and change the place.' "[16]

But first, shortly after the Asbestos strike ended in February 1950, Trudeau decided to go to Ottawa as an economic advisor in the Privy Council Office. He was motivated in part by his usual desire to be where interesting things were happening. The Liberals under Louis St. Laurent had swept to a majority victory on June 25, 1949, and the Privy Council Office would be at the centre of what promised to be an exciting period of innovation. But, more importantly, the move to Ottawa was yet another step in the long pedagogy of Pierre Trudeau: Having studied political theory and economics and having explored the political and social systems of different countries in his travels, he now wanted to observe the workings of government from the inside — and the central office of the federal government was a logical vantage point. He conducted his observations diligently, as Pelletier points out in his introduction to *Réponses*, a 1968 book of Trudeau quotations: "When we arrived [in Ottawa] as MPs after the last election and had to undergo a difficult apprenticeship, Trudeau was already ready for action. He knew the milieu, the institution, the officials. He was effective from the first day, which partly explains his rapid rise despite his 'inexperience', which was much more apparent than real."[17]

Trudeau commuted to Montreal from Ottawa every weekend for meetings with Pelletier and a handful of other, like-minded intellectuals to lay concrete plans for *Cité Libre*, the political magazine which had been tentatively conceived in the long discussions during his year in Paris. The first issue of the magazine (which was supposed to be quarterly, but actually came out for the first few years whenever it happened to be ready) appeared in June of 1950. In it, Trudeau, who was the central figure and intellectual leader of the project, served notice that *Cité Libre* had been conceived as a weapon in the anti-Duplessis battle for modernization and democratization in Quebec: "We wish to testify to the Christian and French fact in North America. So be it; but let us make a clean slate of all the rest. We must submit to methodical doubt all of the political categories that the previous generation bequeathed to us: the strategy of resistance is no longer useful for the full flowering of the City. The time has come to borrow from the architect that discipline that he calls 'functional', to throw out the thousand prejudices with which the past burdens the present, and to build for the new man. Let us cast down the totems, break down the taboos. Or better, let us consider them void. Dispassionately, let us be intelligent."[18]

"*Cité Libre* was a curious affair," Pelletier says. "We would meet every week, and anyone who had written an article read it to the others for criticism. That is why the publication came out so irregularly — just whenever we had time. The meetings were quite informal. We brought our wives, and Pierre brought his girl friends. I would preside, and he would get very impatient if I tolerated any digressions."[19] It was only after 1954, when Jacques Hébert became production manager and a member of the editorial board, that *Cité Libre* was able to expand its reach and influence by settling down to a regular schedule and developing an efficient distribution system. Trudeau divided his time between Ottawa and the *Cité Libre* meetings until late 1951, when he left the Privy Council Office to devote full attention to his activities in Quebec; he gave up the PCO job both because he had already extracted as much as he needed to learn from the experience and because the magazine had become too political for his association with it to be compatible with his status as a civil servant.

The main thrust of his writings in the 1950s, whether in *Cité Libre* or in other publications such as Hébert's short-lived crusading newspaper *Vrai*, was twofold: opposition to nationalism, and advocacy of democracy. Those themes were, in fact, the main frontiers of the battle between the province's reformers and the alliance of Duplessis and the Catholic Church. Over the years, Quebec's political leaders and the religious establishment had developed an intricate and devastatingly effective formula for maintaining their own power: Together, they incessantly preached that Quebec had a special destiny that could only be fulfilled by remaining outside the mainstream of modernization; that preservation of Quebec's French society could be achieved only by maintaining a siege mentality toward Canada and the rest of the world; and that political authority was bestowed unchallengeably by God.

The prevailing nationalist view of Quebec's role in the 1950s was still the one articulated in 1902 by Msgr. L.-A. Paquet, a leading French-Canadian theologian: "It is our privilege to be entrusted with this social ministry, reserved for élite peoples. . . . Our mission is not so much to manipulate capital, as to handle ideas; not so much to light the fires of factories, as to maintain the luminous hearth of religion and of thought, making it radiate afar. While our rivals are laying claim to the hegemony of industry and finance, we shall strive above all for the honor of the doctrine and the palms of apostleship."[20] Paquet's view of political authority, too, remained the generally accepted one: "All authority other than God's own comes from divine authority. . . . The idea of authority born of the free will of man, and constituted according to human calculations alone, has thrown into the world a social conception which is only a cause of trouble and a source of instability. . . . What must not be admitted is that the people itself is sovereign, and that, in choosing the members of a legislative assembly, it delegates to them the power to govern."[21]

On such foundations, the Duplessis régime and the Church establishment together had erected a powerful barrier against any real democracy. "The legislature of Quebec is a fortress," Duplessis typically intoned in 1948, "that we must defend without failing. It is that which permits us to construct the schools which suit us, to speak our language, to practice our religion and to make laws applicable to our population."[22] And, on the morning of the 1956 provincial election, the sentiments of the Church were typically expressed in a "Morning Prayer" broadcast on French-language CBC radio: "It is therefore a complete error . . . to claim that authority does not belong to those who exercise it, but that they hold it only by virtue of a mere mandate that can be recalled by the people at any time."[23]

Doing battle against these widespread assumptions gave Trudeau an opportunity to hone both his political ideas and his skills as a communicator. His writings of the period are striking for their distillation of sophisticated and diverse political theories into lean, pungent, and elegantly crafted sentences, and for their closely reasoned argument from first premises in the best Cartesian style inculcated by the Jesuits.

Attacking the Church's views on political authority, for instance, he wrote: "Some take the easy way out by reiterating that authority comes from God. They omit to explain why God conferred it on a Stalin or a Hitler; or why, in our democracies, God would choose to express himself through the intermediary of electoral thugs or big campaign contributors.[24] . . . Human societies, then, differ from the beehives in that men are always free to decide what form of authority they will adopt, and who will exercise it. And it really is men who have the responsibility of taking these decisions — not God, Providence or Nature. In the last analysis any given political authority exists only because men consent to obey it. In this sense what exists is not so much the authority as the obedience."[25]

He treated defensive nationalism with similar disdain: "For a long time, adversity gave us a rule of action. To say no was our whole policy, and with good reason we considered as leaders those who spearheaded an effective resistance. Our people was at that time surrounded by real dangers, especially ethnic and religious assimilation, and our welfare lay in refusal. But it is not everything to avoid evil, one must do good. . . . Alas! it is the fate of certain peoples that, having battled too long, they end up thinking that virtue is a negative."[26]

But, in the writings as in the man, there was also an element of hardness, a willingness to be blunt in ways that could wound. He didn't hesitate to savage, at one time or another, not only most political parties and politicians, but also French Canadians as a society, criticizing them with a clinical aloofness that would later cause his critics to argue — wrongly — that he was in fact a French Canadian who despised his own people. In 1952, for instance, he wrote: "In our relations with the state we are fairly immoral: we corrupt civil servants, we use blackmail on MPs, we put pressure on the courts, we defraud the treasury, we obligingly look the other way when 'it concerns our interests'. And in electoral matters, our immorality becomes really scabrous."[27] Or, on another occasion: "The shameful incompetence of the average Liberal MP from Quebec was a welcome asset to a government that needed little more than a herd of trained donkeys to file in when the division bell rang. The party strategists had but to find an acceptable stable master — Laurier, Lapointe, St. Laurent — and the trained donkeys sitting in the back benches could be trusted to behave."[28]

Such comments couldn't fail to make him enemies, but their explanation lies not in any hostility toward Quebec society but rather in a combination of intense feeling for it and impatience with its shortcomings. His upbringing, cosmopolitan education, and travels made him a Quebecer unlike most others, one who could view the province from a critical distance and diagnose its failings. But his writings were intended to expose those failings to Quebecers themselves, not outsiders, and their brutal tone was intended not as a condemnation but as a prod toward change. The intensity of his feeling for Quebec is the reason, too, for his ferocity toward the Duplessis nationalists of the 1950s and the separatists of today: He displays the visceral vehemence of a man confronting people he perceives as the corruptors of something he holds dear.

If Trudeau's *Cité Libre* comments about democracy and narrow nationalism seem today to be innocuous statements of the obvious, they were nothing short of revolutionary in the context of Quebec in the 1950s. But they didn't exactly set the province afire, if only because they weren't all that widely read. The magazine's circulation was only a few thousand copies, and it was aimed not at a mass readership but at a relatively small élite of progressive intellectuals. But for those intellectuals, who comprised the vanguard of reform, it played a most important role: By publicly and fearlessly making arguments that were anathema to the oppressive Duplessis régime and the prevailing public opinion, it served as a morale-booster and rallying point; and the quality of those arguments and the clarity of its analysis provided a philosophical underpinning for the Quiet Revolution, giving the reformers lines of attack to use in conditioning public opinion toward change.

In 1956, Trudeau figured prominently in an effort to carry the anti-Duplessis battle a step further by uniting all the forces of opposition. The vehicle for this attempt at unity was an oddly vague new organization called Le Rassemblement, of which Trudeau was first the vice-president and later, briefly, the president. Its 600-odd members were drawn from across the spectrum of opposition parties, labour groups, academic institutions, and intellectual forums. The only common denominator was a desire to further the cause of democracy, using Le Rassemblement as "a movement of education and democratic action". The basic idea was that there was strength in numbers, and that by pooling their efforts the various foes of the Duplessis régime could devise new ways to educate the public about democracy. Although it may have played some role in stimulating individual members to new initiatives within their respective organizations, the Rassemblement had no power base and it became too bogged down in squabbles over ideology and strategy to have any visible impact.

In 1958, Trudeau supported an attempt to turn the Rassemblement into an active political coalition, the Union des forces démocratiques, which would try to defeat the Duplessis government. In the pages of *Cité Libre*, he wrote: " 'Democracy first!' should be the rallying cry of all reforming forces in the province. Some may be active in the chambers of commerce and others in the trade unions; some may still believe in the glories of free enterprise while

others spread socialist doctrines. There is no harm in
long as they all agree to work out democracy first of all. A
it will be up to the sovereign people to opt freely for the c.
they prefer."[29] But this idealistic political vehicle, corroded by
ternal ideological bickering and overtaken by the rush of outside
events, never really got out of the workshop. In September of 1959,
Duplessis died suddenly, and his successor as National Union leader
and premier, Paul Sauvé, suffered a fatal heart attack after only
three months. In the election of June 1960, Trudeau urged *Cité
Libre* readers to support the provincial Liberals under Jean Lesage,
who proceeded to defeat the disorientated Union Nationale and
usher in an era of modernization and reform.

But Trudeau's support for the Lesage Liberals had been tentative
at best, and it didn't take long for him to become disillusioned with
them. Lesage had recruited some of the best political talents in the
province, broken the hold of the Church over education, and begun
to drag Quebec into the twentieth century. But he soon yielded to
the temptations of a *politique de grandeur* and started to replace
the passive nationalism of Duplessis days with a more aggressive
challenge to national unity; in 1962, he ran an election campaign on
the slogan "Maîtres chez nous" ("Masters in our own house") and
by 1963 he was speaking of "the hour of the last chance" for Confederation. At the same time, a new separatist movement was beginning to gain momentum, especially among the young, and in
1963 the terrorist FLQ sprang into existence with a spate of mailbox
bombings.

For Trudeau, this meant that the battle against nationalism had
not ended, just entered a new and even more bitter phase. As early
as 1961, he was twitting the Lesage administration for its failure
to snap Quebec out of its nationalist tendencies: "Let's open the
borders — this people is dying of asphyxiation!"[30] Then, in 1962,
he let fly at nationalism and separatism with both barrels in a long,
carefully reasoned, and impassioned *Cité Libre* essay entitled "The
New Treason of the Intellectuals": "Now, except for a few stub-
born eccentrics, there is probably not one French Canadian intellectual who has not spent at least four hours a week over the last
year discussing separatism. That makes how many thousand times

two hundred hours spent just flapping your arms?[31] . . . The ultimate tragedy would be in not realizing that French Canada is too culturally anemic, too economically destitute, too intellectually retarded, too spiritually paralyzed, to be able to survive more than a couple of decades of stagnation, emptying herself of all her vitality into nothing but a cesspit, the mirror of her nationalistic vanity and 'dignity'."[32]

Two years later, in another *Cité Libre* article, he summed up his disillusionment with the course of events since the collapse of the National Union: "In 1960, everything was becoming possible in Quebec, even revolution. In fact revolution would probably not have been necessary, so wide open was the road to power for all who had mastered the sciences and the techniques of the day: automation, cybernetics, nuclear science, economic planning and whatnot else. A whole generation was free at last to apply all its creative energies to bringing this backward province up to date. Only it required boldness, intelligence and work. Alas, freedom proved to be too heady a drink to pour for the French Canadian youth of 1960. Almost at the first sip it went at top speed in search of some more soothing milk, some new dogmatism . . . and it took refuge in the bosom of its mother, the Holy Nation."

Though Trudeau identified himself as a socialist throughout most of his *Cité Libre* days and had a long-standing mistrust of the federal and provincial Liberals, he never fully cast his lot with the CCF or its successor, the New Democratic Party. "I didn't enter the NDP in earlier years because I was not ready to make up my mind, and later I didn't believe in it, because the ideology was wrong."[33] The ideological falling-out began when the socialist party made it clear that it wanted to concentrate most of its energies on the federal scene rather than on pursuing reform in Quebec, and it became complete when the NDP later espoused the idea of some form of "special status" for the province.

In addition to his involvement with *Cité Libre* and later the Rassemblement as well, Trudeau divided his time among an array of other activities. The Quebec intellectual world consisted of a number of interlocking discussion groups, and he was at the core of several of the most influential. He practised law from time to time, taking on only cases which particularly interested him; these tended to be in the areas of labour law or human rights, as well as any litigation involving one of his friends, such as Jacques Hébert's protracted contempt-of-court battle over a book he had written alleging that a man had unjustly been hanged. He remained deeply involved with Jean Marchand's labour movement, not only as a legal advisor and occasional negotiator, but also as a teacher: his frequent travels to remote parts of the province to give workers lectures in basic political and economic theory provided an opportunity to broaden his knowledge of Quebec and its people, as well as to exercise his taste and talent for teaching. In 1961, he became a teacher in a more formal sense, as an associate professor of law and founding member of the Public Law Research Institute at the University of Montreal, from which he had been barred during the Duplessis era. And, amid all these activities, there were his frequent and extensive travels.

It was because of these travels and his lack of any single full-time occupation that Trudeau acquired a reputation as a dilettante. It is a reputation that still rankles: "My acquaintances would say, 'He has no office, he never works, what does he do?' But, you know, I'd be working bloody hard — at writing articles and preparing my dossiers for whatever conciliation procedure I had or at administering my father's estate, which my brother and sister had no inclination to do, or at receiving clients or visiting the labour groups. . . . All my friends were joining the labour movement, or setting up an office with a colleague — I didn't want it. I wanted to be my own agent, and I'd take some cases and not others. . . . I appeared not to be adjusted, and people wouldn't see me at the office; they'd either reach me at home or they'd hear that I was off in Africa or something, and the assumption was that I wasn't working. Well, I think that I was working a great deal, either reading or writing or teaching or whatever. The explanation is that I didn't want to tie myself down to *an* office. I had too many things that I wanted to do."

Though Trudeau's record until his entry into politics is not one of avoidance of work, it clearly constitutes a constant flight from commitment. He laboured intensely at whatever he happened to be doing and he did quite a variety of things, but — with the exception of *Cité Libre* — he always gave the impression of doing it with one foot in and one foot out, poised to move on to something else. This reluctance to commit himself stemmed partly from a fear of real responsibility and partly from a determination not to allow himself to be locked into any one option until he had completed his process of self-training; that process appears to have extended right up to his election to Parliament in 1965.

CHAPTER SIX

The Reluctant Leader

LOOKING at Trudeau's career with hindsight, it is tempting to imagine that much of his life — the relentless self-training, the education, the travels, the stint in the Privy Council Office, the building of a following with his *Cité Libre* articles — was a methodically planned preparation for high political office. His meteoric rise in the twenty-nine months after his election in 1965 certainly looks, from outside, like a cunningly conceived and boldly executed assault on the pinnacles of power. Even Lester Pearson assumed that his successor's professed reticence was just political posturing, telling *Time*'s Martin Sullivan in 1968: "We have never had anybody in the leadership who hasn't given the impression that he didn't particularly want it but that everybody wanted him. . . . So Trudeau is following along in the tradition of being dragged to the Speaker's chair, as it were, reluctantly but not too reluctantly."[1] But the reality is quite different: Trudeau is that rarity among politicians, a leader who did not crave power but rather tried consistently and genuinely to avoid it. His enjoyment of his office and its power is not the triumph of a man who has successfully captured a long-sought prize, but the surprised delight of one who finds himself revelling in something he hadn't really wanted.

Though his training and his general intellectual interests seemed to point him toward political life, Trudeau's personal inclinations made him a most unlikely politician. From earliest youth, his pre-occupation with his freedom made him shy away from any leadership role; to be a leader is to sacrifice some measure of solitude, and that, not surprisingly, held no appeal for someone who had identified even in childhood with Cyrano's "To climb not very high, perhaps, but all alone": "I never liked to be a leader in anything. I never liked to be responsible — you know, I never sought to be chief of a Boy Scout troop, or if we were a gang off hiking, I never tried to be the first one; I'd sort of rather follow on my own and go off. I didn't want to lead the people along, to be the first in the path and so on. Very often they would thrust me into that position — I'd think up the idea, 'We've got to go up to James Bay,' or 'We have to canoe down to wherever-it-is,' or 'We've got to surge through the bush between the St. Maurice River and Lake St. John,' and then I'd find a group who would be willing to do it and they would sort of say, 'Well, it's your idea.' But I wouldn't like it when I'd walk with people on my heels; I'd like distance between me and them. If I couldn't be far enough ahead, then I'd let them go ahead and walk in the rear. I guess I like to be with myself. . . . I never had contempt for leaders. I don't think it's a useless function. But I didn't aspire to be one myself.

"Well, let's be honest: There was probably an element of not wanting to assume responsibility. You know, freedom is also that, and it's perhaps a lack of maturity — when you lead you have to be answerable to those you've led, and they say, 'You got us lost!' or something. . . . It's the same thing with marriage. Why did I get married so late? I always say it's because I liked to enjoy my freedom and so on, but obviously there was probably the feeling that I wasn't ready to bear that responsibility."

Though he had many of the attributes of a natural leader — strength of will, force of personality, superior intellect, audacity, and the indefinable quality that commands the confidence of others — his disinclination was so obvious that none of his associates in the 1950s and early 1960s could envisage him in a leadership role. Says Marchand: "He was always considered as a very valuable intellectual, but not as a leader. I don't remember anybody asking Pierre to lead any group. We were all happy to have him with us, you know — but not as a leader. Unless you talk about intellectual leadership: that, maybe. But as a leader of an organization or a group, I don't remember anybody suggesting that."

There was, accordingly, no stage of Trudeau's life before the

1960s when he seriously entertained the idea of going into active politics. "I can't honestly say what I thought in my early teens or in my first ten years, because sometimes I will meet some very aged friend of my mother's or some distant aunt who will say, 'We said you'd be prime minister some day, and you said you would, too.' I would be inclined to say that if I ever said that, it would be much in the sense that I said I'd be a cowboy, or I'd be a fireman, or an explorer. Kids identify with things that are exciting. But it certainly wasn't one of my motivating ideas in any relevant part of my formative years."

His later studies at the University of Montreal, at Harvard, and in Paris and London were focussed on the political process in its broadest sense, but his intended destination was the sidelines rather than the centre. "I think I hoped to be part — as an economist or a sociologist or a jurisprudent would be — of guiding humanity, or Canada, in a way that I thought preferable. But I didn't see that role exercised from a politician's point of view." His interest was in the broad strokes, the large sweep of events and social forces, rather than the practical details of running a country. "I don't know if it was general in those days, but I didn't have all that high a regard for contingencies, for the everyday life as a Mackenzie King was administering it in those days. I had in those very early days a very high disdain for what was going on today and to-morrow — you know, newspapers and the radio and discussions in college or even university. They had clubs where they would dis-cuss politics, and I was much more interested in Plato or in Aquinas than I was in a discussion of yesterday's budget.

"Later, too, I can't recollect ever having formed the intention of becoming prime minister. I didn't see myself as leader of a group. I like to communicate, I like to convince people, I like to push ideas and reforms, and in that sense I liked teaching, when I could, or haranguing, or something like that. . . . When I got to a stage when I was involved enough with politics to write about it — after all, that's only when I had about reached my thirties — it's at that point that I realized that I wouldn't be accepted in any of the estab-lished parties, therefore I might as well accept to be a kind of rebel or a critic or an essayist. I'd admire more a Chesterton or a Léon

Daudet, I'd know more about him than I'd know about an Asquith or a Poincaré. So I didn't identify with the prime-ministerial or the political figures of the time, and therefore it's unlikely that I ever wanted to be one. I did identify with those who were writing about politics and speaking about it and thinking about it."

This is confirmed by Marc Lalonde, who has worked closely with Trudeau since the beginning of the 1960s: "Certainly he was not planning his life saying, 'I'll be prime minister one day.' I'm convinced of that. His whole life was more finding satisfaction in being excellent at whatever he did. That had its satisfactions in itself. He was a guy with a social conscience; he kept a continuing interest in public affairs; in his actions or in his writings, he was on the side of the progressive theories. But his going into politics in 1965 was almost a chance affair. It was just that Marchand insisted he wouldn't go into politics without Trudeau and Pelletier. There was no great pressure in the Liberal Party to get Trudeau to run. Nobody in 1965 said, 'Here goes the next PM.' Not even his own friends. Even when he was appointed minister of justice, I saw it as a very remote possibility. He still had this image of a semi-dilettante, and therefore that he would be a kind of patrician in politics — you know, do it for a while, and then go on to something else."

The origins of Trudeau's entry into politics really go back two years earlier, to the period preceding the federal election of 1963. By then he was disillusioned with the Lesage government as well as with the Quebec labour movement's increasingly nationalist orientation. Moreover, the strength of Quebec nationalism under the Lesage administration had begun to so weaken the central government that Trudeau felt the whole federal system was threatened. In his analysis, this system was essential not only to the welfare of Quebec but also to the preservation of individual liberties, and his theory of counterweights told him that it was time to start strengthening the federal side. And, most important, he had by then concluded that the means to dissipate Quebec nationalism lay not within the province, but in the country as a whole. As he and Pelletier jointly put it in *Cité Libre* two years later: "We believe that extremist nationalism is almost always the product of a failure:

the incapacity of the previous regimes to establish justice in the ethnic field. No doubt the most effective way to heal nationalist alienation is to establish a better regime. It is at this that we want to work."[2]

The federal Liberals under Lester Pearson were out of office and preparing for an election. They wanted very badly to recruit Marchand, who by then was the powerful and widely respected president of the CTCC's successor, the Confederation of National Trade Unions. Marchand, politically astute enough to realize how easily a lone Quebecer could be swallowed up in the party and in Parliament, insisted that he would run only if Trudeau and Pelletier joined him. The three decided to give federal politics a try. But then, while they were waiting for the beleaguered prime minister, John Diefenbaker, to call an election, in January of 1963 Pearson suddenly reversed his long-standing opposition to nuclear weapons on Canadian soil and pressed the Diefenbaker government to accept them. Trudeau, Marchand, and Pelletier were strongly opposed to the weapons, and the reversal on such an important issue made it impossible for them to support Pearson. His candidacy scuttled, an outraged Trudeau proceeded to excoriate Pearson and the Liberals in a *Cité Libre* piece that colourfully vented his feeling of personal as well as political betrayal: "I detect among the old guard the same brutal cynicism; I see in the youth associations the same selfish docility; and between them, men of my generation who tremble with anticipation because they have seen the rouged face of Power. . . . What idiots they all are!"[3]

The Liberals formed a minority government. Two years later, preparing for another election and increasingly worried about the militancy of the Lesage government and the terrorism of the FLQ, they were again almost desperate to woo Marchand as a candidate. They didn't much care about Pelletier, and had real misgivings about Trudeau. But Marchand again insisted that it was all three or nothing; after some intense behind-the-scenes manoeuvrings, Pearson's emissaries — Guy Favreau, Maurice Lamontagne, and Louis Giguère — finally agreed. Trudeau, for his part, was prepared to put pragmatism ahead of principle in joining the party he had so recently denounced. The Liberals could scarcely have undergone a miraculous transformation in less than two years, but he liked their approach to federalism, and he was more convinced than ever that the federal side needed reinforcement. The NDP was too far removed from power to be of interest; the Tories were out of the question because of Diefenbaker's erratic leadership, their attitudes toward Quebec, and their general conservatism; and Trudeau's experience with the stillborn Union des forces démocratiques had taught him the futility of trying to work from outside the system.

But his commitment to this political adventure was by no means passionate. The Liberal hierarchy had decided to run him in the Montreal riding of Mount Royal, both because it was a safe Liberal seat and because the prosperous, predominantly English-speaking, and largely Jewish population was considered sophisticated enough to accept an "unusual" candidate like Trudeau. But when Trudeau heard that Victor Goldbloom, a prominent paediatrician, was also interested in the riding's Liberal nomination, he almost backed out, Marchand says: "When he knew he would have to run against Goldbloom, he almost changed his mind. He started saying, 'Well, you know, Goldbloom is a good man, maybe I shouldn't,' and playing Gaston and Alphonse. That's the attitude Pierre had all the time."

While Marchand was still working to convince sceptical Liberals that his colleague should be accepted as a candidate, Trudeau almost compounded their misgivings by turning up for a crucial pre-nomination meeting with Liberal organizers dressed in an open-collared sports shirt, a suede jacket, a beat-up old peaked hat, muddy corduroy slacks, and sandals. He was intercepted as he stepped out of his Mercedes SL-300 and sent home to change into more conservative attire before the Liberal organizers could see this further display of unconventionality. The nominating convention itself also had a rather strange twist, Marchand says: "It was the most awkward convention I have ever seen, with Goldbloom saying that Trudeau was the best candidate, and Trudeau saying that Goldbloom was the best candidate." But once he had the nomination, Trudeau settled down to a trouble-free, low-key campaign and was elected by a 13,135-vote margin on November 8, 1965, joining Marchand and Pelletier in going to Ottawa as a team that the press promptly dubbed the "Three Wise Men" from Quebec.

The trio's entry into the campaign attracted considerable attention in the rest of Canada. An editorial in the *Toronto Star*, for instance, called it "an event of high and hopeful import for Canada as a whole. . . . Three of the best minds and hearts in French Canada have decided to join in the main task of nation-building, on the basis of a real partnership between the two major cultural groups established by Canadian history." And University of Toronto historian Kenneth McNaught wrote, with arresting prescience: "Trudeau's political fate will likely be the political fate of Canada." But Trudeau himself indicated, during the campaign, that he was pursuing only a limited political involvement: "I was not offered a cabinet post. I made it clear I did not want such a post before anyone had the chance to offer me one."[4]

Marchand was brought into the Pearson cabinet almost immediately, in December, as minister of citizenship and immigration, and he set about trying to find powerful positions for his two partners. By January, Pearson was ready to make Trudeau his own parliamentary secretary, explaining that "I had read his pieces for years, and was impressed by them, particularly by his detailed technical knowledge of economics and constitutional law. We're into a period where that's very important, and we'll be dealing a lot with Quebec. Pierre is a Quebecer, and seems to be the kind of qualified person we need."[5] Trudeau accepted the post — reluctantly — and used it as a platform for his views on the constitution and dealing with Quebec; he also gave his fellow MPs an informal series of lectures on political theory and its application to the problems of the day, and quickly began emerging as an intellectual leader of the caucus. Marchand, meanwhile — aided by Pelletier and other reformers such as Jean-Pierre Goyer, Maurice Lamontagne, and Jean-Luc Pépin — concentrated on wresting complete control of the Quebec caucus from the party's Old Guard.

By late March of 1966 — less than five months after their election — Trudeau, Marchand, and Pelletier had established such a solid beach-head that they were able to dominate the founding convention of the Quebec wing of the federal Liberal Party, established in response to the Lesage administration's insistence that the federal and provincial Liberals split into distinct organizations. With Trudeau leading the attack in the role of constitutional expert, they beat back all talk of special status for Quebec or massive constitutional change, and persuaded the convention to adopt resolutions which took exactly the line Trudeau had been preaching in his writings for more than a decade.

A year later, on April 4, 1967, Pearson — by then thoroughly impressed with Trudeau and beginning to ponder possible successors as he contemplated retirement — appointed him minister of justice, put him in charge of constitutional negotiations with the provinces, and encouraged him to proceed with overhauling divorce laws and the Criminal Code. The man who, as a student, had been so fascinated with law as an instrument of social control suddenly found himself at the controls of that instrument. As he put it shortly after taking office: "Justice should be regarded more and more as a department planning for the society of tomorrow, not merely the government's legal advisor. It should combine the function of drafting new legislation with the disciplines of sociology and economics, so that it can provide a framework for our evolving way of life. Society is throwing up problems all the time — divorce, abortions, family planning, LSD, pollution, etc. — and it's no longer enough to review our status every 20 years. If possible, we have to move the framework of society slightly ahead of the times, so there is no curtailment of intellectual or physical liberty."[6]

But for all the apparent relish with which he discharged his functions, first as parliamentary secretary and then as justice minister, Trudeau had not leaped on these promotions as steps up the political ladder. On the contrary, he had resisted each time, still reluctant to accept direct responsibilities and the accompanying limitation of his freedom. Says Marchand: "When Pearson asked Pierre if he should make him his parliamentary secretary, Pierre's first reaction was negative. He said, 'I didn't come here for that.' I had to convince him. After many meetings, he accepted — but reluctantly. It was the same when he was named minister. He said, 'Why the hell are they in such a hurry? I've been here less than two years.' That was Pierre's attitude: he had no political ambition at all. Each time, I was the one designated to meet with him, to convince him to accept the promotion."

From the moment of his entry into cabinet, Trudeau was the object of fascinated attention from the press, most of it initially focussed on the fact that he was such an unusual minister. In the grey, cautious Ottawa of the day, his sporty, casual taste in clothes, his image as a swinger, his reputation as a radical, and his candour, all marked him out as someone very different from his colleagues. Wrote Dennis Braithwaite in the *Globe and Mail*: "Pierre Elliott Trudeau . . . is surely the most singular Minister of Justice in our long, ambiguous history. . . . Even if he goes all the way to a pompadour and rumpled three-button suit, he will remain the most arresting TV personality the Government's got and the closest thing to a Kennedy image in Canadian politics. Trudeau is handsome, he has the well-known Gallic voltage, he is cool, intelligent, amused, articulate; and he speaks English with scarcely a trace of accent." Peter Newman, writing in the *Toronto Star*, described him, three weeks after his entry into cabinet, in almost ecstatic terms: "His intelligent, skull-formed face (which might have been carved in alabaster to commemorate some distant war of the crusades) is a pattern of tension, subtlety, unrest and audacity. He is a man who both in his physical presence and intellectual discourse manages to maintain a detached view of his environment, yet at the same time give the impression of being responsive to the play of political forces around him. Unlike the unreconstructed political dinosaurs of the Liberal Party who still occupy most of its positions of power, Trudeau is an agent of ferment, a critic of Canadian society, questioning its collected conventional wisdom. He mistrusts rhetoric, has only disdain for pomposity, and longs for contemporary fulfillment through experience."

Then, gradually, attention begun to shift toward Trudeau's statements on the constitution. All through the summer of 1967, while the idea that Canada urgently needed a new constitution was gaining momentum, he kept forcefully arguing the opposite case. "If there were a specific constitutional issue, I would be glad to give it high priority," he told the Commons standing committee on justice and legal affairs in late June. "But this is not the case. In the circumstances, I feel it is much wiser to keep repeating that the constitution must be obeyed . . . that we do not feel it advisable to disrupt the fabric of the country by sitting down now and attempting to redraft it."[7] But then Pearson, under pressure from the provincial premiers, agreed to convene a federal-provincial conference on the constitution early in the coming year, and Trudeau decided to make the best of it by seizing the initiative. In September, in a major address in Quebec City to the Canadian Bar Association, he abruptly reversed his field: "The federal government henceforth declares itself ready to discuss any constitutional changes that are proposed."[8]

He went on to make a concrete proposal of his own: the process of change should begin by entrenching a bill of rights, binding on both the federal and the provincial governments, in the constitution. That, in turn, would lead naturally to other changes, including the finding of a formula for amending and patriating the British North America Act. The proposal was a remarkable indication of the degree to which he was succeeding in bringing the whole Pearson government around to his own constitutional theories. Years earlier, in almost identical terms, he had advocated in *Cité Libre* "the essential stage of a declaration of rights entrenched in the constitution which would be binding on all Canadians and on all our governments . . . that would enable us to agree on basic principles and lead us even, I think, to a formula for amending the constitution, which in turn would enable us to repatriate the constitution."[9]

But if the neophyte justice minister began impressing the public with his forcefulness and lucidity during this period, he also demonstrated the capacity for snappish, even vulgar, bluntness that was to continue to cause him trouble in later years. When he announced in May the appointment of Carl Goldenberg and Ivan Head as special advisors on the constitution, he was asked what he would tell critics who complained that both men were anglophones. "I would tell them," he replied in French, "*merde.*" (The word's literal translation is "shit", but in this context its meaning would be closer to "screw you".) And at the same Canadian Bar Association convention where he gave such an elegant, persuasive speech on the constitution, he later became irritated by the questioning at a press conference and lapsed into the tone and language of a street-fighter. He described talk of special status for Quebec as an "intellectual hoax" and *"une connerie"*, a very vulgar, anatomically derived French term for foolishness; English Canadians who accepted such a deal, he added, would be "saps". He thus managed, as the French-language press was quick to point out, to first open the door to constitutional negotiations and then in the next breath to insult the constitutional option favoured by Quebec Premier Daniel Johnson and a significant segment of Quebec opinion.

All this, however, was in the realm of words. The public saw no real action from the much-publicized new justice minister until year's end, because he was busy supervising the drafting of legislation and rebuilding the morale and effectiveness of a department which had been allowed to slip badly in the preceding years. Then, in December, in quick succession, he introduced two important and politically daring pieces of legislation: a new Divorce Bill on December 4, and an omnibus bill to overhaul the Criminal Code on December 21.

The common threads running through these two bills were modernization and secularization. They revamped antiquated laws to keep pace with changing attitudes, and in the process they created a new distinction between the standards of morality preached by various religions and the rules that the state should impose on its citizens. In the case of divorce, this meant broadening the grounds beyond adultery to such causes as perversion, certain criminal offences, physical and mental cruelty, and — most important of all — the catch-all concept of "marriage breakdown". The Criminal Code amendments — which died on the order paper and were not reintroduced until after Trudeau had become prime minister — proposed to decriminalize sodomy, bestiality, and "gross indecency" between consenting adults in private; homosexuality between consenting adults; therapeutic abortions performed in hospital on the recommendation of a medical committee; and lotteries organized by governments or charitable institutions. At the same time, they proposed to introduce breathalizer tests to curb drunken driving, and to impose new restrictions on the sale and possession of fire-arms.

If the two pieces of legislation were dramatic in themselves, public interest was compounded by the quality of Trudeau's performance in introducing them; the press carried glowing accounts of his coolness under fire, his skilful handling of Opposition questioning, his superb command of the facts, and his eloquence. And his widely quoted words were persuasive in themselves. Explaining the divorce bill, he said: "With laws dating back to 1870, in a society which has moved so quickly and so far in the intervening 97 years, it is not astonishing that the present divorce laws and the way in which they govern our society are highly unsatisfactory and indeed produce some very evil results. . . . We are now living in a social climate in which people are beginning to realize, perhaps for the first time in the history of this country, that we are not entitled to impose the concepts which belong to a sacred society upon a civil or profane society. The concepts of the civil society in which we live are pluralistic, and I think this parliament realizes that it would be a mistake for us to try to legislate into this society concepts which belong to a theological or sacred order." And, defending his Criminal Code amendments, he coined the memorable aphorism, "The state has no place in the bedrooms of the nation."

At any other time, all this might merely have won him high marks as a promising new minister. But timing is everything in politics, and in the winter of 1967-68 the Trudeau reforms coincided with a peculiarity in the public mood. The just-ending Centennial Year celebrations had been a psychological milestone, an occasion for Canadians to tell themselves they were now a fully grown, mature nation. And Expo 67 had given that sense of maturity a particularly dynamic direction: the World's Fair had been a triumph of modernity, innovation, and flair, applauded by visitors from around the globe. Canadians didn't want that euphoria to evaporate; they were in a mood to innovate, to outrace a past that suddenly seemed unexciting, to Be Modern. They would gladly have embraced as their slogan Trudeau's call of seventeen years earlier: "Let us cast down the totems, break down the taboos." Trudeau's assault on the Victorianism of the laws, and the flair with which he executed it, suited that mood perfectly; as a result, he found himself rocketed toward the status of a national hero.

Trudeau's performance in December also coincided with another development: the official opening of the Liberal leadership race. It had been on, unofficially, since at least the previous spring, when Pearson had indicated to his ministers that he was thinking of retiring in 1968. Even earlier, it had been generally assumed that Pearson, having failed to win a majority in two successive tries, would not lead the party in another election. Then, after the Tories had replaced Diefenbaker with Robert Stanfield on September 9 and taken a commanding lead in the Gallup Polls, the prime minister's imminent departure was so universally taken for granted that he had trouble restraining his ministers from devoting all their energy to campaigning for the undeclared vacancy. Finally, on December 14, Pearson announced that he was retiring, and a few days later the leadership convention was set for April 4 to 6.

The press, already singing Trudeau's praises over the divorce legislation — and about to have further cause for enthusiasm over his Criminal Code amendments — promptly began touting him as a major contender for the leadership. If there was any manipulation in the timing of Trudeau's two major offerings so close to the opening of the campaign, it was engineered not by the justice minister — who neither wanted the leadership nor intended to contest it — but by Pearson himself. The prime minister favoured Trudeau as his successor — or, at the very least, wanted him to be the French-Canadian candidate and to make a strong showing — and he may well have timed the introduction of the legislation and his own resignation announcement in such a way as to give Trudeau a boost.

It was only after his handling of the divorce legislation, in fact, that Trudeau's candidacy for the leadership was entertained by anyone as a serious possibility. There was no doubt, from the outset, that there had to be a strong French Canadian contender, and the Liberal Party's tradition of alternating French and English leaders meant that this contender would have a good chance of becoming prime minister. But Trudeau had no real public existence, except as something of a curiosity, before December, and his associates also knew that he wasn't interested in the top job. Most insiders, including Trudeau, expected that the candidate would be

Marchand. The only catch was that Marchand really didn't want the job either. He felt that his English wasn't good enough and that he lacked the requisite physical stamina; moreover, his wife didn't want to leave Quebec or to live the life of a prime minister's consort. A few of Trudeau's closest associates — Marc Lalonde, who by then was a constitutional advisor in the Privy Council Office; Jean-Pierre Goyer, a young MP and former *Cité Libre* colleague; and, of course, Pelletier — had come to feel that he had the makings of an eventual prime minister, but before December it seemed like an impossible dream.

Says Marchand: "During 1967, after we knew the leadership would soon be open, a few friends in the cabinet — Edgar Benson, Larry Pennell, Walter Gordon, Pierre, and myself — had meetings to discuss who the next leader should be. My name was being put forward, and I always disagreed. We talked about other names, but the results were not very good, none of them were right. There was no question of Pierre being proposed as leader. Nobody suggested it. He wasn't interested. It never came to mind, until the first debate in December about amending the divorce law. From that moment on, I said, 'Pierre, I think you will have to change your mind.' "

Trudeau demurred both privately and publicly, telling his friends that he wasn't ready for that sort of venture and insisting to reporters that there was no question of his becoming a candidate. He would have had valid strategic reasons for taking that position even if his real intentions had been different: both his Criminal Code amendments and his role at the crucial federal-provincial conference in February might have been compromised if he had been performing as a leadership candidate vulnerable to the suspicion that all his motives were self-serving. But his deep reluctance was genuine. "He really let himself be dragged into it," Lalonde recalls. "I remember him going to Tahiti over Christmas, 1967 — he left us with no indication that he was interested at all; if anything, the indication was no, he was not interested. He really felt that Marchand was the guy who should run, that he owed it to Marchand to rule himself out. It was a matter of respect for Marchand's political sense, and the fact that Marchand had been more or less the political leader of the three. But then, even after Marchand was out, we still really had to work Trudeau over. He also felt that he didn't know the party, that in that sense he was a neophyte in terms of party politics. I remember him raising the point that he had not been a minister for long, that he did not know the workings of government very well."

In mid-January, after Trudeau had returned from a two-week holiday in Tahiti — where, incidentally, he met Margaret Sinclair, who was later to become his wife — Pearson called him and Marchand into his office, stressed to him that Marchand had definitely decided not to run, and told him that he was the only possible French candidate. But Trudeau still refused to commit himself. The idea had begun to tantalize him, but he still had a great many doubts. He was worried about his inexperience and his lack of contacts within the party. He was sceptical about his alleged popularity, pointing out that it might be an illusion created by a press which tends to create and encourage fads and then abandon them for something new. He feared that a run for the leadership could end in ignominious defeat, destroying his credibility and undercutting everything he, Marchand, and Pelletier had come to Ottawa to accomplish. And, underlying it all, there was the ever-present matter of his personal freedom. As he puts it:

"I remember the argument I was giving Pelletier and Marchand for not accepting to run for the leadership of the party. The argument I was giving them was that 'I don't know this party, they don't know me. I just entered in '65; let me work with it another five or ten years, and then I will have built my power bases, and I'll have learned something about politics and the House of Commons and the party and everything else. And then I'll do it.' And this was true, but there was obviously an element of rationalization there. You know, I just had butterflies in my stomach, that suddenly I was going to lead and therefore I was going to lose my liberty in the sense that I'd be responsible to a cabinet, to a party, and the country for the direction in which I led them."

But while Trudeau held back, events around him were already building up their own momentum. From late December on, Marc Lalonde was busy building the organizational infrastructure for a Trudeau candidacy. The key people around him included Gordon

Gibson, 30, a young British Columbian with an MBA from Harvard, who was executive assistant to Northern Affairs Minister Arthur Laing and who had concluded as early as the fall of 1967 that Trudeau should be the next prime minister; Jim Davey, 38, a British-born, Oxford-educated physicist, computer expert, and management consultant; Pierre Levasseur, 29, an MBA and former Quebec civil servant whom Marchand had manoeuvred into the pivotal position of executive director of the Liberal Party's Quebec wing; and Donald Macdonald, then a young Toronto MP who served as the campaign's link with an influential coterie of supporters in the Toronto intellectual community.

In mid-January, to get Trudeau some additional national exposure, Lalonde persuaded Pearson to send the justice minister on a whirlwind tour of provincial capitals in preparation for the federal-provincial conference. Then, on the weekend of January 27, the annual convention of the Liberal Party's Quebec wing became — thanks partly to the efficient behind-the-scenes organizational work of Marchand and other team members — another Trudeau triumph; followed through the halls of the convention hotel by gaggles of adoring teen-agers and bathed at every move in the glare of TV lights, he dazzled the delegates with his performance in a question-and-answer session on the constitution and federal-provincial relations. Next, in the first week of February, came the federal-provincial conference, a nationally televised political spectacular which accomplished little of substance, but showcased Trudeau's toughness and eloquence as he clashed with Quebec Premier Daniel Johnson over special status for Quebec and the need for a constitutional bill of rights. And, finally, on February 9, there was the Ontario Liberal Association's annual convention in Toronto: he was mobbed by the 1,400 delegates and carried around the room on the shoulders of his supporters.

By this time, Trudeau was not so much resisting a run at the leadership as testing the waters. He still would have preferred the whole question to go away for a while, but it clearly would not, so all that remained to be established was whether he really had a serious chance of winning. After the Toronto meeting, Marchand and Lalonde began putting even greater pressure on him to make up his mind. "He still said, 'I would prefer to wait,' " Marchand recalls. "I said, 'If you don't go in, Hellyer or Winters will be the next leader, and how long will he stay there?' When he finally agreed, it was very reluctantly. He was not enthusiastic at all." Adds Lalonde: "When we were arguing with him he brought a couple of us in and said, 'If I go in, I want a commitment that you'll be around. I want to be sure you're not sending me out to war alone.' He was afraid that if the Gallup would show that we were still trailing the Tories if he was leader, he would be left all alone holding the bag. In that sense, you could say he was somewhat concerned he would be unable to cope. But I can't remember him appearing to me as a guy who had very serious misgivings about his ability to do the job."

He finally made up his mind on February 14 and announced the decision two days later, giving reporters at his press conference an analysis of his candidacy that most took as just another example of his cool, self-deprecating humour. In fact, it was an entirely serious statement of his view: "To be quite frank, if I try to analyse it, well, I think in the subconscious mind of the press it started out like a huge practical joke on the Liberal Party. I mean that. . . . It seemed to me, reading the press in the early stages a couple of months ago, it seemed to me as though many of you guys were saying, you know, 'We dare the Liberal Party to choose this guy Trudeau. Of course, we know they never will, but we'll just dare them to do it and we'll show them that this is the man they could have had as leader if they had wanted.' . . . And what happened, I think, is that the joke blew up in your face and in mine. You know, people took it seriously. I saw this when — not when the press thought I had a chance and that I should run and so on — but when I saw the response from political people, from members of the party and responsible members of Parliament."[10]

Once he had entered the race, Trudeau threw himself unsparingly into the effort to win the leadership. But he insisted on pursuing it on his own terms. "I was serious from the moment I decided to run," he said later. "The state of mind which is true — and which perhaps I should not confess too openly — is that it is not important for me to be prime minister at any price."[11] The price he refused to pay was to tailor his behaviour or his policies to anyone else's dictates, or to promise anything he didn't genuinely want to deliver. It was this lack of driving ambition, both before and after entering the campaign, that ironically proved to be one of his strongest political assets, because it left him free to be more candid, more relaxed, more outspoken — and, hence, much fresher — than fellow politicians whose fears of a career-damaging misstep led them to plod along with constant caution. In the campaign, he held the leadership at arm's length and simultaneously used that very detachment as an aid in pursuing it, a delicate balancing act exemplified by his performance in a televised question-and-answer session at Toronto's St. Lawrence Hall. How badly, he was asked, did he want to be prime minister? "Not very badly," he replied, then added in the next breath: "But I can give you another quotation, from Plato — that men who want very badly to head the country shouldn't be trusted."

Trudeau operated throughout the campaign on two levels. At private meetings with delegates he was restrained, candid, quietly charming, and meticulous about outlining his policy views in detail; occasionally, the charm would momentarily vanish behind a cloud of professorial irritation, and he would deal impatiently with a questioner who hadn't paid sufficient attention to earlier answers. At public gatherings, usually with the press watching and the cameras rolling, he adopted a more playful posture, sliding down banisters, kissing pretty young girls, nibbling at flowers.

This flamboyance was, more than anything else, an essentially shy man's instinctive way of coping with all the sudden attention; it enabled him to hide his reticence and appear cheerfully outgoing without really yielding up much of his inner self or his privacy. It was also a display of the streak of show-off in him, the urge to assert his individuality at boring or unpleasant moments through startlingly inappropriate behaviour — the same tendency that eight years earlier had made him suddenly turn a somersault during a guide's tedious lecture in China, or that nearly a decade later would make him execute an elaborate pirouette in London at the end of a photo session with the Queen and other Commonwealth leaders, or brace his hands on House of Commons desks and swing his legs toward the Opposition like a gymnast on parallel bars. And, finally, it was an expression of the instinctive actor and showman in Trudeau, who has a remarkable ability to sense and take on the coloration of any particular event. In his movements, his dress, and his speech, he has a sense of drama and timing that most professional actors would envy. Watching him walk across the tarmac en route to a campaign appearance, with his trenchcoat draped over his shoulders like a cloak, a newsman remarked on the image of Napoleon it evoked. "No," a colleague corrected him, "Marlon Brando *playing* Napoleon." And his appearance onstage at the leadership convention for his pre-balloting speech — the pause at the top of the stairs, head bowed, shoulders slumped in an attitude of humility as the roar of the crowd washed over him — was an instance of the actor's craft at its finest.

None of this was planned image-making, in the sense that none of it originated anywhere but within the man himself. Indeed, few image-makers would have dared to gamble that Trudeau's insouciant behaviour wouldn't backfire disastrously. Says Lalonde: "The guy just bloomed that way. It was just the way he developed during the campaign. I can assure you, there was no scenario that said, 'You have to act that way.' He always had in him a little bit of the trait of a prankster, if you read all the crazy things he did when he was younger. In the campaign, he just decided he might as well have fun. To say that he and his experts decided he would play this role — no bloody way! There were a lot of young people with talent around the campaign, and they just produced the gimmicks to go around the way Trudeau developed."

Trudeau was backed by what was probably the most efficient organization in the campaign. The style of his candidacy made it important for his organization to give the impression of an amateurish, spontaneous crusade of enthusiasts. In fact, it was amateurish only in the sense that most of the human cogs in the campaign machine were not seasoned political pros, but rather outsiders to the game of power politics. They were almost all young — the median age in Trudeau's organization was somewhere under thirty — and, because they were outsiders, they differed from the aides of other contenders in that they were interested solely in achieving their candidate's victory, without being distracted by concerns about maintaining or improving any political positions of their own. But if the operation was amateur in that sense, it was crisply professional in other ways. The key Trudeau people were outstandingly bright, and expert in such fields as advertising, management planning, and organization. When they focussed their various skills on the improvisation of a leadership campaign, the result was a combination of dynamism and hard-nosed efficiency that the other candidates could scarcely hope to match.

Even though the key figures were either outsiders or newcomers to Liberal politics, moreover, the Trudeau candidacy itself was not really an assault on the party Establishment by alien forces. Pearson might easily have scuttled the justice minister on at least a half-dozen occasions; instead, he gave the candidacy at the very least his tacit support. Revenue Minister and Treasury Board President Edgar Benson was national co-chairman, with Jean Marchand, of the Trudeau campaign. And Finance Minister Mitchell Sharp, a pillar of the Liberal Establishment, had decided months earlier that unless his own candidacy miraculously took off, he would throw his support behind Trudeau at whatever moment it would do the most good; had Trudeau entered the race earlier, Sharp probably wouldn't have bothered to run at all. As it turned out, his decision to withdraw and to throw his support to the justice minister on the eve of the convention contributed immeasurably to Trudeau's momentum and credibility.

The press, too, played a key role not only in launching the Trudeau candidacy, but in propelling it toward success. A study conducted in the political science department of Laval University found that between January 1 and March 20, with nine candidates — Trudeau, Sharp, Eric Kierans, Paul Martin, Paul Hellyer, Robert Winters, John Turner, Allan MacEachen, and Joe Greene — in the race, sixteen major newspapers across the country had given Trudeau twenty-six per cent of their total campaign-related coverage.[12] Press coverage cannot do the trick alone — Sharp was second to Trudeau in volume of coverage with sixteen per cent, yet his campaign went nowhere — but coupled with the other factors in Trudeau's favour, the enthusiastic attention of the press was a vital asset.

Although he arrived at the convention as the clear leader and maintained his position with strong performances in the policy workshops and in his main speech to delegates, Trudeau's victory was by no means certain until the fourth and final ballot; even after the third ballot — in which he had 1,051 votes, Winters 621, Hellyer 377, and Turner 279 — he might still have been defeated if Turner had thrown his support behind Winters instead of staying in the race to the finish. But, throughout the convention, Trudeau maintained the same cool detachment he had shown during the campaign. Two weeks earlier, he had taken the very large gamble of vetoing plans for the traditional type of demonstration, with marching girls and a band, to precede his crucial Friday night speech to the convention. He had argued, characteristically, that if the delegates really wanted him, they would pick up signs left beside their seats and applaud, without requiring the stimulus of a contrived demonstration. That combination of sang-froid and theatrical instinct paid off handsomely: When the justice minister was called to the microphone Friday night, the Ottawa Civic Centre hall came electrifyingly alive with a great whoop of "Trudeau!" from the audience and a sudden forest of Trudeau placards.

All through the gruelling tension of voting day on Saturday, April 6, Trudeau remained impassive. He went through lunch with a few key aides immediately before the voting without making a single reference to the convention. Back in the Civic Centre, he maintained an air of serene detachment as the pandemonium around him mounted during seven and a half hours of voting. He mugged for the cameras, waved periodically to his supporters, played at throwing grapes into his mouth from aloft, toyed with a flower. He was, in reality, not uncaring but fatalistic. Trudeau is an intensely competitive man and, since he had come this far, the fighter in him intensely wanted to win. But victory would also mean a threat to another vital element of his personality — his solitary nature, his pursuit of freedom unfettered by commitments, his uneasiness about the responsibilities of leadership. It was a threat that he had concluded he could handle, but his feelings were mixed. His outward calm was the stoicism of a man who had reconciled himself equally to either outcome.

During the third ballot, one of the young, orange-jacketed

Trudeau "hosts" ringing his box leaned through the throng of journalists and hangers-on and asked the justice minister for his delegate badge as a souvenir. Trudeau smilingly put him off, explaining that he still needed it. The young man persisted: Could he have it when the voting was over? But Trudeau appeared not to hear. Just before 8 p.m., the results of the fourth ballot boomed over the public-address system. "Trudeau, 1,203" — then bedlam. The arena erupted first in a great roar, then shouts of "Trudeau!", then a swelling chant, "Trudeau, Canada, Trudeau, Canada!". The band beside the platform struck up "Happy Days Are Here Again". As the final "3" of the vote tally came over the speaker, Trudeau leaped to his feet. Everyone around him was hugging him, pumping his hand, clapping his shoulder. A flying wedge of policemen formed to propel him to the stage to be hailed as Canada's fifteenth prime minister. But first he paused, took off his delegate badge, reached through the tumult, and handed it to the young man who had requested it two hours before.

On April 19, after a brief working holiday in Florida to plan the composition of his cabinet, Trudeau was sworn in as prime minister. He moved into 24 Sussex Drive with a grand total of two suitcases — "One of the two," he recalls, "is one that my mother bought for my brother and me when we toured the United States and Canada in 1938 or '39" — which he carried himself. Three days later, he called a federal election for June 25.

The campaign quickly became one of the most remarkable phenomena in the politics of Canada or any other democracy. It is not uncommon for the public to heap adulation on a national hero or a spellbinding orator, but Trudeau had credentials as neither. In a campaign that often seemed more like a joyous coronation, crowds gathered by the tens of thousands, not to hail his past accomplishments or hear his rhetoric, but simply to see the man — and preferably to touch him. Wherever he went, he was mobbed like a pop star; fingers grasped toward him for a handshake, a touch, or a snatched souvenir; at one stop his watch was ripped from his wrist, and late in the campaign pubescent girls took to trying to pluck hairs from his balding head. The most frenzied scenes were caused by youngsters, most of them below voting age, but adults in the crowds were scarcely less affected. If not Trudeaumania, they succumbed to Trudeauphilia — a vast outpouring of visceral *liking* for this dynamic, quiet-spoken man with the tough yet hopeful words and the shy smile.

What made the phenomenon all the more remarkable was that Trudeau was not, in conventional terms, a particularly good campaigner. His speeches were delivered in a dull monotone, and when he improvised he sometimes leaped from thought to thought to the point of incoherence. When he read from a prepared text, it was even worse. His speech-writers saddled him with excruciatingly turgid prose, full of sentences like "this more active concern of the federal government for the problems of the manufacturing industry can be ascribed to the changing balance of the economy and the necessity for improved industrial performance as a prerequisite for general economic growth,"[13] and he made no effort to hide his own boredom. Though he was sometimes adept at putting down hecklers, there were numerous instances when they threw him completely off stride. He also showed flashes of snappish irritability that would have badly damaged most politicians. In Dartmouth, N.S., for instance, he mistakenly thought that cheering and heckling near the stage was drowning him out, so he cut short his speech, glared at the friendly crowd of two thousand, snapped, "Well, if you don't want to listen to me, I'll just ask you to vote for Arnie Patterson, Liberal candidate," and stalked off.

But Trudeau could do no wrong, and substance was secondary in the appeal of his campaign. His itinerary was designed for maximum exposure, and each stop was not so much a speech as an appearance. He would come to a riding and travel in a convertible — or, better still, a gaily decorated antique car or float of some sort — in a slow motorcade through crowded streets, always to the accompaniment of perky go-go music or a marching band. The parade would make its way to a shopping-centre mall or town square, where time would be set aside for him to be mobbed while he worked his way on foot through the throng. Then he would mount the stage and deliver a short — seldom more than ten to fifteen minutes — address, usually combining several set themes:

the beauty and promise of Canada; the exciting future that lay ahead if Canadians had the courage to excel and innovate; the need for a united country where all Canadians, regardless of language or origin, are equal; and the threat posed by those who would divide the country or tinker with dangerous formulas like special status. Whether he was speaking French to a Quebec audience, or English in some other province, he would invariably switch in mid-sentence to the other language at some point in his speech — and the audience would invariably applaud. He didn't really *say* very much in these speeches, but he conveyed a great deal: a sense of vitality, an invitation to involvement, a promise of exciting innovation.

Though substance was secondary in the campaign, it was by no means non-existent. Anyone who studied what he said, particularly in question-and-answer sessions and press interviews, could have had a reasonably good idea of what he was about. In fact, the only real difference between the 1968 campaign and the one in 1972 was that by 1972 the kissing had stopped and the public mood had curdled. In both campaigns, the main theme in his speeches was the need to accept limits on what could be expected of government. And, in both campaigns, he made it clear that he saw the politician's role as that of an educator. In 1968, the public was dazzled when, instead of offering solutions, he simply explained the nature of problems and outlined the choices that would have to be made; in 1972, the mood had changed, and the same display of professorial detachment infuriated the voters.

"We are not promising things for everybody and we are not seeing great visions," he said in 1968. "We are trying to make the people of the country understand that if they are to be governed well they will have to participate in the governing; that there are no magic solutions; that there is no charismatic leader with a magic wand which will produce great solutions; that the solutions for this country will be as difficult as they are for any other country; and that if we want to sell our produce, if we want to progress in terms of our productivity, we will have to invent new things and we will have to find new markets and fight for them."[14] And, more bluntly: "You know that no government is a Santa Claus, and I thought as I came down the street and saw all the waves and the handshakes that I'd remind you that Ottawa is not a Santa Claus. We don't intend raising taxes any more than we have to, and therefore we aren't making many promises this election."[15]

He demonstrated right from the beginning that beneath the shy smile and the sometimes diffident manner there was a steely toughness. Asked when he called the election whether any ministers had opposed the move, he retorted that anyone who dissented would have to say so himself — and would do so at his own peril. Then, his expression hardening, he served notice that he wouldn't tolerate the sort of leaky, publicly squabbling cabinet Pearson had endured: "If they don't agree with cabinet decisions, they won't be ministers for long — not for very long at all."[16] And, late in the campaign, on the day Senator Robert Kennedy died of an assassin's bullet in Los Angeles, Trudeau again showed his toughness in the cold, controlled fury he turned on separatist hecklers in Rouyn, Quebec. Eyes blazing, finger jabbing the air, he battered them with putdown after putdown: "The men who killed Kennedy are purveyors of hate like you — those who refuse to discuss! There won't be free speech in your Québec libre, monsieur. . . . It's not me you're insulting. It's your fellow citizens. . . . If you want to get rid of foreigners, of the English, of American capital, it's easy. You only have to continue the violence. But you're going to be left behind by the 20th Century."[17] Finally, on the eve of the election, he gave a physical demonstration of courage by refusing to leave the reviewing stand at the St. Jean Baptiste parade in Montreal while a bloody riot raged across the street and other guests of honour scurried for cover from a shower of broken glass. It was scarcely surprising that the man who had earlier sought out the most brutal wars in his foreign travels would refuse to be panicked by a flung pop bottle, but it was a display of flintiness that contributed to the size of his victory the next day.

He also made clear from the outset that he was inclined to be a confrontationist rather than a conciliator on matters that involved Quebec. During the leadership campaign, he charged that France had put the tiny African republic of Gabon up to inviting Quebec to an international conference of education ministers — an invitation that led to the suspension of Canada's diplomatic relations with Gabon — and he disregarded the usual diplomatic niceties in giving France a stern warning: "If France were ever to do that — invite a province to sit at a conference as an independent state — in such a case, we would have to treat France as we treated Gabon."[18] During the federal campaign, he deliberately made a major issue of the Quebec government's international aspirations, declaring that "This is the type of issue which the Canadian people have a right to make a judgment on."[19] He argued that "there is one way to keep Canada united and that is to make sure Canada speaks with one voice in the world" and flatly stated that "the federal government will not condone or accept"[20] Premier Johnson's attempts to carve out an international role. He also virtually dared the Quebec premier to involve himself in the federal campaign, provocatively noting that Johnson wouldn't want to risk "a humiliating defeat" by actively working against the Trudeau Liberals.

On both the Quebec issue and the general nature of his campaign, Trudeau walked a precarious tightrope by simultaneously appearing to do one set of things and loudly insisting that he was doing something else. He quite consciously used his firmness toward Quebec's constitutional aspirations as a major element of his campaign, thereby feeding assumptions he was a prime minister who could "put Quebec in its place". But at the same time, he kept insisting, quite truthfully, that he should not be mistaken for a Quebec-basher and that his intention was to increase, not diminish, the role of Quebecers in Canada's life. In the same way, the man whose political motto was "reason over passion" ran a campaign that was stronger on emotion than on specific content — and simultaneously insisted that the emotional aspects weren't what counted: "I do not want to prevent people from liking me, goodness knows I get a great kick out of enthusiasm, no matter where I find it, but I keep telling people that they should not choose politicians or parties on the basis of any fad or anything which is as transient as personal popularity. I hope they will choose leaders not by the emotion that they draw forth from teenagers and not by the ethnic background they have . . . but by their ideas and by their approach to Canadian problems."[21]

In fairness, Trudeau did not originally set out to create Trudeaumania on purpose, and there was no way that he could have killed it outright during the campaign without damaging himself and h. party. He was, in fact, deeply ambivalent about the phenomeno... As an intellectual, he recoiled at the idea of political choices being made on the basis of emotional attraction rather than ideas. As a practical matter, he also worried that the hero-worship would eventually backfire: "This kind of mania chews up its heros pretty quickly, and I do not intend being chewed up."[22] But as a politician and an individual, he enjoyed the public's enthusiasm — perhaps even assuring himself that it was rooted primarily in admiration for his policies — and recognized it as a vehicle for winning the election without having to make many concrete commitments. He was not innocent of deliberately feeding Trudeaumania, because he accepted a campaign strategy that was conceived as a triumph of style rather than substance.

By voting day, anyone who was paying attention to such things could also have been aware of two Trudeau faults that later were greeted with apparent surprise: his capacity for cutting nastiness when attacked, and his occasional insensitivity to things that are important to other people. In February, during the leadership campaign, the Liberals managed through inadvertence to get themselves defeated on a tax bill. The Opposition argued that the government had fallen and an immediate election was required, and the Commons was in an uproar. Defending the government's refusal to call an election, Trudeau spoke in quietly professorial tones, but found himself attacked by a chorus of Opposition hecklers. He retorted icily: "When you howl like animals, I cannot very well hear the questions you are asking me. If you want to ask me questions, I will reply. But to moo like a herd, that doesn't advance the decision much."[23]

The insensitivity was displayed right at the beginning of his prime-ministerial tenure. First, to maintain the option of calling an election for June 17, he advanced the date of his swearing-in by two days, thereby depriving Pearson of the sentimentally important opportunity to step down exactly five years after taking office. Much worse, he then handled the announcement of his election call in Parliament in such a way that he cut off the opportunity for party leaders to pay tribute to the outgoing prime minister. Instead of leaving time for the tribute before he made his announcement, or asking MPs to remain in the chamber afterward, he was coldly logical: Since the governor general had already granted dissolution, it was inappropriate for anyone to speak. The result was that Pearson, who had chosen not to run in the election, found himself leaving Parliament for the last time, without a formal word of farewell.

If Trudeau's faults were openly displayed, he was also remarkably candid about some elements of his psychological make-up. "I am not pitting myself against other people," he declared several times during the campaign. "I am trying to do as good a job as I can and I am not really worried about the others."[24] Unnoticed in 1968 and bitterly resented as arrogant when they were repeated in 1972, these statements in fact revealed an important element of Trudeau's political attitude. Just as his inner-directed, self-testing attitude made him shun competitive sports in favour of more private ones when he was younger, so Trudeau dislikes regarding political life as a competition between himself and other leaders. "I've often said it at election times," he recalls now. "People say, 'You're fighting to beat Diefenbaker's record' or 'You're fighting to beat whoever the leadership contender was' or 'You're fighting to beat Joe Clark.' And my answer is, 'No, I'm fighting against myself.' You know, I want to do better for me, and I refuse to be judged by the standards of others. I set my standards as high as I can from time to time, and I want to judge myself by them."

His unwillingness to make conventional political promises was also largely the product of his psychological make-up — namely, his determination to relinquish as little of his freedom as possible. "I have not made any promises," he told a TV interviewer in mid-campaign. "I have not said to anyone, 'If you run, you will be a minister.' Or I have not said to anyone who has asked me if he should stay on in the party or withdraw, 'Well, stay on, there is a great future for you. You will be a minister some day.' It is not that important to me to be prime minister. It is very important to be prime minister in order to get my ideas across, but in order to get them through I have to feel free and I do not want to be saddled with 100 promises or 200 that I cannot fulfil. So in that sense, when I woke up after the convention I was very happy, because I won that convention without promising anything to any-body."[25]

He also made clear from the outset in 1968 that in his view elections should be decided not on specific policy issues, but on the over-all orientations and talents of the various parties. As he put it in a convoluted but revealing reply to a radio interviewer: "I suppose the main issue is which party will the people elect. Is it a party like the Liberal Party or is it a party like the Conservative Party? Who do they want to govern them? And we as a party are attempting to put as many ideas as we can in front of the people to show them that we do not have the solution — the answer — to all the problems, but that in a country like Canada, which is not only changing fast but which in order to continue progressing must adapt to that change and be ahead of the times rather than following the times, we want to make sure that we have members of Parliament and a government which is able to tackle all the problems without any doctrinaire approach — without any hard line, as it were — but which is prepared to accept the challenge of change and meet it."[26]

This broad approach has its dangers, because it smacks of the very charge Trudeau levelled at the Liberal Party in his *Cité Libre* days: "The philosophy of the Liberal Party is very simple — say anything, think anything, or better still, do not think at all, but put us in power because it is we who can govern you best."[27] If people are to decide which party is best suited to govern, they like, reasonably enough, to be able to do it on the basis of com-paring specific policy stands on issues which concern them. But logic is on the side of Trudeau's perception, however unpalatable it may seem at first glance, because events these days move too fast to make detailed election platforms very meaningful. The position taken on a specific matter before election day may be totally unsuitable by the end of the first year of a five-year man-date, because intervening events have totally changed the situation; a promise to deal with a specific problem may be rendered totally irrelevant within months by an entirely new and unexpected problem which forces a change in priorities. The only reliable criterion, consequently, is a judgment based on how skilfully and desirably the various parties are likely to deal with *whatever* problems arise, as well as on the attractiveness of the general directions in which they propose to move the country.

In the 1968 campaign, in any event, the appeal of the Trudeau Liberals was conveyed not in crisp policy statements, but in vague *impressions*. And most of those impressions centred on Trudeau. The campaign, as seen on TV by most Canadians, was a succession of memorable tableaus: Trudeau in British Columbia, holding a handful of flowers, surrounded by little children, smiling beatifically, looking remarkably like a politicized version of St. Francis of Assisi; Trudeau, eyes blazing, forefinger jabbing, barking out his words ferociously as he does battle with separatist hecklers; Trudeau, head bowed, feet shuffling awkwardly, looking like an embarrassed little boy abashed by the wild cheers of a crowd; Trudeau, grinning wickedly, executing elaborately clumsy dives into a swimming pool to parody how rival party leaders Tommy Douglas and Robert Stanfield might perform on a diving board.

In his words, as in such scenes, there was something for everybody to single out and identify with. Conservatives could detect a kindred spirit in his talk of fiscal responsibility and his repeated warnings that government was no Santa Claus. Reformers found a spokesman in his talk of innovation, progress, and the challenge of building a better, more just nation. The young saw in his candour and spirited antics evidence that he was of a new generation, while their elders found reassurance in his insistence that the kissing and the banister-sliding weren't what really counted. Because of its vagueness, his campaign became a sort of hollow vessel into which everyone could pour his own hopes and aspirations, then interpret them as what Trudeau was offering.

This applied not only to political matters, but to more personal matters of identification as well. His effect on women was devastating. Here, for the first time, was a leader to whom they could relate as a *man;* with his predecessors, the question simply didn't arise in those terms. Trudeau was not only single and relatively young, he was highly attractive. Though not handsome in a con-

ventional sense, his features were found by women to be rich
in sexual fascination; an airline stewardess, seeing him in person
for the first time, looked him over carefully, and reported: "He's
got sexy eyes — and that mouth! He needs love and affection,
and not the motherly kind." He was also rich, sophisticated,
athletic, tough and cold enough to carry a tantalizing hint of
wickedness and danger, and yet also oddly vulnerable because of
the shy sensitivity that could be glimpsed beneath the protective
shell. For women who weren't inclined to perceive him in terms
of sexual fantasy, the trace of vulnerability evoked another reaction: the mothering instinct.

Men, meanwhile, found in him a reflection of how they would
like to perceive themselves: the shimmering intelligence, the physical prowess, the much-reported taste for adventure and danger,
the combination of toughness and grace, the appeal to women. A
slightly different mix of the same qualities in another man might
have evoked hostile envy; in Trudeau, it tended rather to create
a feeling that by supporting him and identifying with him, men
might affirm the same qualities in themselves.

As for the spell he cast over youngsters, it can be explained
to a large extent by the special affinity for children his sister
recalls from his younger days. He genuinely enjoyed the company
of youngsters, and he knew just how to handle them. He didn't
talk down to them or make them feel they were intruding, but he
didn't try to be one of them either. He maintained a certain
friendly distance, putting down impertinence with mock severity,
and the young sensed his liking for them.

All these factors accorded happily with a national mood that,
at that particular moment, was peculiarly hungry for a leader like
Trudeau. Besides the afterglow of Expo, the mood was conditioned
by nearly a decade of jealousy. Canadians had enviously watched
the presidency of John Kennedy, and had continued to wish for
a leader like him. The Kennedy envy had been rekindled early in
1968 by the ascendancy of his brother Bobby. Then there was the
hunger of a whole young generation for real political power: the
1960s were the period of idealistic student radicalism, of sit-ins
and protests, and in the United States the young had already

succeeded in bringing Lyndon Johnson to his knees. In Trudeau, Canadians saw a "young" leader with the grace of a Kennedy and a vitality that made him a generation removed from the governing greybeards of the day.

And, finally, in that peculiar national mood, Trudeau's candidacy corresponded with a new anti-materialism, a burgeoning nationalism, and a still-unarticulated love of country. Trudeau managed, on a few memorable occasions, to articulate that feeling and speak eloquently to Canadians of matters which touch not the body but the soul. On a balmy June evening in Fort Langley, B.C., he talked quietly and spontaneously to a crowd of some two thousand; he spoke of Mozart, of the brave and generous St. Exupéry, of human frailty, and of a nation sweeping eastward "to ocean waves breaking in on the granite coast of Newfoundland". Then he went on: "Some people despair because they fear the future may escape us. But I speak to those who know the future cannot be guaranteed to any person, province or country — and that the future will be what we make of it. It is up to us to know what to do with this country we love."[28]

In those few sentences, he captured the mood of a nation at once hopeful and uneasy about its unsolved problems. "Take a risk on the future," he invited on another occasion. "We're not really doing what we should with this country because we're hamstrung with the past. We're afraid to change. We think the people of Canada are not prepared to take a risk. Well, they are."[29] Canadians responded, on June 25, by giving him 155 seats in the House of Commons — the clear majority that had so painfully eluded Pearson — and 45.3 per cent of the popular vote.

The meteoric rise of Pierre Trudeau between that December and June was a remarkable phenomenon, but not a unique one. John Kenneth Galbraith, in an earlier article in the *New York Times* entitled "The Build-up and The Public Man", had come very close to describing it:

"The autonomous build-up always strikes someone who is already in the public eye. Perhaps he has earned a measure of public esteem for doing an important and difficult job in a restricted area of public endeavor. Or he has made a promising start on such a job. Or, in a common case, he has just assumed public office after a respectable private career.

"Then comes the build-up. He is a man transformed — indeed he is no longer a man but a superman. His eccentricities become the mark of unique personality. His hobbies are the refreshment of an intense and active mind. . . . But most remarkable of all are his qualifications for the job he has assumed. Where others ponder, he has solutions. That is because he is able to separate the essential from the non-essential, and then find a painless course of action by shooting straight for the target. It has been the fault of lesser men that they have left the impression that there was a choice only between equally grim alternatives. . . .

"The build-up is particularly likely to occur at a time when problems are numerous, vexatious and incomprehensible. Not knowing how to control nuclear energy, disarm, increase needed expenditures, balance the budget, eliminate farm surpluses . . . we find it desirable to invent people who can do these things. The press and the networks, sensitive always to the needs of the customer, assist. . . . They create the master statesman who will see us through.

"Such statesmanship, as a career, is not especially secure. The job turnover is very high. That is because, while it is easy to place a man on a pedestal, it is not at all easy to keep him there. A pedestal is a peculiarly public place. Since the build-up is indiscriminate in its selections, some rather grievous shortcomings may thus be revealed . . . to a public whose expectations are inordinately high. There is a convention which allows those who have taken part in the build-up to participate actively in the ensuing deflation. The build-up rarely lets its man off at his point of departure. When working with ordinary efficiency, it leaves him well below zero."[30]

Galbraith wrote that piece fourteen years earlier, about the build-up as it affected Eisenhower. But with a few minor modifications, it might have been a description of Trudeaumania and its aftermath in the following four years.

CHAPTER SEVEN

Political Philosopher, Philosophical Politician

When Canadians elected Pierre Trudeau as prime minister, they bestowed the mantle of leadership on a most unusual political creature: a social thinker and critic, without either the burdens or the benefits of long years of political experience, suddenly granted the opportunity to translate his theories and beliefs into reality from the apex of power.

It was, in a limited sense, an experiment with the Platonic concept of a philosopher-king, a leader chosen exclusively for the quality of his thought. He didn't have the absolute power of Plato's mythical perfect ruler, of course, and there was another important limitation: In the first mandate of his prime-ministry, he didn't have the political expertise or confidence to give free rein to his theories; and by the time he had totally mastered the intricacies of the job, he had already become much more politician than theorist. But Trudeau, far more than most Western leaders, came to power with a coherent and painstakingly developed political philosophy. And he still operates not by instinct or improvisation, but by constant reference to an elaborate philosophical framework.

There is little that is original in his philosophy; stripped to its essentials, it consists primarily of an overlay of Acton, de Tocqueville, Montesquieu, and a host of other thinkers on a foundation of the classical liberalism of John Stuart Mill and John Locke. But what Trudeau has done — and what makes his political thinking something more than just the general erudition of any well-educated man — is take the parts that appeal to him most in various philosophies and construct them into a structured, closely reasoned system of his own. If his thinking has changed so little on such subjects as federalism and nationalism over the years, it's because it is so deeply rooted in a whole chain of reasoning that begins with the role of the individual, works its way through the function of the state, and goes on from there to various specific political problems. Four themes dominate the theory: the absolute value of the individual, the supremacy of rationality, the constant struggle between totalitarian and democratic tendencies in society, and the obligation of every individual to involve himself in the political process.

Trudeau has never set forth his philosophy in any single place, but it comes through clearly — in bits and pieces — in his writings between 1950 and 1965, particularly his articles in *Cité Libre* and *Vrai*. He says he cannot think of any instances where his years in power have caused changes in the philosophy articulated in those days. What has changed, rather, is his degree of adherence to his theories: He has no qualms about making decisions as prime minister which fall short of, or even appear to contradict, some of his stated beliefs. When challenged about those instances, he falls back on the distinction between the critic or teacher and the man of action: "When you're teaching, you must as much as possible preach ideal solutions. When you're in politics, you must preach solutions which are possible . . . you must seek ways to accommodate absolute truth to the facts around you. I'm not embarrassed at all for having chosen the political career, and therefore I am not at all ill at ease at following the rules of that particular avocation, politics, the art of the possible rather than the art of the perfect and ideal."[1] But if it is easy enough to find instances where his philosophy is not readily reflected in his political actions, that philosophy still provides the framework for his over-all approach to government and is the key to understanding many of his attitudes.

Trudeau's political theory, like the man himself, is preoccupied with the individual and his freedom: "What takes priority over every other consideration in choosing a political system is the human person. Not the person as an abstract notion; what counts are very concrete people."[2] And what counts for these people, what makes them human, is their freedom. "Freedom is a free gift, a birthright that distinguishes man from beast.[3] . . . For humanity, progress is the slow journey toward personal freedom."[4] In singling out freedom as the distinctively human quality, Trudeau equates it with reason: Man is free because he has the power of reason, the ability to make considered choices, and the only free — and, hence, truly human — actions are those which are rational and intelligent.

This intertwining of freedom, rationality, and humanity has several important consequences. First, the emphasis on rationality introduces an element of intolerance into a system which otherwise is designed to encourage diversity. Trudeau doesn't really acknowledge the individual's right to choose to be *irrational*, to put more weight on emotion or instinct than on intellect. He assumes that other minds function like his — and, indeed, have comparable intelligence — and shuns any other approach as a failure to meet the standard of acceptable human behaviour.

The second consequence is his insistence on "cold, unemotional rationality" in politics: "If not a pure product of reason, the political tools of the future will be designed and appraised by more rational standards than anything we are currently using."[5] That is the essence of Trudeau's idea of "functional politics", a concept whose lasting importance to him may be deduced from the fact that it was the title and theme both of the first article he wrote for *Cité Libre* in 1950 and of the manifesto he wrote with Marc Lalonde and several others in 1964. His "functionalism" is not so much a theory as a state of mind: a pragmatic willingness to tackle each problem on its own merits, without reference to dogma or ideology. He abhors ideologies, considering them irrational in that they dictate approaches without reference to the particular facts of each situation: "I early realized that ideological systems are the true enemies of freedom.[6] . . . I am a pragmatist. I try to find the solution to each problem as it comes up in order that it be the best possible solution for the present situation, and I do not feel myself bound by any doctrines or any rigid approaches to any of these problems."[7]

To appeal to people in politics through their emotions is, in Trudeau's system, to strike at their freedom; hence, in part, his hostility to nationalism, which must always have an emotional base. That is also why he mistrusts any charismatic form of leadership and refuses to use the force of his personality to sway the public toward acceptance of any given policy or direction. His willingness to play the political game by its own rules permits him to use charismatic appeal to win or retain power in an election, as he did in 1968 and 1974; but to use anything but low-key, reasoned argument in selling any policy, however desirable, is in his view to undermine the rationality, and thereby the freedom, of the public. And, conversely, he also requires of the public the same rationality that he demands of politicians. Participation by the individual in the political process must be rational to be meaningful; as far as he is concerned, unsubstantiated opinions or gut feelings carry no persuasive weight.

Although freedom is the highest value in Trudeau's system, it is not the ultimate objective. The real goal is individual self-perfection, and Trudeau has the classical liberal's belief in the infinite perfectibility of man. He accordingly defines ideal freedom in its broadest sense, to mean the absence of all obstacles — physical, material, or cultural — to a self-fulfilment whose precise nature each person must decide for himself.

Self-fulfilment is the reason people live in society. Social life is an inescapable human need — "God created man with a nature that compels him to live in society"[8] — but the only legitimate purpose of any society is the well-being of the individual: "Men live in societies so that each may fulfil himself to the maximum; and there is no justification for authority except to make possible the establishment and the development of an order which facilitates such fulfilment.[9] . . . Societies exist precisely in order that, through mutual help, cooperation and the division of labor, people may fulfil themselves better than if they lived apart. If people couldn't direct their collective efforts toward this goal, they would do better to go live alone in the woods or on the hills."[10]

All this is fairly conventional liberal thought, although Trudeau places somewhat more weight on the individual than do the philosophers on whom he draws. But he veers off in a direction rather more his own in the overwhelming emphasis he puts on the individual's political responsibility within society. He approaches political participation not as a right, like the liberal philosophers, but with the more Platonic view that it is an inescapable and fundamental human duty. The state is a tool for the direction of a society by that society, and its role is to perform society's mission of liberating the individual. Since it is a collectively owned and operated tool, every member of the society must share responsibility for its actions and omissions. "When a given form of authority unjustly bullies a man, it is all other men who are guilty of it; for it is they who by their silence and consent permit the authority to commit this abuse. If they ceased to consent, the authority would collapse."[11]

Trudeau's views of the state and citizen participation are shaped by his constant fear that authoritarianism is lurking just around the corner. "There nowhere exists a power which does not seek to increase itself: it's a universal law."[12] The state is an indispensable instrument, but it is also a threatening force that must constantly be held at bay lest it oppress the individual. Participation by everyone in the control and guidance of the state is therefore a moral imperative as well as a practical necessity; politics, as the act of preserving and expanding freedom, becomes the most important of human activities.

He cites approvingly Plato's dictum that "the price people pay for not concerning themselves with politics is to be governed by people worse than themselves" and adds: "A state in which the citizens take no interest in political matters is doomed to slavery."[13] Moreover, enlightened self-interest combines with morality to require that each person participate in the governance of the state with an eye to more than his own welfare. "A society of egoists quickly becomes a society of slaves; for each man, taken individually, is quite incapable of shaking an established government: such governments are not in the least weakened when a dissatisfied citizen no longer agrees to obey the authorities, for they will simply put him in jail. To remain free, citizens must seek their well-being in a social order which is just to the largest number; only large numbers have the power to make and destroy governments. Thus men can live free and at peace only if their society is just."[14]

If everyone has an obligation to take an interest in how society is being governed, Trudeau sees a corresponding duty for government not only to accept but to encourage the involvement of its citizens. "To claim that one or several leaders know better than the greatest number what set of actions is good for everyone, is to strike at the very foundations of social morality.[15] . . . What do the citizens want? That is the question a democratic government must constantly ask itself. . . . For if it wants to establish an order which the citizens will consent to accept, the state must not merely inquire into their needs; it must also encourage them to demand what they consider just. In this way, democracy becomes a system in which all the citizens *participate* in government: the laws reflect, in a sense, the wishes of the citizens and thus benefit from the special wisdom of each one."[16]

This belief in encouraging citizens "to demand what they consider just" is the explanation for Trudeau's often-disconcerting tendency to fire questions back at the public rather than provide answers himself. He still does this occasionally, but particularly during his first term in office the Socratic teaching method was one of his favourite techniques. At town-hall meetings and on open-line radio programs, he would repeatedly stress that it was the public, rather than the government, that had to decide what priorities and directions Canada should adopt; he would respond to questions by outlining the options, then asking the audience some pointed questions of his own about what they wanted.

Government's role, he believes, is not merely to run a society but to educate it, and he sees his own role as largely pedagogical. "I suppose I consider politics as another form of teaching.[17] . . . I think it's important to create confidence in the people about the ability of this society to work out its problems. Creating confidence really means talking, explaining. It's having a seminar all the time — with Parliament, with cabinet, with the caucus, with the country, with the student, with whomever you're meeting."[18]

But, contrary to what his writings might suggest, encouraging the public to make additional demands is not necessarily a prelude to meeting those demands; on the contrary, it may often be a matter of encouraging people to voice their expectations so that Trudeau may then explain why they are being unrealistic. As he put it in a 1971 interview: "I think that in the free societies we have to realize more and more the uncertainties, the credibility gaps, particularly the gap between rising expectations on the one hand and the possibility of fulfilling those expectations. . . . I think the only way of avoiding that increasing gap between the desire, the expectation, and the fulfillment [is] by repeating the truth to the people and getting them to participate in the decision — not in order that it be better, but in order that they realize for themselves that their expectations cannot be fulfilled and that the problem is more difficult of solution than the dreams would reveal."[19]

Trudeau's concept of participatory democracy involves, first of all, the removal or reduction of obstacles to active public involvement in politics; in practice, that has meant attempting to broaden the base of the Liberal Party and make it more open to divergent views, democratizing his party's constituency nominating conventions, and legislating restrictions on campaign spending by all parties to reduce the natural advantage of the affluent. Secondly, it involves intensified government efforts to be aware of the public's general mood and concerns, whether through such experiments as his ill-fated regional desks, the use of opinion polls or sophisticated analyses of incoming correspondence, or direct contact through open-line programs and public meetings. And, finally, it involves giving the public ample opportunity to have its say on major policy proposals before they become law; hence his extensive use of white papers on policy proposals, particularly during his first term.

What it does not involve, however, is sharing government's actual decision-making role with the public in any way — nor even necessarily allowing public opinion on any given issue to prevail. "Parliamentary democracy," he wrote in 1958, "does not require that the governed exercise a right of decision over each of the technical problems posed by the complex art of governing in the modern world. It would be illusory to hope, for instance, that one could have recourse to a popular vote to establish the details of a fiscal policy, a war budget or a diplomatic mission. The whole of the citizenry cannot judge such measures except by the results they have produced, or seem likely to produce, for the well-being of the whole."[20] Or as he put it more bluntly in 1970: "I think there is perhaps a distinction which isn't always understood, between participation and decision-making.[21]. . . Participation doesn't mean participating in the decisions. In a society there is always some tool or instrument for somebody making a decision at some point. In our form of government, it is the cabinet. But what people want to know and be assured of, is that their point of view has been considered."[22]

In practice, Trudeau's idea of participation may mean scarcely more, on the government's side, than carefully explaining policies — that's why he considered Information Canada, the ill-fated federal publicity and information agency established in 1970 and dismantled in 1976, an instrument of participation — and knowing but not necessarily heeding public opinion: "My view of participatory democracy is that the people who govern are well aware of the problems and ideals of those who are governed, and that we are in constant touch with them." And, for the public, it may mean no more than taking an interest in government, coherently articulating concerns and wants, and then voting intelligently at election time — on the basis not of specific issues, but of over-all performance and capabilities. "Modern democracies make only exceptional use of the plebiscite, which requires every citizen to pronounce himself on a problem which is often too technical. On the contrary, the electoral system only requires each citizen to pronounce himself on a general set of ideas and directions, and on the men capable of formulating and implementing them."[23]

What is essential for Trudeau is that the public have a realistic and involved view of government, recognizing that it is neither a remote force that is irrelevant to their daily lives nor a "Santa Claus" from whom goods and services may be extracted without cost. This limited concept of participation is far less than many people expected in 1968 and it coincides only imperfectly with his general political theory, but it is by no means valueless. Government can, and should, go against public opinion in certain instances, but political realities dictate that no government can consistently ignore the public will and remain in power. To the extent that he succeeds in encouraging the public to take an interest, make policy choices, and forcefully state its views, Trudeau increases the policy pressures his administration can ignore only at its own peril.

Any more direct form of participation would be incompatible with Trudeau's own personality, as he himself admits: "People who know me well enough realize that basically I'm pretty rigid and pretty set in things that I believe in deeply, and much of my consultation and participation is done in the hopes that people will come in the end to see things as I do — which is a form of leadership, perhaps it's the only form of leadership in a democracy. And indeed, if I consult, it's because my mind is not absolutely closed. But there is a conflict there in the sense that I always feel that it is our job to decide, and if we do what most people thought was right, that's good; but, as with the death penalty thing, if I still think the other course is right, then people say, 'Then why did he ask us?' I don't think that applies to techniques, the way in which we draft the law, or what particular budgetary policy or exact tax points you should have, and so on. I'm not an expert in most of these technical fields, and if somebody after consultation shows me that I would achieve the same goals by doing something completely different, then that's been a very useful consultation. So on the means, I think consultation and participation are still very important. On the goals, I suppose this is my political message: basically on some things if you don't agree with me, then you have to change your leader, change your prime minister."

Since the state exists only to enhance the freedom of the individuals who comprise it, Trudeau sees its power as both a useful tool and a danger. It must function, in his view, as an expert, mandated servant, in the same specialized sense that a physician who is trusted to heal is a servant. That, in turn, requires that the state's role be strictly defined within the framework of a constitutional, representative democracy. "Freedom, say the English, is bought at the price of eternal vigilance. But to be vigilant, one must first know one's rights. We must know on what our status of free men is founded, and in what respects the state has the authority to restrict it . . . we must establish strict limits within which one man has the right to command another."[24]

Those limits, he believes, must isolate individual morality as a deeply private matter into which neither society nor other individuals may intrude. "The state must take great care not to infringe on the conscience of the individual. I believe that in the last analysis, a human being in the privacy of his own mind has the exclusive authority to choose his own scale of values and decide which forces will take precedence over others."[25] Hence his famous statement "The state has no place in the bedrooms of the nation," and his reforms of the divorce law and the Criminal Code.

Though private morality ends at the point where the rights of others are affected, Trudeau stresses that the state may only encroach on the freedom of the individual to the absolute minimum necessary for the common good. "The state must not use force except to the extent that persons or organizations try to use it themselves against the common good. If it is true that in the final analysis the state must hold the monopoly on force, it is not so much to use it as to prevent others from usurping it."[26] But he is by no means the advocate of a weak state, since he assigns to it a positive duty to protect the individual from others who seek to infringe his rights or liberty: "In a modern society like ours, the citizen runs a strong risk of being hamstrung by a web of very complex social, economic and administrative institutions. For instance, the ordinary citizen has neither the time nor the means to check whether a given public service is charging him fair rates, whether a given monopoly is selling to him at reasonable prices, whether a given cartel or association is exploiting him to death. And even if the citizen knew he was the victim of an injustice, he wouldn't have the power to come to grips with such offenders. Therefore, if the citizen wants to avoid being commanded against his will at every turn, he must give himself as a protector a state strong enough to subordinate to the common good all the individuals and organizations who make up society."[27]

That is why Trudeau, in the name of protecting society against the breakdown of constituted authority or the threat of further lawlessness, had no qualms about invoking the War Measures Act in 1970; why he has always supported the legalized use of wiretapping by police to combat crime; and why he opposed granting public servants the right to strike against the state. "I never thought that the state should be weak in front of the individual," he says. "I thought it should never be oppressive, but I never thought it should be weak."

His overwhelming emphasis on the freedom of the individual is the reason for Trudeau's intense hatred of nationalism in general, and of Quebec nationalism in particular. Though he dislikes all forms of intense, flag-waving nationalism as being too irrational, it is not the existence of sovereign nations to which he objects; Trudeau is no internationalist or world federalist. What he loathes is a very specific type of nation: one whose sole *raison d'être* is a single ethnic group or race which is considered synonymous with the nation itself.

His objection is that when the nation — defined in its sociological sense as a single ethnic community sharing a common language and customs — becomes the basis of the state, the individual is no longer paramount. It is no longer a matter of the state existing only to serve the individual, but vice versa: the individual is defined as only an instrument in the battle for a higher good, the good of the Nation, which is viewed as an organic entity that comprises its living members, its dead, and its future generations. As he puts it:

"The nationalists — even those of the left — are politically reactionary because, in attaching such importance to the idea of nation, they are surely led to a definition of the common good as a function of an ethnic group, rather than of all the people, regardless of characteristics. That is why a nationalistic government is by nature intolerant, discriminatory, and, when all is said and done, totalitarian. A truly democratic government cannot be 'nationalist', because it must pursue the good of all its citizens, without prejudice to ethnic origin."[28]

Nationalism and its inherent intolerance, he believes, naturally tend toward wars. "The tiny portion of history marked by the emergence of the nation-states is also the scene of the most devastating wars, the worst atrocities, and the most degrading collective hatred the world has ever seen. Up until the end of the eighteenth century it was generally the sovereigns, not the nations, who made war; and while their sovereigns made war the civilian populations continued to visit each other: merchants crossed borders, scholars and philosophers went freely from one court to another, and conquering generals would take under their personal protection the learned men of vanquished cities. . . . In our day, however, we have seen nations refusing to listen to Beethoven because they are at war with Germany. . . . The nation-state idea has caused wars to become more and more total over the last two centuries. . . . Besides, each time a state has taken an exclusive and intolerant idea as its cornerstone — religion, nationhood, ideology — this idea has been the very mainspring of war."[29]

He divides nationalism into two forms: aggressive and defensive. "Nations that were dominated, dismembered, exploited, and humiliated conceived an unbounded hatred for their oppressors; and united by this hatred they erected against aggressive nationalism a defensive nationalism."[30] Applying this analysis to what he calls "the sub-sub-species Quebec of the sub-species Canada",[31] he concludes that "Anglo-Canadian nationalism produced, inevitably, French Canadian nationalism."[32]

But the more nationalist Quebec becomes, in his theory, the more it becomes a perverted society in which the individual is subjugated to the supposed good of the collectivity. And, indeed, one need only look at the Parti Québécois government's insistence that "collective rights" take precedence over individual rights in the field of language freedom to see elements of Trudeau's analysis translated into reality.

It follows from these premises that Trudeau regards Quebec independence as both philosophically and practically abhorrent:

"To insist that a particular nationality must have complete sovereign power is to pursue a self-destructive end. Because every national minority will find, at the very moment of liberation, a new minority within its bosom which in turn must be allowed the right to demand its freedom."[33] Hence his argument, however fanciful, that if Quebec can separate from Canada, perhaps Westmount or Hull would have to be considered equally free to secede in turn from Quebec.

He argues, in fact, the exact opposite of the nationalists: The cause of human welfare can best be served by a state which is deliberately pluralistic and multicultural. He takes as his own the words of Lord Acton: "The coexistence of several nations under the same State is a test, as well as the best security of its freedom. It is also one of the chief instruments of civilization. . . . The combination of different nations in one State is as necessary a condition of civilized life as the combination of men in society."[34]

If his emphasis on individual freedom turns Trudeau implacably against nationalism, that same emphasis is the basis of his enthusiasm for federalism. He regards federalism not merely as a fact of life in Canadian politics, but as the most theoretically desirable of systems for all those who believe in the liberty of the individual.

Federalism, first of all, through decentralization of power, puts many areas of government activity much closer to the individual. While a centralized state may make the average citizen feel too far removed from the power centre to be comfortable in dealing with the state, federalism "seems to be the ideal means of remedying this fatal indifference, by making the contacts between the governors and the governed frequent and vital. . . . True [decentralization] . . . will involve giving real powers to local governments, and leaving as much responsibility as possible within easy reach of the people. It will also encourage the principle of self-government in semi-public bodies: unions, parish corporations, student associations and the rest."[35]

His second reason for equating federalism with freedom is that it fragments the power of the state, making it easier to supervise and control. "In too centralized a state, executive and legislative burdens would become extremely onerous. The government would be forced to rely on an increasingly large and powerful bureaucracy, which would be less and less controllable. The people would have difficulty following the ever more complex debates of the chamber, and couldn't make a valid appraisal of the MPs; the MPs, over-loaded with legislative (and electoral) duties, couldn't adequately discuss the policies of the executive; and the latter would find it impossible to keep the civil service adequately supervised. The certain effect of excessive centralization would be that bureaucrats would exercise, as they pleased, exorbitant powers they held by delegation, under laws which they themselves had prepared for the blind approval of the MPs. The servant of the people would then become in reality its (more or less?) benevolent despot."[36]

Trudeau's fear of bureaucratic power stems from two premises: that since unelected officials are not directly responsible to the public, their exercise of power becomes undemocratic by definition the moment it is inadequately supervised by elected representatives; and that a bureaucracy, by its nature, tends to be more preoccupied with efficiency than individual rights. "What seems certain is that all centralization is tyrannical, if the increased power of the bureaucracy is not subjected to more energetic control by the repre-sentatives of the people or by the judiciary."[37]

Apart from being the system most likely to safeguard democratic freedom, Trudeau also regards federalism as the most efficient, be-cause it allows different problems to be tackled by whatever level of government can most effectively deal with them, and doles out as much power — but *only* as much — as each level needs for the assigned tasks. "The ideal state would therefore seem to be one with different sizes for different purposes. And the ideal constitu-tion for it would be one that gave the various parts, whatever their size, the powers they needed to attain their own particular objec-tives. In practice, the federal state comes closest to this ideal."[38]

True to his pragmatism, Trudeau doesn't attempt to define philo-sophically what the balance between centralization and decentral-ization should be — "In the final analysis, only the citizens as a whole can say at what point a stop must be put to centralization"[39] — but he has some general thoughts: "For example, in social or cultural matters, where needs often vary from region to region and where a citizen must feel that he can communicate directly with the source of power, there is an advantage in limiting the territorial jurisdiction of the state. In other areas, such as economic matters, it is much more efficient for the geographic unit to be considerably extended."[40]

Since the role of society and the state is to promote individual fulfilment, Trudeau recognizes that simply maintaining order and protecting people from oppressive forces isn't enough. He assigns to the state a more active responsibility for ensuring that no one is denied the basics — economic, social, and cultural — that are a precondition to any real freedom and development.

"The case for economic rights," he wrote in 1962, "might then be stated as follows: Since economic goods are necessary to satisfy the needs of mankind, and since these goods — to become serviceable — must in some way be produced, it follows that every social order should guarantee the rights of man, as a consumer and as a producer. As a producer, man has a right to demand from society that it offer him a market for his useful labor or produce. As a consumer, man has a right to a share of the total production of society, sufficient to enable him to develop his personality to the fullest extent possible."[41]

Trudeau is not, by inclination, an economic interventionist. As long as the economy is operating in accordance with the general good of society, he believes, the state should leave it as free as possible to develop on its own. "Economic forces operating . . . according to certain laws but unhampered by administrative red tape or territorial barriers will tend to enrich the community as a whole."[42]

But he believes that the state must encourage industrial democracy and must also intervene in the economy to whatever extent is necessary to ensure that its general course serves the common good rather than a few private interests. "Man does not live by bread alone, and he will never be content until the dichotomy between those who may arbitrarily command and those who must humbly obey is abolished, even in the economic sphere. . . . Even today men are laboring to lay the foundations of a society of equals; and the sooner such problems as price arbitration and cooperative management or ownership of industry can be seriously discussed, the better this society will be equipped to prevent the industrial revolution from turning into a violent one.

"The ancient values of private property have been carried over into the age of corporate wealth. As a result, our laws and our thinking recognize as proprietors of an enterprise men who today hold a few shares which they will sell tomorrow on the stock-market; whereas workers who may have invested the better part of their lives and of their hopes in a job have no proprietary right to that job, and may be expropriated from it without compensation. . . . The same erroneous concept of property has erected a wall of prejudice against reform, and a wall of money against democratic control. As a consequence, powerful financial interests, monopolies and cartels are in a position to plan large sectors of the national economy for the profit of the few, rather than for the welfare of all. Whereas any serious planning by the state, democratically controlled, is dismissed as a step toward Bolshevism."[43]

His conclusion is that "if this society does not evolve an entirely new set of values, if it does not set itself urgently to producing those services which private enterprise is failing to produce, if it is not determined to plan its development for the good of all rather than for the luxury of the few, and if every citizen fails to consider himself as the co-insurer of his fellow citizen against all socially-engineered economic calamities, it is vain to hope that Canada will ever really reach freedom from fear and freedom from want."[44]

In this, Trudeau sounds like a standard democratic socialist. But where a democratic socialist would smoothly pass from such premises to decisive action, Trudeau's view is constantly tempered by the other side of the argument — the danger that too much state intervention on a continuing basis could inhibit the economy and, worse, that it could itself become an intrusion on freedoms.

He puts great emphasis on economic growth, but not as an end in itself. It is a means to achieve social objectives, which are more important to him than economic ones, but which he realizes cannot be attained without a healthy level of prosperity. "It would be a great oversimplification to adopt the attitude: social needs first, then economic. . . . It is a rare state that can disregard economic or technological laws with impunity. A government trying to do so, even though for excellent social motives, would so impoverish its economy that its social goals became unattainable. In fact, unless the economy is fundamentally sound, a strong, progressive social policy can be neither conceived nor applied. All social security measures, from family allowances to old age pensions, from free education to health insurance, must remain theoretical if the economic structure is incapable of bearing the cost."[45]

His social objectives "in a very general way consist in so organizing a political community that all its members have the essential before a few are allowed to enjoy the superfluous."[46] But here again, Trudeau recognizes no absolutes: "Of course, the concepts of the 'essential' and the 'superfluous' will be defined variously in different countries and at different times; and even in one country at any given time they will be defined according to each person's social philosophy."[47]

In the cultural field, too, he sees an important but carefully limited role for the state: "We have seen that the state must occasionally intervene in the play of economic forces to better ensure the pursuit of social objectives. But it must not stop there; if it does, we could find ourselves promoting the development of a community that was rich, technologically advanced, equitably structured, but completely depersonalized. . . . Technology, which brings abundance and material happiness, presupposes an undifferentiated mass of consumers; it also tends to minimize the values that let a human being acquire and retain his own identity, values that I am grouping here under the vague term 'cultural'. . . . The state must use its legal powers to compel the economic community to favor certain values that would otherwise be destroyed by the pressure of economic forces. In other words, just as the state intervenes in economic matters to protect the weak through social legislation, so it must intervene to ensure the survival of cultural values in danger of being swamped by a flood of dollars."[48]

But, just as in the case of economic and social measures, Trudeau also stresses the dangers of such intervention. "It supposes that the state knows better than the citizen what is 'good' for him culturally, and such a hypothesis must always be applied with utmost prudence and consideration. More than any other, this kind of value is international and common to all men; in the long run, then, the state should ideally promote an open culture. There is also a danger that cultural protection, like its economic counterpart, would tend eventually to produce a weak, 'hot-house' culture."[49]

In each sphere of state intervention — economic, social, and cultural — Trudeau doesn't accept that there are *a priori* standards that define how much is proper. He sees government, rather, as a constant tightrope act, maintaining a precarious and ever-changing balance between what is too much and what is too little. Too little intervention in the economy, and it may either stumble or operate only to the benefit of a handful of corporate interests and to the detriment of the majority of citizens; too much, and it may wither, or excessive zeal by the government may encroach excessively on the freedom of the producer and the consumer. Too little intervention in the social field, and individuals may suffer unjustly; too much, and freedom of choice may suffer, incentive may be curtailed, or the economy may be weakened to the detriment of all. Too little government involvement in culture may produce a sterile society; too much will infringe on the individual's freedom to choose his own cultural values.

This constant need to maintain a finely tuned balance is the basis of Trudeau's devotion to the theory of counterweights. What began in his childhood as a desire to assert his individuality, to be 'un original' who would applaud English victories when all his classmates were cheering for the French, gradually evolved into the key element of his whole theory of government. As a man in a light canoe must shift his weight in the opposite direction from the pressure of a wave, so too government can only keep a stable social order from capsizing by constantly shifting its weight and direction to counterbalance changing excesses and pressures.

"The theory of checks and balances, so acutely analysed by [Montesquieu and de Tocqueville], has always had my full support. It translates into practical terms the concept of equilibrium that is inseparable from freedom in the realm of ideas. It incorporates a corrective for abuses and excesses into the very functioning of political institutions. My political action, or my theory — insomuch as I can be said to have one — can be expressed very simply: create counterweights."[50]

This goes hand in hand with his pragmatism, his advocacy of "functional politics". In the name of maintaining what he considers an appropriate balance, he feels free to act, on different issues or at different times, like a conservative one day and a leftist the next. For all his talk of the social role of the state in the early 1960s, he did not hesitate in 1968, after the progressive social legislation of the Pearson era, to declare: "It is my belief that we have enough of this free stuff. We have to put a damper on this revolution of rising expectations."[51] And although he is uncomfortable with excessive state intervention in the economy and had long and consistently opposed price and income controls, he was not squeamish about deciding in 1975 that a breakdown of responsibility by business and labour required the introduction of a controls system.

"This is something I've always not only believed in as political theory," he says, "but it's something that I've tried to make part of my rule of life. I don't like excesses. And when some tendency is going too strong, I feel that society will be better balanced if you press from the other side."

Even though he differs from most government leaders in having an elaborate and clearly stated political theory, Trudeau's behaviour in office makes him far more difficult than most to categorize politically. This is due in part to the pragmatism that is built into the theory itself, and to his willingness to depart from the philosophy altogether when he deems it necessary. But, even more, it is the result of the remarkable way he has chosen to handle the challenge of being a social critic suddenly catapulted to active political power.

He has not wholly abandoned either role for the other. Rather, to the confusion of much of the Canadian public, he has chosen to operate on two levels. On one hand, we still have Trudeau the thinker and educator: Still wearing the mantle of activist reformer and champion of social justice, he is in the forefront of progressive thought among world leaders as he highlights society's failures and the directions in which we must move. But there is also Trudeau the legislator and prime minister, and this is an altogether different creature: a much more cautious and conservative leader whose prime concerns are to achieve consistency and rationality across the whole spectrum of policies and to balance the demands of competing interests.

It was Trudeau the dynamic reformer — the leader with the intellect to diagnose society's shortcomings and the toughness and guts to remedy them — that the public embraced in 1968 and 1974. And it was his replacement, both times, by Trudeau the cautious legislator that dashed the expectations raised in his campaigns and laid the foundations for widespread disenchantment. Between elections, the two Trudeaus tend to alternate in a pattern of bold, innovative speeches and slow, cautious policies that leaves the public bewildered and sometimes furious.

In his continuing role as public thinker and educator, Trudeau feels free to act as a goad, a provoker of thought. What he says in that capacity, particularly in off-the-cuff remarks, isn't meant to be taken as notice of any intention to act; he may, in fact, be tossing out ideas before he has fully thought them through, or even be playing devil's advocate. "It's hard to say this," he explained shortly after taking office, "but people who think in terms of clichés think of the prime minister as like the Pope or something, who always must speak in encyclicals that are written by hordes of cardinals. You know, things move too fast for that. You've got to get the people used to accepting ideas that are put to them for purposes of discussion, or of reflection, not necessarily of legislation or immediate action. The important thing is that the democracy be alive, that there be some source of thinking coming out of Canada, out of the government, some incentive to think. I don't feel that I must state ultimate wisdoms every time I open my mouth. . . . If I speak as the prime minister and I make announcements to the House of Commons, or I announce a decision of cabinet or something, that's the prime minister speaking, the chief of the executive. But if I am arguing with a bunch of students, obviously I am not talking ex cathedra; I am talking as a human being trying to understand things and trying to get explanations across."[52]

This approach is rooted in Trudeau's determination to retain his individuality, to maintain an identity distinct from his role as prime minister. But behind it is also a conscious desire — based on his dislike for blind faith in any form of authority — to demythologize the office of prime minister. "I think that proceeding the way I'm attempting to do means that I'm destroying a little bit of the aura of authority around the office of the prime minister, and one who does that cannot rely merely on the prestige of his function to be effective. In other words, by admitting that I don't always speak ex cathedra, I'm admitting that the Canadian people shouldn't always put the ultimate weight on every one of my words. And I'm saying that, unlike most leaders, I have this peculiarity that I am not infallible. I am teaching people that they shouldn't obey the government blindly or listen to the prime minister with blind faith."[53]

The technique has backfired so regularly that he has used it far less since the 1972 election. But he used it again in his infamous 1975 year-end television interview, in which he alarmed a public already made jittery by the imposition of economic controls by saying that the free-market system had failed and the future held the prospect of even more pervasive government authority. This was yet another misunderstood instance of Trudeau the social critic being mistaken for Trudeau the legislator.

Even in more formal, prepared speeches, he is often attempting to provide intellectual leadership without signifying any accompanying intention to legislate. It is as social critic that Trudeau talks, compellingly and eloquently, of the need for new values domestically and for a greater sense of sharing internationally, of massive shifts of emphasis from consumption to conservation and from quantity of goods to quality of life. But although those standards may influence over-all government policy in a vague way, Trudeau the legislator is prepared to allow energy-conservation measures in Canada to lag far behind even those of the United States, to hold down foreign-aid spending in the name of restraint, and to slap a protective quota on textile imports from developing countries despite his talk of sharing with the Third World.

"I suppose one of the roles of the politician is to be an educator and a preacher, and to get people used to even thinking about new directions, long before the government is able to act in those directions," he says. "And my other comment is that it's hard to judge whether any of these ideas have been either active or dormant unless one could — and it would be a thankless task — examine every decision that has to be taken." In a great many instances, he argues, the general policy directions he has articulated serve as a touchstone for the cabinet in deciding whether a given proposal should be accepted or rejected — and, consequently, his public theorizing is more than an abstract exercise.

But when he enters the cabinet chamber, Trudeau generally leaves his mantle of social critic at the door and becomes a far more cautious and pragmatic legislator. Says Mitchell Sharp, a senior member of Trudeau's cabinet from 1968 to 1976: "How far the PM's speeches influence government policies is a great puzzle to me. I'm not sure I understand his approach in that area. As a leader in cabinet, he deals with the decisions that have to be made; I suppose in his speeches he's trying to alter the atmosphere in which decisions are made. He doesn't talk like that in cabinet, or very rarely." Sharp says Trudeau has never come into cabinet and said, in effect: "We've got to move toward new values, a greater sense of sharing, lowering materialistic expectations — how shall we do it?" Rather, the veteran minister finds, "his general approach seems to be to direct his philosophy not so much at the cabinet as at the public. On the discussions about a guaranteed annual income, for instance, he looked at the decisions in cabinet in a very solid way. He looked at the costs, at maintaining the motivation of people to work."

In his actions as prime minister, Trudeau has been an innovator, but not a drastic reformer. He has been eager to experiment with new techniques for solving various problems — whether it be through the creation of a new department or the establishment of an imaginative new program like Opportunities for Youth or Local Initiatives Program — and he puts a considerable premium on capacity for innovation in his choice of deputy ministers. But he mistrusts daring, sweeping reforms. As Jean-Paul Desbiens, one of Quebec's leading social critics during the Quiet Revolution under his pen-name of Frère Untel, once put it: "The paradox of Pierre Trudeau is to bank on a continuum of changing interpretations rather than propose abrupt change."

On matters involving the individual's right to be free from en-croachment by the state, he is an ardent liberal. But in his govern-ment's concrete actions in many other areas, he has been cautious, if not conservative.

In matters of government spending, his inclination from the outset has been to dampen expectations rather than shell out more cash. He served notice even before taking power that the era of new, universal welfare programs was at an end. He has attempted to combat poverty instead through indirect measures such as the Department of Regional Economic Expansion and through modest, gradual increments in existing programs. If government spending has increased vastly during his tenure, it is primarily due to in-creases in the costs of established programs and revenue-sharing agreements as well as growth in the federal public service, rather than any great government largesse in creating new programs or doling out money. Says Marc Lalonde: "He's a rather conservative economist. On the financial side, he's a Scot, a conservative — a penny saved is a penny earned. He lives very austerely, he has never been a conspicuous consumer; in that sense, he believes in the virtues of saving; his philosophy is 'look after yourself for your old age.' It's part of his ethic."

In a great many other areas — law reform, gun control, energy conservation, efforts to help developing countries, to name only a few — the government has been much more cautious than its preachings would lead one to expect, unwilling to risk bold moves for which the public might not be ready. This has been particularly true since the near-defeat in 1972, which Trudeau attributes — not altogether accurately — to having attempted too much in the first four years. Says Donald Macdonald: "Particularly after 1972 when we took the big shock of a near-defeat, I think we all became more cautious. When you look at him over the spectrum, though, before he went through the experience of near-defeat, he was prepared to be very much a reformer. After that, it probably is true to say that he was very much more cautious."

In most of the areas in which Trudeau has been particularly active, his main preoccupation has been structural: He is more con-cerned with the creation of mechanisms — to make government more efficient, to alleviate regional disparities, to establish institutional bilingualism, to deal more effectively with an entity like the European Economic Community — than with the achievement of immediate, dramatic results. Even his Just Society proved to be not so much a program of reform as the pursuit of a certain state of mind: "What is the definition of justice? It is to give to each man his due. . . . And when I say a Just Society, I am thinking of letting the people know that the values we are seeking are those that they feel important — not some objective test of greatness, but some subjective one of: are they happy in this society, do they feel they are getting their due out of society?[54] . . . As a general approach, I would say it means that we must get people involved in the society, feeling that government is not something up there which is run by wicked men in order to help one section of the population and harm another, but government is part of the population."[55]

If his actions have on the whole been less daring than his words, it may be in part because — with the exception of national unity and human rights — there are few issues which he approaches with visceral feeling rather than just rationally. As Ivan Head, one of his closest aides since his days as justice minister, puts it: "It may come down to his virtual refusal to accept a degree of emotion in what he's doing. There's never been a reformer and certainly never a zealot that didn't have a great degree of emotion about how he went about things. Thus when the PM meets the counter-arguments — and they are always there from the public service — about this or that course of action, he's very willing not necessarily to accept their advice but certainly to weigh it, and not to assert himself as someone who just has it within his gut that 'this has to be done, this just has to be done.' "

But even more, the answer may lie in Trudeau's whole personality. Says Jim Coutts, who has had the opportunity to observe him closely from the vantage point of principal secretary: "In his head, he's a reformer, always asking, 'Why does it have to be this way, what can we change, how can this be better?' But in his gut, he's a conservative; he's a product of a certain class of society, an élite — I don't mean that pejoratively — with a great belief in the order of things."

Trudeau himself doesn't really dispute this view: "I hope the first part of the phrase is right; people rarely come to me with something where I don't say, 'Well, couldn't it be better and let's argue it.' On the second part, about being a conservative, I wouldn't object strenuously to that, either. I dislike the connotation of it being a class thing. I do like the 'order of things'. I do believe in the order of things, I believe that true liberty can only come out of order, not anarchy.

"I don't have my mind working in one direction and my gut working in another. I am an integrated personality, and it would be better to say that my mind operates on two levels or my gut operates on two levels. In other words, I'm not subscribing to the metaphor, but I'm subscribing to the idea that in me there are two tendencies, one wants to conserve order and the other wants to improve on the established order. I think in their guts human beings like to have peace and security, so in that sense they are conservatives. But in their minds they are discoverers, they are adventurers, and this leads to changes. Now I've always believed those changes should be gradual rather than violent and structured rather than anarchical. And that is the history of my life, of my public life and of my private life."

CHAPTER EIGHT

The Machine That Pierre Built: PMO and Cabinet

ON JUNE 26, 1968, the newly elected prime minister found himself with a clear majority mandate, undisputed control of his party, and a vast outpouring of public confidence. Counterbalancing those formidable assets were two very large liabilities: great inexperience in government, and a potentially crippling lack of contacts across the country. Trudeau's priorities when he took office were shaped by those political liabilities, by his insistence on order and rationality in politics, and by his impressions of government in the Pearson cabinet. Those factors impelled him to make changes in the Prime Minister's Office and in the cabinet system which may prove to be among his most important and lasting legacies.

"Trudeau arrived with very short experience as a minister, no record in the party, having been out of Ottawa before for about fifteen years," says Marc Lalonde. "He had very little knowledge of the administration in terms of the people. Moreover, he was a different personality from Pearson. There's no way he could have lived in the disarray that existed under Pearson.

"Pearson was a man who had tremendous breadth of experience in government. He was a top bureaucrat made prime minister. Public administration held no secrets for him. In a way, he could handle both government and administration — but only he could do it the way he did it, because he was so much a part of the establishment. It didn't matter so much if his office was run like a railway station. Almost everybody had access to him, and no one knew if he was coming or going, but he always managed to fall back on his feet because of his knowledge and the loyalty he inspired."

For Trudeau there could be no question of such informality and improvisation. Both his inexperience and his abhorrence of any form of disorder dictated that his personal circle of advisors be large and carefully structured. The creation of that sort of Prime Minister's Office (PMO), with Lalonde as its head, became the first order of business.

But improvisation, before Trudeau's arrival, had also extended far beyond the Prime Minister's Office into the whole political arena, and he had observed with growing horror the chaos and daily crises of the last Diefenbaker years and the Pearson minority era. Ever worried about the fragility of democracy, he had become convinced that the central government was breaking down and that the consequences could be disastrous. "Why did Fascism arise in Italy, and why did Naziism arise in Germany? Why did Gaullism arise in France? It arose because in the country the judgment was made that Parliament couldn't answer the questions, could not settle the issues fast enough," he said in 1969. "This is absolutely vital and I repeated it even during the election, that this is my fear, that Parliament might lose its credibility; that the government is elected to do a certain number of things, to meet a certain number of problems, and if it doesn't do those things and meet those problems, the judgment of the people will be, 'Parliament is just not good enough. Let us look for a strong-man.' "[1]

The Pearson years struck him as a constant, inadequately planned scramble. "I felt that the five years of minority government that we went through were a kind of situation where we weren't able to plan our legislation, we weren't able to bring in all the necessary reforms . . . and I was quite concerned about the machinery of government. . . . One of the reasons why I wanted this job, when I was told that it might be there, is because I felt it very important to have a strong central government, build up the executive, build up the Prime Minister's Office, strengthen Parliament."[2]

Lalonde sums up the incoming Trudeau team's perceptions this way: "The big impact that there was on a lot of us working under

Pearson was the kind of happy-go-lucky approach that Pearson had to cabinet decisions. There were always so many balls up in the air, and somehow a decision was made. Pearson was no great co-ordinator of actions.

"Judy LaMarsh would go into a tantrum one day, another minister the next, and finally one day an arbitrary decision was made. Where it had come from, how it was made, nobody knew. It was crisis management, all the time. The big issues that took up the time were relatively picayune things. Then the budget would come, be decided, ministers would have maybe ten minutes to talk about it. Pearson felt he never had the time to discuss the broad issues. It was the weekly crisis, the weekly depression of this or that minister, that we had to deal with. There was no long-term planning, no possibility for even middle-term planning, no possibility for co-ordination of activity. There was a feeling that whoever had the strongest voice or happened to come in at the right time could carry away all the loot."

Encouraged by Gordon Robertson, the career civil servant who had been secretary to the cabinet and clerk of the Privy Council since 1963, and by Michael Pitfield, who was then an assistant secretary to the cabinet, Trudeau immediately set about imposing a new order and rationality on the decision-making process. The cabinet committee system was overhauled and strengthened to take much of the planning and detailed analysis of legislation out of the hands of the large, unwieldy cabinet and into the care of small, specialized groups of ministers. At the same time, the changes were designed to shift more of the real decision-making power from the bureaucracy to the ministers.

Under Pearson, the Prime Minister's Office had been a relatively small and loosely structured circle of advisors and aides. In 1967, it had a total of forty employees: a principal secretary, an executive assistant, three special assistants, a private secretary, a four-person press office, a twenty-two-person correspondence section, and eight secretaries. What Trudeau wanted was an expanded and more formally organized prime-ministerial *machine*, and Marc Lalonde was the logical choice to build it. Since he had worked in both the

PMO and the PCO, he had first-hand knowledge of both operations and enjoyed a good working relationship with Gordon Robertson and his PCO officials. He was also one of a rather small field of contenders from among whom Trudeau could select his principal secretary: as an inexperienced newcomer with few established contacts, the new prime minister felt compelled to surround himself with the few associates and advisors he already knew and trusted.

Lalonde's approach was to identify the various functions Trudeau had to fulfil as prime minister, and to so structure the PMO that at least one official would be responsible for helping him with each function. A prime minister has a dauntingly large array of duties — as chief policy-maker, chairman and arbiter of the cabinet, parliamentarian who must answer questions on a wide range of subjects, head of government who must deal with his counterparts around the world, MP with his own constituency to represent, personnel manager for the hundreds of important posts that lie at the prime minister's discretion, party leader, and public figure. Those responsibilities put tremendous strain on the time and resources of any prime minister, and especially of one like Trudeau who believes in exercising the powers of each role to the full.

That, in Trudeau's system, is where the PMO comes in. The members of his personal staff map out his time, regulate the flow of documents he must see, handle his correspondence, brief him on the issues he must understand, write his speeches, arrange his contacts with the press, and provide him with political advice on the various decisions he must make every day.

Above all, when he set up the new system, Trudeau wanted the PMO, through the functions of its individual members, to function as his eyes and ears. Unlike a prime minister who had risen more conventionally and slowly through the system, he didn't have the personal contacts that would enable him to telephone sources across the country and ask what people were thinking or how they were reacting to his policies. And he also had a special need to guard against becoming a *de facto* captive of the bureaucracy: he didn't have a sufficient number of contacts within the public service, or enough knowledge of the system, to be certain that officials were telling him the whole story on any issue. His solution was to rely on his personal staff to provide him with independent information and advice.

Says Lalonde: "I think you have to go back to the fact that he moved into the job with experience in justice, and as a parliamentary secretary. He had very little knowledge of what was happening in other departments. Trudeau has always been a thorough worker, and he wanted to know what he was being asked to decide. He would therefore request pretty extensive briefing notes with alternatives, while Pearson would more or less tend to act out of the vastness of his experience — or fly by the seat of his pants. For us there needed to be better co-ordination and better organization of the office on the political side, because Trudeau had had so little contact within the system. In terms of political information, our greatest efforts were made in planning the PM's travel across the country, much better backgrounding, and better information regarding his correspondence flow."

The result was a PMO more than double the size it had been in Pearson's day, numbering eighty-five by 1970. It comprised a number of entirely new positions, ranging from an advisor on foreign relations to an aide in charge of recommending and screening nominees for prime-ministerial appointments. The most original — and controversial — of the new positions were four "regional desks", one each for the Maritimes, Quebec, Ontario, and the West. Their purpose was to keep the prime minister abreast of regional problems and public opinion across the country, and to provide liaison between Trudeau and various groups. The desk officers met with provincial government officials, business and labour leaders, students, and Liberal Party members, and reported back to Trudeau on their suggestions and complaints. They also planned and organized his trips into their respective regions. It was a theoretically good idea, but it was laden with practical political pitfalls: MPs bitterly resented the desks as an attempt to circumvent their own role as the link between their area and Ottawa, and the system was quietly dismantled after the 1972 near-defeat. Similar regional functions are still discharged by various staff members, but now it is done on a much more informal basis.

Another change Trudeau brought to the PMO was his decision to cut it loose from the federal bureaucracy. In Pearson's day and before, all the prime minister's aides were members of the civil service. Trudeau broke those links, preferring to make it clear that his staff — as distinct from Privy Council officials — was intended to be political, partisan, and answerable only directly to him.

The most important positions were filled by people Trudeau already knew and trusted because of their roles in his ascent to power. Lalonde, of course, had been one of the key architects of his leadership campaign. Jim Davey, another key campaign figure, became program secretary, in charge of helping Trudeau co-ordinate policies, keep them in tune with changing times, and maintain policy liaison with the Liberal Party. Pierre Levasseur, who had played a vital role in the conquest of the party's Quebec wing, was put in charge of the regional desks. Gordon Gibson became Trudeau's first executive assistant. Ivan Head, Trudeau's constitutional advisor when he was justice minister and the writer of many of his campaign speeches, went through a succession of roles as legislative assistant, speech-writer, and foreign-policy advisor.

The PMO has undergone several changes of style and emphasis since 1968. Under Lalonde, it was highly visible — if secretive — and more concerned with policy than with partisan politics. When Martin O'Connell, a defeated minister, took over as principal secretary after the 1972 election, he drastically lowered its profile, restrained its activities, and shifted the emphasis from policy to politics. Under Jack Austin — a hard-driving but thoughtful former deputy minister, lawyer, and businessman who replaced O'Connell in 1974 — the PMO put more or less equal weight on policy and partisan politics. With Coutts, who became principal secretary in 1975, the Prime Minister's Office is at its most political, staffed by a corps of pragmatic Liberal Party professionals. But, except for the abolition of the regional desks in 1972 and much periodic tinkering with titles, the over-all distribution of functions within the PMO has changed relatively little from the structure established in 1968.

As of August 1977, the PMO had a total staff of eighty-six. Only twenty-three of them were classified as officers — that is, actual aides and advisors — while the rest were secretaries, clerks, technicians, and so on. Five of the officers were in the press office, three in the correspondence section, and the remaining fifteen were scattered over a broad range of functions. Roughly a third of the total manpower — thirty persons — is in the correspondence division, a sophisticated, partly computerized operation which answers and analyses the prime minister's mail.

At the apex of the PMO's organizational structure is the principal secretary. He runs the operation and serves as Trudeau's chief political advisor. He attends Privy Council Office meetings to maintain liaison, and sits in on various sessions of cabinet committees. He is also the chief link between the prime minister and the Liberal Party, and he occasionally acts as Trudeau's emissary in private meetings with business, labour, or other interest groups.

The executive assistant has a double role — as the keeper of Trudeau's schedule, and as his closest personal aide. The scheduling is a remarkably complex job. Requests from outside the government for Trudeau's time — a meeting with a committee of labour officials, a speech to a Canadian Club luncheon in Moose Jaw, his presence at St. Jean Baptiste Day celebrations in Shawinigan — go first to an appointments secretary, who screens them and solicits the opinion of an appropriate PMO advisor. If it's an invitation from abroad, for instance, she would consult Ivan Head as to whether it should be accepted; if it's from a group in Ontario, she checks with the staffer who has regional responsibility for that province.

The invitations that survive this screening go to a program committee, chaired by the executive assistant, which meets roughly once a month to plan the major events in Trudeau's schedule for six months ahead. The other members of the committee are the principal secretary, the appointments secretary, Head, a representative from the press office, and Trudeau's speech-writers.

In addition to this six-month schedule which maps out the big events — primarily trips and speeches — the executive assistant prepares a weekly schedule comprising any major event taking place that week, plus cabinet meetings, caucus, the morning staff meeting, and all the other fixed elements in Trudeau's program. And, finally, the remaining openings in the prime minister's timetable are filled with appointments in a daily schedule that is prepared one day ahead — and then juggled as necessary as the day actually unfolds.

The other part of the executive assistant's job, as the aide who is physically closest to Trudeau's side at any given moment, consists of trouble-shooting and providing whatever assistance is necessary. This involves him, first of all, in a "move-along" function: he is responsible for keeping Trudeau on schedule by intervening at the appropriate moment in any meeting or appearance to tell the prime minister that it's time to move along to his next engagement. Beyond that, his job is largely a matter of co-ordinating details: making sure that a briefing book Trudeau needs for a meeting arrives on time, seeing to it that transportation arrangements work smoothly, and passing on details of Trudeau's future engagements to all the staffers who will in any way be involved. And, finally, there is also a personal-service function: carrying Trudeau's briefcase or briefing books to leave him free for hand-shaking, taking care of any gifts that are presented to him during a visit, or fetching anything he needs.

Ivan Head, his foreign-policy advisor, is mainly concerned with personal relations between Trudeau and foreign heads of government, but he also briefs and advises him on other foreign-policy matters. In an era of summitry when heads of government act largely as their own foreign ministers, Head fulfils a function quite distinct from the external affairs department. When he travels abroad as Trudeau's emissary to confer with a foreign leader or his top officials, he speaks not for the government of Canada but for Pierre Trudeau; that often permits a degree of candour, informality, and blunt political argument that would not be possible through normal diplomatic channels. And, through a network of international contacts, he acts as Trudeau's eyes and ears in the outside world, just as other staffers keep him briefed on developments within Canada.

Richard O'Hagan, the special advisor on communications, supervises and advises on all aspects of the prime minister's media relations, communications, and general image-making, while other members of the press office deal with day-to-day press inquiries and such related matters as making accommodation and travel arrangements for journalists on Trudeau's trips.

The prime minister's legislative assistant anticipates the questions he is likely to be asked in Parliament, suggests answers, and keeps him informed on all important parliamentary developments. She is also the conduit through which he obtains general news, in the form of a digest of major domestic and foreign developments, as well as a selection of the newspaper clippings, editorials, and cartoons she thinks he should see. When he is travelling abroad, she cables him a brief newsletter to keep him abreast of events in Canada.

The nominations secretary is, in effect, Trudeau's executive head-hunter for the 400-odd order-in-council appointments made each year. She seeks out suitable talent across the country for various positions, screens the suggestions proffered by other ministers, and consults with the various interest groups that may have a stake in any given appointment.

Trudeau's administrative assistant and constituency liaison officer, Mary Macdonald, who was Lester Pearson's powerful private secretary and general advisor, has two separate functions. As administrative assistant, she is in charge of his paper-flow. All documents for him are channelled through her; to protect him from being swamped, she doles them out in manageable doses based on her estimation of what is most urgent for him to see on any given day. As constituency liaison, she is Trudeau's link with the Mount Royal riding he represents as MP. She handles routine constituent requests and problems herself, and brings more special or complicated matters to his attention.

Trudeau's several policy advisors study policy proposals from a political angle, keep in touch with the views of the Liberal Party, and act, in effect, as regional desk officers. Each is responsible for maintaining contacts in one province or region and advising Trudeau on all matters involving that part of the country, whether it be appointments, travel plans, the state of the Liberal machinery, or changing political attitudes.

The PMO also comprises at least two speech-writers — one

English, one French — and a changing procession of special advisors who are hired on a short-term basis to contribute their expertise to some specific area of planning.

Though Trudeau's expansion of the PMO has provoked considerable criticism and even suggestions that he is somehow "presidentializing" the system, in reality nothing more sinister is involved than bringing the prime-ministerial apparatus fully into the twentieth century. As the scope of federal government activities and the complexity of issues have grown over the years, the staffs of prime ministers have steadily increased to keep pace. When Alexander Mackenzie became prime minister in 1873, he didn't even have a secretary to answer his mail. By 1935, R. B. Bennett had a staff of twelve. It grew to thirty under Mackenzie King, and remained at that level in the St. Laurent and Diefenbaker years; Pearson increased it to forty. But the administrative dishevelment of the Pearson era was ample evidence that this did not suffice, and Trudeau's abrupt doubling of the PMO's size was simply an acknowledgment of changing times. As Lalonde points out: "When C. D. Howe decided to build a pipeline, the only issues were: can we get the money, what's the deadline, and so on. It's another world now, in just twenty years. On the Mackenzie Valley pipeline question, there were twenty-nine departments and agencies involved."

If he is to exercise effective supervision over the increasingly complex activities of some thirty government departments, Trudeau needs a staff large enough to keep him adequately informed and to ease the pressures on his time. But this enlarged PMO endows him with no new powers, nor do his aides have any authority of their own; they can act only on his behalf, and he remains fully accountable for all their actions and omissions. If his power is in any way augmented, it is only in the sense that there is more power in efficiency and good information than in confusion. Inevitably, however, this efficiency and information is bought at a price — not to the system, but to the prime minister himself. A staff large enough to shield him from excessive pressures is also large enough to determine much of what he sees and hears, and to damage him politically if its advice is unsound. There is also a risk that staffers may misrepresent his views to others or act in his name in ways that he never wished, leaving him to suffer the consequences.

As one veteran minister observes: "There is a terrible habit among subordinates everywhere to attribute views and decisions to the boss — views and decisions which aren't there at all. A large part of the impressions of Trudeau within the government are gathered not from direct contact with him but through his staff. And if all you knew of Trudeau was what you heard from some of the people around him, you'd get the impression that this fellow Trudeau had very strong views on almost everything and was quite dictatorial — and that's not so."

A more pertinent question, consequently, is not whether the PMO is too large — indeed, any successor is likely to maintain its basic structures in only slightly modified form — but whether Trudeau's choice of personnel has been good enough. The record is mixed, at best. The size and organization of his staff have enabled Trudeau to function with a degree of efficiency that would otherwise have eluded him, but the quality of its advice has been spotty. The Lalonde PMO was composed of aides who were intellectually formidable but politically naive, and the resulting isolation from reality was a large factor in his near-defeat in 1972. The Coutts operation, a decade later, tends toward the opposite extreme, putting so much emphasis on political expediency that it risks being too clever by half.

Trudeau's restructuring of the PMO was not an end in itself, but merely a preparatory step toward a much broader objective: the introduction of greater rationality and planning into the whole federal decision-making process. The ultimate locus of that decision-making is the cabinet, and it is the operations of cabinet that Trudeau set out to change. His main purpose in revamping the PMO was to give himself the capacity to replace the ad-hocery of Pearson and his predecessors with an orderly system, and then to manage it effectively.

Until 1940, the cabinet operated with almost bizarre informality. There was no agenda, no secretariat, no one to record what went on, no listing of decisions taken, and no system for communicating those decisions to the departments affected. In 1940, with the issues arising from Canada's involvement in the Second World War increasing the pressure on the cabinet's decision-making capacity, Mackenzie King took the first reluctant steps toward formalization of procedures. He created a small cabinet secretariat to serve the ten cabinet committees that had been established at the end of 1939 to manage different aspects of wartime government. In reality, only one of those committees, the War Committee, had any real and active role, and it was this committee that the new secretariat served. By 1945, this slightly more structured approach had proved to be so useful that King agreed to having an agenda for the cabinet itself and to the recording of cabinet decisions. After the war, a number of new committees were created, but they played little real role until Lester Pearson revived the system in 1964.

Under Pearson, there were ten standing committees of cabinet and at least a dozen special ad hoc committees to deal with everything from criminal and penal matters to veterans' affairs. Instead of being discussed first by the full cabinet and then sent to a committee if further study was required, as had been the practice until then, the Pearson system required proposals to be presented in the appropriate committee first.

But all real decision-making still took place in the cabinet itself; the committees could only make recommendations, which then had to be debated in cabinet. And, in committees and cabinet alike, the system was closer to a federation of ministerial fiefdoms than to any real collective decision-making. A minister presented a proposed course of action in its final form, and the only real option his colleagues had was to approve or disapprove; there was little opportunity to explore alternatives or recommend detailed changes.

That approach might have been adequate in simpler times, but it was rendered obsolete not only by the increasing complexity of the issues under discussion, but also by the increasing recognition of their interrelation. The great socio-political discovery of our time is that everything connects, and that gain in one sector is accomplished only at the cost of loss in another; there are no solutions in government these days, only trade-offs between competing interests. For example, the environment can be protected by ordering a manufacturer of farm chemicals to stop polluting a river; but if he complies by ceasing or reducing production, workers will be laid off and the environment will have been improved at the cost of higher unemployment; whether the manufacturer curbs protection and thereby creates a shortage of the chemicals, or complies by installing costly anti-pollution equipment, the result will be higher prices to the farmers who must buy those chemicals; that, in turn, will lead the farmers to reduce their production, pass the higher cost on to consumers, or both; the resulting changes in the food supply situation may increase inflation or affect Canada's export commitments.

Since different ministers and their departments are responsible for different aspects of national management, this chain of inter-relationships inevitably creates conflicts and dilemmas: the environment minister is determined to reduce pollution, the agriculture minister worries about the impact on farmers, the finance minister argues that the economy may be adversely affected, and so on. In the Pearson days and before, there was nothing to do except battle it out — without clear ground rules and often at the expense of bitter cabinet splits — among ministers who could do no more than accept or reject each other's proposals. In practice, what very often happened was that the battles were settled and the trade-offs decided not by the ministers but among senior bureaucrats.

Says a former deputy minister and political insider: "Deputy ministers would meet over lunch at one of their favourite watering-holes, such as the back room on the second floor of Madame Burger's restaurant in Hull. They would meet up there and have informal discussions, and they would come to their policy conclusions. They would agree on what advice to give, and then each deputy minister would go back to his minister with pretty much the same view and the same advice. And, lo and behold, that advice would be reflected in cabinet."

When Trudeau came to power, he resolved to replace the im-

provisation and disorder of the Pearson cabinet with a framework
that would permit detailed and rational discussion of issues among
ministers; to develop mechanisms for long-range planning, co-
ordination, and priority-setting; and, in keeping with his view
of bureaucratic power as essentially undemocratic, to wrest more
of the real decision-making function away from top officials and
back to the elected officials.

To achieve these changes, he overhauled and strengthened the
committee system. A full cabinet of some thirty ministers is simply
too large and unwieldy a forum to permit coherent and systematic
discussion. It is also an arena that lends itself less well to concessions and compromise than a small committee. On most issues,
there are unlikely to be more than a half-dozen ministers very
directly involved. If they are split down the middle as to what
should be done, and the question is fought out in full cabinet,
three ministers will win and three will lose face — in front of
twenty-four others.

In Trudeau's system, the previous welter of committees has
been pared down to only eight — four policy committees that
deal with various areas of government activity, and four co-
ordinating bodies. Each minister sits, on average, on two committees. Unlike in Pearson's day, every committee meets at the
same scheduled time each week, thereby increasing ministerial
attendance and making it possible for the committees to operate
systematically.

One of the biggest changes from the Pearson system is that the
committees no longer just make recommendations which must
then be debated by the full cabinet: everything goes to committees
first, and they are expected to make provisional decisions. On each
matter that it studies, a committee must give the cabinet either
a report — that is, a decision — or a recommendation. These
reports and recommendations are listed in an annex to the next
cabinet agenda. On receipt of the agenda, any minister may ask
to have any provisional decision discussed and decided by the full
cabinet; where no such request is made, committee decisions are
deemed to be decisions of the cabinet and become policy without

any further debate. If a committee is deeply divided or unprepared for some reason to make a decision, it can either refer the matter to the Priorities and Planning committee, or give cabinet a recommendation rather than a report; the recommendation tells cabinet what the committee is inclined to favour, but leaves it to the full cabinet to discuss a final decision. In practice, only about twenty per cent of the matters discussed in committee result in a recommendation rather than a report, which means that the cabinet's time is left free to discuss only the thorniest and most contentious matters.

Another vitally important innovation introduced by Trudeau is that no committee is presented with a simple "yes or no" choice on any proposal. Instead, ministers are for the first time involved in the actual shaping of policies outside their own departments. A minister can no longer simply tell his colleagues what he proposes to do; he must share all his background material with them and let them know the various options, enabling them to recommend changes or alternative courses. As Sharp, a veteran of both the Pearson and Trudeau cabinets, explains:

"In the Pearson government, we discussed and agreed or disagreed with recommendations of individual ministers and accepted responsibility for the actions of our colleagues resulting from cabinet decisions. However, Mr. Pearson did not require ministers to document their proposals fully and did not, generally speaking, require detailed scrutiny by other ministers. Under the Trudeau system, all proposals must be fully documented, their conclusions and recommendations based on a careful consideration of alternatives and presentation of the arguments pro and con. Where appropriate, financial implications must be specified. Caucus consultations must be described or reasons given why they have not taken place. Effects on federal-provincial relations must be described, and if an announcement is to be made, the arrangements for publicity must also be specified."

In addition to all this written information, the committee studying any proposal is able to question not only the sponsoring minister, but also his senior officials. The minister, consequently, can no longer fall back on vague references to expert departmental advice; the experts themselves appear before the committee, and the quality of their reasoning can be probed.

These changes shift the locus of much decision-making power from the senior echelons of the bureaucracy to the elected ministers. They also shift the exercise of power from the individual minister to a collectivity. A powerful, skilled minister may still be able to bull his proposals through cabinet unscathed, but he will at the very least have to explain them much more fully than in the past. Far more often, ministers now have a hand in shaping each other's policies, reaching into a colleague's proposals and saying, "You'll have to change such-and-such."

The four policy committees are Economic Policy, External Affairs and Defence, Social Policy, and Government Operations. Every area of government activity is classified as the appropriate domain of one of these four. The co-ordinating committees are Legislation and House Planning, Treasury Board, Federal-Provincial Relations, and Priorities and Planning.

The areas of responsibility of the first three policy committees are exactly what their respective titles imply, while Government Operations deals with routine federal operations and services — transportation, communications, and public works, as well as routine decisions in the fields of industry, trade and commerce, and agriculture (matters such as import tariffs, agricultural subsidies, or farm quotas).

The main responsibility of the Legislation and House Planning co-ordinating committee is to supervise the process of turning policy decisions into concrete legislation. The policy committees operate not with proposed bills but with memoranda outlining what should be done and why. Then bills are drawn up in accordance with these committee decisions, and submitted to the Legislation and House Planning committee for approval. This committee's task is to go over the proposed legislation section by section, line by line, and ensure that it is in accordance with the policy that has been approved, that it doesn't go beyond what was decided, and that it is technically and legally sound.

Treasury Board is both a committee of cabinet and a central

organ of government with a sizable bureaucracy of its own and vast influence as guardian of the federal purse and employer of the entire public service. All proposed government spending must be channelled through Treasury Board for approval, and it is here that the nuts-and-bolts spending decisions are made. The finance minister is responsible for the general economic stance of the government, and the Priorities and Planning committee decides, within that framework, which areas of spending should have priority over others. But then it is the Treasury Board committee, with the advice and assistance of its bureaucracy, which translates the policy directions and priorities into over-all spending plans. It reviews the existing and proposed spending programs of each department, evaluates their effectiveness and importance within the general scheme, and allocates or refuses the requested funds.

Although they are separate committees in theory, Federal-Provincial Relations, and Priorities and Planning have become the same body in practice; they have exactly the same membership and the same meeting time, functioning some weeks in one capacity and some in the other. The chairman, in both capacities, is Trudeau himself, and these are the only committees he chairs.

As Priorities and Planning — or P and P, as it is known — this committee is at the apex of the cabinet structure, providing the planning capacity that Trudeau found lacking in the Pearson era. Instead of merely dealing with proposals as they arise and having the resulting decisions build a federal policy incrementally, Trudeau uses P and P to try to decide, *a priori*, what the government should be doing. These decisions on over-all objectives are then communicated to other ministers and departments with instructions to bring forward proposals for attaining the stated goals.

P and P is also the forum for deciding how trade-offs should be made when a situation or proposal creates a conflict between several objectives, and it serves as the cabinet's "supreme court" for adjudicating policy clashes between ministers. In addition, several types of issues — personnel planning, budget planning, Throne Speech planning, or any particular problem Trudeau decides to single out — go directly to P and P rather than to one of the policy committees.

In its planning capacity, P and P has often functioned as a kind of freewheeling, élite seminar, dealing with such abstract philosophical questions as government's role in society, the status and importance of the work ethic, and the balance to be drawn between economic growth and the quality of life. "We're setting up machinery which will permit us to deal with the important and not only with the urgent," Trudeau explained in 1969. "Ever since I can remember governments, it was [a matter of] rushing from one urgent thing to another urgent thing, settling them as they arose but never finding time to look at the non-urgent but extraordinarily important questions which would become urgent in three or five years' time and which perhaps by then would be pretty well beyond solution. We must avoid becoming Coney Island cowboys, just shooting at targets as they appear and doing a little bit here and a little bit there to solve the problems as they arise."[3]

The philosophizing approach Trudeau brought into P and P is almost unprecedented in modern politics, and it puts considerable strain on the participants. But although it was carried to extremes between 1968 and 1972, it is a general direction to be welcomed by anyone who believes those who govern a society should occasionally pause to think about what they're doing. Says Mitchell Sharp: "When this sort of study began, I remember I said, 'It's better than any university.' We had long discussions on law and order, for instance, in 1968 and 1969. There they were — Marchand, Pelletier, Turner, Lang, MacEachen, Trudeau — a remarkable group of people, some of the most eminent lawyers in the country among them, and the discussion carried on was most remarkable.

"I think it's too much to expect from a group of practising politicians that they can direct their time and energy to that sort of approach. It has at times, though, had considerable effect. I remember the discussion of NATO, which had not been attempted that way before by any government. The prime minister insisted that we examine all the options — non-alignment, neutrality, membership without contributing forces, membership with forces committed but not in Europe, membership with forces in Europe, and all the options on how many troops in Europe. We went through that whole exercise, step by step, it drove us up the wall and took days and days. But no one could say we hadn't studied all the options."

The Trudeau system is, in a sense, "automated", with a minimum of squabbling as to which forum should consider a given proposal or where it should appear on the cabinet agenda. In the normal course of events, a proposal goes first to the appropriate policy committee. If a major impasse develops between the interests of two or more ministers or departments, or if the committee feels there are implications for the government's over-all policy to be considered, the matter is referred to P and P; usually, once the particular difficulty is settled, the memorandum is returned to the committee to complete its work. If there is new spending involved, the policy committee passes the proposal to Treasury Board for comment. Then it goes on the cabinet agenda, as either a report or a recommendation from the committee, and is either automatically accepted or debated in cabinet.

To avoid the skirmishing for position that existed in previous governments, the cabinet agenda has been standardized so that everything falls into predetermined slots. Business of the House is first, followed by reports from the committees, which appear in the alphabetical order of committee names; then committee recommendations are listed, in the same alphabetical order. Items are debated, where necessary, in the order in which they appear on the agenda. Once a policy memorandum has been accepted by cabinet, the appropriate legislation is drafted and sent to the Legislation and House Planning committee. When that committee has finished, it too makes a report or recommendation to cabinet, and the cycle is completed.

Trudeau's reforms have succeeded, to a remarkable extent, in replacing improvisation with a structured, smoothly functioning decision-making machine. No proposal becomes policy until it has had thorough study by a committee whose small size and limited agenda make it a more efficient instrument of scrutiny than the full cabinet. An attempt is being made, for the first time, to treat each proposal not in isolation but in the context of a carefully constructed framework of objectives and priorities. The full cabinet is freed from the burden of routine clutter and given more time to concentrate on the most important matters. The involvement of ministers in each other's policies at a relatively early stage has increased cabinet cohesion when those policies later have to be defended, and has reduced the number of open cabinet splits.

But all these improvements have been bought at a price. The increase in the number of stages each proposal must pass through, combined with Trudeau's insistence on full and rational debate, has lengthened the time it takes for any decision to come out of the system. The demands of committee work and the volume of cabinet documents to be studied have reduced the time ministers can devote to other duties, including running their own departments and staying in touch with the public. To get high marks in Trudeau's system, a minister must develop expertise not only in his own area of responsibility, but in the issues and operations of half a dozen other ministries — and that imposes a crushing workload.

If the more collegial approach to decision-making increases cabinet solidarity, it also somewhat blurs individual ministerial responsibility. Since a minister is no longer the sole author of his department's actions, he cannot as fully as in the past be held accountable by the prime minister or his colleagues for any failures.

It is possible, too, that collegial decision-making has actually changed what type of individual can thrive as a minister. This possibility is difficult to assess, because the new interrelationship of issues, even without Trudeau's structural changes, would have reduced the independence of ministers. But there is no doubt that Trudeau's system puts a premium on a different set of ministerial qualities than in the past: it is best suited not to the aggressive, independent, take-charge minister who decides what his department should be doing and battles it through to completion, but to a rather more bland, technocratic compromiser and team player who is prepared both to share his decision-making powers and to take the trouble to master the intricacies of his colleagues' portfolios.

"I'm pretty sure," says Gordon Robertson, "that C. D. Howe would have gone mad. Jimmy Gardiner would never have worked in this system." It may be no coincidence that a great many of the ministers who have voluntarily left the Trudeau cabinet — Eric Kierans, Paul Hellyer, Bryce Mackasey, James Richardson, John Turner — were among its more idiosyncratic types, unable or unwilling to adjust to being homogenized into a collectivity.

Regardless of the individual merits of those who left and those who have taken their place, the change in predominant ministerial type from aggressive individuals who function largely by political instinct to more cerebral team players may in itself have affected the government's whole direction. "As the influence within cabinet of ministers of a cerebral type increases," speculates one Trudeau associate, "then more and more the result is a kind of conservatism. Lacking a Marchand and a Mackasey, you don't have a guy that comes into that cabinet room and says, 'I entered politics because, by God, I was going to do this and that.' And therefore they all fall under the sway of this emotionless, sometimes vapid, gentlemen's club which is the cabinet, in which no one raises voices and in which there has to be a consensus. That kind of activity, in my view, favours a relentless, insidious kind of unattractive 'business as usual' attitude."

Trudeau has succeeded in turning the cabinet system into a smooth-running decision-making machine that is much better equipped mechanically for running the country than its predecessors. But the product of any machine is only as good as the quality of its essential components, and Trudeau's system makes such heavy demands on the intellects and energies of its ministers that they must be individuals of the highest calibre if the quality of actual decisions is to match the sophistication of the machinery. For a variety of reasons — some Trudeau's fault, others largely beyond his control — the general calibre of the members of his cabinet has become far from imposing.

One reason is that Trudeau has never had much taste for going out and recruiting new talent. In his view of politics, and indeed of life, it is not for him to persuade people that they are needed in government and should run for office. That, he believes, is something every individual must decide for himself. As he put it in 1972: "I'm one who always repeated that the first law of politics starts with the facts, starts with the data, and I'm not too inclined to go outside the party and to bring some people in. I'm told the business world thinks that they don't have a real spokesman in cabinet or in the party; well, I'm not going to go and get one elected artificially in order to say we have a spokesman. If business thinks it should be more interested in politics, let it send some people."[4]

Even if Trudeau did want to personally recruit people of established stature as candidates, it would not be easy, because the democratization of nominating procedures in the Liberal Party — and, for that matter, among the Tories as well — has been accomplished at a price. The requirement that candidates be elected by a wide-open constituency nominating convention has made it far more difficult for a leader to bring people of his choice into Parliament. By putting a premium on personal contacts within a riding association and on organizational ability, the democratization also makes it more difficult for many individuals of cabinet calibre to win the nomination on their own accord. A first-rate businessman, academic, or physician who seeks to make a contribution in government is more than likely to lose the nomination to, say, a local salesman who has "paid his dues" by working for years as the riding association's secretary — or who has the organizational ability to sell a few hundred membership cards and bring in busloads of supporters. There is no reason, obviously, why the salesman should not be the candidate, but it can't work both ways — a system designed to make it easier for the ordinary, average person to enter Parliament can't be expected to produce a cabinet full of brilliant, outstanding leaders.

Another factor limiting the kind of talent Trudeau can draw on for his cabinet is the change in public attitudes toward politics and politicians. Political office used to be considered a creditable form of public service, and it was fairly normal for a person who had achieved success and prominence in the private sector to cap his career by running for office and becoming a minister. But public cynicism has grown to the point where politicians tend to be scorned as parasites or manipulators, and few people who have already achieved success in some other field are now eager to enter this bruising and unpopular arena. The result is a new breed of politicians: young, ambitious men and women with little prior record of achievement, who enter politics as they would any other profession, prepared to slowly work their way upward. Both the Liberals and the Tories now find that, instead of ready-made, mature cabinet material, their parliamentary parties consist of swarms of young apprentices who need years to develop in stature. And some never do develop adequately, because too much and too early exposure to politics without counterbalancing experience in other fields can stunt their perceptions.

Faced with a shortage of illustrious talent for his cabinet, Trudeau has not been innovative or daring in his choice from what was available. Instead, he has clung quite closely to the long-standing convention that the cabinet must be built in accordance with intricate formulas of geographic, linguistic, and even religious representation — a system which has its merits, but which allows a Joe Guay (more notable for his lung power than his intellect) to find his way into cabinet because he happens to be one of only two Liberals elected from Manitoba, while a much more impressive MP like John Reid waits years on the back-benches because he comes from a northern Ontario region which already has a minister, Robert Andras. And, except for the time when he axed three ministers after the 1974 election, Trudeau has been a most reluctant political executioner, allowing ministers to remain in cabinet long after they have demonstrated their mediocrity or have visibly grown weary.

Standing at the controls of a decision-making machine which functions much more smoothly than its predecessors, but not nearly as well as it would with better ministers, Trudeau himself admits: "I used to say, 'If I ever become prime minister, I'll choose my ministers according to ability, not according to French-English, east-west, north-south, ethnic grounds and so on.' I must confess that, in that, I have been much more conventional than I had thought I would be. If I have too many good ministers from one particular area, I may be inclined to choose one from another area even if he is not quite as good, but for geographical reasons, or for reasons of English-French balance or ethnic participation or whatever it is."

CHAPTER NINE

Trudeau in Cabinet: "Consensual, but..."

OF ALL Trudeau's functions as prime minister, none is more important than directing the formulation of his government's policies. Since the decision-making takes place behind closed doors and since a prime minister is ultimately responsible for everything his government does, it is conventional to attribute all policies to him — to speak of "Trudeau's agriculture policy" or "Trudeau's foreign relations" or "Trudeau's price-and-income controls". But, in reality, different prime ministers impose their stamp on policy-setting to varying extents and in different ways. How many of the decisions of the last decade are really Trudeau's, and how does he operate as the chairman of cabinet and its top committees?

"It would really surprise most Canadians, I think," says former cabinet secretary Gordon Robertson. "I've sat in cabinet and cabinet committees with four prime ministers — Mackenzie King, St. Laurent, Pearson, and Trudeau. And of those four prime ministers that I've seen in action, I'd say that Trudeau probably was the most likely to be guided by consensus and the least likely to assert his own views.

"Most people have the impression that Trudeau is sort of an authoritarian person who imposes his views in cabinet or in cabinet committees. But he's the most patient person in the world. He allows all kinds of discussion, invites it, encourages it, shows enormous patience, usually hangs back so that he won't inhibit people in what they say. But his mind and his analyses are just first-class tools in seeing that people dwell on the things that are important and decide the things that are important, and then he's remarkably likely to be guided by the consensus, having influenced that consensus."

This view is echoed by minister after minister. Says Donald Macdonald: "I've always thought that one of the least justified characterizations of his methods was to say that he was extremely arbitrary and knew what he wanted in advance and really insisted on getting it. There have been a very limited number of cases where it has been pretty clear that his mind is firmly made up, but in the vast majority of cases he operates on a consensus-gathering basis." Says Mitchell Sharp: "Some think that he dominates the cabinet by saying, 'This is my view, do you disagree?' That's very seldom the way he works. He asks questions, really uses a Socratic method. He doesn't so much express a viewpoint as ask questions and steer the discussion." And C. M. Drury concurs: "He is basically consensual, except for a few issues in which he has a particular personal interest."

But to say simply that Trudeau operates by consensus would be to stop far short of the total picture. His is a managed consensuality, a selective consensuality, and a consensuality in which all ministers do not carry equal weight. Dictated initially by his own personality and his political liabilities, this managed consensuality is a technique designed to obtain greater commitment by all ministers to the policies eventually adopted, to ensure that every decision is extensively and rationally debated, and still to let him have his own way when he feels particularly strongly on an issue.

"I'm more inclined," Trudeau explains, "to be a loner and to want to do things on my own and not have to drag a lot of people along with me, and if they agree, fine, and if they don't, fine. And I guess that was the pattern of my life until I got into politics. I never liked to be a leader in anything. . . . So, in getting into politics, into a party in which I had no roots and very few acquaintances, I found it very necessary to change my ways. And rather than being authoritarian, saying, 'this is what we are going to do, come along,' I developed, I suppose, a much greater penchant for consensus-seeking than I had ever had to have in any of my previous avocations. That was an empirical and pragmatic decision, that I was the head of a team — cabinet, caucus, the party itself, in a sense Canada — and I had to make sure that people were prepared to support what I thought was right.

"That's the genesis of it. In practice, I guess it depends. In some areas, in cabinet, I am much more of a leader than in others, depending on the particular thing we're discussing. If it's something on which I have strong feelings and definite principles, then I generally make sure that the decision comes out my way. But on many problems of administration, it's a matter of finding what is more practical at a given time or can work best, and I am open to persuasion. And I don't attempt to lead, I attempt to see what the consensus is, and then I declare it. In areas where I think the consensus is wrong, I do say, 'Well, I'm sorry, but the decision is this.' "

The levers of prime-ministerial power in Trudeau's system extend far beyond the cabinet room. Through the information-gathering and disseminating facilities of the Privy Council Office (the PCO), Trudeau is able to pervade the whole policy process and monitor every step of the decision-making chain. The PCO has a dual function: to assist cabinet and its committees with record-taking and co-ordination, and to serve the prime minister with policy information, analysis, and advice. Since the PCO is basically "the prime minister's department", the two functions intertwine to his advantage.

The PCO acts, first of all, as the funnel through which the prime minister's thinking is disseminated to the top echelons of the bureaucracy in each department. The secretary to the cabinet and one of his assistants attend each cabinet meeting. They then report to other officials in the PCO what was said, and each of those senior officials is responsible in turn for maintaining liaison with a certain number of deputy ministers. Each deputy minister is briefed by a designated PCO official, after each cabinet meeting, on anything that touches on his department's sphere of responsibility. The same kind of reporting procedure is used for the Priorities and Planning and Federal-Provincial Relations committees. Thus, any opinion

Trudeau expresses, however casually, in cabinet or committee on the directions in which a department should be moving is immediately communicated back to that department's policy-makers and begins to shape their thinking and proposals. And this, in turn, means that Trudeau is influencing the policy process long before a proposal reaches the stage of committee discussion.

The PCO also functions as a funnel in the opposite direction, giving Trudeau an unrivalled knowledge of everything that is happening throughout the policy system. PCO officials attend every meeting of cabinet committees or of interdepartmental committees of deputy ministers. They also keep track, in their co-ordinating capacity, of proposals that are being prepared for presentation to a cabinet committee. And, as the prime minister's policy advisors, they discuss these proposals with the ministers and bureaucrats involved. By pooling all this information gathered by its various officials, the PCO is able to keep Trudeau informed of all the proposals coming through the system.

This enables Trudeau to head off anything he finds unacceptable long before it reaches the consensus-seeking arena of cabinet. "If I know that I am going to have a confrontation in cabinet, if a minister is recommending something and I think it's dead wrong, I won't let him put the thing to cabinet," he says. "I'll see him in my office, I'll set up an interdepartmental committee, I'll meet him privately, I'll say, 'Look, we're on a collision course, this can't possibly be right.' The whole role of the PCO, and the PMO to a certain degree, is to inform me of the genesis of the discussion, how it's going. And if I think it's going in a way that I approve, fine, I'm happy to let the consensus develop. If I think it's not going in the right direction, I ask them to arm me with the arguments and facts and figures."

When it comes to chairing cabinet or one of its committees, Trudeau arrives fortified with the power that lies in unshared knowledge. For each policy memorandum to be discussed, the PCO equips him with a concise memo about two pages long, outlining the positions of the various key ministers and their bureaucrats, the areas of disagreement, a substantive PCO analysis of the issue, and sometimes a recommended position for him to take. He alone comes to the cabinet table knowing beforehand what every other participant is going to argue, and that exclusive view of the total picture gives him a formidable advantage in the ensuing debate.

Trudeau describes his approach in cabinet and committee this way: "Generally I let the lead minister speak, the guy who is making the presentation, and a great number of times I'll then talk right away and say, 'Well, you know, you're wrong,' or 'You can't do it that way because . . .' Then he comes back and says, 'I thought of that, but here's the answer,' and so on. I'm trying to lead him away from his decision, either towards mine if I have one, or towards an improvement of his if I'm not certain if he is right or wrong. I hope I am reasonably good in bringing people around to accepting my point of view."

In such debate, his advance knowledge is not his only built-in advantage. As Sharp puts it: "I have said that Trudeau never came into the cabinet and said, 'This is what we will do.' But at the same time, we recognized that we were a majority party in 1968 because Trudeau had been the leader. We all had the sort of feeling that we were there because Trudeau was the prime minister. It wasn't as if he laid down any policy approach, but we realized he was the man who had brought us where we were. Pearson was merely one of us, whereas Trudeau was not — he was someone extraordinary." The psychological edge provided by Trudeau's electoral appeal is compounded, as Sharp notes, by a more practical consideration: "The prime minister is in a very strong position because he controls the appointment of ministers." However consensual the process, a minister who consistently allows himself to be at odds with his leader risks his chances for advancement.

And, finally, Trudeau also brings to the search for consensus the advantages of his own intellect and debating skills. Says Gordon Robertson: "He's got such a superb mind, and such an intellectual command of any given subject, that this in itself probably impedes people from introducing their comments, because they are rather concerned that they may make fools of themselves. It isn't that he lacks patience, it's just that they know that his mind is a lot better than most of theirs." Adds another top official: "This is a prime minister who is very confident of his intellectual skills. In discussion, in the forum of cabinet, this prime minister is a wicked opponent. If you disagree with him, he's got a good memory for facts and arguments, a very sharp tongue, he can wear you down."

Trudeau can be sharply cutting in debate — particularly if he feels a minister hasn't done his homework or is trying to argue from intuition rather than logic — but for the most part he keeps the atmosphere in cabinet formal but relaxed. He functions much like a seminar leader, encouraging participation, probing positions with tough questions, keeping the discussion closely focussed on the matter to be decided. He is skilful at cutting ministers off if they digress or ramble on too long, without wounding their sensibilities. He also takes pains to draw out the opinions of the more reticent participants, and to protect them from being interrupted or ridiculed by their colleagues. Says one insider: "Someone like old Dan MacDonald from Prince Edward Island will start relating some issue to the problems of potato farmers or something, and others around the table will just tune out or start making wisecracks — but Trudeau shuts them right up, and says, 'Yes, Dan, go ahead, tell us more.' "

In practice, Trudeau is involved in open debate on only a tiny fraction of all the issues decided by cabinet — those few that are referred to Priorities and Planning, sent back to full cabinet from committee with a recommendation rather than a report, or appealed in full cabinet by a minister.

It is in P and P rather than full cabinet that disputes between ministers are usually settled, and in those instances Trudeau seeks to function as a conciliator. Says Donald Macdonald: "When there's a pretty solid difference of opinion between two ministers or between groups, he's got very considerable clarity in setting out the issue, and then he'll call upon the protagonists to speak. And the leadership there is really, in many cases, by cross-examination, by trying to find the weak points in the protagonist's case — and he's equally likely then to go after what he perceives to be the weak points on the other side. Then at a certain point, he'll start saying, 'Look, I think that we therefore can agree on this and this,' and very often that is the case and then he'll gradually narrow it down to the points of agreement. And very often from there he'll go off in private with the ministers on a question, and ultimately he'll say: 'Okay, well look, we've got to put this thing to bed. This is what we are going to do.' And it's generally not a Solomon-like decision of cutting it in half — he really does have to pick choice A or choice B, and he will do that. But it can be a rather protracted process. This is very often why decisions which were expected at a certain time go on and on and on, because he tries to get agreement."

Perhaps the best illustration of Trudeau's approach to conciliation is his handling of the potentially explosive disagreement that developed in P and P between Lalonde, as minister of health and welfare, and John Turner, as finance minister, over Lalonde's proposal to overhaul the welfare system by introducing a guaranteed annual income program. Lalonde had spent several years preparing the proposal, but when he confidently began stating his case at the crucial P and P meeting that was to decide its fate, he found himself caught in a political ambush: the finance department had held back from his officials some important calculations on the possible fiscal impact of the plan, and Turner began peppering him with questions and alternative hypotheses he couldn't answer.

The situation was rich with potential for a nasty cabinet split. Turner was hinting that he wouldn't stay in cabinet if Lalonde's proposal were accepted, and Lalonde would have little choice but to quit if he felt humiliated in cabinet and abandoned by the prime minister. An insider describes what happened:

"Trudeau kept it from becoming a personal confrontation between the two. He called John in and talked with him about his arguments, and then called Marc in and talked about his arguments, and he postponed the crisis for several weeks after the P and P thing. There was more than one P and P meeting on this problem. There was the one classic where Marc comes in bushy-tailed and loaded for bear and gets trapped in an ambush, but Trudeau spread it out for at least four or five more meetings while different parts of everybody's arguments got arrayed and aired. And eventually the Lalonde forces were exhausted. They had nothing new to say and the cabinet was siding with John.

"But they never took a vote. Therefore, the PM said, 'We accept the program, the question is when we can afford it.' He had slowly, gradually defused it. What happened was that it gradually became so clear where things stood that the PM could come down and say, 'The policy is great, but the timing is not good,' and that was the common ground that Marc could buy and John could buy."

In addition to the channels of intervention open to him on specific issues, Trudeau can also shape the consensus by determining the framework of priorities within which decisions must be made. In the first mandate, the government's over-all objectives were mostly determined by Trudeau and his advisors and communicated downward through the system. After the 1974 election, an attempt was made to reverse this approach by means of an elaborate priorities exercise in which all ministers were asked what they felt the government should be doing and then the composite results were weighed by Trudeau. This approach never led anywhere, however, because events overtook the government and priorities had to be revised in the light of spending restraints and the controls program. Apart from such major planning exercises, Trudeau can exercise his direction-setting prerogative in the planning of throne speeches and in chairing the Priorities and Planning committee.

For the most part, however, Trudeau plays only a limited role in the initiation of specific policies and programs. He tends, rather, to focus attention on problems or on objectives which he believes should be met, and then to delegate the responsibility of devising proposals for concrete action.

"I get together with a few people, or I come back from a summer vacation and I've thought of what I think the session should be doing or what I think our strategy should be," Trudeau says, "and I discuss it with a few people and we begin setting a framework of action, whether it be a sketch of the Speech from the Throne or a list of priorities. And then we go to the ministers singly or collectively and say, 'Here is a background, let's work on this and let's add ideas to it or criticize it and so on.' So, in that sense, policy directions are initiated by me, but very little detailed application of particular housekeeping items or general run-of-the-mill legislation.

"I can remember the times when I'd be reading something or

discussing with someone or looking at statistics and saying, 'Gee, we're going to be hit with heavy unemployment of youth next summer.' That's how the first idea for Opportunities for Youth came about: It was up at Harrington Lake. I was discussing this problem with a couple of people, and we were in the confrontation '60s, nothing was being produced beyond the traditional hiring of the kids by the bureaucracy and getting the private sector to hire some, and so I said, 'That's not good enough, go out and find something that we can offer these kids and get them to do, and we'll pay them for it.' Same thing with Indians, I guess — I've changed my mind on some aspects of that, but the thrust that we had to break that logjam, the decision of putting things in a hierarchy in cases like that and setting other things aside obviously originates from me. That doesn't mean that if another minister comes up with a good idea, it's not acceptable in that framework that I put forward."

What is generally lacking in Trudeau's approach to policy initiation is the articulation, to his government and to the nation, of a clear set of goals. He nudges a given policy in this direction or that, directs the attention of his ministers to areas where he wants more action, and determines what should be pursued as priorities and what should be put on the back burner. But, with the exception of national unity matters, he seldom infuses the policy process with a discernible sense of over-all purpose, preferring to keep most of his goals to himself until and unless they come to fruition.

Says Sharp: "It's not his style to articulate directions. I don't really recall anything like that. The PM retains many of his characteristics as an academic. He has a sceptical mind. He doesn't go off on great enthusiasms or anything like that. He may indicate that this is the way he thinks we should move on something, but with no great feeling." Adds a close Trudeau advisor: "If one is the kind of person — and I would think most people are of this kind — who wants to be associated with someone else to be 'turned on', to 'have his fire lit', to 'join with him in his crusade', Pierre Trudeau is not the guy, and this is what has turned an awful lot of people off on him. Working with some ministers, one has that sense of enthusiasm and zeal and common purpose that makes for winning football games, you know, when everybody knows that that's the goal line and the object is to get the ball over there and you know you can do it. With Trudeau, it's difficult to detect what the motivating force is or what he wants to come out of any particular issue, very difficult."

Trudeau himself explains it this way: "I like to think that I'm helping bring Canada up to date on its problems and to cut through much of the hesitation which has prevented us from solving problems in the past. There were several things in foreign affairs, domestic affairs, in government reorganization, approach to the budget, approach to the control of spending, operation of the Prime Minister's Office, recognition of Peking or the Vatican, reassessing our role in NATO — these are all things that I wanted to do. And I suppose as one gets on, one realizes that one has only done them in part, and that the rest of the time has been occupied by dealing with the urgent problems that come our way and hopefully solving them.

"What's important is that I don't try to sound as though I've thought up a whole lot of new ideas and brought them into government. I would put it differently. I can't say that I was much of an original thinker in government; I hope I was in my academic life. But what I've tried to do in government is be sensitive to the institutional, ideological, and social realities, and to make sure that we were responding to them. And whether it be Galbraith or Heilbroner, or Plato or Aristotle for that matter, there are certain things that I believe to be right and true, and I want to make sure that they are not neglected in the process of government."

If Trudeau's ministers still consider him consensual despite the number of levers he can pull to impose his will, it is because he uses those levers rather sparingly. His handling of cabinet decisions falls into three rough categories: issues which he stakes out as his personal domain, in which he claims a prerogative to decide what should be done and how; issues in which he feels strongly about the goals to be attained, but is open to discussion as to the means; and issues in which he takes no great personal interest, as long as what is being done strikes him as reasonable and consistent.

These categories are by no means rigid, since different policy areas move up and down in his hierarchy of importance over time, and a particular problem within a subject area normally in the second or third category can have implications which move it into the first. Thus, for instance, although transportation matters would normally tend to fall into the second or third category, the importance of Western transport problems to national unity sometimes moves them into the first category.

Every prime minister has certain subject areas which he considers particularly his own; in Pearson's day, for instance, Mitchell Sharp recalls that foreign policy was rarely discussed in cabinet. For Trudeau, that principal subject area is the whole field of national unity, defined broadly to encompass federal-provincial relations, the constitution, language policy, equalization payments, and manifestations of the federal presence.

That subject area is fundamental to his whole involvement in politics, as he bluntly stated in 1973: "Every man has his own reasons, I suppose, as driving forces, but mine were twofold: One, to make sure that Quebec wouldn't leave Canada through separatism, and the other was to make sure that Canada wouldn't shove Quebec out through narrowmindedness."[1]

Asked now how he would like history to complete the phrase "Pierre Trudeau was the prime minister who . . .", he answers revealingly: "Pierre Trudeau is the one that succeeded, or didn't succeed, in getting Canada to accept that it had two official languages and that there was equality between them. Point number one. Point number two: Pierre Trudeau is the one who, because of his approach to this, as well as his approach to correcting regional disparities, really had Canadians from all parts of Canada come to the realization that they were better in a united country than in one which was divided either by separatism or by exaggerated decentralization, that they had common interests in the political and economic and sociological sense which made the country they were in much more worthwhile. That's what I fight and win election campaigns on, that's what the people want, and that's what I got into politics to give."

On anything directly related to those objectives, Trudeau does not operate by consensus. In a showdown in cabinet on anything he considered fundamental to national unity, he would be more likely to say, "Find yourselves a new leader if you don't agree," than to bow to the wishes of any majority.

Also of direct personal concern to Trudeau, though on a less intense basis, are some specialized aspects of foreign policy — particularly relations with the United States and the whole question of a "New Economic Order" in relations between developed and developing countries — and the general supervision of fiscal responsibility in government spending initiatives. In addition, he assumes personal control over anything he considers fundamental to his government's over-all image and policy stance. "He believes," says one associate, "that there are some values which his government basically stands for — whether it be in foreign policy or individual rights or equality of opportunity or anything else — and he won't allow anything he feels is inconsistent with those values."

Beyond the first category, issues are considerably more difficult to classify. Trudeau himself offers little help: "I've been pretty eclectic. There are always some current issues which demand more attention from me and I specialize in those; it's more of a reactive attitude than otherwise. In Planning and Priorities committee, we sometimes deal with food policy, sometimes with energy policy, sometimes with open government, sometimes with organizational reform, and those are the things that I am concentrating on at that particular time. You know, some of the problems I spend most time on are very often problems that wouldn't have interested me hadn't I been in government. The dairy policy caused me to put an incredible number of hours into it, but it's not something I would have been attracted to before getting into the necessities of politics. It wasn't my area, it wasn't my field. . . . I've spent very much time in economic areas. But, you know, I can't say I got into politics thinking that this was going to be one of my aims, to reduce the problem of inflation or see how I could make controls work. Still, it's been basic and vital to our policy in the past couple of years.

"Obviously the constitution, civil liberties, federal-provincial relations, have been precise concerns of mine. I wouldn't say even they occupy me overwhelmingly. . . . But beyond the things I've said, national unity . . . there are not too many things that you would find me pursuing consistently."

Measured not in terms of the time invested but of the type of authority Trudeau exercises, the second category of issues comprises those to which Trudeau attaches major importance but on which he is willing to discuss and delegate the concrete pursuit of stated objectives. These include the specifics of regional economic expansion programs, the general workings of the economy, social policy, food policy, energy matters, some elements of Indian affairs, most aspects of foreign policy, and some transportation and justice issues. When something like an oil crisis in the energy field takes on dimensions that can affect national unity or federal-provincial relations, Trudeau may step in more actively and take personal command. On the other hand, some routine aspects of an area like agriculture policy may preoccupy him so little that they are really in the third category.

In this second category, says a close associate and advisor, Trudeau "functions at quite a high level of abstraction in his decision-making. As long as the main outlines of a policy proposal are within the guidelines of where he wants the government to be heading, he won't tell the ministers how to decide. And those main guidelines are very broad. On food policy, for example, it's a question of ensuring that a certain balance is sought between the interests of producers and consumers. Once he's got it, the rest of it, as far as he's concerned, is up to the ministers — and what's important to them is not the balance between producers and consumers, but practical things about broilers and turkeys and farm quotas. On the Long-Range Patrol Aircraft question, he felt that the Russians had become more powerful, NATO should be strengthened, and Canada should play a larger role; I don't think he cared personally which aircraft was chosen, as long as the choice was soundly made. On competition policy, I don't think he gave a damn whether there would be a tribunal or not, but he believed we should be seeking to extend certain aspects of competition policy."

Before 1972, Trudeau tended to take very limited personal interest in economic management and to rely almost completely on advice from the department of finance. But after his government's clumsy handling of unemployment and inflation contributed heavily to his near-defeat in 1972, economic management rose considerably in his hierarchy of personal interests. From 1974 until the election of the Parti Québécois in Quebec in 1976 diverted his attention, he became increasingly intrigued by the general workings of the economy — the relative power of various groups, the distribution of wealth and production, and the other structural problems that contribute to inflation. Because of its vital importance to the country and to his government's whole program and image, Trudeau played a powerful role in shaping the decision to impose price-and-income controls, insisting on a limited scheme rather than an across-the-board freeze.

But on most economic matters, he remains highly consensual. Says Donald Macdonald: "I think you'd find on economic issues that he inclines to be very, very dialectical. He'll keep debating them around and around, and he is really prepared to take almost just the best consensus he can get. He's rather eclectic in his choice of economic conclusions, and I think that indicates that in the economic area he doesn't have as deeply held convictions as he does, for example, in language relations."

In the preparation of a budget, Trudeau may press his minister to put greater emphasis on either inflation or economic growth. But he leaves the details of budget-making almost entirely to the discretion of his finance minister. "I don't think," says a well-placed insider, "that when Turner was minister, Trudeau liked his boondoggles to the middle class, things like the Registered Home Ownership Plan — he thought they were silly. With Don Macdonald, I don't think he was enamoured with the way Finance handled corporate depreciation; he thought maybe there should be more money instead for fighting unemployment. But in his view, those are proper decisions for the minister of finance to make, and it's not for him to interfere." Adds Marc Lalonde: "When Turner was here, on all financial and fiscal matters the PM would not push John around. All the fiscal decisions were John's."

For all his emphasis on social policy in his earlier writings, and his talk of a "Just Society", the social policy field has never been dominant among Trudeau's preoccupations as prime minister, and welfare matters are seldom mentioned when he enumerates the things he entered politics to accomplish. His decision to make Lalonde minister of health and welfare and to give him Al Johnson, one of the best and most progressive bureaucrats in the federal administration, as deputy minister reflected an intention to overhaul the welfare system. But when economic conditions changed and the scheme ran into strong opposition from Turner and finance officials, Trudeau allowed the proposal to sink into limbo without indicating any strong personal commitment to it.

Although it is an area that has contributed handsomely to his prestige, Trudeau came late to an interest in foreign policy, and his involvement in it remains quite selective. Says Ivan Head, his foreign-policy advisor: "He's a man who had probably done more foreign travel than any person who has ever come into high public office in Canada, and yet who was willing despite that background to be quite indifferent to foreign affairs. That was not what interested him, not what he regarded as important. It was something he was quite willing to delegate to others from the very beginning and have nothing to do with. As he's become aware of not only the usefulness but the personal interest to him — the attractiveness to him as a person — of personal diplomacy, often in the form of summits, that has changed."

Trudeau regards foreign policy, for the most part, as the pursuit of Canada's domestic interests abroad, and he is sceptical about assigning the country any larger international role. "We shouldn't be trying to run the world," he has said. "We should be trying to make our own country a good place.[2] . . . We're perhaps more the largest of the small powers than the smallest of the large powers.[3] . . . Personally, I tend to discount the weight of our influence in the world. If we have influence, so much the better. But I don't think this should be our purpose, sort of, to tell the world what is morally right and what is morally wrong and go around voting properly on the right issues and being all things to all men."[4] His foreign-policy goals are accordingly modest: to assist Canada's economic growth, to further the cause of national unity at home by ensuring that Canada maintains a fully bicultural presence abroad, to avoid excessive dependence on the United States by strengthening Canada's ties with other countries, and to make whatever limited contributions to world peace our circumstances permit.

Relations with the United States are one of the few foreign-policy areas to which Trudeau accords "first category" attention. Here, as in most other fields, his preoccupation is with maintaining a fine balance. On one hand, he considers a certain amount of domination by the United States inescapable, if only because few Canadians would be prepared to pay the economic price that would be required to end it: "I think the problem of economic domination is somewhat inevitable, not only of the United States over Canada but perhaps over countries of Europe as well. . . . These are facts of life and they don't worry me.[5] . . . If the whole country became nationalistic in an economic sense, it would soon find itself trying to eat its pride, you know, but you don't go far on a proud stomach."[6] But, on the other hand, Trudeau believes it is his government's role to ensure that this domination does not extend so far as to cause serious damage to Canada's economic, political, or cultural well-being or sense of identity. This, to him, is less a matter of erecting across-the-board barriers to U.S. influence than of determining on a case-by-case basis whether a threat exists, and what protective action is required. In such subjective judgments, of course, his perception is quite different from that of economic nationalists who are convinced that the present level of U.S. ownership in this country is, in itself, a threat to Canada.

Trudeau's pursuit of what he considers a proper balance in the Canada–United States relationship takes two forms. First, it involves an attempt to wean Canada away from over-dependence on its southern neighbour by developing closer economic and political ties with other countries. This strategy constitutes the "Third Option" outlined on behalf of the government in 1972 by Mitchell Sharp, who was then external affairs minister; the other two options identified and rejected by the Trudeau government were to leave the Canada–United States relationship unchanged, or to move deliberately toward closer integration between the two countries. As Trudeau explains it: "The object of our policy, simply stated, is that we are trying to create counterweights. . . . It's a very simple strategy of creating other channels of interest than the automatic, easy, north-south, Canada–U.S. ones in which we are always the smaller and minor partner."[7] This strategy of diversification underlies much of Trudeau's foreign policy, including the recognition of China, the rapprochement with the Soviet Union, and the pursuit of closer and more active relations with the countries of the Pacific Rim, Latin America, and the European Economic Community.

The other element of Trudeau's approach, which has sometimes been misinterpreted as anti-Americanism by the United States and even by some Canadians, involves selective government intervention to assert or protect Canada's independence. As Trudeau puts it: "We can't expect, without becoming much poorer, to control all of our economy. What we can do is make an effort to control those economic or financial institutions which are of greater importance in the free development of this society. . . . The same thing in cultural fields."[8] These selective interventions have included blocking the sale of Canadian uranium mines to U.S. interests, introducing legislation to prevent the World Football League from expanding into Canada, encouraging the Canadian Radio and Television Commission to impose stringent Canadian-content requirements on broadcasters, and driving the Canadian editions of *Time* and several other U.S. publications out of the country by ending their tax concessions. Apart from such specific interventions, Trudeau also established the Foreign Investment Review Agency, a screening body whose limited mandate is designed not to block or discourage foreign investment but to ensure that it takes place in forms which carry some benefit for Canada. In a more general sense, Trudeau has also periodically asserted Canada's independence by pursuing policies — such as trading with, and even visiting, Cuba — that defied pressures from the United States, by vigorously resisting the extraterritorial application of U.S. laws to American corporations operating in Canada, and by such actions as making American draft-resisters and deserters welcome in this country during the Vietnam War.

A second area of foreign policy to which Trudeau accords "first category" attention is the matter of nuclear non-proliferation. The intensity of his feelings about nuclear weapons and the prospect of their use has changed little since he wrote in 1961: "Massacres is too weak a term. Twisted, charred, liquefied, vanished into thin air. . . . Of all humanity nothing will remain but traces of shadows stamped on the concrete debris, on the stones in the fields, on the cliffs of the ocean, as if they were so many stains on a bad photographic plate."[9] He has not been prepared to take Canada out of the business of making nuclear reactors — which, although designed for peaceful purposes, can be used to produce nuclear bombs — but he has insisted that those reactors be sold under safeguard agreements which greatly reduce the danger of misuse, and he has consistently pressed the issues of non-proliferation and disarmament in his talks with foreign leaders.

The third foreign-policy area in which Trudeau takes a strong personal interest is the changing relationship between developed and developing countries, a subject on which he said in 1968: "We must recognize that, in the long run, the overwhelming threat to Canada will not come from foreign investments or foreign ideologies or even — with good fortune — foreign nuclear weapons. It will come, instead, from the two-thirds of the people of the world who are steadily falling farther and farther behind in their search for a decent standard of living."[10] He believes that Canada, because it is both an industrialized nation and a country whose economy is heavily dependent on the production of raw materials, can well understand the problems of both developed and developing countries and therefore can sometimes serve as a bridge between the two. Though domestic economic and political considerations have deterred him from matching his sympathy for the concerns of developing countries with concrete generosity, he has succeeded in establishing close personal rapport with such leaders of the Third World as Julius Nyerere of Tanzania, Lee Kuan Yew of Singapore, and Michael Manley of Jamaica.

In addition to those issues, including aspects of foreign policy, which Trudeau considers his personal domain and those in which he cares strongly about the end result but not the details, there is also a third category of issues that come before cabinet: those in which Trudeau has no great personal interest. This large group of subjects is where Trudeau is at his most consensual. He insists that the decisions be carefully and soundly reached and that they not conflict with the government's priorities and over-all directions, but he makes little effort to determine the outcome. "On ordinary public business," says Sharp, "he tries to reach a consensus. He wants order, he wants decisions to be reached logically, and he insists that decisions be made."

Consensus, to Trudeau, does not mean simple majority rule. Issues before cabinet almost never come to a formal vote; it is Trudeau, at the end of a debate, who interprets the consensus and declares it. On a few relatively unimportant decisions in which he took a straw vote just to see where everybody stood, Trudeau has even playfully asserted his power by announcing: "It's 18 to 12 — the 12s have it." In reality, on most important questions, what matters to Trudeau is the consensus of ministers whose judgment he respects.

"I perceive it," says Lalonde, "as being consensus in an in-group. With thirty men and women around a table, it's unavoidable that some people in the decision-making process carry more weight with the PM in a decision. It depends to a great extent on the value of the contributions of these people, the political weight they carry. I find the PM is a guy who is very rational, an intellectual; he likes an intellectual challenge, he likes a guy who runs his show well on his own. For that guy, the PM in cabinet will be a consensus man."

Trudeau does not appoint and retain his ministers solely on the basis of their talents. Such considerations as maintaining geographic balance also play a part, and that means there are always a number of ministers whose opinions — particularly on matters outside their own portfolios — Trudeau does not greatly value. To a minister who consistently argues from premises different than Trudeau's or who has given the prime minister reason to mistrust his judgment, Trudeau may appear not very consensual at all. And even among the ministers he does respect, there is a hierarchy of policy weight: even a very competent minister would have to produce powerful arguments indeed to persuade Trudeau to overturn a conclusion reached by the ministers on the Priorities and Planning committee.

The policy weight of ministers in cabinet does not necessarily correspond to their popularity in the country at large or even to the importance of their portfolios. Bud Drury, for instance, had no national following, yet even when he occupied the relatively minor portfolios of public works and science and technology, his influence with Trudeau was immense; the prime minister not only attached great weight to his opinions in cabinet and committee, but also frequently solicited his advice in private. Bryce Mackasey, on the other hand, enjoyed a high degree of national popularity and was respected by Trudeau for the quality of his political instincts, but — because he tended to argue from instinct rather than careful documentation — his impact on policy outside his own portfolios was small.

The weight of various ministers' opinion also varies from issue to issue. On an energy matter, for instance, the position of a certain group of ministers might constitute a consensus for Trudeau, while on a question of foreign policy ministers with different orientations and expertise might prevail. And, on decisions that directly touch only Quebec, the decisive consensus — to the extent that he seeks one at all — is likely to be limited to Quebec ministers. Complains one minister from Ontario: "It is a significant point that what goes on in Quebec is never quite fully revealed to English-speaking ministers. There is always an element of mystery."

In general, it's safe to deduce that the ministers Trudeau names to the P and P committee carry more policy weight than most of their colleagues, because he would not have appointed them to his most important planning body if he did not particularly respect their judgment. Beyond that group, it's simply a matter of individual qualities, and the balance shifts as ministers earn or forfeit Trudeau's confidence.

The quality he most values in a minister is independence — a willingness to take positions on issues solely on their intellectual merits, rather than engaging in political gamesmanship by supporting or opposing various proposals in exchange for the support of colleagues for one's own initiatives. "In the case of Drury," Trudeau explains, "what I liked about him was that he was of no particular clan in caucus or in cabinet. I knew he would give his advice regardless of whether some ministers would be sore at him for not having supported their point of view. When that sort of minister says something, it could just as easily be contradictory of my position as it could be supportive. But I know he's doing it because he believes it, and not because at this particular stage of the game it's better to be with this particular group of ministers even if it means telling Trudeau he's wrong.

"I think that's what I look for most in this game. I think there were prime ministers or leaders who governed through cliques; I've never had the ability or the desire to do that. And if somebody is a member of a clique, I'm rather more distrustful of him than I am inclined to say, 'Jeez, I need this guy because he's got a lot of followers.' You know, I don't think I could operate in the kind of government system they have in Japan, for instance, or even Israel for that matter, where each minister brings his own power base and so on. . . . So that's probably one of the main tests of whom I ask for advice: 'Will it be given objectively and with the interests of the party and the leader at heart, or will it be with some other calculation?' — which isn't necessarily a bad or a venal calculation; some people are clannish and some are not. I'm not, and therefore I'm probably more attracted to those who are not."

In addition to independence and intellectual acuity, Trudeau also values a certain toughness in a minister, a willingness to stand up to him in argument. He has no taste for yes-men. When challenged or criticized in debate, Trudeau fights back ruthlessly. But unless he is personally insulted, Trudeau has far more respect and admiration for an opponent who stands his ground effectively than for one who yields. Hence his high regard for Don Macdonald, a minister who was more likely than any of his colleagues to be abrasively argumentative with Trudeau. "He liked Macdonald because Don would stand up to him," says a close Trudeau advisor. "Don wouldn't pull any punches, and Trudeau liked that. They'd have a hell of a row in cabinet, and the PM's esteem for him would just soar."

This weighting of ministerial opinions, coupled with his varying degrees of intervention on various types of issues and his ability to shape policy before it ever reaches the cabinet stage, makes Trudeau's a complicated, selective consensuality. Or, as he puts it: "Yes, consensus-seeking — provided I'm sure that I can share the consensus."

CHAPTER TEN

"What's he really like?"

"**I**F YOU'RE writing a book on Trudeau, maybe you can tell me: What's he *really* like?" asks a man who has worked with him for the better part of a decade. Strange as it sounds, there is nothing at all facetious about the question. Like many successful leaders, Trudeau displays different facets of his personality to different observers, being careful not to let any one aide or minister see the total picture. To be fully known and understood is to be vulnerable, and Trudeau has until now been almost passionate in his avoidance of vulnerability. He has preferred, often at considerable political cost, to shield himself in office behind a thick buffer zone of myth and speculation about his true nature. And just as his personality is far more complex than that of the hard, emotionless man his image portrays, Trudeau as prime minister is often surprisingly different from the impression he creates.

Behind the shield of apparent confidence, there are startling vestiges of the shy, insecure boy who was too easily moved to tears by praise or blame and who harboured suspicions of inferiority. Far from being arrogant in the exercise of power, he is in reality curiously unassuming and even diffident about some aspects of his prime-ministerial role.

"If I'm introduced as 'the leader of our country', I feel a bit shy about that," he says, "because it's really the office that's being introduced and not me. I guess basically I'm saying that I'm still not quite used to thinking of myself as prime minister, in certain emotional circumstances. To give a good example of that, I was at a recent citizenship ceremony in Montreal, where a lot of new Canadians would just sort of hold my hand and have tears in their eyes and say, 'We need you, Mr. Trudeau, to save our country.' Well, that makes me rather moved, but it also leaves me a bit shy, because, you know: 'Who am I? I'm Pierre Trudeau, I'm not the leader of a country.' And then I sort of realize, 'Well, yes, I am, so don't be shy about it.' "

If Trudeau still sometimes has trouble identifying with his prime-ministerial role after a decade in office, he has even greater difficulty in bringing himself to use its moral authority and persuasive power in certain situations. Like many seemingly outgoing performers who are quite shy in private life, he has no problem handling relatively impersonal interactions with large audiences. "I'm not shy about speaking to a crowd of a thousand and saying, 'Gee, you've got to vote for me, you know, you need leadership and I'm going to give it to you.' And if it's in the middle of Calgary, I say to myself, 'Jeez, there's not one out of fifty that's going to vote for me, but what the hell. . . .' " But when the performer-audience role-playing across the footlights is replaced by a one-to-one relationship, fear of rejection sets in.

"When it becomes personal and there's a chance the guy will say no, I suppose there's a feeling of fear of being rejected at some point," Trudeau says. "And it's not very rational. Sometimes I have to pick up the phone and phone someone I've never met before and say, 'Look, I'd like you to become a senator' or a chief justice or something. Not very many chances that he's going to say no, but, in fairness, I'm a bit shy about it. You know, I can't say: 'Hi, there. I'm glad to talk to you. How are things? How's your wife and the kids? Look, I've got a tremendous thing for you. I hope you realize I've put a lot of thought into it and really I'm doing you a big favour. Do you want to be president of this particular commission?'

"I guess I'm afraid. . . . I don't say that, because the guy could say: 'Look, fella, I know you're the prime minister, but I'm very happy down here and I don't want that job, don't make it sound like a big deal — it ain't.' There's a bit of that, I guess, and maybe that's not using the resources of my leadership. I've been so often asked to pick up the phone and tell so-and-so that I needed him as the candidate in the next election and so on, and I just can't do it. I don't say I never do it, but I'm shy in those circumstances."

The same sort of diffidence also carries through occasionally into his activities in the international arena, particularly at multilateral summits. Says Ivan Head: "I'll pass him a note at an international gathering and say: 'Make this point.' And he'll turn to me: 'But who am I to make that point?' It's a feeling that it would be ostentatious or arrogant or presumptuous. And I lose some of those and I win some. There's a real dogfight to tell him that they are waiting for him to say this, or that his word might tip the balance: 'Oh, surely not, surely not. If the issue is not self-evident to these others, why would anything I say one way or the other win it?' And it's not by any means a lack of courage on his part or a lack of willingness to see the importance of the goal or the desirability of getting there, but it's a disclaimer that anything he can do will be of any use at all."

This tendency toward self-deprecation is compounded, in domestic matters, by Trudeau's acute consciousness of his lack of roots and contacts in the Liberal Party. "It's been a weakness of my time as prime minister that I did not have the roots in politics and in particular in the Liberal Party that a guy who hadn't been catapulted so fast would have. It's why I was perhaps more bound into at least a more apparent consensus-seeking role than to real leadership or real giving of directions. I don't have the power bases within the party that a Mackenzie King had or a Laurier had. I can't phone up Mr. X or Mr. Y and say: 'Look, we're old friends, you've known me from 'way back. Take my word for it, this is what's happening and this is why. Go out and spread the word.'

"You know, the name of the game is power. And the more power bases you have, the more autonomous you are in facing a college of colleagues who have different geographical, social, and economic interests to represent. It's a handicap for me, and it's perceived as such, that I don't have a great deal of friends in the other provinces, except perhaps in the universities, that I don't have a great deal of old acquaintances in the various levels of the Liberal Party in the various parts of Canada. And when I got into the job of prime minister, I had to be so absorbed in the job because of my inexperience that I couldn't spend very much time cultivating what little power bases I had."

One of Trudeau's close associates also perceives a reflection of another form of insecurity in the prime minister's choice of some of his social contacts: "There's an apparent willingness on his part to find attractive a certain level of society, a certain kind of person in society. I'm talking about the Rockefellers or the Kennedys or the Aga Khan or the King of Jordan — not necessarily the jet-setters, but the persons of substance and influence, people of position as distinct from the ephemeral political position. It's out of keeping with the guy's character and yet it's there. One finds not a fawning, but a very real sense of uncertainty and therefore eagerness to accept hospitality or invitations from this sort of people."

This associate theorizes, further, that Trudeau's taste for this sort of company may be part of the explanation — over and above the man's formidable intellect — for the enormous influence of Michael Pitfield, scion of a patrician and wealthy Montreal family. "Michael is one of those guys who is never caught in an embarrassing moment. The rest of us find our tie in our soup on occasion or say the wrong thing sometimes, but Pitfield is a guy who's always cool, always impeccable, and it may be that the PM finds some sense of stability in keeping an eye on, and relating to, this kind of person who always seems to know how to behave himself and how to act and how to react. I think the PM has regarded Michael as a guide and a beacon in many instances, or as an advisor in what Michael senses as correct socially."

Except when he is among people he already knows as friends, Trudeau is often ill at ease in social situations in ways that are mistaken for arrogance or lack of interest. Despite the impression he sometimes gives, he actually enjoys meeting people and prides himself on his ability to establish rapport even in the briefest encounters: "I relate very directly and intensely to people. People have told me that with my children or other children or somebody I'll meet or somebody speaking in caucus, I'm very attentive to the individual. I've seen other politicians — I'd almost be inclined to name some — going through a crowd, sort of 'Hi, there! Hi, there!' and they're shaking hands with this one and already looking for the next hand, and then that one over there. Or they're talking to somebody at a cocktail party and sort of, 'Well, this guy is not all that important, is there someone more important over here that I can see?' I don't think I do that. I think I'm very present to the person or persons who are with me."

That's true, as far as it goes: If someone, even a total stranger, is speaking to Trudeau, he appears genuinely interested and attentive and usually prolongs the conversation by asking questions. But unless the other person brings up a topic of conversation after being introduced or approaching Trudeau, the prime minister is usually at a loss. He doesn't have the politician's knack of opening up conversations with people who may themselves be too shy or awed to think of anything to say; he is more likely, in such situations, to smile pleasantly and move on to the next person.

Recalls an aide: "There was a staff gathering one evening a little while ago, a buffet supper at someone's house with spouses and girl friends and so on, and the PM was clearly so ill at ease and didn't know how to handle himself, didn't know how to respond. And so I went up to him and started discussing a matter I hadn't had a chance to bring up in the office. It was a business kind of thing, but it was also just something to talk about and I wanted to help him out. And you know how most people would feel if a subordinate came up to them under those circumstances and started talking business: 'For God's sake, it's Friday night, leave it.' But he just sort of locked in on it — it was like a space ship coming in and the collar locking, and he was at ease there and he sort of clung and didn't want to let go. You know: 'What else? What else? Is there anything else that's happening that we haven't had a chance to talk about?' It was really an escape for him. . . . He is not at ease with new people. He's very, very reticent, and it's a strange combination of characteristics that this man who is so confident of his own mental power and his own sense of judgment is at the same time so lacking in confidence as to how to deal with others."

These traces of self-doubt, coupled with his view of politics as a process in which all citizens must share responsibility, go a long way toward explaining a certain lack of dynamism in Trudeau's leadership. Except in a few special instances, he believes it is not up to him to tell the people what they must do; he prefers to say what he thinks *should* be done and to leave it to the public — with a minimum of persuasion from him — to decide whether it agrees. More than most leaders, he has the ability to sell policies and shape public opinion through sheer force of personality and intellect, but he has no enthusiasm for that sort of aggressive persuasion. Who is he, he often seems to feel, to try to impose his will on a nation? And, as in dealings with individuals, to put himself totally on the line in pressing for acceptance of any proposal by society would be to risk a painful rejection.

As Trudeau puts it: "If I think some idea is headed completely in the wrong direction, when it is turning to violence or something like that, I suppose I have no choice but to get out there and say, 'Stop! We must go in some other direction.' I would think that can only be done exceptionally and I think also it should only be done exceptionally. . . . I think a government should be slightly ahead of the people. It must not only be contemporary with the issues, but it must indicate directions which it thinks the society should follow if it is going to be happy and if it is going to be able to respond to the challenge of change. But I have always said and believed that you can't be that far ahead of the mass of the people that you are isolated from it. If you're that far in advance, you can only lead if you're a dictator, or else you cease leading because the people say, 'You're too far out, man, we can't go along with you.'. . .

"You can't lead the people like you lead a horse, you know, by sitting on it and knowing the laws of physiology and mechanics and saying, 'Well, if I lean a little bit forward and prod the horse with this leg, he will jump into a canter on that side,' and the horse moves on as an animal. The people are spread all over the map in Canada, geographically, linguistically, and therefore you can't expect leadership in the sense of a horseman leading his horse along a path."[1]

Traces of self-doubt, however, are only one element of Trudeau's make-up, an element that he usually takes pains to suppress or camouflage. He is, at the same time, a tough, combative man who well understands the uses of power. And if he is somewhat unsure of himself in personal relations, he is supremely confident —

and intensely competitive — in his physical and intellectual prowess.

Says Ivan Head: "I particularly remember one occasion during the Commonwealth Conference in 1973 at Mont Tremblant, when all the leaders had gone back to Ottawa on the special airplanes we had for them, and the PM had asked me to stay behind and come back with him in the helicopter. And in that interval between the airplanes' leaving and the helicopter's departure, he said: 'Let's go water-skiing.' Neither of us had water-skied all that summer, but each of us — it was unstated — was determined he was going to outdo the other guy. We went at it until we almost sank into the lake. For example, he was determined that he could do a deep-water single-ski start. Now that's a tough thing to do until you've got the knack of it, and if you haven't practised it for a while. . . . But he stayed at that, I don't know whether it was six, seven, or eight times, until his arms must have been just about pulled out of their sockets. And the next day, he must have felt like I did — that his legs were just about falling off him, that his arms were terrible, the worst neck-ache that you've ever had — and he was in an intolerable mood and so was I. But he just had to do it.

"The bobsled run in St. Moritz was the same kind of thing. He didn't know how dangerous it was, but insisted on doing it because he was challenged. And when he did it, I was crazy enough that I wasn't going to permit a guy ten years older than me to do it, I had to do it better than him. As soon as he saw that my time was better than his, he insisted on doing it again, and this is the kind of person he is."

In intellectual matters, Trudeau functions in two gears. He is gentle with simple people whom he doesn't expect to know a great deal, and vastly tougher with those whom he presumes to have a certain level of sophistication and expertise. Says his sister Suzette: "Pierre's very impatient with people who should know better or do better, who were prepared to do better. On the other hand, he wouldn't lose his temper with somebody who was not too intelligent and he wouldn't lose his temper if he didn't feel the person was able to do better."

Confirms a close associate: "He tends to expect people with the intelligence to know better, to in fact know better. If you're the minister of xyz, he expects you to think like the minister of xyz. He can be merciless on someone who doesn't know his brief." Trudeau's rather formalistic view of who should know what, this associate observes, can occasionally lead him to shift from one gear to the other in mid-discussion: "There was one absolutely remarkable conversation he had with a well-known economist. Until he knew she was an economist, he was answering some rather sophomoric questions with rather patient, simplistic answers. When she identified herself as an economist, he asked her a couple of questions about where she had done her economics. Having decided she was really presenting herself as an economist, he forgot she was also a lady and just demolished her."

In argument with people whom he expects to be knowledgeable, Trudeau is viciously combative. When challenged, he becomes, in the words of one aide, the verbal equivalent of "a street slugger, the kind of guy whom you don't want to give even the slightest push, because he'll break off a wine bottle and start slashing back." In that mood, Trudeau becomes less concerned with the intellectual quality of his arguments than with winning, and is quite prepared to score points by saying things he doesn't really believe or which are scarcely worthy of his intelligence.

"No matter how well you score and how convincingly you score," says Head, "he shakes that off. No matter how weak a point apparently made or a serve put across the net by an adversary — and it doesn't have to be an adversary, it's anybody conducting a discussion with him — he'll return it with full force. He's like the guy who's always up for that game of tennis but whom you never invite to play a social game of mixed doubles, because, by God, when he can put the ball between the eyeballs of the woman at the net, he'll do it. He can't lob. You know, he's volleying full force intellectually all the time."

Trudeau has two favourite debating tricks which he uses to great advantage on unsuspecting opponents. The first is to exaggerate and extrapolate the other person's argument to the point of absurdity, then demolish the extrapolation: If you're arguing against A, you must also be saying B and C, and to argue C makes you a fool or a knave. The second trick, particularly useful when called upon to defend a given policy, is to turn the question back on the interrogator, inviting him to state what he would do differently; Trudeau then attacks the suggested alternative instead of debating the merits of his own course. Consider this exchange with an African journalist:

Q: "How are you fighting apartheid in South Africa?"

A: "How are we fighting it?"

Q: "Yes, how do . . ."

A: "How are *you* fighting it?"

Q: "Well, we show opposition to it. We . . ."

A: "But I haven't seen any African soldiers disembark in South Africa."

Q: "No, that's not what we say you should do, Mr. Prime Minister. How do . . ."

A: "Well, perhaps *I'm* saying *you* should do . . ."

Q: "How do you consciously show that you disapprove of apartheid in South Africa?"

A: "Every resolution on the subject which comes through the United Nations — we supported one again last fall. We indicated our condemnation of that regime, and if it's moral support you want, you have it completely. If it's military support through freedom fighters, I'm suggesting that we're not getting involved in civil wars, and we have the example of countries that do get involved in them, like in Vietnam, and they're generally blamed by the whole world for doing so. . . . I couldn't get the Canadian people to start a war with South Africa."

Q: "I believe that apartheid is a form of slavery and a crime against humanity."

A: "Sure. But what are you doing to help the persecuted in other parts of the world?"[2]

If Trudeau will almost never concede a point in argument, let alone openly admit that he has been wrong about something, he nevertheless does not resent criticism from people he respects. He defends himself fiercely, but he accepts it. A man who was present describes one such instance in 1968 after Trudeau, in the midst of his leadership campaign, had marred the effectiveness of his speech to the Canadian Bar Association by following it with a crude attack on the constitutional arguments of the Quebec government:

"At the conclusion of the conference, there was a small session in the minister's office in Ottawa, and Marc Lalonde took off into Trudeau and just tore strips off him. It was a civilized kind of thing, but all the more rough because of it. You could tell that Marc was just distraught over this kind of thing, and saying: 'Listen, you know we are your friends, we are your supporters, we are your advisors, and we've had such high regard for you, and this kind of activity on your part just makes us wonder.' I have never in my entire adult life heard such a sustained and close to vicious attack on someone, certainly not someone of higher authority. And I just shivered. I was embarrassed to be involved in this. I knew that he and Marc had been colleagues for some time, but not for that long, and I didn't know how Trudeau would react to this.

"And he sat there and it was like water rolling off, there was just no evidence whether any of this was striking home or not. And then he started back at Marc when Marc had finished, and he gave better than he got. But it was in this totally cool, dispassionate way, whereas Marc had had tinges of emotionalism — and of course Marc's was the more human thing, but the PM was all the more devastating because there was none in his. He defended himself, and in a debating sense or even in a dramatic sense I don't know whom you would have awarded most marks to. But it was just incredible how he came back and took it. But I noted the point that should an occasion arise when he had to be told that, in your view, what he had done was absolutely unacceptable, you didn't have to beat around the bush. You have to be ready for what he's going to come back with, for his response, but you do it."

Trudeau slips into a combative mood the moment he feels directly challenged or invited to justify himself: his eyes narrow and become colder, his face hardens, his voice takes on an edgy impatience. If the other person persists, Trudeau's cold anger visibly compresses itself into an icy fury that becomes almost a physical force radiating out toward his antagonist, an effect impressive enough to intimidate all but the most self-assured challenger. Once a question or a remark, however casual, has made Trudeau feel combative, he remains in that mood for the duration of the conversation and it is virtually impossible to get him out of it; even the most innocuous subjects then draw either a cautious or a point-scoring response. On the other hand, if the tone from the outset is mellow and the approach oblique rather than challenging, Trudeau is likely to respond in kind even on subjects he finds unpleasant.

Despite his verbal toughness, Trudeau is a most reluctant butcher of personnel and can seldom bring himself to fire anyone. His reluctance allows ministers and aides to remain on the job long after they have demonstrated their inadequacy. Says Marc Lalonde: "He's not a good manager of personnel. When I was in the PMO, I managed the office. There were some people on staff he was very unhappy with, but he wouldn't fire anyone, he wouldn't tell anybody he was generally unhappy with them. He would complain to me." Head confirms this view: "He has certainly had some persons on staff that he had no confidence in, but he didn't do much about it."

Trudeau's attitude toward his staff is a mixture of consideration and insensitivity. Although the workload itself can be gruelling and he expects his staff to put in whatever long hours are necessary, he takes pains not to intrude unnecessarily on their time. "I've found him extremely considerate to work for, in terms of my own needs and time," says executive assistant Murdoch. "He's always very concerned that he's interfering in my personal life because of my job. He's not the sort of person who makes unreasonable demands that you work late into the night. He has a family that he enjoys being with, and he assumes that other people do, and he's frequently saying, 'You don't have to do this,' or 'You don't have to go there, take some time and be with your family.'"

Trudeau himself puts it this way: "Except in rare occasions, I feel that the problem doesn't have to be solved at half past two in the morning on a Saturday night and therefore I don't want to be disturbed about it, and therefore I feel the same thing about others. I very rarely ever phone them at home and say, 'Gee, this is not a good piece of work, I'd really like you to start over and get it in first thing Monday morning,' or 'Please rush out here with those documents, I don't think it's a good draft and I want you to . . .' "

This is partly a matter of consideration, and partly a reflection of his own desire to maintain a clear division between his work hours and his free time. "I don't bring my government problems to bed with me, and I don't let them invade the absolute time I need for rest or reflection or physical maintenance. And it's in that sense that I don't let those who work with me phone me on a Saturday or a Sunday unless it's absolutely vital. It's for that reason that I don't, except on rare occasions, have staff meetings on Saturday or cabinet gatherings on a holiday. I think it's absolutely vital to my performance, and probably that of my staff, to have a normal family life, and time when they don't have to worry about me and the job."

In addition to respecting the private time of his aides, he is also thoughtful in other ways. He sends flowers to the wives of staff members at Christmas, for instance, and he invariably takes the time to listen and offer advice if a staffer comes to him with a personal problem. But he can also, on occasion, be crashingly insensitive to the feelings of those around him, criticizing their performance or ridiculing their ideas in front of others. Says a close aide: "He'll be as nasty as anyone can possibly be to some-body, and often in front of others. There's a sadistic quality to him sometimes, no question." This aide recalls one particularly painful episode of Trudeau nastiness: "It was back in the days when we had large speech meetings, and we would go through a kind of rehearsal where the person who wrote a speech would read it out and it would be discussed. And on this occasion, the person had really worked his guts out on a speech, and when he finished reading it, the PM uttered just one sentence: 'I'd rather die than give that speech.' In front of all those people! Well, at that point, you know, you just want to say: 'You son of a bitch!' "

Each Trudeau aide goes through a series of phases with the prime minister. When he first joins the staff, there is a period of testing during which Trudeau keeps asking questions about his area of expertise and his work, trying to satisfy himself that the aide knows what he's doing. Once the testing period is success-fully passed, Trudeau tends to step back and delegate a great deal of responsibility to him in his area of specialization. And, finally, if he is really impressed with someone, he may solicit that person's opinion occasionally on matters outside his own assigned field. As long as he is satisfied with the quality of work being done, Trudeau likes to delegate as many tasks as possible. Says Head: "He's very willing to put full responsibility on those he trusts to do things when he delegates. It's not a question of saying, 'I don't want to see this again or hear about it.' It's a full placing of confidence, total confidence, which in itself makes one feel very close to the guy, saying to yourself: 'God, he's really giving me an open-ended letter of credit here!' He tells you, in effect: 'I haven't got time to work out the strategy with you, or the tactic. You know what has to be done. Do it.' " And Trudeau himself says: "I am a great believer in delegation, even in politics, and when I centralize it's because I discover it's the only way in that particular instance to get the thing done."

As he has two gears for dealing with different types of people in discussions, Trudeau also has two operating gears: one for day-to-day business, another for crisis management. In day-to-day decision-making, Trudeau tends to be cautious, slow-moving, in-clined to drag out even minor decisions until they have been examined from every possible angle and a consensus is reached on what should be done. As a top aide puts it: "His biggest fault is that on small things he insists on too much study. Decisions take too long on things that aren't all that important."

But when it comes to crisis management, Trudeau becomes totally different — bolder, crisply decisive, and somehow more serene. Observes Murdoch, in a perception echoed by staffer after staffer: "The more difficult the situation becomes, the more easy he becomes. If things are really tough, he becomes even more considerate and easier to get along with, and he becomes calmer. He's a very calm guy anyway, but as the situation gets tougher he seems to relax."

"In a way," says a veteran minister, "he'd probably be a better prime minister if it was a crisis situation all the time. He's just a different man then — quick, tough, decisive. No more agonizing and mulling over every last detail, just 'yes, to this; no, to that; we'll risk this; I can't accept that other thing.' It isn't that he doesn't consider the decisions carefully, it's just that he's more willing to trust his snap judgment instead of plodding along step by step. And the decisions that emerge are at least as good, and probably better." The whole minority government period between 1972 and 1974 was, in a sense, an instance of Trudeau the crisis manager. Says Head: "In terms of his acting with decisiveness, without hesitation, in those areas where he felt action was necessary, that period was outstanding. There was, I suppose, a sense that this was survival day by day, and that ministers had to be so involved with that survival process that there was no time for the luxury of fiddling about with jurisdictions or niceties or other things. There was no haggling. It was very decisive. It wasn't that he accepted everything, but everything was a quick decision, yes or no."

When he has successfully steered his government through a crisis, or achieved some other success of which he is particularly proud, Trudeau has a habit of rewarding himself with a period of drastically reduced activity. "A strange trait of Trudeau," says one of his closest associates, "is that when he does something well, he'll take a day off, a week off — a year off. It's a reward-for-effort response." The roots of this habit go back to long before he entered politics. "I have always had a peculiar way of working," Trudeau says. "I generally worked very long hours and many weekends at teaching, at writing, or at going around the province for the labour unions. And then I'd take long vacations. Every three years or something, I'd take three or six months off." His duties as prime minister make it impossible for him to leave physically on protracted vacations, but he has translated this habit into a pattern of peaks and valleys in the intensity of his prime-ministerial activities. Every so often, under the guise of pondering a future course, he — and consequently his government — becomes less active and less visible for periods of varying duration. As an associate puts it: "He alternates between an operative mode and a contemplative mode." It was Trudeau's retreat into this contemplative mode, partly as a reward to himself for having survived the tense and hectic minority period, that helped produce his government's nearly disastrous year-long slide into lethargy after the 1974 election.

In this approach to his work, as in some other areas, Trudeau exhibits an occasional tendency to fluctuate between extremes. Says an aide: "There sometimes seems to be a missing element — a missing piece of the mechanism of his monitor, of his balance wheel — that permits him to move in excessive changes of course." This tendency is a product of his determination to do everything to the fullest: he can't lob. He may pay little attention to a given policy area or course of action for years, but once it has captured his interest and imagination, he's liable to pull out all the stops.

A minor, but revealing, example of this tendency was Trudeau's extensive and expensive redecoration of 24 Sussex Drive during the minority government period in 1973. During the three years he had lived in the Château Laurier Hotel and his first four years in the prime minister's official residence, Trudeau took absolutely no interest in the décor of his living quarters. Then, on an official visit to London after the 1972 election, he attended a dinner at 10 Downing Street and was impressed by the changes Prime Minister Edward Heath had wrought on Britain's equivalent of 24 Sussex Drive. In office only a short time, Heath had hastened to imprint his own taste on the residence, which had not been redecorated for several decades, and an aide recalls Trudeau saying: "Isn't it something what he's done with this place. Damnit, when the moment comes, I'm going to do that at 24 Sussex. Why should it be a shabby place? It shouldn't be — it's the showplace of Canada to leaders from abroad."

On his return, Trudeau promptly set about ordering a complete refurbishing of the residence. There was nothing wrong with the initiative as such — Trudeau subsequently declared that he would buy back from the government when he left office any of the costly antique furnishings it might not want to keep at taxpayers' expense — but the scope of the work was politically dangerous and inappropriate at a time when the nearly defeated prime minister was trying to demonstrate humility. Having suddenly decided after all those years to take an interest in his quarters, however, Trudeau preferred to take the political risk rather than settle for half measures.

Despite his obvious enjoyment of such perks as the comfortable prime-ministerial residence, the Harrington Lake retreat, the attentive household staff, and the ease and comfort of his travel, Trudeau does not like the more ostentatious aspects of the prime-ministry. He values those privileges of office which enhance his comfort and convenience, but finds public ostentation embarrassing. "He resists strongly the sort of imperial aspects of being a a prime minister, in terms of going around with a lot of staff or a lot of bodyguards, for instance," says Murdoch. "The trappings have always been things that he's been resistant about rather than encouraging about. Large numbers of staff in public, security, uniforms, big cars, motorcycles — all that kind of stuff, he's been terribly resistant about.

"Motorcycle escorts, for instance: although he really admires the guys who drive motorcycles, he doesn't like those escorts at all, and whenever we can get rid of them, we do. We have them to get us through traffic on trips, because in a big metropolitan centre the only way you can be on time is if you have traffic control, and you either have motorcycles or marked cars. But the moment he can say, 'Well, gosh, I'm going home now and I don't have any other appointments,' that's it. Same thing on staff. I always have to think about the number of people every time we go some place, because he's always saying: 'Haven't we got too much staff along? Why do I need so many people around me?' "

The most ostentatious trapping of Trudeau's prime-ministry, the $76,000 armoured Cadillac limousine, is also not a matter of Trudeau's own preference. He much prefers driving around in his own Mercedes convertible, but he accepted the advice of RCMP security experts that it was essential he use an armoured vehicle for his public travel. Once that decision was made, Murdoch points out, it was inevitable that the vehicle would be big and luxurious: "If he has to have an armoured car, then you're stuck with: 'Well, who makes armoured cars?' You get a Cadillac or you get a Lincoln because that's what there is." Of course, Trudeau drew more attention to the vehicle and increased public suspicions of showboating by opting for a striking silver colour rather than a more conventional black. But Murdoch argues: "I think the colour is a question of personal choice and certainly not a question of saying, 'I'm going to have something that distinguishes me from other people.' We gave him a choice of colours and he said, 'Well, I think I'd rather have this colour than a black one.' "

Trudeau also dislikes having too great a fuss made about his personal safety. Recalls aide Colin Kenny: "On a visit to St. Pierre–Miquelon, we had flown in with two helicopters. The regulations are quite strict for flying the PM over water; he's only supposed to fly if there's a back-up helicopter to pick him out if he goes down. Well, on the morning we were supposed to leave, the place was fogged in, and the Canadian Forces pilot came in and started explaining to the PM that the back-up helicopter was grounded in St. John's and that because of the safety regulations, the PM wouldn't be able to leave on schedule. When he had finished explaining, the PM looked at him and said, 'Major, if I were a general, would we make this flight?' The pilot said: 'Oh, yes, the regulations only apply in your case, because you're prime minister.' The PM said: 'Start the plane.' "

Trudeau especially likes those prime-ministerial perquisites that save him time. Despite the efforts of his staff to ease the burden wherever possible, the demands on his time and attention remain enormous, and time is a commodity Trudeau guards with the utmost jealousy. Any request that he devote some of it to a particular meeting or trip quickly becomes a bargaining session: if an aide asks him to spend half an hour at some event, he wants to know whether it's absolutely necessary, and whether fifteen minutes wouldn't suffice; if a three-day trip is suggested, he presses for a reduction to two. "He's very rigorous when you're presenting time proposals to him," says Murdoch. "It's always 'why? why? why?' "

These time pressures spill over into his private life as well. "I know every evening that I take off during the week, whether it be to go to the ballet or to spend a long dinner with friends, means that I have to work that much longer on the weekend catching up whatever I didn't do that particular night," Trudeau says. "This is not a line that I'm a terribly hard worker, this is a line that there's so much work to do and . . . I'm always surprised to hear that, you know, Mackenzie King was always having people in to dinner and staying late and so on. Well, heck, I thought that would happen a little bit when I married Margaret, that it would get more active. But rather than she influence me, I ended up influencing her. We'd always say, 'Well, we've got to change that, see more people' — and we never would."

Because of these pressures on his time and energies, Trudeau lives in a curious kind of intellectual isolation. He almost never reads a newspaper from beginning to end, relying instead on his staff to prepare a digest of what they think he should know. He finds time to read very few books, except on vacation; before each holiday, he asks a few people whose judgment he respects to each recommend one book he should read. He tries to keep up with changing ideas and trends mostly through meetings and correspondence with primary sources, people as diverse as Alvin Toffler, Herman Kahn, Marshall McLuhan, and, on occasion, someone like John Lennon. He seldom watches television, and sees relatively few movies. The result is that, in a sense, he lives in a different world from most of the public: he doesn't get the over-all impression others do from fully reading a newspaper, doesn't see the TV programs that are occupying or numbing people's minds, doesn't read the latest best-seller that everybody is talking about.

Not only does he find little time to reach outside for new ideas, the emphasis on the here-and-now in his work is also such that Trudeau finds relatively little time to simply think as an intellectual. Asked his thoughts on man's first landing on the moon in 1969 more than two weeks after it had taken place, Trudeau replied: "This is the type of question which makes me feel there are some disadvantages to my job. This is an event of tremendous significance and I really haven't had time to reflect on it. I can't give you the answer I would like, any more than I can give a very well informed answer on other important technological innovations." The "disadvantages", which Trudeau recognizes but is relatively powerless to offset, include the fact that opportunity for intellectual self-renewal while in office is severely limited. As he puts it: "Until I got into politics, I spent the previous ten to fifteen years accumulating ideas about how society should be run, keeping up on all the literature . . . reading what was said, and so on. . . . In a sense, that baggage of acquisitions, intellectual and other, that I had when I came into the party, I'm not able to renew."

If Trudeau has been unable to replenish his intellectual baggage, he has nevertheless matured visibly during his decade in power. Although he still approaches the leadership function with somewhat less enthusiasm than many other politicians, he no longer fears responsibility. "In a sense, the revelation of all this latter period of my life is that I bear responsibility so lightly. Criticism doesn't really demolish me. I don't mean that I am not influenced by it, but it doesn't give me ulcers, and I don't say, 'Gee, we should have done it differently, if only we had done this. . . .' "

He has also recently begun to lower some of his rigid defences, to be more willing to risk being open and vulnerable in talking about himself. Says an advisor and former aide: "For most of his life, he's been what I would call a 'control freak', determined to control any situation he's in, not to leave himself open. Now, being a guy who wants to try everything once, I think he's become more willing to try the other way."

At the same time, paradoxically, greater maturity has also led Trudeau to learn to control himself better in public. There have been far fewer incidents in recent years of unsuitable attire, inappropriate behaviour, and insulting and ultimately self-damaging remarks. Where the earlier Trudeau would undoubtedly have blown his stack, he endured questioning by journalists about his marital troubles in 1977 with great tact and dignity; throughout that difficult period, his remarkable self-discipline allowed him to operate quite normally under close scrutiny, betraying to neither staff nor outsiders his private pain.

Those marital troubles were, in a sense, part of the price he has paid for being prime minister. When any man marries a woman nearly thirty years his junior, there is a good possibility of strain in the marriage. When the man is as inner-directed, disciplined, and rational as Trudeau, and the woman is as outgoing, demanding of attention, and emotionally flighty as Margaret, the chances for serious trouble are greatly magnified. And when, on top of all that, the marriage must cope with the tremendous pressures that a prime minister's job puts on his time and attention, and the strains of living in the limelight, the formula for domestic grief is complete. Margaret's realization, in the wake of the separatist victory in Quebec, that her husband would be unlikely to contemplate getting out of politics for at least several more years was probably what tipped the scale in her decision to leave him in the summer of 1977.

For the most part, despite its personal toll and the aspects he finds difficult, Trudeau thoroughly enjoys his job as prime minister. Though he prefers the broad strokes of government to the day-to-day details, he says: "It's my astonished realization that I can also enjoy administrating. I can rise to that challenge of clearing my desk and making sure that the decisions are taken. But it's not the part of my life that I prefer, and as I've said time and time again to my caucus, 'If we're just here to administer, what the hell are we wasting the best years of our lives for? Let the Tories or some other gang administer. But we're here to try to give direction to the country.' When I feel that I am only administering, that I can't contribute to the creation of tomorrow, certainly I won't have the patience to stay on here."

He finds the work rewarding, on the whole: "I'll concede that I didn't do anything close to what I was hoping to do in terms of quantity and quality, but I am not that frustrated at being able to do nothing that I sort of give up this job in despair. . . . I sort of say I am staying in office because I still think that the kind of realization I am able to do and policy I am able to fulfil, faulty as it may be, is better than [others] would be able to do. In terms of absolutes, I am not doing anything near the kind or the quantity of the things that I would like to be doing. But I'm still immodest enough to think that the kind of government I'm providing, by and large, is chalking up a better record than I think my opponents could do."

Trudeau seldom expresses his innermost feelings, but Ivan Head recalls at least one occasion when he communicated his enjoyment of the job in more visceral terms: "It was around 1970, and we were driving back from a very good meeting at Montebello with a bunch of top people in the international development field, a really stimulating group of people to be with. And during the drive I raised a number of proposals that were attractive to him, and then he turned to some cabinet documents he had to read. And I guess the first one was pretty good, he was only part way through it and he took off his glasses and was looking out the window, and then he turned to me with a big smile and said: 'Ivan, government is fun, isn't it?' "

After a decade in power, some of that initial sense of fun and novelty must inevitably have faded. Had it not been for the victory of the Parti Québécois in Quebec, Trudeau might well have begun contemplating his retirement. But as one of his closest associates and advisors puts it:

"He probably came to be prime minister more against his will than any of the previous ones that I've known. But once he's got the office, he wants to stay on in it — partly because he's got nothing better to do, partly because he thinks he's needed in it, partly because he enjoys it, and partly because his competitive nature and ego drive him against allowing anybody to take it away from him."

CHAPTER ELEVEN

Point of Weakness

To be prime minister is to pose before the nation as an amalgam of diverse and rare talents — as wise and dynamic policy-maker, inspiring national leader, shrewd partisan politician, eagerly followed captain of cabinet and party, deft crisis manager, and efficient administrator. Every occupant of the post is expected to have all those skills in full measure, and none does; each is inevitably deficient in some area, the only question being how grave the flaws are and whether they ultimately prove to be crippling. In Trudeau's case, the greatest weakness is in the human-relations aspects of political leadership.

It is here that his sensitivity, his self-discipline, and his pursuit of his own freedom combine to cause him serious difficulty. Sensitive, he protects himself by holding the people around him at arm's length, behind a barrier of apparent coldness. Having disciplined himself to be immune to most forms of criticism or praise, he cannot understand why others are not similarly indifferent. And, determined to preserve his freedom and independence, he cannot bring himself to admit that he needs or depends on anyone else. The result is a style of leadership quite different from the informal, pep-talking, manipulative approach most North Americans have come to expect; in its austere aloofness, it comes somewhat closer to the manner of French presidents. And its price — politically costly at times — is to make him a leader respected and followed, but generally unloved.

Says Mitchell Sharp: "One of Trudeau's serious faults is his lack of sensitivity to human relations. He has never been able to generate a feeling amongst his followers that any individual follower is important to him, except for close personal friends like Marchand and Pelletier. He doesn't have any skill in human relations. He told me once: 'I find the most difficult part of this job is dealing with people.' He's a man who inspires, but who seems to lack warmth in his personal relations. I've heard this from so many people. They're here, they're gone, with never any appreciation expressed. He never says, 'I'd like you to help me.' It has had an understandable effect. A minister said to me the other day: 'Why is it that whenever Pearson was in difficulty everybody came to his help, and with Trudeau everybody says he can take care of himself?' I think that's why."

Echoes Donald Macdonald: "There's one area where he does have weakness, and that's dealing with people. You know, he's a very private person himself and he doesn't, I think, have a great deal of empathy for other people, and he can fail to comprehend or sympathize with other people's situations. I don't think he's deliberately callous, but the opportunity to be warm and sympathetic on some particular question — the kind of thing which instinctively comes to many people — won't come to him, and some of the difficulties he's had with colleagues have been related to that."

And Marc Lalonde puts it this way: "He has never been a manager of people. He was very much the individual working on a project. His staff will say, 'You should mention something to this minister, congratulate him.' And sometimes he will do it — but very rarely. He's not the type of guy to whom it will come naturally to go out of his way. A guy like Pearson was continually pouring oil over the system, and everybody always came to his rescue because he needed help. Trudeau never appears to need help, he is not a guy who is inclined to go out and ask for help — he will not do it. Is it pride? I don't think so. It's being his own free man."

Trudeau's avoidance of the personal touch sometimes goes to strange and self-damaging lengths. He deeply wounded Sharp, one of his most loyal ministers, by never once inquiring about Sharp's first wife during the many years she suffered an incapacitating illness before her death in 1975. Similarly, when the wife of another senior minister underwent major surgery, Trudeau never expressed a word of sympathy or concern.

The explanation does not lie simply in coldness or lack of in-

terest, because on other occasions Trudeau has been strikingly
solicitous. When Ivan Head was at a crisis point in his marriage
and deeply upset, the prime minister insisted on clearing large
chunks of his schedule and spending hours sympathetically discussing the situation. Recalls Head: "He said, 'This is more important. If we can't take time to be human in our own relationships,
what the hell is the rest of it worth?' It was an absolutely incredible
kind of thing. If one is in difficulty or has some overwhelming personal problem, he — unlike almost anyone I have ever known —
can sense that and is willing to cancel appointments, virtually to
put the ship of state in neutral."

Another man, with whom Trudeau has had occasion to work
closely but who is by no means a personal friend, had a similar
experience: "On the day my wife and I separated, I asked to see
the prime minister, because I felt he should know. I'd never talked
to him about a personal thing in my life, and I just said: 'I think
you should know that today I've separated from my wife.' And he
said, 'Well, I'm not inhibited by any particular knowledge of your
wife, but this has happened to a lot of my friends and a lot of
people in this age, and it's not a problem as far as working with me
is concerned.' And then he said, 'Look, why don't you come up to
the house tonight and we'll just talk about it.' Well, I hadn't come
to him for sympathy, and I was just taken aback, because I don't
think he reaches out to many guys like that."

These instances, in the way they differ from the experiences of
Sharp and the other minister, suggest a partial explanation of
Trudeau's attitude: In the instances where he showed interest and
sympathy, it was the other person who took the initiative in mentioning the problem. It seems that Trudeau's over-developed sense
of privacy inhibits him from initiating any mention of the private
problems of others, even to express sympathy, for fear that he
might be intruding. In Head's case, he had known about the marital
difficulties for months, but said nothing until Head broached the
subject. "I told him I had problems," Head recalls, "and he came
back and said, 'Yes, Margaret had told me six months ago that you
and your wife were having problems.' He had known for six
months, but he was not going to take the initiative."

Another part of the explanation seems to be a feeling that expressions of sympathy do nothing to help the recipient; rational to a fault, he apparently believes that a person who has troubles won't feel any better just because Pierre Trudeau says he's sorry. If an aide has suffered an accident or other misfortune, Trudeau will ask others about it with great concern, but will seldom say anything directly to the person. Instead, he will go out of his way to be friendly and considerate in some other manner, most often by paying the person the compliment of soliciting his advice or discussing his proposals with particular interest. "If you have troubles, he won't talk about it," says Jim Coutts. "But he feels the best and nicest thing he can do for you is to take your ideas seriously."

If Trudeau has offended some people by appearing indifferent to their problems, he has forfeited an additional measure of loyalty from most others by refusing to give his working relationships a personal dimension. His work and his private life are kept rigorously separate, and he does not normally socialize even with the most senior ministers. "Mr. Pearson was a friend," says a veteran of both men's cabinets. "I don't look upon Pierre Trudeau as a friend. He's friendly enough, but he's not the sort of person I would ever want to discuss personal problems with. I would never ask anything from him. My feeling would be that if I were to ask anything from him, it would diminish me in his eyes. He would never ask me for anything, I would never ask him for anything. You would think that over a period of years, relations would be different, that some sort of feeling would develop. . . . Perhaps that's good for a prime minister, not to extend himself — but I never felt that way about Pearson."

One reason for Trudeau's unwillingness to socialize with his ministers is that he does not find politicians, as a breed, particularly interesting private company. Outside his work, he much prefers to be with people with whom he can discuss philosophical ideas or explore interests outside his areas of greatest expertise, whether it be deep-sea diving, or architecture, or sociology, or a host of other subjects. He also finds it necessary for his general equilibrium to distance himself from politics in his free time: "It's a desire to save part of my life for myself and my sanity. I don't know if it's singular to me, but it's a need to be removed from the scene of the battle from time to time, and seeing somebody who's battling along with me might tend to drift back to the job. I mean, you know, politicians get together even over dinner and they end up talking politics, so the result is that not too many politicians end up having dinner with me."

The wall of privacy Trudeau has erected is so forbidding that even the associates who are closest to him and like him most feel there are barriers they ought not cross, a feeling that results in an extraordinary mix of attitudes.

"I do like him," says Marc Lalonde. "I'd go to war for him. But it's not the type of warm friendship that you would feel with a guy you would call a real pal. I would have to force myself a lot to phone him and suggest a movie or something. I would feel I was imposing on him."

Says Head: "He's one of the few men that I unabashedly say I love, in the sense that you love your family. He has an immense attractiveness to me as a person who represents something, a guy who is committed to discharging a terribly important task that he did not seek for himself, and who, when you scratch down deep enough, is really a very unassuming, compassionate human being." But Head also says that when Trudeau's first son was born in 1971, he had great difficulty deciding whether to call and offer congratulations: "I had to debate with myself, I remember batting it back and forth with my wife: 'Do I phone to congratulate him, or how would he react to my interfering in his personal life?' And she was pretty disgusted that I would even hesitate on this kind of thing, and I finally decided to phone. He was at the hospital, of course, and his response was just overwhelming. You know, he was just so pleased, and it was clear that nobody else had dared do it."

Even within the sphere of political activity, Trudeau refuses to employ the conventional artifices of leadership. When one of his ministers gets into political trouble, Trudeau is loyal — sometimes to a fault — and will never throw anyone to the wolves. But beyond that, he makes no active effort to inspire individual loyalty. He won't make any minister feel specially important, won't express gratitude, and won't ask anyone to remain in office as a favour or a duty. "He doesn't play cliques and insists on remaining an honest person," says one of his closest advisors and associates. "He doesn't get into bed with you politically, doesn't give the impression of saying, 'Come on, we'll screw so-and-so.' That's a basic attribute of Anglo-Saxon leadership, that sort of camaraderie, but that would be a dishonest game in Trudeau's mind, and he won't play it."

Trudeau's unwillingness to express appreciation is rooted in the basic elements of his personality. If the early Greek philosophers believed that man is the measure of all things, Trudeau too often believes that he is the measure of all men. Because he has trained himself to be inner-directed and not to depend on praise — indeed, to sidestep it whenever possible — he assumes that others feel the same way. And even when he realizes that this is not the case, something still inhibits him from expressing appreciation.

"I think it's a flaw in my character, quite frankly," he says. "When I see the pleasure I could give people by saying, 'Jeez, you've been doing a good job,' you know, and I don't do it . . . there's something wrong. I should be . . . I guess in a sense it's perhaps a different code of behaviour. It seems to me when you're on a team and you're doing a good job, if you're kept on the team that's the proof that you're doing a good job. But it probably would be nice if one expressed it.

"Maybe there's a family trait there. We were never a gushing family, never great extroverts, and rather early on — I mean after we'd ceased being kids — we kind of made an agreement that we weren't going to spend our life exchanging gifts on a birthday or on a Christmas or a New Year's or an Easter. We know we love each other in the family, and we don't spend our time telling it to each other. Phone calls between my brother and myself and my sister or nephew are very few and far between. If my friends knew that, they wouldn't feel sort of left out as friends, because they'd know that's the way we are. And we know that if there's a jam or a problem, then we can see each other and we'll do a hell of a lot for each other. But it's the kind of thing that almost goes without saying. That's amongst adults; kids, yes — I always take a day or two off before Christmas to try and find something for my nieces and nephew, things like that. But I won't bother shopping for my sister or my brother.

"It's, as I say, a kind of flaw in our characters, a desire to be absolute individualists and assume that the other is the same way, and that therefore we don't have to spend a lot of time telling him that he's a good man, because he should see it in your eyes, I suppose."

Trudeau's reluctance to express appreciation is exceeded only by his unwillingness to ask anyone for help. Cyrano's "To climb not very high, perhaps, but all alone" is still his motto in that sense, buttressed by a fear of rejection and by some very rational — but psychologically unsound — ideas about what should motivate people to act. Whether he is dealing with individuals or with the nation at large, Trudeau can almost never bring himself to make appeals on a personal basis, even though he realizes that failure to do it can be politically costly:

"One of the things that I'm often told by Liberals or advisors or something is, 'Go out and tell the people that you really need them, and that you need their help and so on.' And my first inclination is to say: 'Well, you know, if they believe in the things we're fighting for, it's obvious that I need them and therefore why should I tell them?' But sometimes it comes. It comes instinctively on the question of national unity. I was telling ethnic Canadians at a recent meeting, 'We really need you to help Canadians understand what they're doing to themselves and what they can be doing.' But in a sense, it's less me crying for help from them, it's telling them, 'Jeez, the country needs your help.'

"I guess there's a bit of pride there, too. A mixture of pride on the one hand, of not wanting to go around begging people to help me, much more the attitude of 'Well, if they think I'm right, they should be helping me; if they don't think I'm right, they shouldn't.' But it's also a feeling that the object of the exercise is not to help me, it's to help whatever ideas or legislation or policy or cause we believe in. I know this is not good in terms of human relations. . . . I don't know what more I can say."

This reluctance to ask for help also extends to an unwillingness to pressure ministers or senior aides into remaining on the job if they want to leave. Says a top civil servant: "There have been resignations from his personal staff and PCO staff, some of them very key people, where the PM could have got one of those people to stay by saying, 'Don't leave, I need you,' or 'You owe it to your country.' The PM has not, to my knowledge, used that approach on anyone. The reason, he has told me, is because it's repugnant to him. He believes that at particular points in time people become ripe for a change, and they are the only ones who can judge when that time has come. There was a point when I decided to return to private life, and I went to the PM and he said: 'Fine — a man's life is like a fruit on a tree, there's a point at which it ripens to the point where he must drop off.'

"That's not at all what Pearson would have done. He would say: 'For God's sake, you can't leave me now.' He would have said that even if he knew he was resigning tomorrow and you had a once-in-a-lifetime opportunity for which tomorrow would be too late. A prime minister has every right to act that way. That's one of the differences between the two men. Trudeau would not interfere with anyone's private life. He would act as if you were just not necessary — although, having dealt with those situations, I know he's desperately anxious that the fellow not do it."

Trudeau has a fundamental belief that it would be a misuse of power for him to use the moral authority of his office to pressure any individual because, as he puts it, "the individual destiny is more important than the institution." Unwilling to have anyone impose fetters on his own freedom of choice, he cannot bring himself to do it to others. But his sense of freedom also plays a role in another way: to express a vital need for any individual is to become beholden to him if he agrees to stay on, and that debt of gratitude would strike Trudeau as a limitation on his own independence.

Trudeau's impersonal approach is, as he himself recognizes, an abdication of some of the levers of power available to a prime minister. People's emotional needs don't always correspond to the laws of rationality, and being leader of a nation endows a man with a special emotional role. The job itself makes him an embodiment of cherished values, and the people who work with him are likely to be motivated to some degree by admiration and respect. His word, therefore — be it to praise, blame, or persuade — carries a weight immeasurably greater than anyone else's, even among presumably sophisticated and hardened aides and ministers. His commiseration on a misfortune is likely to be viewed not as intrusion but as the sealing of a human bond; his praise of a given piece of work, far from being irrelevant, may be essential to an individual's continued good performance; his urgings that a minister or aide remain on the job might be not unfair arm-twisting, but needed reassurance that the person's contribution is really important and appreciated.

Considering that he never had to motivate or manage anyone except himself until he became justice minister at the age of forty-seven, he has not fared as badly as he might have: he has succeeded in imposing order and cohesion on his cabinet, with few leaks or noisy cabinet splits. His ministers respect Trudeau and few are eager to cross swords with him. But what his style fails to inspire is any sense of loyalty or dedication to him as a person; most people have no urge to make personal sacrifices to help this prime minister. In a sense, he has created exactly what his style invites and what he professes to want: a government of autonomous individuals who feel they owe their leader nothing personal and who make their career decisions on the basis of what strikes them as rational for their own good, with scant concern for the impact on Pierre Trudeau and his fortunes. However comfortably that may fit with Trudeau's personality, the political consequences have sometimes cost him dearly.

Trudeau's weakness in human relations was never more costly than when it contributed in 1975 to John Turner's departure from the government, a departure that deprived the cabinet of its strongest member from English Canada, weighed heavily in the decision to impose economic controls, and helped put the government into a tailspin from which it might never have recovered had it not been for the separatist victory in Quebec. Turner did not leave over any policy dispute. A variety of factors — financial, domestic, and political — went into his decision to retire, but above all he left because he had grown bored and frustrated working with a prime minister who didn't particularly like him, who seldom praised him, and who refused to make him feel special. Trudeau himself recognizes this:

"I had a lot of admiration for Turner, I had a lot of time for him in a political sense. He generally was right on when we'd be talking about politics and his feeling for the country and whether we could get by with this now or whether we couldn't. He wasn't always right, nobody is. But, you know, he's the kind of guy that in political terms I thought was one hell of a guy. And I think he knew that, because when there was an important political decision to make and I'd bring in a few guys to make the end decision, Turner was always one of them. It wasn't just because he had clout and a strong backing, it was because I thought he was a good politician.

"I think what went wrong is that we both sensed it was too bad that there wasn't more than that to it, that we weren't also closer personal friends, and that, for instance, I'd see Gérard Pelletier more often than I would John Turner. But what John probably doesn't realize is that with Pelletier, we'd talk about other things than politics. . . . Long before [Turner left], I sensed a certain malaise, but I didn't think it was a political malaise. I thought it was the fact that the guy has a hell of a lot of qualities and why the hell should he stay in a job that was without . . . well, when the boss or prime minister isn't his friend and associate and so on. John and I both made efforts to see a little more of each other, and when we did, it was fun. You know, we met in Jamaica once and we'd invite each other over to dinner from time to time, but I guess the problem is it was always business, very rarely just pleasure. And when John told me, 'I'm getting out because I want to have more time with my family and kids,' to me it meant exactly that. . . . I accepted that decision because I respected it, and I think he was telling me the truth rather than looking for a way out. There may have been a lot of other reasons why he also found the life unsatisfying, and I've tried to be candid in saying that it was perhaps not the kind of camaraderie that John likes to see in the people he works with."

Despite his outward confidence, Turner was the sort of politician who badly needs to be appreciated and who suffers most from the aloof Trudeau style. The product of a social if not an economic élite, he regarded political office as a sort of priesthood, a public service that deserved constant acknowledgment of the self-sacrifice involved. "He needed people to tell him all the time, 'It's really great that you're doing this, you could be doing anything, you could be off making $500,000; it's great that you're doing this for your country,' " says an insider who knows him well.

Instead, he found himself with a prime minister who considers political involvement a basic human duty and who didn't think Turner was being particularly heroic at all. Worse, Trudeau wouldn't even fulfil Turner's need to be considered special within the cabinet; the prime minister acknowledged that Turner was probably his heir apparent, but refused to provide a sense of camaraderie, a feeling that he and Turner were running the country together. Turner considered himself superior to every other minister in the cabinet, and desperately wanted Trudeau to tell him: "It's you and me, John. If it weren't for you and me . . ." If pressed hard enough, Trudeau would probably have told him instead that yes, he was a good and valued minister, but so was this or that cabinet colleague. Another prime minister, sensing this need in one of his ministers, would probably have flattered him a little and told him what he wanted to hear; words of praise, spoken in private, are relatively cheap. To Trudeau, however, that would have been both dishonest and distasteful, and he rejected it as too high a price to pay for Turner's loyalty.

Besides feeling these increasingly gnawing frustrations, Turner felt politically trapped. He wanted very badly to become prime minister, and the finance portfolio is the traditional graveyard of such ambitions. Trudeau showed no signs of wanting to let him out of it, and Turner could see that the economy was heading into ever more stormy waters. He had a terror, too, of becoming another Paul Martin, a political face grown stale and over-familiar in a society that craves novelty. He concluded by the summer of 1975 that if he had any chance left of salvaging his prime-ministerial dreams, it lay in leaving the government and then returning — fresh and hopefully untarnished — whenever Trudeau vacated the leadership.

That conclusion had been building for several years. Says Senator Keith Davey, the Liberal Party's chief political strategist:

"Turner is a very old friend of mine — we've been great friends since 1962 — and once a quarter we'd have dinner and just kick things around. When my appointment was about to be made in 1973 as the campaign chairman for the next election, I talked to John and said I wanted to know what he thought about it; he was all in favour. And I said: 'Well, John, I just want to make one point — to the extent that I succeed [in winning the election for Trudeau], you may never be prime minister of Canada.' He said: 'I understand that. Give it all you've got.'

"Then, in the course of the campaign, I said to him: 'Early on, at some point, what we've got to do is assess your position once the election is over.' On election night, John came into 24 Sussex with his wife and he came over to me and congratulated me and said: 'Remember our last conversation? Let's get together soon.' So we got together within two or three weeks of the election; we had dinner and we decided that John should make an assessment in two years. If the prime minister was going to stay on, John should leave and get into private life and make some money. If it looked like he was going to leave, John should stay and contest the convention. Well, by the middle of 1975, John had decided that he didn't want to be this generation's Paul Martin, so he opted out.

"Knowing John very well, I'm sure he'd want the prime minister to get down on his bended knee and say, 'John, we've got these terrible problems. We can solve them together, and please don't leave.' The prime minister didn't do that. He was very professional. He urged John to stay, but John was determined to leave and I think it's just that simple."

What happened in Trudeau's office on September 10, 1975, was a classic example of failure to communicate. Turner had already told his deputy minister, several friends, and at least one journalist that he had decided to resign, but he was still ambivalent. His decision to leave was genuine, but he also believed that he was indispensable to the government, and he wanted to be pressed into making the sacrifice of staying. But the atmosphere between the two men was by then so guarded and bristly that they missed each other's signals. Trudeau wanted Turner to stay, but the minister's ambivalence was so alien to him that he didn't recognize it; rational as ever, he assumed that a man of Turner's experience and stature wouldn't insist that he was leaving unless he meant it. Had Trudeau recognized that Turner literally wanted to be begged, of course, it is still most unlikely that he would have done so.

Turner opened the exchange by saying, in effect: "I've decided to get out." Had Trudeau said, "I understand what you're going through, how tough it is, but I need you and the country needs you, what you're doing is so important," the lines of communication might have remained open. Instead, the prime minister expressed puzzlement: "That doesn't make any sense. Why would you want to get out? You're likely to be the next leader, you've got everything. I don't understand." Turner went through all his reasons, and Trudeau responded, in effect: "Well, if you've made up your mind, I respect your decision. What are you going to do?" Turner said he didn't know, and Trudeau asked if he'd like to be a senator or a judge. Turner took the offer of those traditional resting places for burnt-out politicians as an insult, and the tone of the conversation became considerably sharper. Later in the discussion, Trudeau offered to move him out of the perilous finance portfolio, perhaps to transport, but by then Turner was in no mood to consider anything. He found himself — somewhat to his own surprise — actually implementing his decision to leave politics, and he strode out of Trudeau's office feeling furious and betrayed.

Trudeau recognizes his role in Turner's departure: "I probably should have made John feel more wanted, more necessary, more desired, more useful, and in the interview when he told me that he was leaving, I probably should have pressed him a hell of a lot more to stay on, and used all those phrases that we need him and he should be here and so on." But that admission is made in a tone that brings to mind an old European proverb that Trudeau sometimes quotes: "If grandmother had wheels, she'd be a trolleybus." For Turner to be dissuaded from leaving would have required more than just pressure; it would have taken outright pleading, what Keith Davey calls "an un-Trudeau-like statement" — and that would have been so foreign to Trudeau's character as to be outside the realm of possibility. To most conventional politicians in that situation, the right words of flattery and appreciation would have come almost instinctively, without qualm or hesitation. But Trudeau is no conventional politician, and that unconventionality — a virtue in some contexts, a vice in others — gives a human-relations mishap like Turner's departure an air of historic inevitability.

Trudeau's weakness in human relations also extends, at times, to dealings with the press and the public as a whole. His relationship with the press has been an unusual one, characterized by a curious detachment on his part and an intense personal dislike on the part of many journalists. Though the relationship has improved markedly since the separatist victory in Quebec, Trudeau has managed — through his own fault — to spend much of his prime-ministry being seen by the Canadian public through the eyes of a press that viewed him with sour hostility.

In his handling of the press, as in his manner of dealing with ministers and aides, Trudeau renounced one of the traditional levers of power available to a prime minister. The opinion most Canadians have of their prime minister is derived not from personal contact, but from the impressions they form as a result of what they read in their newspapers and see on TV. And that journalistic coverage, in turn, is inevitably shaped by the perceptions and attitudes of individual reporters; political journalism cannot be "objective", only fair, and even the most fair journalist cannot entirely avoid having his perceptions of a leader's actions and likely motives coloured by any intense liking or dislike he may feel for the man. Most politicians, realizing this, go out of their way to court the press and maintain friendly relations, but Trudeau has been uncompromising in refusing to disguise or embellish his true feelings.

He recognizes the power of the press, and rather mistrusts it. There is a danger, he wrote in 1967, "that mass media — to the extent that they claim to reflect public opinion — constitute a vehicle for error, if not indeed an instrument of oppression. For my part, I have never been able to read newspapers without a sense of uneasiness, especially newspapers of opinion. They follow their customers and are therefore always lagging behind reality."[1]

He still holds that view today: "I do feel that the press can exercise a tyranny, and they are a power which like every other power has to be analysed, studied, controlled, and criticized if necessary. I would suppose I am critical of the press in the same sense that I am critical of, say, a provincial government doing certain things, or of our own government, or of corporate power or trade union power doing certain things. I think the press is as deserving of criticism as are the executive, legislative, and judicial branches of government. They are the fourth estate and they exercise a lot of power and I look at them critically. I don't think I am more unfair or hostile to them than I would be to others exercising power; I think the press, the media, are more sensitive to criticism than most others and for that reason I think that they sometimes submit to double standards. But I think they have a very important role to play, and I by no means would try to suppress that role. . . . And one thing is certain: I have no vendetta, I have no grudges with the press."

Trudeau is right in his perception of the press as rather thin-skinned, but what has wounded the sensibilities of individual journalists even more than his occasional criticisms is the impression he gives of simply not caring. Trudeau has always, even before entering politics, kept newspapers and TV at arm's length. Indeed, for a man who prides himself on being knowledgeable in a broad range of fields, he has always manifested a curious lack of interest in day-to-day news. Even in the 1950s, when he was actively involved in commenting on developments in Quebec and abroad, he was disinterested in newspapers: "I never read in those days *La Presse* or the *Montreal Star* or *The Gazette* or the *Globe and Mail* or *Le Soleil* or *Le Nouvelliste*. I did read *Le Devoir* off and on. . . . It wasn't because I despised in any sense these people, or thought that they weren't doing a good job, it's just an aspect that didn't interest me very much. Before getting into politics, I wasn't very much bothered by day-by-day events and I'd rather read a book a week than seven newspapers a week."

Even now, Trudeau virtually never reads a newspaper from beginning to end. "I do look at the *Globe and Mail* a few minutes in the morning when I have time, but certainly don't read any article that's on the inside pages. And that's not through contempt. I think it's the job of the people around me to keep me posted about the important facts of the day or of the hour. . . . I look at the first pages of *Le Devoir*, *The Gazette*, and the *Globe and Mail*. And in the evening occasionally I'll look at the first page of the *Citizen* and the *Journal*. Just luck of the draw, these are the papers that happen to come to Sussex Drive. I suppose if they sent the *Toronto Star*, I'd probably look at the first page of that, too. And when I have a bit of time, I'll look at the editorial page — very rarely to read it, but to look at the subjects they deal with, relying on the almost-certainty that if there is something of importance to me it will be put in my clippings and then I'll glance through them during the House."

In making no secret of the fact that he seldom reads or watches the news, Trudeau wounds journalists in their sense of self-importance. Worse, he underlines to them how little weight they carry with him, taking pains on occasion to emphasize how little importance he attaches to what is written about him: "I suppose this is not flattering, but I can't remember the names of those who have been particularly unkind to me. And if I meet them, I'm just as liable to smile at somebody who has been unkind to me as at one who has been very kind to me. So I'm not overly bothered by it. I think they have an important role to play, but as one who doesn't like to be tyrannized by public opinion, I guess I don't let myself be overly influenced by the press."

Unlike most politicians, Trudeau makes virtually no personal effort to secure sympathetic coverage. He is not above manipulating the press through the timing and manner of making announcements, but he refuses to seek favour by catering in any way to the wishes and vanities of journalists. "I don't have much time for anybody in this job, including my wife and kids, and even less for my friends, and therefore I don't have much time for the press, in the sense that I don't curry their favour or try to be palsy-walsy with them or butter them up. I know that some politicians think it's part of their job to be nice with the press. You know, it pays off. I don't despise those who do that, I just don't have time to do it. And, you know, I've been told hundreds of times I should have four or five press people at the end of the afternoon having a drink around this office. Quite frankly, at the end of the afternoon when I finish my work, I'd rather go home and see my kids."

When he does meet with journalists, particularly in press conferences and broadcast interviews, Trudeau tends to be far more candid and outspoken than most political leaders. He will sometimes sidestep a question or slough it off with an inadequate answer, but surprisingly often he says exactly what he is thinking. Unfortunately for his relations with the press during most of his years in power, what he was often thinking was that the reporter asking the question was rather stupid.

Trudeau's view of journalists — like his view of ministers, officials, and other people carrying out specialized functions — is quite formalistic: anyone who presents himself as qualified to perform a given task must be presumed to have all the expertise desirable for that task. Applied to journalists, that means expecting them to be thoroughly knowledgeable about any subject on which they want to question him. In theory, that's a fair expectation; in practice, it doesn't work that way. A reporter in Ottawa may have to cover as many as two or three stories a day, ranging across as many possible subject areas as there are departments. On any given day, he may find himself having to report on charges that federal energy officials helped form an illegal uranium cartel, a protest by a group of Indians over the federal stance in negotiations on a land claim, and an announcement by the agriculture minister of a change in milk subsidies. And he must, to report each story, become an "instant expert" on some area of activity that occupies the full-time attention of dozens of bureaucrats, if not of a whole department. Under those conditions, no one can develop really satisfactory expertise in any one area. A certain number of journalists are nevertheless able to do a remarkably good job of quickly assimilating, assessing, and conveying new information; many others — undereducated, underpaid, and overworked — aren't. For broadcast journalists, especially radio reporters, the situation is further complicated by the eccentric demands of the medium: they are expected to ask questions which will elicit short, punchy answers that can be edited to fill perhaps thirty seconds of on-air time — a requirement that scarcely lends itself to thoughtful, subtle inquiries.

For too long, Trudeau didn't understand these limitations. If a journalist betrayed ignorance of his subject matter, asked Trudeau a question that struck him as silly, or couldn't grasp one of his answers, Trudeau made no attempt to hide his scorn. He would cut down the questioner with abrupt impatience or withering sarcasm, thereby earning the victim's lasting enmity. Beneath their veneer of professional cynicism, most journalists are as sensitive to the special aura of a prime minister as the next person, and they are secretly eager to have him respect them and consider them intelligent. Every time Trudeau made one of them look silly in front of colleagues with a cutting put-down, he made himself another enemy just itching for the chance to demonstrate in print or on the air that this prime minister wasn't so clever himself.

✓ Trudeau's treatment of journalists has improved considerably in recent years. At the weekly press conferences he instituted after the Parti Québécois came to power — he had actually offered such regular conferences after the 1972 election, but had been turned down by the Parliamentary Press Gallery, which feared news management — he has been soft-spoken, witty, and sometimes gracefully candid. His view of the press as an institution hasn't really changed, but he has shifted the blame: "I don't think there is enough professionalism among members of the press. . . . I demand of them standards of professionalism, and I don't think they always meet those standards. . . . But I was once very annoyed at some bad reporting, and somebody told me: 'Do you know how much these people are paid?' And really, you know, they are very badly paid when you consider the role they have to play, to inform a whole nation of what has been done or said by a government or a minister or some important person. It's bad work, but it's done by unprofessional guys who perhaps have to moonlight or who don't have time to do good work. That's all! And I think this is a reflection not on my attitude to the press, but perhaps the attitude of newspaper owners and publishers toward the importance of the job. What are they trying to sell?"

As Trudeau has curbed his tendency to be sharp with journalists, his mellower attitude has paid dividends. Much of the Press Gallery membership, viewing him with new respect in the light of his efforts to preserve national unity, has in turn warmed to him to a surprising degree. In fact, the atmosphere at his press conferences has at times been somewhat too cordial and deferential rather than hard-hitting, as if people feared to shatter the newly found rapport.

The tempestuousness of Trudeau's relationship with the Canadian public has similarly been due, at least in part, to his uncompromising attitude toward human relations. People are used to having their politicians approach the electorate in a suppliant pose, asking for votes and support, but Trudeau won't play that game. Instead, he says, in effect: "I am what I am — take it or leave it."

As he puts it: "I want to do better *for me*, and I refuse to be judged by the standards of others. I set my standards as high as I can from time to time and I want to judge myself by them, and I guess that's also the explanation why I am not, or pretend not to be, too influenced by the judgment of others, particularly the media. I don't care what they think, it's what I think which is important. . . . I don't care if I don't make it, providing I don't need anyone else's help, providing what I do make I make alone, without begging for favours. That's why I say from time to time, 'If people don't want to vote for me, they don't have to vote for me.' And I really feel that way deep down. As a matter of fact, I feel more that way deep down than I feel so officially, because in the operative sense of course I need their votes if I want to implement the kind of policies I believe in and if I want to lead the party I'm leading. And I'm not a fool enough not to know that when the Gallup Polls are very bad, people in my party will begin to say, 'Gee, . . . '. So, in a superficial sense, I'm not insensitive to praise or blame or to positive or negative Gallup Polls."

As he resists telling people in government or the press what they want to hear, so too Trudeau has no taste for buttering up the public. He hasn't hesitated to scold Canadians as group, to say their priorities are wrong, their expectations unrealistic. Indeed, some of his earlier episodes of behaviour inappropriate for a prime minister may have been, at least subconsciously, attempts to prove he was still his own man. He himself, referring to "some hostility that I have towards authority which makes me love freedom so much", suggests that "hopefully now I'm more mature and I am more, I guess, identified with authority and I have accepted that you can be free within social constraints and rules and so on." But it isn't necessarily quite that simple. Becoming the nation's highest authority figure didn't necessarily leave him without any authority to resist against; it may simply have changed the identity of that authority. If the ordinary individual in society is subject to the authority of the state, the highest authority for the leader of a democratic state is the public. When he behaved and spoke in ways he must have known the public would find unacceptable, Trudeau may simply have been challenging the latest authority in his life just as he had challenged his teachers, his church, and the state.

Although he no longer displays that sort of immaturity, he still insists on a verbal honesty that sets him apart from most politicians. He is determined in most situations to say exactly what he thinks, whether it will please or offend, and he goes out of his way to resist when advisors urge him to restrain himself.

Says a close associate: "During the 1974 election, the support of the *Toronto Star* was considered crucial. Coutts took him up to see their top people and he told Trudeau, 'We can probably get them, just go along a bit on economic nationalism.' Trudeau said he wouldn't. Coutts and Davey said, 'So don't, we'll get around it somehow, we'll make sure it doesn't come up, don't say anything about it.' Well, I don't know if he mentioned it himself, but one way or another the topic came up, and he made it clear what he thought of economic nationalism — and the whole thing blew up."

Davey recalls another similarly hair-raising experience at the start of the 1974 campaign when Trudeau was introduced to a key group of new Liberal organizers at Toronto's Lichee Garden restaurant: "He came down there and it was really an incredibly awful performance. One of these guys said, 'I have a friend, Mr. Prime Minister, a kid who lives in Scarborough, who wants very much to buy a house and he just can't afford to, the prices are so terribly high. What will I say to him?' And I remember the prime minister saying: 'Tell him to move to Regina.' And it was just — God, it was just awful!"

Trudeau's forthrightness only occasionally reaches such self-damaging extremes, but he always puts strict limits on the personal concessions he will make to court public favour. Says Coutts: "He's got a different style for every occasion. On how he says things, he's open to advice. You know, 'Should we do the fighting stance, or be very philosophical, or very quiet, or sneak up on them?' But what he won't change is the substance. He just won't say something he doesn't believe." The public, unaccustomed to such an uncompromising attitude in a politician and lacking a better label for it, tends to call it arrogance. It is actually something far more complex, a guarding of identity that requires no small measure of confidence, and it alternates between being a political blessing and a curse. When people are generally dissatisfied with him, it turns their irritation into fury; at other times, it is seen as a reflection of a steely inner strength and independence that contributes mightily to his charisma.

CHAPTER TWELVE

The Trudeau Years I: Experimenting with Power

TRUDEAU's decade in power breaks down into four major periods, each distinct not only in the tone and style of his government but also in the incarnation of the man himself: the 1968-72 experiment; the 1972-74 scramble to survive as a minority government; the lethargic decline between the 1974 election and November 15, 1976; and the beginnings of the struggle to preserve the nation in the wake of the separatist victory in Quebec.

The first period is in many ways the most interesting, because it embodies to a remarkable extent both the views Trudeau had preached for years and the kind of "New Politics" leadership the public had professed to crave. True to his writings that "the political tools of the future will be designed and appraised by more rational standards than anything we are currently using," the novice prime minister approached his job methodically, with a neatly Cartesian timetable: the first year would be spent overhauling the machinery of government, getting a firm hold on the levers of power and laying plans; the next two would be dedicated to preparing and introducing legislative reforms; and in the last year, while the benefits of earlier actions began to be felt, the government would pave the way to an election with particularly attractive legislation and a few political goodies. Unfortunately for Trudeau, however, the true arena of government is not a tidy chart but a messy, turbulent world of unpredictable people and

235

uncontrollable events, and his elaborate timetable inevitably went awry.

Trudeau began the planning process by setting up task forces to review virtually every area of government activity and determine where change was desirable. By the fall of 1968, there were task forces studying foreign policy, defence policy, housing policy, communications policy, tax policy, information policy, sports policy, prices and incomes policy, and a number of other areas. This was Trudeau the free-thinker at work, the man who wanted to "cast down the totems, break down the taboos", insisting that nothing was sacred and that every major policy field had to be re-examined from first principles. But it was also Trudeau the gut conservative, unwilling to change anything until it had been studied from every conceivable angle, and the most immediate result of his studious approach was to make the government appear inactive.

The initial emphasis on slow, careful planning got Trudeau's administration off to a highly unorthodox start. Most new administrations try to maintain their campaign momentum by making a show of bold, decisive action as soon as they take office. Trudeau, instead, quite consciously set out to dissipate some of his government's momentum, attempting to damp down the fires of public enthusiasm without extinguishing them altogether. He had, in the campaign, promised virtually nothing; but in promising nothing, he had appeared to promise everything, and had kindled extravagant hopes of dramatic change. Trudeau recognized that the intensity of those hopes was politically dangerous to him, and it also conflicted with his political theory: he wanted a society and a government soberly and thoughtfully planning the future together, not slavishly following a single man. His government's first throne speech on September 12, 1968, was, accordingly, a dull, careful document that might have been ghost-written by Mackenzie King.

To a nation that expected a stirring call to action, it offered instead yet another restatement of the limitations on government: "Across the land there are great expectations of what this government will produce. My ministers recognize the responsibility for leadership which these hopes entail. They are determined to do all that they can to carry out the mandate they received from the people of Canada in the recent general election. They recognize their duty to ensure that the wishes of Canadians concerning their government be fulfilled as quickly and as completely as the general advantage will allow. At the same time my government is conscious that aspirations and their realization have to be tempered by a sober awareness of reality. In the complexities of modern society, effective programs take time to develop and more time to implement. At all stages they require financial and intellectual resources which are not unlimited and must be used with careful planning and the hard judgment of priorities. It is a simple fact of life that everything cannot be done at once." The speech went on to enumerate — in flat, almost bureaucratic language and with little detail — the various areas in which the government planned to act, and then it acknowledged a reality that was to be at the core of the public's disappointment: "The legislative program that the government proposes is very extensive but many of the items have been seen before or are of an uncontroversial nature."

When newsmen later asked him where all the dynamism had gone and how he could hope to keep younger Canadians excited about government with such a prosaic document, Trudeau reiterated the austerely rational view of government that informs all his writings: "I really don't want to gain them by words and show of fireworks and exciting phrases. If we can't satisfy them and the others by good legislation, by progressive action in Parliament, by forward-looking policies, all of which I suppose you and they will have occasion to study and criticize, I don't want to gain plaudits for merely words and enthusiasm which isn't followed up by action."[1] If Trudeau's position had the appeal of honesty, he also betrayed a certain romantic naïveté about the political process and a soon-to-be-damaging overestimation of the electorate's collective rationality when he continued: "You know, the purpose of government is not to look good. . . . I think it's important perhaps, for obvious reasons, close to an election to look as good as you can, and every politician does this instinctively, I think. But the purpose of government, once again, is to get down to the business of governing. . . ."

This was a dominant theme throughout Trudeau's first mandate. Government was serious business, not entertainment, and it would be both dishonest and time-wasting to expend much effort on cosmetics. Trudeau intended, he repeated in an interview at the beginning of 1969, to keep to his timetable of planning and study, even if that seemed unexciting to outsiders. "Governing is not only solving day-to-day problems, but it's making sure that you're prepared to meet the unexpected problems and this means projecting your thoughts into the future, trying to assess where the trouble may arise and trying to create the solutions before the crisis breaks out. And if you do that, if you solve the crisis before it exists, people will say, 'Well, nothing is happening,' and people can get bored, I suppose, with good government — but we'll think of that in the last month of our mandate."[2]

Trudeau managed, with this approach, to head his government toward political disaster along two seemingly diverging paths: On one hand, he overestimated the public's collective intelligence, assuming that people would judge government actions on their merits without requiring any political niceties; on the other, he simultaneously underestimated that same intelligence, believing that if the public should prove dissatisfied with his government, it could be appeased with some fancy footwork "close to an election" or "in the last month of our mandate".

In addition to wanting to take stock and to dampen unrealistic expectations, Trudeau was restrained at the outset of his term in office by an even more compelling consideration: lack of money. The social programs introduced in the Pearson era were proving immensely costly and there was simply no more leeway for major new expenditures. "Not only can we not come up with any new programs," he said in early 1969, "but we can't even continue the old ones. We are at the stage where we must take all these laws in hand, examine them and realize that if we want to introduce new legislation, for instance to correct regional disparities, we must discontinue certain old programs or interrupt them or reduce their scope. Since we've been in power, we've cut a number of things, for instance winter works, the causeway to Prince Edward Island, the telescope in British Columbia. . . . Despite all these cuts, you see that spending forecasts keep increasing because all the plans on which we have embarked for health, hospitals, education, etc. . . . the costs are climbing at a frightening pace. We've cut a lot everywhere, and we're still short of money."[3]

While longer-term planning and study was under way, the new government busied itself with cost-trimming and with legislation that didn't entail major new expenditures, thereby disappointing a public that had come to associate dramatic reform with dramatic spending. Trudeau had warned all along that his government wouldn't be a Santa Claus, but his message hadn't sunk in.

Much of Trudeau's most important activity at the beginning of his mandate — his extensive restructuring of the Prime Minister's Office and the cabinet system — took place out of public view. But his parallel attempts to reform the workings of Parliament were very visible indeed, and the public wasn't at all sure it liked what it saw. Streamlining parliamentary procedures had in fact been one of Trudeau's few concrete commitments during the campaign, and he had worried publicly that the public was losing confidence in government because of the slowness of the decision-making process. He got his time-saving efforts in Parliament off to a bad start, however, by trying first to save the time of his own ministers: instead of having every minister available in the House each day for Question Period as had been traditional, he set up a roster system whereby each minister would be in the House only three days a week. Though the change was hardly drastic, Trudeau handled it tactlessly by denying opposition leaders the courtesy of advance consultation about the proposal, and the opposition predictably stormed that the prime minister was trifling with the rights of Parliament.

When he introduced his main reform proposals in December, the opposition had already been made edgy by his abruptness and was suspicious of his motives. In reality, the changes made parliamentary scrutiny of legislation and spending slightly more efficient, reduced the level of uproar without significantly changing Parliament's real power — and failed to achieve any notable increase in the speed of processing legislation. As with the cabinet, Trudeau's main change was a strengthened committee system.

In the past, spending estimates of government departments had to be considered and approved in the House of Commons in so-called "supply debates". The opposition was able to use these occasions to embarrass the government by protracting debate and withholding approval of funds until there was a "Perils-of-Pauline" situation in which the government was literally in danger of running out of money, but there was no real scrutiny of spending estimates. Trudeau's reforms shifted the study of estimates from the whole House to eighteen standing committees of MPS; in exchange for this, he gave the opposition twenty-five "opposition days" a year during which it could debate any topic of its choice.

Similarly, detailed clause-by-clause examination of virtually all bills was transferred from the whole House to these committees, enabling MPS to develop expertise in their committee's subject area and to summon the testimony of expert witnesses. The use of committees to study estimates and bills has improved the scrutiny of both, and produced some good suggestions for the improvement of various items of legislation. But many of the committees are too swamped with work to do a really first-rate job. To improve the quality of analysis and criticism of legislation, Trudeau also introduced the innovation of giving the opposition parties and the Liberal caucus federal funds to enable them to hire research staff.

These changes have made Parliament slightly less tumultuous and have made it possible for spending plans and legislation to be examined in a calmer, more thoughtful setting. What they have not done, however, is make the parliamentary process any faster. Between 1960 and 1963, when John Diefenbaker was prime minister, Parliament sat for a total of 457 days and passed 158 public bills, for an average of fractionally less than three days per bill. In the five Pearson years between 1963 and 1968, Parliament sat for 680 days and passed 252 bills, which works out to 2.7 days per bill. In a marathon 255-day session between September 30, 1974, and February 27, 1976, a Parliament fully accustomed to the new system, under a fully experienced Trudeau majority government, passed 83 bills — for an average of three days per bill.

But Trudeau's problem when he introduced the changes was not doubt as to their efficacy, but rather the suggestion that they might be *too* efficient. The opposition was suspicious of all the proposals, but it was particularly vehement about another rule which would have made it easy for the government to limit the length of debate on any bill. The result was that Trudeau found himself peppered with accusations of dictatorial intent, and the news media took up the cry. He finally agreed to send the time-limiting proposal back to committee for further study on condition that the opposition would accept the rest of the reform package. Then he made matters worse by publicly boasting that he had out-foxed the opposition, having deliberately made the time-limiting rule unacceptable so that the other parties would accept everything else just to get rid of it.

If, by the end of 1968, the public was already receptive to charges that Trudeau was undermining Parliament, it was because the context for judging the new prime minister's behaviour had already begun to change. As early as August 1968, Trudeau had slightly tarnished his image by carelessly quipping "Where's Biafra?" when he was asked what Canada might do to ease starvation in the secessionist Nigerian state in the midst of a civil war. The remark was neither as cruel nor as thoughtless as it sounded: The Trudeau government was convinced that reports of widespread starvation were being stage-managed by the Biafrans to win world sympathy, and the prime minister's professed ignorance of Biafra's location was meant to underline that he recognized the existence of no such entity; there was only Nigeria. Still, it sounded terrible, and the flippantly callous tone set many people's teeth on edge. That jolt was followed by a vague, building sense of letdown: the throne speech was unexciting, Trudeau was too busy and too business-like to radiate the charisma he had shown in the campaign, and the government seemed to be simply plodding along.

People began to suspect that they had somehow been fooled by the campaign, that Trudeau wasn't what they had imagined him to be. That suspicion abruptly changed the context of his behaviour. The offhand remarks, blunt statements, and exuberant antics that had seemed charming when Canadians were dazzled by Trudeau suddenly became offensive when people started to feel — however unfairly — that they had been conned. When Trudeau went to a Liberal dinner in Winnipeg in December and began his response to a question about selling wheat by saying, "Well, why should I sell the Canadian farmers' wheat?", that incautious opening sentence stuck in the public's mind and quite overshadowed the serious exposition of federal wheat policies that followed; thus began Trudeau's losing of the West. When he made his debut at a Commonwealth prime ministers' conference in London in January, he plunged himself into more trouble. At the conference itself, his listen-and-learn approach to his first such meeting clashed with the Canadian public's expectation of bold leadership. Outside the conference, he publicly dated beautiful young women, was embarrassed when one of them started gossiping to the press about him, and then gave the press a nasty tongue-lashing for "crummy" behaviour. What came through to Canadians in the resulting news stories was the impression of a frivolous, ill-tempered dilettante.

It was against this background that the public assessed Trudeau's actions in Parliament, and things became even worse in July when he blew his stack over opposition filibustering of a revised version of the time-limiting rule for debate. He called the filibuster "stupid", accused opposition members of "hypocrisy", and was in turn reviled with accusations of "fascist tendencies" and shouts of "Heil Hitler". The rule — which has, in fact, had negligible impact — was finally rammed through, but tempers kept mounting from day to day until Trudeau finally responded to opposition taunts with a coldly sarcastic outburst which ended memorably when MPS started to drift out of the chamber: "I think we should encourage members of the opposition to leave. Every time they do, the IQ of this House rises considerably. . . . When they get home, when they are out of Parliament, when they are fifty yards from Parliament Hill, they are no longer honourable members — they are just nobodies."

This performance should not have come as such a great shock, since Trudeau had already offered a glimpse of this side of his personality when, while he was still justice minister, he had accused the opposition of "mooing like a herd". But his behaviour toward the opposition on this and other occasions was intended to reflect not a lack of respect for Parliament as an institution, but rather a feeling that others were not adequately respecting it. To him, Parliament should be a high-minded, serene forum for the rational debate of laws and issues, a gathering of serious men reasoning together. He finds the raucous, often juvenile heckling and point-scoring deeply offensive, both because of the personal insults levelled against him and because it violates his view of politics as a rather solemn activity. As he puts it: "When I say I don't like the Commons, it's because it's a place where men are shouting, where people yell at each other — yell as one wouldn't dare in a classroom. I find that vulgar. It offends me."[4] Trudeau's combative instincts also come into play, and he has never learned like most parliamentarians to regard the exchange of insults as part of a game; he takes the taunts personally, his "inability to lob" takes over, and he volleys back with devastating verbal over-kill. His victims, sensing that his contempt is much more genuine and deeply felt than theirs, are outraged, but he cannot understand the distinction.

While the public uneasily tried to decide what to make of Trudeau, a great deal of important activity took place in that first year. It just didn't seem exciting enough, and therefore went largely unnoticed in the over-all perception. In the summer of 1968, the government announced a number of major foreign-policy initiatives, including the first steps toward recognition of China, efforts to broaden relations with Latin America, and a re-evaluation of Canada's role in NATO. In October, the Official Languages Act, one of the most important pieces of legislation in the nation's history, was introduced. In April, the Department of Regional Economic Expansion came into existence. In the same month, after a long and noisy debate, the NATO decision was announced: a fifty-per-cent cut in Canadian forces in Europe. In May, the ill-fated Prices and Incomes Commission under Dr. John Young was created. In June, the Criminal Code amendments originally introduced by Trudeau when he was justice minister became law.

Other important changes were brought in over the next three

years, but the public was never really impressed. The government's initiatives were scattered over too broad a range, they were too inadequately sold politically, and there was too little discernible over-all sense of purpose. Worse, a pattern began to emerge: Dramatic change was heralded in some policy area, there was great and bitter debate over its merits, and then the government plumped for some halfway measure which dissatisfied both the proponents of change and the defenders of the status quo. Trudeau's popularity eroded slowly but inexorably. In the fall of 1968, his government had 52 per cent support in the Gallup Poll; by April, it was down to 47 per cent. In June of 1969, 38 per cent of the public disapproved of Trudeau's performance in office; a year later, disapproval had risen to 41 per cent. After Trudeau's powerful handling of the FLQ crisis in October 1970, his personal popularity and that of his government soared spectacularly to nearly 60 per cent, but then a steady decline set in again.

The irony of Trudeau's souring relationship with the electorate was that he was doing almost exactly as much — or as little — as he had expressly promised. He had offered himself as a man who would modernize the machinery of decision-making and take a fresh look at all the nation's outstanding problems, but who had few brilliant solutions of his own in mind and who would refuse to spend lavishly. He failed to deliver not the little he had expressly promised, but the very much he had implicitly offered: an inspirational style of leadership that would challenge the nation with the boldness of its initiatives and unite Canadians in a shared sense of purpose and involvement.

That failure was not entirely through lack of trying. To a far greater extent than was noticed at the time, Trudeau experimented in his first mandate with techniques of participation intended to involve the general public in the shaping of a national consensus. One such experiment was the three-phase policy exercise launched in late 1969 with a Liberal Party teach-in at Harrison Hot Springs, B.C. Liberal delegates from across the country were briefed, quizzed, and challenged on the coming issues of the 1970s by an impressive array of thinkers and experts. These Liberals were then supposed, as the second phase, to go back to their ridings and mobilize the general public to participate in workshops and debates on these issues, with a view to preparing resolutions for the Liberal Party's policy convention in November of 1970, which would comprise phase three. This was a remarkable attempt, entirely consistent with Trudeau's theories, to reach far beyond the party and involve the nation at large in a debate on future directions. But it fizzled out in the second phase when the riding-level efforts failed to catch fire. The policy convention ended up being just another Liberal Party gathering, not the sort of great national conclave Trudeau had vaguely visualized.

Another technique, not much more successful, was the extensive use of white papers and other forms of invitation to open discussion prior to introducing legislation. Instead of simply announcing plans and defending them, the government put tentative policy proposals before the public in the hope that great national debates would ensue on each issue. The government would watch a consensus emerge, and then shape its legislation accordingly. But even when Trudeau encouraged his ministers not to worry about cabinet solidarity and to act as cheerleaders for various debate factions by advocating their own respective views on issues such as NATO, the national debate never really got off the ground. Powerful interest groups lobbied strenuously for their own ends, while the general public hung back in bewilderment. Instead of making the government appear supremely democratic, these tentative proposals merely made it look indecisive. And since white papers on such sensitive matters as tax reform were made public without careful prior scrutiny of all their political implications — on the grounds that these, after all, were merely ideas for discussion and not final plans — flaws were often discovered which made the government look not only indecisive but stupid.

Trudeau's commitment to involving the public in the political process was also reflected in his travels across the country. More than any other leader in a major democracy, Trudeau made a sustained effort to engage in a real face-to-face dialogue with the public. He made himself available, at town-hall meetings and at sessions with students, for questioning by the citizens. In these meetings, Trudeau functioned more as teacher than politician.

✓Where a more conventional politician would have ducked behind a "no comment" or a glib promise, he responded candidly and bluntly to nearly every question or argument. Between 1968 and 1972, there was almost certainly not a single major issue on which Trudeau's personal stand was not known, and this in itself gave rise to a certain form of public participation: people might agree or disagree, but it was difficult to be indifferent to him because he had pronounced himself so sharply on so many contentious issues. Unfortunately for Trudeau, this outspokenness — coupled with his inclination to "demythologize" the prime minister's role by thinking out loud, even at the risk of saying something careless — probably offended more people than it pleased. Virtually everyone found something in Trudeau's thinking to disagree with vehemently, and the reaction was to curse him over that area of disagreement rather than laud him for his candour.

In this as in other areas, it gradually turned out that the public hadn't really wanted the sort of "New Politics" leadership it had professed to crave before Trudeau came on the scene. There was a great hunger, in the pre-1968 period, to replace the disorderly squabbling and scrambling of the Diefenbaker and Pearson years with efficient planning, and to find a leader who did not pretend to have all the answers; who said what he believed instead of hiding behind plummy circumlocutions; and who challenged people to face hard choices instead of holding out false hopes of satisfying everyone.

But Trudeau was precisely that sort of leader, and suddenly the reality didn't look as attractive as the vision. The pursuit of efficiency in government was regarded as cold and somehow vaguely anti-democratic; planning was equated with procrastination; Trudeau's admission that he lacked answers to certain problems was scorned as a dereliction of duty; his outspokenness was interpreted as arrogance; and his emphasis on the limitations of government was judged to be callousness. This reaction was due partly to Trudeau's style and his political inexperience, but it also resulted from the ambivalence of a public that simultaneously wanted to be challenged and coddled.

The same ambivalence also extended beyond perceptions of

Trudeau's approach, to concrete matters of policy. If any specific expectation had been attached to Trudeau's talk of a "Just Society", it was above all that he would mount some sort of dramatic war on poverty. In theory, that was what the Canadian public, in its reform-minded mood of 1968, wanted: a crusade for social justice, an effort to share society's wealth a little more equitably. But when the Trudeau government took a modest step in that direction in 1970 by proposing to increase Family Allowance payments to the poor and finance the increase largely by cutting off Family Allowance for families with incomes over $10,000, the howls of middle-class outrage could be heard from Bonavista to Nanaimo.

While all these factors harmed Trudeau's relationship with the public, the greatest damage was done by his government's handling of the economy. Determined to lick inflation, Trudeau allowed the Bank of Canada and Finance Minister Edgar Benson in effect to declare war on the economy, clamping it down by increasingly painful turns of the screw. In December 1968 the central bank raised its discount rate to 6.8 per cent; it was increased again in March, June, and July until it reached a record high of 8 per cent. The money supply was reined in sharply, and Benson added to the pressure with a restrictive budget in June 1969, warning grimly: "We really mean business in the fight against inflation." In August, Trudeau threw the full prestige of his office into the battle, personally announcing a virtual freeze on federal spending and a cut of 25,000 jobs in the public service. The toll in mounting unemployment began to assume staggering proportions, but the inflation psychology was not broken and prices kept rising. Ignoring warnings from the Economic Council of Canada that the government was underestimating the impact of its policies and courting disaster, Trudeau declared at a pre-Christmas press conference at the end of 1969: "We can only get tougher, we can't get weaker. I'm afraid there are a lot of people who are bargaining that the government can't act tough for too long because it will only get frightened if it sees unemployment go up to 6 per cent. . . . But if people think we are going to lose our nerve because of that, they should think again because we're not."

Between December of 1968 and February of 1971, unemployment virtually doubled, from 343,000 to 675,000. When the government began easing the pressure in the summer of 1970, it discovered to its horror that the economy was not responding. The seasonally adjusted unemployment rate in September 1971 was 7.1 per cent — the highest in a decade — and the government began piling on stimulation with the same frantic zeal with which it had imposed restraint.

To a public that saw unemployment rising to appalling levels and the prime minister calmly saying it might go even higher, the inflation war looked like supreme callousness. But the real explanation for Trudeau's creation of this economic mess lay in his belief that even greater harm would come to low- and middle-income Canadians if inflation were not fought at all costs. As he put it at the end of 1969: "We have no choice but to fight inflation. . . . Not fighting inflation would mean that we would be creating misery for vast segments of the population. You know, a third of the workers are organized and a third of the people in industries can sort of protect themselves by bargaining hard. . . . But the two-thirds of the workers who are not organized, or the fixed-income people, or all those people who can't in some way protect themselves against rising prices — you know, many housewives and so on — these are the people who will be destroyed, the stability of their lives will be undermined if we don't fight inflation. If we don't fight inflation, we'll lose our foreign markets. If we lose our foreign markets, we'll have an exchange crisis. If we have an exchange crisis, we'll have to devalue the dollar. We'd be upsetting the whole economy. . . .

"And in a year from now, when we would have had the exchange crisis, when we would have been forced to devaluate the dollar, when we would have lost our foreign markets, then we would have terrific unemployment. But we'd have it at a much higher level of inflation, a dollar would be worth less and in a year from now we'd be making the fight that we're making now, but we would be making it from a much more precarious point."[5]

In this, Trudeau was accepting without qualification the arguments of the finance department, largely because his own attitudes made him uniquely susceptible to those arguments. Says Marc Lalonde: "He was reacting to advice from finance and the Bank of Canada, who were very exercised about inflation. He's a rather conservative economist. On the financial side, he's a Scot, a conservative, a penny saved is a penny earned. Look at his own personal ethics, his attitude vis-à-vis spending or high living. . . . In that sense, he believes in the virtues of saving, his psychology is 'look after yourself for your old age'. It's part of his ethic, inflation is contrary to all those functions, so it was easy for him to fall into the type of economic approach that finance was strong on at the time. He supported the policy, but he was not the one who originated it. He makes no pretence of being a good economist; he was relying very much on his financial advisors."

Once he accepted the premise that inflation absolutely had to be licked, the tendency that an aide calls "a missing piece of the mechanism of his monitor, of his balance wheel" came into play, and Trudeau allowed himself to go to extremes: if the battle had to be fought and won, it wasn't going to be lost through any weakness or flinching on his part. And, as he so often did in those days, he overestimated the rationality of the public as a body and assumed that if the right buttons were pushed, the right appeals to good sense made, the public would automatically do the government's bidding. While the finance department made the fatal error of underestimating the time-lags required for its measures to take effect and kept piling on new restraints until their cumulative effect was devastating, Trudeau kept thinking that the public would soon join ranks in fighting inflation and make further measures unnecessary.

"The main error I made," he admitted in 1973, "was to think that the anti-cyclical policy would have much stronger and faster psychological effects. In other words, when I said that we were prepared to fight inflation even if unemployment reached 6%, it shouldn't have been interpreted as a desire to see unemployment reach 6%, nor even as an acceptance of that, but as a warning to all sectors of industry that if they didn't cooperate with what was then a policy of voluntary restraint, my God, the consequences could be disastrous for everyone. Therefore it was a

political error much more than an economic error. I didn't think
we would obtain so little cooperation. . . ."[6]

While the battle against inflation badly tarnished Trudeau's
image, the unemployment insurance reforms designed by Labour
Minister Bryce Mackasey and brought into force on July 1, 1971,
simultaneously eased the burden on the jobless and inflicted
further political damage on the government. Those reforms were
a remarkable piece of work. On one hand, they were perhaps the
most socially progressive piece of legislation passed in that first
mandate, nearly doubling the unemployment insurance benefits
and making coverage universal. On the other hand, they were a
political booby-trap deliberately tied by Mackasey to the government: the plan was designed in such a way that when unemployment stood at no more than 3.5 per cent, the cost of benefits
would be almost completely covered by contributions from workers
and employers; but as unemployment rose, the burden on the
federal treasury would steadily increase. At 6.5 per cent, the
government would have to pay about one-third of the total cost
of benefits — about twice as much money as under the previous
system.

Disagreeing with Trudeau's willingness to tolerate high unemployment for the sake of controlling inflation, Mackasey had devised a scheme which would force the government either to reduce
unemployment or to compensate the jobless at ruinous cost to
the federal treasury; any government that allowed unemployment
to rise above four per cent would have to pay for it and face the
headache of trying to find the money. "That's the way the plan
was designed," he later admitted proudly. "It's beautiful; I wrote
it myself. Get the unemployment rate down around four per cent
where it belongs, and it will be one of the cheapest plans in the
world."

Trudeau and his advisors somehow failed to spot the time-bomb
implications of Mackasey's reforms, and the whole thing exploded
just as the election was starting to draw near. The government
found itself with whopping UIC cost overruns, and under simul-
taneous attack from left and right. Critics on the left were furious
that the government had caused widespread hardship by allowing

unemployment to rise so high, while more conservative voters blamed the level of unemployment and the soaring UIC costs on the generous Mackasey reforms which they believed had undermined people's will to work.

The political impact of the novice prime minister's various mistakes was increased by his failure to keep the Liberal Party in happy fighting trim. Normally, the members of the government party can play an important role in their communities between elections, spreading the word about government accomplishments, explaining and defending controversial policies, and warning the administration of any major grievances developing at the grassroots level. But Trudeau's Liberals between 1968 and 1972 became increasingly alienated, discouraged, and finally lethargic.

In a structural sense, Trudeau tried to increase the role and policy input of the party through policy conventions, the regional desk system, and such other measures as requiring that the caucus be consulted on new legislation before it was introduced. But politics at the party level is not a matter of structures but of human relations. While political professionals may be motivated by a taste for power, the opportunity to implement their ideas, or the prospect of benefit to their careers, the amateurs who are the lifeblood of the party system have few such rewards. What motivates them is a sense of involvement in the running of the nation and, at a personal level, the *illusion* of power. The party worker in Thunder Bay or Matane doesn't really expect that his individual policy views will sway the course of the government, but he does expect that they will be taken more seriously than those of his neighbour who has not laboured to put that government into power. Above all, he expects access — the opportunity to communicate more directly with the decision-makers than people outside the party, and the feeling that he enjoys a privileged relationship with the prime minister of his nation. Trudeau gave the members of his party cold, shiny new structures, but he denied them that personal dimension and made them feel that they weren't important to him.

Part of the reason was simply his unfamiliarity with the Liberal Party and its members. "The whole thing was so sudden that a lot of people who were working for me loyally in the leadership convention and close to me, I didn't even know all their names. And when it was over, I was sort of writing thank-you letters to a lot of them, and some of them I couldn't identify. 'What did he do?' or 'What role was she playing?' You know, it would be an important role and 'Gee, I didn't know that.' . . . Part of the unsuccess is due to my real lack of knowledge of the people. After the '68 election, I wasn't even quite sure who my national organizers were, let alone my regional and provincial ones. These were so many names of people I'd seen in the confusion of that election, who would meet me at airplanes and bring me around, but . . . I'd been through a leadership campaign which lasted a few months, where I was meeting fifty people a day who were my key supporters and whom I had never known from Adam, and I'm told today, 'So-and-so, he was your key man in this particular area.' And, 'Gee, I didn't know that.' So that would explain that they probably didn't feel that I appreciated them."

Trudeau strongly denies, however, that he had too little real interest in the party between 1968 and 1972. "It's true that I wasn't successful in convincing the party that it had a large role to play, or perhaps even in giving it a large role to play, but my attempts were nonetheless evident. And my desire — precisely because of my lack of roots in the party — my desire to establish roots in the party was very, very real. And in order to bridge this gap, this failing, I right away in the election of '68 began saying: 'And if I'm elected, I'll draw the party in and I'll set up regional desks, so that everybody around the country, including members of course, will feel that they have a direct line into my office.' . . . And it was me in that period who created what we have since then learned to call 'political cabinet', having meetings of cabinet where we would talk of nothing else except politics and party affairs. And it was certainly me who, to make up for my lack of knowledge of the party, insisted that I spend a lot of time travelling around the country, meeting people and so on. I made speeches around that period, '68, '69, where I used to expand on my dream of a mass party which would be the focal point of all the dissidents. . . . And very early on, I began getting our people to work on election expenses legislation so that the party would be forced to be more democratic. So I'm not bragging about the results, I'm just saying that it's not correct to think that it wasn't an area of importance to me."

But the party was important in a mechanical sense, as an entity, not in terms of the individuals working within it. Trudeau didn't understand the need for — and seldom bothered with — the individual ego-massaging that is such an important part of a party leader's work. His attitude was typified by an incident in 1969: The Ontario Liberal Party, which in those days was the same body at both the federal and the provincial levels, was holding a convention in Ottawa to be attended by 2,000 Liberals. Trudeau didn't want to go to the gathering at all; he felt that it sufficed for his contacts with the party to be through the National Liberal Federation, and he didn't want to set the time-consuming precedent of attending meetings of provincial organizations as well. At the insistence of one aide, he finally agreed to go — and stayed for only fifteen minutes.

Whatever was going on in his mind, Trudeau certainly gave the people working with him during the first mandate the impression that contacts with the party weren't high on his list of priorities. Says one such aide: "After the 1968 election, the big shooters around the PM were Lalonde, Jim Davey, Roméo LeBlanc, and Gordon Gibson. They had perhaps worked as Liberals at riding level, but never at the provincial level, and they were not really familiar with the party. The role of the party during the leadership campaign was primarily an inhibiting one. The party would say, 'You can't do this or that, these are our parameters and you must operate within them.' Partly as a result of that, between 1968 and 1972 the party was viewed as something to be gotten around or managed. It tended to be inarticulate, inconsistent, in a way indifferent — it just didn't do its homework on a lot of things. So the feeling was that the party didn't really have a lot to offer in the way of advice or inputs. The feeling was that it played the same role as the caucus in conveying the mood of the moment, except that the caucus was a hell of a lot less ungainly and far more efficient."

Despite his various errors of style and strategy, Trudeau's accomplishments in the first mandate were substantial. He modernized the structures of the Prime Minister's Office, the cabinet, and Parliament. He took an important step toward combating regional disparities by creating the Department of Regional Economic Expansion, and created new ministerial functions — in environmental affairs, urban affairs and housing, and communications — to formally involve the federal government for the first time in these emerging social problems. He established two imaginative new programs to harness community energies: Opportunities for Youth and the Local Initiatives Program.

The Trudeau government raised the old age pension and guaranteed income supplement and indexed it to the cost of living. It overhauled the Criminal Code, amended the Bail and Detention Act, and established a Law Reform Commission to ponder ways of reconciling laws more closely to the changing needs of modern society. It attempted — though the attempt was marred by silly errors in judgment on the part of Solicitor General Jean-Pierre Goyer — to bring the long-overdue concept of rehabilitation into Canada's inadequate penal system. It revamped the unemployment insurance system in a way that was inevitably controversial but that brought the unemployed a hope for decent subsistence. It implemented tax reforms which stopped far short of the Carter Report's recommendations, but which did make the tax structure a bit more equitable, dropping about a million low-income Canadians from the tax rolls, reducing taxes for some 4.7 million others, and increasing the bite for about 1.3 million at the top of the income scale. In foreign policy, there were a number of important breakthroughs, most notably the establishment of diplomatic relations with China before that country was recognized by either the United States or the United Nations, a thawing of Canada's relationship with the Soviet Union, and the unilateral extension of Canadian jurisdiction over Arctic waters. When President Nixon implemented a set of protectionist economic measures in 1971 that threatened the economies of Canada and other countries that exported heavily to the United States, Trudeau's government moved swiftly both to forcefully voice Canada's protests in Washington and to shelter Canadian businesses against the immediate impact of the measures.

In addition to these accomplishments, Trudeau managed — no

small feat for a political novice who had won the leadership convention with only 51.1 per cent of the vote — to take unassailable
control of his party and to rise to such a dominant position in the
nation that he was often able to shape public perception of events
according to his own scenario, weathering potentially dangerous
setbacks like the resignations of Paul Hellyer and Eric Kierans from
his cabinet with scarcely a ripple. And even more importantly, he
succeeded in four short years in revitalizing the political process, in
making people keenly aware of their government; he made it difficult to be apathetic about the prime minister. In a country where
the governing greybeards used to plod along almost unnoticed and
people focussed their attention on the government only when there
was a scandal or a crisis, that was a cardinal accomplishment.

It was ultimately not lack of accomplishments but deficiencies of
attitude that came so close to making Trudeau's first mandate his
last. He had surrounded himself in office with advisors who were
intellectually formidable but politically inept and naïve, an élite
team of rationalist intellectuals who believed, like their leader, that
it was only necessary to be right and the rest would take care of
itself. Even when the planning went on too long and the inflation
battle and the FLQ crisis upset the four-year timetable, bringing controversial legislation too close to the election and giving too little
time for benefits to be felt or particularly popular steps to be taken,
they believed that no harm was done. With his perceptions shaped
by the advice of these aides, Trudeau gradually became isolated,
not from physical contact with the public but from an adequate
understanding of what was happening to its view of him. Power
had come too easily to Trudeau, and he did not realize how easily
it could also slip away. He was convinced that a careless remark
here, a failure in human relations there, didn't really matter in the
final analysis; when the election came, the public would look only
at his substantive achievements and decide accordingly.

But what the public saw, and increasingly resented, was an aloof,
seemingly arrogant leader who appeared to feel that he owed the
electorate and its sensibilities nothing. Worse, he gave the impression of considering himself superior to the people he was governing. The dark side of Trudeau's view of himself as a political

teacher was that he too often came across as the sort of teacher almost everyone remembers having had and hated at some point: sarcastic, condescending, and cuttingly impatient with the failure of his pupils to be as brilliant as he. And perhaps most damaging of all was the feeling that, having been entrusted with the nation's highest and most honoured position, Trudeau cared little about keeping it. "I'm not really governing to be re-elected," he said in the midst of his inflation-fighting efforts in 1970. "If the Canadian people don't like it, you know, they can lump it."[7] The desire of a leader to be re-elected is the strongest hold the public has over him, and Trudeau's repudiation of that desire was repeatedly stated in terms that were interpreted not as a selfless dedication to duty whatever the political consequences, but as a supreme disdain for the electorate and its opinion of him.

Still, the public was not unequivocally ready in the fall of 1972 to replace Trudeau with Robert Stanfield. When Stanfield had won the Progressive Conservative leadership in 1967, the craggy-faced, dour-looking, slow-talking former Nova Scotia premier had briefly captured the public's imagination. With his somewhat Lincolnesque image, his leadership campaign slogan, "The Man with the Winning Way", and his no-nonsense style, he had seemed an attractive alternative to Lester Pearson's fumbling, crisis-ridden approach to government. But then, only a few months later, he had suddenly found himself being measured not against Pearson but against Trudeau — and, though he was only five years older than the new Liberal leader, Stanfield had at once begun to seem a man of the wrong generation, an old-fashioned plodder offering himself to a nation that was in the mood for youthfulness and vitality.

In the four years of Trudeau's first term in office, Stanfield had worked doggedly as Opposition leader, and his accomplishments within his own party were impressive. What he had inherited on September 9, 1967, was not so much a party as an open political wound, ripped asunder in the venomous struggles over John Diefenbaker's fate. By 1972, he had succeeded not only in restoring a semblance of order and unity, but also in subtly redirecting the party's orientation away from its outdated Prairie populism toward a more modern approach to issues. With the public at large, however, he had fared less well. He was liked and respected as a man of manifest courage, decency, and dignity, but there was no clear sense of what he would be like as prime minister. Trudeau created in people's minds an impression — whether it was accurate or not was another matter — as to what he represented: to be for or against Trudeau was to be for or against a certain set of ideas, a certain approach to government and the handling of the nation's problems. Stanfield, on the other hand, never managed to convince enough voters that he stood for anything more profound or politically alluring than being a likable person.

By the fall of 1972, Trudeau's performance had left the public angry, disappointed, frustrated — but most of all confused, uncertain what to make of this extraordinary leader whose glaring faults stood in such striking contrast to the qualities and potential they still recognized in him. This puzzlement was reflected in the titles of the books written about him before the 1972 election by two respected political journalists: *Paradox* by Anthony Westell and *The Trudeau Question* by W. A. Wilson. Westell didn't unravel the paradox and Wilson's thoughtful analysis of the Trudeau years made no pretence of definitively answering the question. But a third book, *Shrug: Trudeau in Power*, by *Maclean's* magazine's Walter Stewart was no less revealing of the public mood. Stewart's book was not an analysis but a polemic that reflected the rage of Trudeau's most bitter critics. But even Stewart didn't expect to see the prime minister removed from power: "In the coming election, Trudeau will be re-elected. . . . Among the first priorities for Canada, therefore, must come the curbing of the prime minister's power through an electoral rebuke; even if he is not defeated, a decline in the Liberal vote and the election of a vigorous, numerous opposition will help to crack the smug circle in which Canada has been driven. Unless that happens, the nation faces the prospect of another full term of shrugs and smiles, of arrogance and autocracy, of a heartless, bloodless, cold administration that lacks even the self-claimed virtue of efficiency, and that threatens to twist the Canadian political system so out of shape that it may never be restored."[8]

Faced with an offended but uncertain public and an Opposition leader who had not made a strong imprint on the national consciousness, Trudeau might have recaptured much of the electorate's esteem with a powerful, persuasive campaign and suffered only relatively minor political losses. Instead, he waged one of the most bizarre and inept campaigns ever attempted by an incumbent prime minister, and brought himself to the razor's edge of defeat.

As Canadians watched in growing disbelief, Trudeau conducted his quest for re-election in September and October of 1972 as a stately, almost languid procession across the country. Although twenty-seven per cent of the electorate was undecided at the start of the campaign, Trudeau showed no fire-in-the-belly effort to defend his controversial handling of government in the previous four years, and made no recourse to his considerable oratorical skills to beat back the opposition challenge. Instead, he announced from the outset that the campaign would be "a dialogue with Canadians". And, true to his dislike for competing against others rather than against himself, he told one of his first campaign meetings: "We're really not fighting any other party. The other parties can fight us if they want, but we're going to be talking to Canadians."[9]

Three weeks into the campaign, columnist Charles Lynch expressed the general puzzlement when he wrote: "Many things about the man are baffling, but this has been the most baffling of all, to see him running as the somewhat stern Prof. Trudeau. . . . He seems only half-involved in the campaign, going through the motions as though he had other, more important things on his well-stocked mind." Trudeau carried his idea of a non-fighting campaign to the point of making it sound as if he considered opposition criticism and attacks on his government's record to be somehow a misuse of the electoral process. At a meeting of Ontario Liberal candidates early in the campaign, he put it this way:

"Other parties may be running against us, they may be trying to catch up with us — I know they won't — but it's fairly true to say that we are not really running against them. We're trying, in this period of two months, to meet intensively with the Canadian people all across the land; we're trying to discuss Canada with them, discuss the future of the country as they see it, as we believe it to be, to order our goals according to a set of priorities which corresponds to the feeling of the Canadian people. . . . We're not going to refuse any debate on any of the issues, but we're not going to seek them. We will be seeking, as I think I am trying to do this morning, seeking to establish better understanding between all parts of Canada. We'll be appealing to all Canadians to look at this election as the one time when Canadians think collectively about their future — no longer about 'well, what has the government done to my business?' or 'what has it done to this province?' or 'what has it done to this particular linguistic group?', but what has it done for Canada and what is it going to do for Canada."[10]

If that sounded complacent, the slogan coined by Toronto advertising executive George Elliott — "The Land Is Strong" — was worse. Under that smugly meaningless banner, Trudeau spoke at rally after rally in subdued professorial tones, outlining his government's accomplishments, indicating vague philosophical directions for the future — and, above all, insisting that present problems weren't serious enough to justify diverting the thinking of Canadians away from the future. As he put it: "A lot of people, a lot of the people in the press, have been saying: 'Well, what are the issues, what are the issues?' One person says jobs, another person says too many people on unemployment insurance, too many bums. You know, I'll send these little minority groups off together and they can argue their heads off. But the Canadian people are not listening to these people and they are not listening to the opposition. . . .

"You know, we don't mind facing any criticism, any one at all. But we don't want the election to be centred on that, because there are things that remain to be done in this country. And they are not piddling little things about trying to correct a little thing here and a little thing there. What we need is to look towards the future. . . . There are a lot of things to be done in this country, and any party or any group or any person who tries to concentrate the attention of the electorate on little things that are going wrong in the system is a person who's a reactionary, a person who is looking backwards."[11]

Trudeau described his government's plans for the future as the pursuit of four main goals: maintaining and enhancing "Canadian integrity" — a nebulous concept that few in the press or among the public really understood; social justice; fulfilment of the individual; and economic growth. His government's task in the mandate ahead, as in the four years past, he told his audiences, would be to strike a proper balance between these sometimes conflicting objectives. At this point, his campaign speeches became little lectures in political theory. Government, he went on, is a never-ending juggling act that seeks to reconcile the needs of competing interests, and at election time the duty of citizens is to put aside their individual wants and needs and ask themselves how well the government has served the country as a whole.

Although this detached approach inevitably seemed arrogant in the context of an angry and troubled electorate, it was in fact simply a politically naïve expression of Trudeau's fundamental political theories. The 1968 campaign had acquired a life of its own, shaped more by an exceptional public mood than by political strategy; in 1972, Trudeau was determined to conduct the campaign exactly as his austere, almost moralistic view of the political process dictated an election should be approached: as a calm, high-minded national debate that appealed to reason rather than emotion; as an invitation to the electorate to judge the government on over-all performance, capacity, and future directions rather than on individual issues; and as an opportunity for the leader and his ministers to improve their understanding of the nation through sustained exposure to the public. Trudeau was so concerned with not being diverted from this approach by a resurgence of the 1968 emotionalism that he adopted a style so low-key that it was almost inaudible.

"It was obviously a mistake," he now says, "but maybe it was more of a mistake in terms of it not being right for that particular time when we had inflation and unemployment and the language backlash and everything else. People weren't all that ready to just listen to what I thought was reason. And I suppose my attitude was almost over-compensating for the emotionalism of the '68 campaign, which I had been accused of winning on charisma and appeals to the emotions of national unity and the greatness of the country and so on. It had happened that way [in 1968] without me actually designing the campaign that way, but I guess I would have felt a bit guilty to run the same sort of campaign again and try that kind of operation twice. (And so the alternative was, 'Let's not talk about national unity and let's not worry about languages and let's not answer the attacks of all the rednecks who were saying we were forcing French down their throats or socialism down their throats or whatever it is. Let's just tell them what we're doing.' "

On the flight back to Ottawa at the end of the campaign, when it was too late for news stories to have any real impact on the voting, Trudeau chatted with reporters and provided another piece of the explanation for his refusal to stress national unity or strenuously defend his government's controversial bilingualism policies: he had felt it would be intellectually dishonest. He would in effect have been telling people they had to vote for him to prove they weren't bigots, he explained, and he likened that to a black man asking a white woman to go out with him and insisting that a refusal could only be due to his colour. The woman might have 101 reasons for refusing, just as people might have 101 reasons for voting against him, Trudeau said, and he hadn't wanted to distort the issue.

Trudeau's approach to the campaign was also shaped, almost certainly, by a great underestimation of the possibility of defeat. He had won the Liberal nomination and election to Parliament in 1965 without much difficulty, and the 1968 election had been more a coronation than a campaign. There was nothing in his experience to drive home the importance of campaign strategy or to make him understand that an election is normally a rough, volatile, and thoroughly unpredictable slugfest. This gap in his political education was compounded by a misreading of the state of his popularity; before and during the campaign, Trudeau interpreted his capacity to draw crowds as proof of continued public esteem, and he was convinced that any traces of hostility would fade as reasonable people heard reasoned explanations of his government's record and plans. Since the key planners of the campaign — Jim Davey,

Ivan Head, and Marc Lalonde — were all amateurs in terms of electoral politics and thought much like Trudeau, there was no trusted advisor to warn him of the real dangers of the situation; when outsiders tried, the prime minister shrugged them off.

In reality, the campaign strategy and the public mood could scarcely have been more badly mismatched. Much of the public was worried and angry over unemployment, inflation, the state of the work ethic, language policy, Trudeau's failure to live up to 1968 expectations, and a host of other grievances. To successfully overcome this mood, Trudeau would have had to meet it head-on, convince the public that he understood its concerns, and explain why some of them were unfounded and what he hoped to do about the rest. Instead, "The Land Is Strong" and Trudeau's cool professorial insistence that all these grievances were exaggerated left people feeling that he didn't understand or didn't care. Already suspecting him of arrogance, they were convinced by the campaign that what was important to them was trivial to him. The reaction of a great many voters was an urge to teach him a lesson at the polls.

The situation was made even worse by the disarray of the Liberals' election organization. The party professionals, dismayed by Trudeau's flaccid campaigning and by his refusal to adopt any coherent strategy, increasingly concluded that disaster was inevitable and went about their work half-heartedly. And the amateurs — the people on whom a party depends to conduct the campaign in each riding — had become so alienated by Trudeau's apparent lack of interest in them since 1968 that they were unwilling to make the all-out sacrifice of time and energy that it takes to win an election.

Says a Trudeau aide: "At the beginning of the 1972 campaign, we began to see the results of the PM's handling of the party. In a riding like Sudbury, when the prime minister was coming on a visit a few years earlier and we were advancing it, we'd get maybe twenty or thirty local Liberals coming forward to help with organization. Now the campaign was starting, and these same people suddenly were going to Florida, they were busy that evening, they'd love to help but they couldn't get a babysitter, and so on."

Late in the campaign, it finally dawned on Trudeau and his key advisors that defeat might really be looming. In an eleventh-hour shift of strategy, Trudeau suddenly moved to a much more conventional style of politics. In Shawinigan, he heralded the announcement of a plan to build a network of leisure areas by speaking of "candies" the federal government would distribute. In Toronto, the Liberals announced plans for a new $30 million, eighty-acre waterfront park. But instead of helping Trudeau, the sudden scattering of goodies damaged him — it smacked of desperation, and the recourse to pork-barrel politics offended many voters by being so contrary to everything Trudeau professed to stand for.

In retrospect, he isn't proud of these ventures, though he considers the Shawinigan episode a matter of semantics. "The one and only speech, I think, where I spoke of goodies was in [Shawinigan] and what I was peddling was a very ingenious and interesting concept called Byways and Special Places, and to me this was part of making the country better for the people. But this was toward the end of the campaign, and people by that time were beginning to worry about whether we would win or lose and began to sort of tell me: 'You've got to speak more the language of the people and have fun with them and so on.' And 'candies', to me, was probably a mistaken effort at being colloquial with the people up there, because it was only afterward that I was made to realize that that's the kind of expression that Duplessis would have used. In that sense, it was a mistake of language rather than of substance.

"The example of the Toronto waterfront park is more to the point. And it was contrived, as I remember the expression, as the 'blockbuster' in an area of Toronto where we felt we were weak and where we were losing votes. You'll recall that we postponed the election from June till October, mostly because the Toronto and area people, including the campaign chairman and Ontario chairman and so on, just said: 'We're going to be clobbered, we've got to find some blockbuster for Toronto.' And to me that was something out of the ordinary, the exception, it was the aberration of the campaign. It was, with hindsight, almost pitiful the way we had sort of husbanded these dollars together and we'd gotten some real estate people to put the package together, and how we managed to scrape a few millions here and a few millions there, and managed to put the whole thing together, and it was going to be a great big blockbuster. You know, it was something that needed to be done, so in that sense it wasn't just buying frigidaires for individuals to catch their votes. . . . I remember sort of saying: 'How can we do this for Toronto? You know, if they can't look after their own waterfront, well, how can we do it for them if we haven't done it for Montreal?' And they'd say: 'Well, Montreal has St. Helen's Island and in Vancouver they've got their Stanley Park or whatever it is.' Well, that's the aberration, and I think it rebounded on us, and it certainly wasn't part of *my* campaign.

"Much more to the point of my campaign is the speech I made in Toronto the night before the vote, or was it two nights. I just talked to the people for an hour or an hour and a quarter very, very calmly, and on the plane back I remember some of the press saying, 'Why didn't you do that before?' I said, 'That's what I've been doing all the time, I've been doing it through the whole campaign.' And they said, 'How is it you haven't been as emotional before now? Tonight you talked to us about our great country and how we had to understand each other and so on.' I said, 'It's true I've said the same things but not emotionally for the past two months, because I was embarrassed to try and win an election this easy way, appealing to people's feelings about Canada.' "

Despite all the flaws in Trudeau's approach, it was by no means clear what the outcome would be until all the votes were counted. Not only the prime minister's performance, but the whole election campaign, had a curiously abstracted quality; it seemed that once the election had been called, no one knew quite what to do with it. Although the constitution required a trip to the polls around that time, the public mood did not: Four years in office had sufficed to take the glow off Trudeau's once-spectacular image, and Canadians were not particularly enthused about giving the Trudeau Liberals another term in office; on the other hand, they had not been itching at the outset of the campaign to turf Trudeau out of power.

In that uncertain mood, Trudeau's campaign style did him serious damage, but the opposition never quite succeeded in winning the public's fancy, either. Robert Stanfield battered away diligently at the Liberals' handling of the economy, but he and the Tories didn't manage to come across as a clearly attractive alternative government in their own right. The NDP made headlines with David Lewis's attacks on corporate welfare bums and ultimately benefited in many ridings from close vote splits between the Liberals and Tories, but its impact on the public can best be gauged from the fact that it increased its share of the popular vote only marginally, from 17.0 per cent in 1968 to 17.8 per cent.

The final result left the Tories still trailing Trudeau and his Liberals in the popular vote, by a narrow margin of 38.5 per cent to 35.1 per cent. But it was a drastically different result from 1968, when the Liberals had received 45.5 per cent of the vote and the Progressive Conservatives 31.4 per cent. What ultimately counts most in an election, however, is the number of seats — and the result on election night was a dead heat, with 109 seats apiece for the Liberals and the Tories.

Subsequent recounts gave the Liberals 109 seats to 107 for the Tories, 31 for the NDP, 15 for Social Credit, one independent, and a "politically unaffiliated" seat won by Speaker Lucien Lamoureux. But on the night of October 30, 1972, it appeared to many that the election Trudeau had described at the outset as "a bath of fire in which you're purified and you settle all the piddling questions of whether this little thing was right or wrong"[12] was about to burn him into the pages of history as a short-lived political comet.

CHAPTER THIRTEEN

The Trudeau Years II:
Fighting for Power

ALTHOUGH some newspapers hastened on the day after the 1972 election to proclaim the end of the Trudeau years, Trudeau himself never seriously considered stepping aside. He had been fatalistically indifferent during the first mandate to the possibility of defeat — "I'm quite prepared to die politically when the people think I should,"[1] he had said in 1969 — but he did not consider the ambiguous election result an outright rejection. And in place of the insouciance with which he had regarded the abstract possibility of losing office, different factors came into play when he found himself so close to the reality: his pride, his combativeness, and his unwillingness to give up the prime-ministry before he had finished the job he set out to do. As he later put it: "I'm that particular kind of person who doesn't like to be kicked out. I don't mind leaving, but I don't like to be thrown out."[2]

Instead of turning the reins of government over to Stanfield and the Progressive Conservatives, he simply extended his campaign argument that the election was not so much a contest as a consultation with Canadians. The consultation had revealed that Canadians were dissatisfied with certain aspects of his policy and approach: "[The] vote has relayed to me and my colleagues better than any other mechanism could do that there have been failures."[3] Revisions would be made accordingly, but there could be no question of his government abandoning its "duty" to lead the nation. Trudeau's public arguments were based on a fiction about the

267

nature of elections — an election is a battle for the reins of government, not a policy consultation founded on the assumption that the administration of the day will remain in place. But as political strategy in the face of an unclear election result, the continued use of that fiction was ingenious. It invited the voters to accept that his continuation in office was a matter of heeding their admonitions rather than defying their rejection, and it left him free — under the guise of obeying the message he had received from the electorate — to "borrow" policies from other parties or adopt courses he had earlier rejected, without appearing inconsistent or opportunistic.

Constitutionally, Trudeau was on firm ground in retaining office, because any government has the right after an election to face the new Parliament and test its support. Politically, the situation was more dicey. The Liberals led in the popular vote and had a marginal edge in the number of seats; but they had, in a sense, been defeated everywhere except in their Quebec power base, trailing the Tories in both seats and share of the popular vote in the rest of the country. If there was nevertheless no national outcry when Trudeau declined to leave office, it was because he was right in his assessment of the situation: the public had formed no positive will to replace him as prime minister with Stanfield.

But the Pierre Trudeau who battled to remain in power was already in many ways not the same Pierre Trudeau the country had come so close to rejecting. The brush with defeat led him, with startling speed, to revise both his theoretical assumptions about the political process and his practical approaches to that process. Trudeau prides himself on his ability to play any game by its own rules, and he concluded in the autumn of 1972 that the rules of politics are rougher, more irrational, and ultimately more cynical than he had believed. "I'd almost say my faith in politics, my faith in the democratic process has changed a bit," he admitted a year later, in December of 1973. "I used to think it would be sufficient to put a reasonable proposition to a person, for the person to look at it reasonably, without passion, but that's obviously not true. Nine-tenths of politics — debate in Parliament, questions, answers, speeches on the hustings, commentary by the media — nine-tenths of it appeals to emotions rather than to reason. I'm a bit sorry about that, but this is the world we're living in, and therefore I've had to change. I used to think it wouldn't matter if I answered a question impatiently. I was thinking that people would look at what I said rather than the tone in which I said it. . . . I think I, in the last campaign, tried to speak the language of reason everywhere. But this isn't good news and I don't think I got through to the people very much. Next time around, I may be more impassioned and a little less rational. Who knows?"[4]

The same sort of disillusionment revealed itself in his performance at a question-and-answer session at McGill University in April 1973, on the fifth anniversary of his accession to the Liberal leadership. Where he had previously talked about government as a kind of partnership between elected officials and the public, his answers on this occasion conveyed a view of the electorate as rather more an adversary, a confused and self-seeking force that had to be appeased rather than reasoned with. Had he been trying, he was asked, to prepare Canada for the day when not every able-bodied person would need or want to work? "If you say that kind of thing," he replied, "you can be accused of undermining the work ethic. In a right-wing society as exists in North America today, including Canada, that is not a popular line to take. So it is much safer to say to everyone, 'Go out, get a job. . . .'" His answers were liberally sprinkled with such rueful references to the demands of the political process. "What kind of fools do governments have to be, not to say at election time, 'We'll give you lower taxes, higher old age pensions, price controls, everything you want'?" he said with considerable feeling at one point. At another, he noted: "If a government wants to do the popular things, it will ruin the economy — real quick."[5]

While not denying the disillusionment that could be glimpsed in his unguarded statements during that period, Trudeau now says that his resentment was directed much more against the opposition parties than against the public. "I think it lowered my opinion of the opposition more than of the electorate," he says. "You remember that speech I made when the House reconvened in

January, which was probably the most unpopular thing I ever did in the House, saying that the opposition had exploited a lot of anti-French-Canadian feelings. I think that was rather my feeling of that election — not that the people weren't worthy of a cool, rational campaign, and neither that I was myself a very poor campaigner, but that obviously I was trying to fight with a sword when the enemy was fighting with a bludgeon, and next time around I wouldn't be so subtle."

As for the public, "perhaps I was a bit disappointed with the political process and felt that if they want blood and guts, I'll give them blood and guts. What I wouldn't allow you to [infer] is any contempt for the people. I've never felt that; I've never felt I can't go out and explain things to them."

The shock of the 1972 election sufficed, in any event, to turn Trudeau into a much more conventional politician. He drastically modified his personal style, his choice of advisors, and his relationship with the Liberal Party. The change was most immediately evident in the PMO, which Trudeau invested with a far more political and less intellectual complexion. Lalonde, who had left to successfully run for Parliament, was replaced as principal secretary by Martin O'Connell, the defeated labour minister whose roots in the Liberal Party went back to the early 1960s. Jim Davey, the brilliant but overly theoretical policy secretary, was farmed out to the transport department and replaced by John Roberts, another Toronto MP defeated in the election. Press secretary Peter Roberts returned to the external affairs department, from which he had been seconded, and the crucial task of dealing with a hostile press was entrusted to a tough-minded and respected Quebec journalist, Pierre O'Neil. Michael Pitfield was promoted, but moved away from the PCO action centre, by being appointed deputy minister of consumer and corporate affairs. Ivan Head remained in the PMO in his capacity as foreign-affairs advisor, but his role as Trudeau's top domestic speech-writer was taken over by Alan Grossman, a *Time-Life* alumnus with a less philosophical style.

While these moves politicized Trudeau's immediate circle of advisors, even more important changes took place in his relationship with the Liberal Party. Realizing both the price he had paid electorally for alienating the party's rank and file and the likelihood that the party would eventually revolt against his leadership unless he mended his fences, he moved swiftly to demonstrate that he had learned his lesson.

One of the first things he did was to contact Keith Davey, the chief Pearson strategist who had been left on the sidelines by the Trudeau forces in the 1968 and 1972 elections. Davey had written Trudeau a letter at about the mid-point of the 1972 campaign, explaining why in his view the Liberals were headed for disaster and making a number of practical suggestions. Shortly after the election, Trudeau summoned Davey, thanked him for having sensed what was wrong and for having conveyed it privately, and offered him the chairmanship of the next campaign. When that appointment was finalized and announced in the spring, it had its controversial aspects — Davey, after all, had failed to win Pearson a majority — but it served as a peace gesture to much of the Liberal establishment and reassured them that the humbled prime minister was at least putting the political side of his government's battle for survival in the hands of a professional.

Trudeau also moved to establish better personal rapport with party members across the country. Wherever he travelled in Canada, meetings were scheduled with small groups of Liberals, and the prime minister would solicit their perceptions of how the situation was shaping up in their ridings, and their opinions of his own performance. "It used to be," says an aide, "that on these trips a half-hour would be set aside for the PM's lunch and he'd go off in a room by himself and have a steak. Now we schedule an hour and a half for lunch, and he meets a group of Liberals around a table." The objective was to have, in each province, at least a hundred Liberals who could respond to criticism by saying: "That isn't true. I talked to the PM and he told me . . ." In Ontario, for instance, an aide says, "there are 120 or so Liberals who can say they have had a conversation with the PM at least twice in the past year, and about 40 who have met with him four or five times."

In addition to these face-to-face contacts, Trudeau also initiated correspondence with Liberal riding presidents, asking them to write back with suggestions, comments, and reports on how things were going in their ridings. "At first," says an insider, "a lot of them were sceptical, they didn't think the PM would ever see the letters, and so forth. But he wrote follow-up letters saying, 'I wrote you a while ago, asking for your comments, and I haven't heard from you yet. I'm serious about this.' And if that still didn't work, he'd write to the riding treasurer or secretary and say, 'I asked your president for comments and I haven't heard from him. What do *you* think?' "

In March 1973, Trudeau also instituted a carefully structured system of regional political responsibility for his ministers, putting each minister directly in charge of a specified number of ridings. Explains an aide: "Up to that time, it was vaguely understood that ministers had some responsibility for their areas, but it was never clearly defined and there were problems nobody was looking at. In 1972, there was an MP who had a drinking problem, another had money for the first time in his life from his MP's salary and was always off in Florida — he was in Florida for the first three weeks of the campaign — and another had health problems and had just stopped servicing his riding. Everyone knew about these problems, but everyone just figured someone else would do something about it. The three things you can do in a riding are find a good candidate, raise money, and recruit members. Everyone would agree on that, and before 1972 we'd have meetings and ministers would say, 'Yeah, yeah, we've got to find candidates, raise more funds, and recruit' — and nothing much would happen."

In Trudeau's new system, which is still in effect, each minister must visit every riding in his area of responsibility at least once every six months; a senior member of the minister's staff must visit each non-Liberal riding in the assigned area every two months; and the minister is to meet the Liberal MPs from his area every two months. Based on these activities by the minister and his aide, each minister must give Trudeau a detailed bi-monthly report on each assigned riding. The report must cover, concisely but in detail: the minister's activity and his assistant's activity; the membership situation, including the target figure and the change in membership from the previous report; finances, including amounts received and objectives; opposition activity in the riding; the riding association's programs; the activities of the Liberal MP, if there is one; the activities of special groups, such as youth wings; and feelings in the riding about the government's performance on both national and local issues.

Each such report is carefully studied by a member of Trudeau's PMO staff with regional responsibility for that particular part of the country, and a detailed response to the minister — often requesting clarification of a given item or demanding improved performance on some particular matter — is prepared for Trudeau's signature. Particularly serious riding problems or shortcomings in a minister's performance are referred directly to Trudeau for his personal attention, and he also periodically schedules meetings with his ministers for face-to-face discussion of the ridings under their care.

With Trudeau's previous disinterest in such nuts-and-bolts political matters still fresh in their minds, many ministers initially didn't take the new system very seriously — until the prime minister promptly demonstrated that he meant business. "He began taking them on one at a time to discuss their reports," an aide recalls. "And the minister would come in thinking it would just be a gab about generalities. Then the PM would say: 'I think the best way to go through this is to go over your ridings in alphabetical order.' The poor minister would start scrambling to get whatever papers he had brought into alphabetical order. Then the PM would say: 'On such-and-such a riding, I don't understand this item in your report,' or 'I see your political assistant didn't get around to visiting this riding — why is that?' And a lot of times the minister hadn't even read his own report; he had just left it to his assistant to write, thinking that no one was going to take it very seriously. One experience like that was all it took to set them straight. Now that he has become involved, the PM really likes the political game and plays it with relish."

All this, however, was merely the building of an infrastructure for political survival. The real battles still had to be fought in Parliament and in the arena of public opinion, and Trudeau's first step was to insulate himself against the threat of premature defeat in the House of Commons. He did this by taking what had previously been improvised — most recently when the Pearson government had accidentally been defeated on a budget resolution in February 1968 — and turning it into a pre-announced principle of action: "Some things for us will be questions of confidence. Some things would mean the demise of the government," he said in the Throne Speech debate when the new Parliament met in January. "If, for instance, there should be a clear vote of no confidence in the government, if the government should be defeated on fundamentals, on basic principles . . . we shall go to the people. . . . But I hasten to add that other questions, if they go against us, will not be interpreted by the government as a defeat of the government. . . . We are not going to abdicate our responsibilities or to bring this Parliament to a premature end just because this House, in the exercise of its judgment, defeats us on some matter that is not a matter of principle, some matter that does not go to the roots of our policy."

To bring down his government, in other words, the opposition would have to openly and explicitly set out to do so, rather than merely defeat a given piece of legislation. And if that happened, Trudeau made clear, he would not turn over power to the Tories but would ask the governor general to dissolve Parliament and call another election. Since the NDP had just acquired its alluring new balance-of-power role and could scarcely expect to benefit from an early election which would be a de facto run-off between the Liberals and Tories, Trudeau's warning served to discourage an early defeat. At the same time, his position left him with another trick up his sleeve: On most issues, the government was prepared to adopt an almost congressional approach, putting forward proposals which could be accepted by Parliament, amended, defeated, or withdrawn in the face of opposition rejection. But some issues would be "matters of principle" whose defeat would require an election — and the government reserved unto itself the right to determine, not necessarily in advance of a defeat, which issues fell into that category. The opposition therefore had to tread carefully, because any bill it defeated — no matter how minor it might seem — could suddenly be interpreted by the government as a matter of principle requiring a trip to the polls.

With the opposition held at bay by this booby-trap, Trudeau had time to concentrate on rebuilding his popularity with the public. "I pointed out to him," says Keith Davey, "that it seemed to me that if he was to win the next election, he had to get two things across. He would have to appear contrite, convey that he had 'learned his lesson'. Whether in fact he had or not, his public posture had to be that the message had been sent and he had the message. And the second part of it was a conviction on his part that he really did want to be the prime minister of Canada."

Trudeau's public act of contrition began almost immediately. In rebuilding his election-battered cabinet, he shuffled the most controversial ministers away from the firing-line. Jean-Pierre Goyer, who had repeatedly gotten the government into hot water as solicitor general, went to the relative obscurity of the supply and services portfolio; Gérard Pelletier, whose innovative programs as secretary of state had stirred the wrath of conservatives, became minister of communications; Jean Marchand, accused of using DREE grants as political patronage and boondoggles for Quebec, was moved to transport; and Bryce Mackasey, whose UIC reforms had become such a hot campaign issue, refused a shift and ended up fuming on the back-benches.

Trudeau also hastened to announce changes in a number of his government's most controversial policies. The open-door approach to immigration, which had produced the beginnings of a nasty backlash, was tightened up. Unemployment insurance rules were adjusted in an attempt to weed out claimants who weren't seriously seeking a job. The plan to cut off family allowance payments to those with incomes above a certain income level was reconsidered. And the deadline for requiring bilingualism in 25,000 key federal jobs was extended. Such changes, Trudeau explained in the Throne Speech debate, were intended "to try and correct those areas in our administration where we had been incompetent, or where we had appeared to be incompetent . . . without in any way turning back on our Liberal principles and without in any way withdrawing from the faith that we, as Liberals, have in the land or the fact that we, as Liberals, always tend to err on the side of liberty rather than on the side of gain."

Hand in hand with these changes went a curious combination of public self-flagellation and self-justification that began even before Parliament met in January. "We got an awful shellacking from the Canadian people," he told a Liberal dinner in Regina in December. "I am disappointed at the results of October 30th, but I am thankful and almost full of admiration for a kind of system which in that sense has given us a second chance. And believe me, the coming weeks and months must be used by us . . . to show the Canadian people that indeed we have understood what aspects of our government, what aspects of our administration they rejected. . . . For instance, I believe that Canadians on October 30th were telling us, the government, that the Canadian economy could perform better. . . . The other area which was of concern to the West, and I believe shared by a lot of other parts of Canada, had to do with an indignation which was expressed on October 30th about the lax administration by the government of some programs and policies, which weren't necessarily rejected out of hand but which were criticized and justly so because we had failed to administer them properly. . . . And the third reason, well, I guess briefly stated I would say we were accused or suspected of undermining the value system. . . . This value system is one which we respect. . . . But there have been some mistakes in the application of our policies, some errors of administration. . . . All I can say is that we will ensure change, but in a way which will not destroy the basic values."

But the show of humility, on this occasion as on others, was always balanced by insistence that the errors had been flaws of detail rather than of principle. Trudeau stood by all his basic policies, admitting a need for change only in some aspects of their implementation. This was particularly evident in the area of national unity and language policy: Trudeau repeatedly referred to the existence of an anti-French, anti-Quebec backlash, but he steadfastly refused either to ascribe his near-defeat to that backlash or to back away from any of his policies in this field. Rather, he argued, the fault had been one of failing to explain and defend the policies adequately. "I said in so many words several times during the campaign, 'The language question, the Quebec question, I won't even talk about it, you know, some people are talking about it but it's settled, and I bet you that in the next general election we won't even hear of the question.' Obviously that was naïve; the land is not that strong. . . . But as a result of the campaign and the way in which it was waged, I realize that the language question for instance is not well understood."[6]

Trudeau felt so strongly about the language question, despite its political risks at that point, that he went out of his way to make a major issue of it when he spoke in the Throne Speech debate. He quoted a *Vancouver Sun* editorial which had argued that it would be wrong and divisive for him to remain in office because he had been "overwhelmingly repudiated by the English-speaking majority". When his reference to this subject brought an angry reaction from opposition members, he retorted that he had raised it "because I know there are members sitting in the Conservative ranks who, during the election, tried to divide Canada." He returned to this theme several times during the speech, in a performance that brought him harsh criticism in the press and clashed dangerously with the humbled image he was trying to project. This was one issue, however, on which Trudeau remained entirely unwilling to compromise, and he later explained the episode this way:

"One of the areas I wanted to touch upon was the important area of national unity and I just touched upon it by quoting an editorial in a Vancouver paper which I think was rather clear evidence of the possibility of the backlash. . . . Well, this wasn't an attack on the Conservatives. . . . This was not an attempt either to blame our defeat on the backlash or to attack the Conservative party. What astounded me is that when I began quoting the editorial, the House erupted into an uproar. I was rather taken aback because it seemed to me I was being told: 'Well, this is the kind of subject you should not deal with. This is taboo. You don't talk about it in polite company. You just sweep it under the rug and pretend it doesn't exist.' Well, this has never been my way in

politics. I frankly couldn't understand why I was generally applauded when I would attack separatism in Quebec to the point,
you will recall, of even sending troops in there and having the
War Measures Act brought in when violence made it necessary —
and this was generally applauded across the country — but were
I even so much as to mention separatism in other parts of the
country or anti-French Canadian feeling in other parts of the
country, suddenly I became a blackguard and the place exploded
and I was doing something which was shameful and so on. . . .

"It really meant that as prime minister of all Canadians it was
all right for me to attack French Canadian bigots but it wasn't
all right for me to attack English Canadian bigots. . . . And that is
why I left the subject and came back to it later in my speech
because I wanted it to be known not only in the House of Commons but in the country at large that it is not a problem that we
should sweep under the carpet. . . . And I want to put people
on notice that I will not be silent on this. I don't want to create
hysteria about it, but I want people to know that wherever I find
traces of bigotry, I will fight it whether it be in the province of
Quebec or in any other province."[7]

But apart from this continued outspokenness on the national
unity issue — the same depth of feeling on this subject led him,
in June 1973, to successfully ask Parliament to re-endorse the
principles of federal language policy — Trudeau made a sustained
effort at the beginning of the minority period to project an image
of chastened humility. He also deliberately assumed a lower political profile, making fewer public appearances and leaving it to
his ministers to answer most questions and defend most policies
in the House. "It's a very conscious strategy, and it was high time
for me to adopt it," he explained. "I think the situation arose from
the particular circumstances of the 1968 election where I had
played the starring role. Since it was thought that people had
elected this government in part because of my personality, it followed that my personality ought to play a large role in the explanation and defence of our policies. . . . In the perception of
people outside the government, as a result of those particular
circumstances [in 1968], the myth developed that this was a one-

man government, which is far from true. But because people thought so, they took to demanding that it be this man who explained everything and also this man who be blamed for everything if things went badly."[8]

Within four months of the election, Trudeau's efforts began paying dividends, with a Gallup Poll in February finding that fifty-seven per cent of the public believed that the election outcome had changed him. Then, gradually, as the Liberals successfully manoeuvred and compromised in Parliament, Trudeau's penitence was replaced by a fighting stance. At the Liberal Party's convention in Ottawa in September of 1973, he delivered the most combatively political speech of his career to that point, an artful blend of emotion, sophistry, and partisan jibing, in which he called Stanfield "a power-hungry Conservative leader" and accused the NDP of "pure sham and pure hypocrisy" for claiming that they were leading the government rather than clinging to its coat-tails. Thanking his party for its continued support, he skewered the Tories for their treatment of John Diefenbaker when that party suffered a similar rebuke in the 1962 election: "The party fell apart. The ministers resigned, the leader was being slowly murdered by his ministers, they destroyed the party themselves. Thank God that is not the kind of dissent that we see in the Liberal Party."

The government had recovered from its setback and was now ready to enter a new phase, he said: "We have in a sense finished the holding action; we have stopped just hanging in there. The convention time, this time, is a time of rebirth not only of the party fortunes but of the party ideas and the party actions. . . . We will not be dared into an election, certainly not by the Conservatives and certainly not by the NDP. . . . We don't want an election, but believe me we are not afraid of an election. If the opposition combined want an election, there will be many occasions to provoke one. . . . And if they cease to implement Liberal policies, we will have an election and they will have the fight of their lives."

The rhetoric of humility and combativeness was only one part of the newly image-conscious prime minister's struggle for political recovery. Accompanying it was a radically changed approach to the actual business of government. There was no more leisurely long-range planning, no more adoption of complicated programs whose benefits wouldn't be felt until years later, no more argument that policies didn't have to please the public so long as they were sound, no more insistence on holding the line on government spending. Instead, partly to keep the support of the NDP and partly to woo the public, the Liberals adopted a crisp, fast-acting style of decision-making and a kind of conservative populism. The conservatism, a response to what Trudeau and his ministers perceived as a rightward shift in the public mood, took the form of a curb on social experimentation in penal reform, welfare programs, and other fields. At the same time, knowing that the NDP insisted on socially progressive measures and that the public seldom spurns direct and simple government largesse, Trudeau increased various forms of transfer payments and cut taxes.

The emphasis was on swift, decisive response to visible problems. Faced with the energy crisis of 1973, Trudeau moved quickly to introduce a package of measures that borrowed heavily from NDP demands but that insulated the public from the threat of oil shortages or skyrocketing prices and left him looking firmly in command. Faced with continued Western discontent, Trudeau invited the premiers of the prairie provinces and British Columbia to a Western Economic Opportunities Conference in Calgary that demonstrated the federal government's concern and produced an array of specific commitments to assist the region. His leadership image also benefited from his visit to China in October of 1973 and his chairmanship of the Commonwealth prime ministers' conference in Ottawa two months earlier.

While some of the initiatives of the minority period — notably the creation of a virtually toothless Food Prices Review Board, and the proposal for a perilously vague and clearly improvised anti-profiteering law — were cosmetic measures to appease the NDP, the government nevertheless accomplished a great deal that was useful and popular in those eighteen months. Old age pensions were increased and indexed to the cost of living. Family allowance payments, Canada Pension Plan benefits, and the veterans' allowance were all increased. There was a tax cut with particular benefits for low- and middle-income earners, and federal subsidies kept down the price of bread and milk. Parliament passed legislation restricting electronic surveillance, an election expenses act, and the Foreign Investment Review Act, and extended the ban on capital punishment for another five years.

The greatest personal accomplishment for Trudeau, however, was his success in eighteen short months in rebuilding his popularity both within the Liberal Party and in the nation at large. Especially since the 1972 electoral setback had been so much a personal rebuke for the prime minister, it would not have been unnatural for his leadership to come under attack within the Liberal Party and for the party to be weakened by internal splits and discontents. Instead, through his new attention to party matters and his feisty leadership, Trudeau not only kept the Liberals united but won from them a degree of admiration and personal esteem he had not attained in the first mandate. As for the public, Keith Davey and other strategists were convinced by the beginning of 1974 that the recovery was so complete that an election with a sufficiently strong campaign could give them a new majority.

Trudeau bought this recovery at a price, however: he deliberately diminished himself into political conventionality and carefully dimmed his originality. It was a price exacted by the electorate, and without paying it he quite probably would have been defeated. Trudeau, true to his pragmatism, decided that it was preferable to adopt a style of politics he had despised than to lose office and be able to accomplish nothing further. When a disapproving interviewer in 1973 cited to him Henry Clay's dictum, "I would rather be right than be President," Trudeau scoffed: "Well, I forget who said that, but he probably wasn't in politics and he probably was never President. You know, if I wanted to be right rather than prime minister, I'd have stayed in university."[9] The more conventionally political he became — the more he over-simplified arguments, appealed to emotion rather than intellect, and presented policies designed more for cosmetic effect than substantive merit — the more the public warmed to him again. The lessons

of this period and of the subsequent election were not lost on
Trudeau, and he permanently transformed himself into a more
effective politician and a less open and unique leader.

By early 1974, the strain of the balance-of-power role was starting to tell on the NDP. The New Democrats became increasingly
worried that instead of being perceived by the public as socially
conscious champions wresting concessions out of the Liberals,
their continued support was making them look like an appendage
of the governing party. And Trudeau, instead of being conciliatory
as might be expected of a minority prime minister, did what he
could to step up the pressure, taunting that the New Democrats
were "hanging onto us like seagulls on a fishing vessel, claiming
that they are really steering the ship." By April, he was openly
mocking both Robert Stanfield and David Lewis and practically
daring them to force an election. "Mr. Stanfield wants an election;
he wants an election before his party breaks up; he wants an election because it is an old tactic when things are going wrong in your
own house, you start fighting against the neighbour," he said at
a Liberal meeting in Hamilton. "And Mr. Lewis — well, he knows
that the only chance he can get of getting a headline, of getting
his picture on the front page, of getting his photograph on television, is to say: 'You know, I am not going to support this government much longer if they don't do this, that, or the next
thing.' " In Sudbury on the same trip, he carried the goading a
step further: "I think the Canadian people have had enough of
this posturing by the opposition parties. We're not calling an
election. We're not rattling any sabres, believe me. But we've got
a sabre to rattle if they want an election."

By the time John Turner introduced his budget at the beginning
of May, the 29th Parliament was visibly dying. The nerves of the
New Democrats were so thoroughly jangled that it was no longer
a matter of conditional support for the government; they were
just looking for an excuse to pull the plug. When Turner presented
a budget that virtually ignored the NDP's demands, even though
it contained a number of measures likely to be attractive to the public, the nearly inevitable happened, the government was defeated
on May 8, and Canadians were on their way back to the polls.

It was no accident that in 107 previous years of Confederation and 22 years of minority rule during that period, only twice before had a government been defeated in Parliament — and on both occasions it had been in extraordinary circumstances. In 1926, Arthur Meighen's Conservatives were toppled after only two days in power, in the midst of a constitutional crisis; in 1963, the Tories were so bitterly divided over John Diefenbaker's leadership and in such internal disarray that they were in no position to defend themselves against the threat of parliamentary defeat. Ordinarily, however, governments abhor defeat in Parliament and will go to almost any lengths to avoid it, either beating the opposition to the punch by calling an election themselves or withdrawing the offending legislation and amending it to win the necessary support.

But the Trudeau Liberals just sailed inexorably, almost serenely, toward defeat and dissolution, with the prime minister insisting that he didn't think it would happen but that he was quite ready for an election if it did. In reality, the Liberals had prepared a budget that would serve them well if the Parliament survived, but they both expected and welcomed an election. They couldn't call one themselves, however, because the public was so uneasy about economic conditions that it would have been dangerous to say: "We've called this election because we've done such a good job that we want another mandate." It was quite another matter to be able to tell the electorate: "We're doing our best, we've been forced into an unnecessary election, give us a chance to finish what we've started." Admits their strategist, Keith Davey: "I was in the gallery desperately hoping we would be defeated, because I knew we would win the election — we had the numbers."

Trudeau's attitude wasn't quite that clear-cut, partly because he couldn't quite believe that the NDP would take an action he considered manifestly stupid and self-defeating. Davey also believes, not necessarily accurately, that "the prime minister was not yet sufficiently political to hope the hell we were going to be beaten. He sat down there during that vote and hoped some kind of miracle would occur and the government would be saved." Once the election was called, in any event, the Liberals were ready with a strategy dictated by their own research. "We had surveyed," says Davey, "and the surveys showed two things very clearly. The first was that when you ran issues of concern in order of priority, you found out that the overwhelming issue was inflation. It absolutely, utterly, completely, totally dwarfed any issue of concern I had seen in the Pearson days. I remember unemployment for example in '62 and '63 — it was huge — but this time inflation had impacted itself about twice as heavily on the public mind as had unemployment in the '60s. And the overwhelming majority, ninety per cent or something, I forget what it was, thought the government was doing a lousy job [in fighting inflation]. The same survey: We run Trudeau against Stanfield, and I'd never seen one political guy rout another political guy so completely. So it was very clear to me that if on election day, the guy is marking his ballot on the basis of 'Hey, are prices too high in this country or is inflation too bad in this country?', we've got to lose. If he's marking his ballot on 'Hey, who do I want to run this country, who do I want as general manager for all the problems?', we've got. to win it. And so our whole campaign was cast on the issue being leadership and inflation being the problem."

Trudeau started off with a considerable built-in advantage, because both the Tories and the NDP were running dismal campaigns. Stanfield made the fundamental mistake of offering, as his central campaign issue, a plan to impose price and income controls. The details of the scheme were so inadequately thought out that he had to keep making adjustments, and the over-all effect was to give up an Opposition's most important advantage in a campaign: the freedom to go on the attack while the government must defend its record. Stanfield found himself acting like the head of an embattled government, defending his scheme not only against Trudeau's scornful attack but against uneasy members of his own party. Lewis, meanwhile, wandered aimlessly through the campaign, lacking impact because he himself didn't know what he wanted to accomplish. He had forced the election, but there was no outcome that would be significantly better than the status quo he had upset: the NDP would either find itself back amid the stresses and strains of holding the balance of power, or have its strength cut and be relegated again to relative insignificance.

While the opposition foundered, Trudeau charged into battle right from the first shot with a style that Canadians had neither seen from him before nor expected — that of conventional, devastatingly effective, gut-fighting politician. In the first phase, eyes blazing, face contorted with anger, gesticulating wildly, the prime minister crossed the country accusing the Tories and the NDP of having defeated his budget because they were more interested in an election than in all his important anti-inflation measures. He rode a train through the Maritimes and Quebec, reciting to audiences at each whistle-stop the defeated budget's "anti-inflation" measures — tax cuts, removal of sales tax on shoes and clothing, tax-free savings for would-be home owners, all financed by higher corporate taxes — and concluding: "When the other parties talk to you about inflation or the high cost of housing, you ask them — ask them why they defeated our budget despite the measures we proposed."

In the next phase, he gradually moderated his tone from fury to scorn, zeroing in on Stanfield's vulnerable freeze-and-controls proposal with simplistic but effective putdowns. Would Stanfield tell Arab oil exporters: "Zap! You're frozen!"? How could Stanfield hope to govern a country when he couldn't keep his own party united on his own controls proposal? And, when the Tory leader began modifying some details of the plan: "Mr. Stanfield's freeze is beginning to drip." As for the NDP: "They've disappeared over the horizon honking like a flock of geese." At the same time, to add a positive dimension, the Liberals started firing off a barrage of policy promises on housing, transportation, consumer protection, agriculture, social security, and several other areas. The content of these announcements mattered less to Liberal strategists than the fact that they were being made, reinforcing the image of an active government with a broad range of plans and producing enough news to overshadow the other parties in the media.

And, finally, while continuing to hammer away mercilessly at the opposition, Trudeau injected an element of the old "The Land

Is Strong" pitch, delivering the upbeat message that only the Liberals shared the confidence of Canadians in the nation's future. "We're not tragic like the Tories, nor angry like the New Democrats," he told a rally in Hamilton at the end of the campaign. "Sit down, relax. Liberal meetings are fun."

Through it all, there was no resemblance to the playful crown prince en route to his coronation in 1968 or the detached professor listlessly traversing the country in 1972. Trudeau spoke at four or five rallies each day, and never slackened his pace. His speeches were down-to-earth, liberally sprinkled with wisecracks and sharp, memorable lines, and delivered in a vigorous staccato style. He thrived on hecklers, cutting them down with razor-edged wit. He avoided interviews, press conferences, open-line programs, and other situations in which he might be questioned and diverted from his chosen pitch; indeed, he gave only a dozen interviews and had a dozen press conferences in the whole two-month campaign. Where he had previously insisted that his family life was separate from his political role, this time Margaret accompanied him during much of the campaign and delivered several impromptu little "apolitical" speeches praising him as a man and a husband. The 1974 campaign, like those of 1968 and 1972, was again a one-man show in the public's perception — only this time the man was a conventional politician, calculatingly emotional rather than coldly rational, verbally blazing away at his opponents like a political gunfighter in a high-noon shootout.

The electorate responded by giving him 141 seats and 42.4 per cent of its vote.

CHAPTER FOURTEEN

The Trudeau Years III: Squandering Power

THE election of July 8, 1974, elevated Trudeau to a new peak of political strength. He had consolidated his control over his party, added the wiles and guiles of conventional politics to his leadership arsenal, and won a fresh majority mandate in which his exercise of power would be assisted by the experience he had gathered over the preceding six years. He had also rebuilt his relationship with the Canadian public, striking a responsive chord with his campaign and eliciting a new outpouring of goodwill and confidence. The national mood was upbeat, transgressions of the past were forgiven, and people settled back to await the dynamic leadership he had promised. Instead, it all quickly started to come unravelled.

Within two short years of the election that had given him 42 per cent of the popular vote, Trudeau found himself plunged to the lowest ebb of his popularity. In August of 1976, his party had only 29 per cent support in the Gallup Poll, a depth unplumbed by the Liberals since Lester Pearson's trouncing at the hands of John Diefenbaker in 1958. And the Tories, led by unproven and un-dazzling novice Joe Clark, were suddenly ahead of the veteran prime minister's forces by 18 percentage points. Once again, as in 1972, the question was: Can Trudeau survive? And this time, amid widespread speculation that he would soon retire if his popularity did not increase, the answer was far less clear.

In retrospect, the fundamental mistake that brought Trudeau into this plight was his decision in the early post-election weeks to devote the first year of his new mandate to a period of low-key, almost invisible government. Energies in that first year were to be devoted to two objectives: clearing up the backlog of legislation — most of it routine and unexciting — that had been left on the order paper when the government was defeated in the spring, and plotting a course for the remaining three years of the mandate. This emphasis on long-range planning had much in common with Trudeau's post-1968 approach, only this time the process was reversed: After the 1968 election, the long-term planning of policy directions and timetables was centred in Trudeau's office and the results were filtered down to the cabinet; in 1974, Trudeau reached out to his ministers and invited them to shape the government's strategy.

This was done by means of an elaborate and cumbersome year-long "priorities exercise" which began shortly after the election. Each minister was interviewed at length by PCO officials on his views as to what the government should be doing. The views of all ministers were then synthesized into a general statement of directions in sixteen "priority areas", and this material was sent back to individual departments for study of ways to turn the broad objectives into action. The process dragged on and on, with Trudeau's aides first touting a Montreal speech in January of 1975 as the event at which he would announce where his government was headed, then shifting expectations toward an announcement in late spring, and finally pinning their hopes on a statement at the Liberal Party's national convention in November. "There are six or seven good papers in the priorities exercise," a minister complained privately amid the delays, "but too much of the material is too general and philosophical. The cabinet is having difficulty making decisions. In a way, we're over-informed — we have so much information, so many alternative proposals, that people get paralysed by it, and a tendency develops to just keep putting off the tough decisions." Meanwhile, as Trudeau and his ministers pondered how to govern in the future, the public saw a government drifting with apparent aimlessness in the present.

"Any study of 1974-75 has to be considered in the light that they really did make a decision to low-profile it for a year," says one of

Trudeau's closest advisors. "That was to be the catch-up year. And the priorities exercise was the far reach of the planning pendulum. It was fairly reasonable that one would say, 'We have gradually developed the techniques of establishing priorities over the past years, so now we are capable of a fairly sophisticated exercise in priority-setting.' It was a natural thing in the first year of a four-year mandate to consider what they were going to be doing. It then followed that this would be the grand-daddy of all priorities exercises, to be followed, surely, by great results. . . . It was the far reach of the pendulum; since then we have gone considerably further back. We still do the examination every year, but not at that level of complexity."

Trudeau himself explains his government's curiously inactive behaviour in that period as simply an attempt to zero in more efficiently on specific policy targets — things like parliamentary reform, the further expansion of bilingualism, the problems of native people's and women's rights, environmental protection, and the reduction of poverty. "What you describe as a low profile I would describe as trying to provide a government and a basis from which to bring in some of the important reforms which we had in mind. . . . And I was realistic enough to know that we couldn't do them unless we could manage the economy well and bring down inflation and so on. And, you know, I would still maintain that that meant giving leadership of a kind that was perhaps less visible. But we spent a hell of a lot of effort in those days trying to seek a consensus to bring down inflation, the ministers spent hundreds of man-hours consulting with various groups and trying to talk inflation down. . . . In this Parliament, we were determined to pursue certain priorities and we enumerated them and they were all there, but to spend less time in the House of Commons trying to improve everything everywhere and concentrate on certain selective priorities. It didn't work all that well, but the effort was to govern less, but not in order to be, shall we say, more small-c conservative, but to govern less in order to pursue more efficiently and more ardently certain priorities which we thought were higher than others."

The decision to get off to such a slow start — despite the lesson of the post-1968 period that expectations of decisive action cannot be dashed with impunity — was not the result of any single over-whelming consideration, nor was it clearly reached at any precise moment. It evolved, rather, from a number of elements in the condition of the Trudeau government at that time and in the personality of the prime minister himself.

In some ways, the causes of what happened in 1974-75 go all the way back to the period between 1968 and 1972. When Trudeau had first come to power, he had launched an intensive program of policy review and formulation. But after his schedule went awry and his government's attention was distracted by inflation and unemployment, he had gone into the 1972 election with many of his carefully formulated plans still unimplemented. When the election result was a minority government, those long-range plans had to be shelved in favour of scrambling for day-to-day survival. And by the time Trudeau won his new majority in 1974, Canada and the world had changed, and the plans first conceived some four years earlier were no longer relevant.

Trudeau found himself with a majority government and an intellectual larder barren of useful, concrete plans; even the policies he announced during the campaign had been snatched half-ready off the drawing-boards and didn't add up to anything approaching a coherent program. In that situation, it became tempting to take the long view again and devote the first year to having the government canvass itself on what to do next.

That temptation was encouraged by the Ottawa bureaucracy for reasons of its own. By 1972, a major rotation in the senior echelons of the public service had become due. A number of deputy ministers had been in their posts long enough and were ready to change departments in what would have been the last rotation of a generation, the group then in their fifties. But the instability of minority government made it necessary to postpone the changes, and after the 1974 election some deputy ministers were already thinking of retirement and others were impatient for a shift. Not wanting to become involved in new initiatives or major policy changes which might postpone their retirements or imperil the rotation, some of these top-ranking civil servants were inclined to agree with the government that a year of stock-taking was desirable.

And the cabinet, too, had reasons beyond those of policy for welcoming the idea of a less hectic year. Thirteen of the ministers had been in the cabinet for at least seven years, and three of the most influential — Drury, Sharp, and MacEachen — had served for thirteen. After the two tense, bruising years of minority government, they were all tired men and the idea of a slow year to catch their breaths was appealing.

Trudeau also had additional reasons of his own for favouring inaction. First, what an associate has called his "reward-for-effort response" came into play: he had achieved a major success in surviving the minority period and winning a new majority, and he was inclined — at least subconsciously — to reward himself with a calmer, more reflective year. Secondly, he was already having difficulties at home with Margaret, who had to be briefly hospitalized a short time after the election for treatment of severe nervous strain, and the distraction of those domestic worries may have made him somewhat more susceptible to the arguments from people around him for a less demanding year. And, finally and most importantly, there was Trudeau's theory of counterweights and his dislike of exaggerated public expectations. After the tense, action-filled, and highly visible minority period and the emotional, expectation-arousing campaign, his long-held views made it natural for him to favour restoring some equilibrium by means of a period of diminished political intensity.

But while all those factors make Trudeau's post-election approach easier to understand, they did nothing to make it less politically disastrous. The relationship between any politician and his constituency is fragile, based as much on expectations and impressions as on substance, and the prime minister's year of apparent inactivity strained it to the breaking point. The campaign had deliberately saturated the nation with images of dynamism: Trudeau, the picture of machismo in his leather trenchcoat, standing on a train platform barking out condemnations of the Tories and the New Democrats for bringing down his government . . . Trudeau, angry and scornful, mocking Stanfield and his controls plan . . . Trudeau, the experienced, confident leader, repeating over and over that "the issue is leadership" . . . Trudeau, leaving a trail of policy announcements across the country, calling for a mandate to swing into exciting action.

And then he disappeared. He allowed eighty-four days to pass between the election and the opening of Parliament, a period of let-down punctuated only by an unexcitingly functional cabinet shuffle and two instances of ministerial ineptitude: With the egg marketing fiasco beginning to explode around him as warehouses overflowed with rotting eggs, Agriculture Minister Eugene Whelan made matters worse by publicly responding, with characteristic grace, to criticism by Food Prices Review Board head Beryl Plumptre, only to be publicly criticized in turn by Consumer Affairs Minister André Ouellet — a spectacle which hardly gave the impression of a smooth-running, cohesive government. Labour Minister John Munro, meanwhile, provided the only other visible government action in the form of a thoroughly botched intervention into a West Coast grain-handlers' strike. He first undercut management's bargaining position in the dispute by warning that Parliament would be recalled to impose a settlement on the terms of a conciliation report if management didn't accept those terms itself. Then management didn't budge, Parliament wasn't recalled, and Munro rushed to Vancouver to intervene personally — and turned out to have nothing useful to say.

When Parliament finally opened on September 30, it was with a bland Throne Speech that contained little fresh policy and even less indication of the kind of general course the government was charting for its new mandate. Then, while Parliament settled down to the uncaptivating task of clearing up its legislative backlog, Trudeau and his administration remained nearly invisible. With the exception of a budget and three important and generally successful prime-ministerial trips abroad — one to Washington, and two to Europe in pursuit of a contractual link with the European Economic Community — there was little positive action for the public to see. What people saw, instead, was a succession of negative incidents. Close on the heels of the antics of Whelan and Munro, the government blundered into making the appointment of James Jerome as Speaker of the House a needlessly controversial issue by denying opposition leaders the courtesy of prior consultation. This was followed in short order by Canada's ill-advised abstention on a United Nations vote on whether to hear from the terrorist Palestinian Liberation Organization, Marc Lalonde's misjudgment in accepting a ride to Israel aboard a private corporate jet, Margaret Trudeau's free trip to Japan provided by a Hong Kong industrialist, Trudeau's characterization of an opposition MP as a "son of a bitch" over a misunderstood remark, and the government's botched handling of a pre-Christmas pay raise for MPs.

All these mistakes were relatively minor, but they cumulatively eroded the image of a government which offered little action to counterbalance the impression created by its pratfalls. And they were particularly damaging to a government which, only a few months earlier, had based its whole campaign on creating the expectation of bold leadership. By year's end, this gap between expectation and performance was being widely noticed, but Trudeau professed to be unperturbed. Asked about it directly at a pre-Christmas press conference, he replied: "I'm a little bit puzzled as to what you and the people mean by leadership. Do they want somebody on a white horse charging forth and saying, 'You follow me,' or do they want to look at the results and ask themselves if this country by and large, given its advantages and problems, has done as well, or better, or worse than most?"

This was entirely in line with Trudeau's long-held views on leadership and his belief that its most direct forms should be used only in exceptional circumstances. On the major issues confronting his government — inflation-fighting, the overhaul of the welfare system, and the framing of a new immigration policy — he was proceeding slowly in accordance with his conviction that the function of government is not to impose solutions to most problems, but to invite society to develop a consensus on what should be done. Since it is almost impossible to obtain a spontaneous consensus on such complicated issues, and since the true task of leadership is not merely to seek consensus but to shape it, it was scarcely surprising that Trudeau's efforts in these areas produced few results.

By March, the impression that the government was drifting had begun to exact a serious toll on Trudeau's popularity. One Gallup Poll found that 43 per cent of Canadians disapproved of the government's performance and only 35 per cent approved; in 1973, the same question had shown 44 per cent approval. A second Gallup, centred on Trudeau himself, found 36 per cent of the public saying its opinion of him had gone down in the past three months, while only 13 per cent said it had gone up. Then, as the government's efforts to find a voluntary solution to inflation-fighting failed, John Turner resigned, and price and income controls had to be introduced, the real trouble began for an already-weakened government.

The tortuous path that led to the imposition of price and income controls on October 14, 1975, really had its beginnings in the earliest years of the Trudeau administration. In 1969 and 1970, Trudeau had experimented with combating inflation through Draconian fiscal and monetary measures; the resulting unemployment and political outcry taught him a lesson he was not about to forget by repeating the experiment. He had also experimented with the idea of a toothless watchdog body, the Prices and Incomes Commission, with a mandate to try to persuade business and labour to avoid actions that would fuel inflation; that, too, had proved unsatisfactory.

With the country facing a new round of mounting inflationary pressures in the post-1972 period, Trudeau didn't have very many untried weapons left in his arsenal. One such weapon was mandatory price and income controls. Although the 1974 campaign deliberately lopped off the subtleties, Trudeau's previous position had always been not that he rejected controls outright but that he considered them inappropriate to the circumstances of the day. "Well, at present we are not for them, and that's why we haven't introduced them," he said in March 1972. "But whether we might have to introduce them in the future, the answer is yes, we might. And that is why we have told Parliament that we had contingency plans for looking at various forms of fighting inflation and this was one of them."[1] During the 1972 campaign, he was even more precise: "If inflation really gets out of hand, [imposition of controls] is a viable option, one which I hope we won't have to use, but which we would be forced to use if inflation got out of hand. . . . It would have to put us in a situation where we would be much worse off, or shall we say noticeably worse off, than our competitors in the trading world, countries with which we have relations."[2]

In the 1974 campaign, he would have been on firm ground if he had confined himself to maintaining that position and to pointing out that the causes of the inflation then being experienced — excessive demand, higher import prices for oil and other commodities, and rising food costs — could not be remedied by the freeze and controls Stanfield was advocating. But in the fighting stance he and his advisors had devised for that campaign, Trudeau allowed himself the luxury of over-kill: Though he must have known that the day might come when he would have to impose controls himself, he went beyond calling them inappropriate to the circumstances and ridiculed them as an approach that had failed everywhere it had been attempted, "a proven disaster looking for a new place to happen". By the time the campaign was over, all that was clear in the public's mind was that Stanfield was for economic controls and Trudeau was against them.

By early 1975, however, the situation had begun to change drastically. The main inflationary pressure was starting to come not from high import and food prices and excessive demand — none of which can be subdued by controls — but from soaring wage settlements as workers scrambled to protect themselves not only against present inflation but also against the inflation they feared in the future; the higher wages, in turn, were pushing up the price of goods and services produced in Canada, thereby fuelling inflation and harming the competitive position of Canadian exports abroad. As Canadian wage settlements developed a pattern of exceeding those in the United States while productivity lagged, the nature of our inflation approached the criteria stated by Trudeau for imposing controls. Those criteria were basically sound: A situation of cost-push inflation spiralling upward as a result of runaway wage demands is the only circumstance in which controls, used as a last resort, have some chance of success.

But in the spring of 1975, neither John Turner, as finance minister, nor the rest of the cabinet were prepared to resort to controls, although some finance department officials already favoured the measure. "In the cabinet discussion preceding the budget of June 1975, Turner put before us three alternatives and said he had no preference: one of the options at that time was price and wage controls, another was voluntary consensus, and the third was fiscal and monetary measures," says Mitchell Sharp. A few ministers were in favour of controls, but the majority view — never opposed by Turner — was that the pursuit of voluntary restraint should be continued. In rather naïve pursuit of a "consensus" among business and labour on voluntary wage and price restraint, both Turner and Trudeau preceded the budget with a scare campaign in which they warned repeatedly that Canada's competitive position was being undermined and the nation was heading for disaster unless inflation was brought under control. The consensus effort got nowhere, but it succeeded in getting the public even more worried about inflation — and then the budget offered no new initiatives to combat it.

"We were trying to read the signs: Was inflation going to get worse?" says Tommy Shoyama, who as deputy minister of finance played a key role in the controls decision. "Up to that time, we were inclined to think that most of the momentum had been spent, but we were worried that it was plateau-ing at such a high level. We had reason to believe the settlements would start to come down, but the question was whether they would come down fast enough."

By mid-summer, finance department officials were pessimistic. At their urging, Turner sought cabinet approval to have the department put more work into the controls contingency plan that had been kept ready on the shelf for years. "We had a rather short, sharp debate in late July, early August of 1975," recalls Donald Macdonald. "Turner was obviously concerned then about the pattern that was showing up in Canadian inflation, and he sought approval to go ahead and have some further elaboration of the internal work of the department. The prime minister recognized all the political difficulties of reversing the position with which he personally had been very much in the forefront in the previous election, but he was prepared to conciliate or mediate an agreement on what should be done. And the agreement he mediated was that, of course, the department of finance officials should be entitled to give some further study to this particular area — all Turner was doing was seeking to have further work done."

The next major development, at summer's end, occurred within the finance department. "At the end of August, the department had its annual seminar where we get senior officials together for a two-day meeting," says Shoyama. "Half a day was spent in a discussion of the situation, and the seminar projected two outcomes. One was that we don't get it under control, it may taper down very slowly. The outcome is unemployment rising to ten per cent, a really severe budget deficit, an impossible balance of payments situation. The alternative was that if we project a push-down [in the rate of inflation], we can carve into the gap with the U.S. and contain unemployment at about the seven per cent level.

"In September, we had to go to cabinet with our regular report on the financial situation and outlook. I guess it was just about the same time that Turner put in his resignation. We drafted a document with these two scenarios, and said there was no alternative but to go to controls. With Turner gone, we had no minister to sign the document, so Drury signed it to get it to the cabinet table. That was followed by meetings with the ministers over the next few weeks, two or three times a week, often late into the night, in which ideas were thrashed back and forth."

In the midst of these discussions, Trudeau approached Macdonald to take the finance portfolio vacated by Turner on September 10. "The PM's stipulation was that, despite my having been an opponent of the controls, I was to be open-minded on the question," Macdonald says. "If after further examination of it the cabinet felt that this was probably the only course of action to be accepted, then I wasn't to get on my high horse and ride out of the cabinet. I was to accept that judgment. That was one of the specific conditions the prime minister made — that I was to be open-minded — and I accepted that."

Following Macdonald's swearing-in on September 26, it didn't take long for officials of his new department to convince him that controls were indeed necessary. By then, most of his senior cabinet colleagues had already been persuaded by the finance department in those long hours of talks. "I guess by the third week of September or so, the consensus among ministers had swung to supporting the idea," Shoyama says. "By the third week of September, the trend was shifting to: 'What *kind* of program?'" When it came to winning the agreement of the new minister, he says, "the written material was very key for Macdonald. He felt he was a new minister and had to rely on the advice of his establishment."

What the finance department originally presented to cabinet — or, more specifically, to the Priorities and Planning committee, in which virtually all the debate and decision-making on the issue took place — was a comprehensive program involving an across-the-board freeze to be followed by controls. Cabinet in general, and Trudeau in particular, rejected this as unacceptable. "The prime minister was absolutely adamant on this point," recalls Sharp. "He said he was not going to saddle the country with a bureaucratic system where everybody would be subject to prosecution, and that it would all be bound to break down. He took the view that he just didn't want to bring into effect a vast bureaucratic structure." Trudeau also rejected the idea of an initial freeze, partly because he didn't believe it would work and partly because that would be too close to the Stanfield proposal he had so recently mocked.

"Finance led with a classic control plan in which everybody was going to be controlled no matter how big or small they were," says a top-ranking insider. "The PM countered with a purely voluntary scheme, and from those two extremes they began trading off." P and P, under Trudeau's leadership, rejected both the first proposal submitted by finance and a second, insufficiently modified one; the voluntary scheme with which the cabinet countered the finance proposals was one that P and P itself wrote from pieces of the finance scheme. "There was a process of negotiation, virtually, between the officials and P and P," this insider says, while Trudeau pressed his own advisors in the Privy Council Office to find some effective alternative to an across-the-board plan. Such a solution was finally found, and "the key trade-off was when the PM offered to accept a control program if it only applied to the biggies. He based himself not on Galbraith but on an observation of the material finance had put in one of the proposals, which he found indicated that most of the biggies were controllable by applying controls to very few numbers. Finance accepted that, and then began to fight for the exceptions."

The plan that gradually developed was patched together from bits and pieces of a variety of proposals: the contingency plan; the guidelines for the abortive consensus scheme, which included the notion of a basic permissible wage increase coupled with provisions to take into account productivity, past experience, and an element of catching up; and a price justification plan developed by the consumer and corporate affairs department, which provided the structural skeleton of a jawboning body which would monitor wage settlements and prices and recommend rollbacks where necessary (which became the Anti-Inflation Board) and a separate enforcement agency (which became the office of the controls administrator). By the beginning of October, Shoyama says, the basic outlines of the plan had taken shape. While the details were being hammered out, various committees — comprising officials from the finance department, PCO, and the departments of consumer and corporate affairs, labour, and industry, trade and commerce — were set up to write the policy paper that would accompany the controls announcement, draft the legislation implementing the program, and begin to handle matters of staffing. All these elements of the program were discussed in almost daily meetings of P and P, and the plans were not finalized until literally the last minute; Shoyama recalls that the policy paper was still being drafted on October 12. On Thanksgiving Day, Trudeau met with the provincial premiers to preview his intentions, and those talks led to further changes, including a last-minute decision to extend the duration of the program from two years to three. Finally, on the evening of Thanksgiving Day, October 13, Trudeau went on national television and announced to an astounded public the imposition of mandatory controls.

For a government which had so recently opposed controls, this move was a desperate political gamble. To some extent, the government itself was responsible for the circumstances which made it necessary. Its actions during the minority period had helped inflation to build up a strong head of steam; in its vain attempt to sell voluntary consensus, the government had deliberately fanned public fears about mounting inflation rates; and then, with the consensus exercise an obvious failure and no other solution in sight, Turner's abrupt and unexplained resignation had turned those fears into something akin to panic. An editorial in the *Globe and Mail* on September 12 was typical of the media reaction that mirrored and contributed to the public's perception: "Unable to arouse the prime minister and his cabinet colleagues to the need for decisiveness to ward off the dangers of collapse, Mr. Turner has taken the only step left to him. He has bolted the either-or-and-on-the-other-hand lethargy of the Trudeau administration." Finance department officials had favoured controls long before Turner's departure, and it is likely that by the autumn of 1975 the measure would have been implemented even without that development, but the public's mistaken interpretation of his basically self-serving resignation gave the cabinet an extra sense of urgency: "I think we would have made the decision in any event," says Sharp, "but we had to make a decision at that time to offset the effect of his resignation. His departure was a very serious matter."

In the circumstances, the controls decision was the right one. Mandatory controls, like many other economic measures, operate not so much directly on the economy as in the realm of mass psychology. And the collective mental state of Canada's economic decision-makers — primarily in organized labour, and to a lesser extent in business — at that point clearly required drastic treatment. If only economic factors had been involved, it is possible that inflation would have begun to abate slowly even without controls; indeed, some economists were already saying that the corner had been turned. But the psychological dimension of the problem was that most Canadians expected inflation to continue getting worse, and a very slow rate of improvement might not have sufficed to keep that expectation from leading to wage demands and pricing decisions that would create a runaway inflationary spiral. What the government's economic experts feared, in short, was an economic equivalent of mass hysteria, and the abrupt imposition of controls had the same mind-clearing effect as a slap across the face of a hysteria victim.

But those controls, like the slap, could only deal with the immediate outburst rather than with its causes. Trudeau himself acknowledged this in his television address, stressing that "the only benefit of having restraint imposed by law is that it gives people time to understand and adopt the real cure, which is a basic change in our attitudes." In a television interview on December 14, he was even more specific: "We only consider these three years of controls as a breathing space. If we don't use this period in order to change our social structure and values in some way . . . then we'll get out of the controlled period with the same expectations, the same motivations, the same economic mainsprings which will create inflation and unemployment all over again."[3]

In a policy statement accompanying the introduction of controls, Macdonald outlined some of the structural changes the government considered necessary: Energy consumption had to be reduced through intensified conservation programs. Special initiatives in housing policy were required to ensure an adequate supply of new housing, and to prevent land prices from soaring by increasing the supply of serviced land for housing. In the area of food supply, measures had to be taken to increase productivity and protect farmers against market fluctuations, and also to improve the functioning of the food processing and marketing sectors. Competition policy had to be refined and strengthened. New approaches to collective bargaining were necessary, including measures that would reduce the fragmentation of bargaining units.

In the months following the imposition of controls, Trudeau took every opportunity to sound his plea for individual responsibility and restraint. It was essentially the same message he had delivered from time to time since 1968, a warning that public expectations about what government, society, and the economy could provide were becoming dangerously unrealistic. But now the selling of that message had become the centrepiece of government policy. As he put it in a speech in Hamilton in December 1975: "What we're doing with this anti-inflation program is buying time, buying time during which we will get to the roots of the evil, but more importantly, buying time so that we will change somewhat the nature of the society which has been developing in the past fifteen, twenty years, since the Second World War — a society which was perhaps too obsessed with material wealth, a society which thought there could be more for everybody, everywhere, all the time, a society which seemed to encourage groups and people to go every man for himself, and the biggest to take the biggest part." But while Trudeau had some success in driving home the theme that the times called for belt-tightening, the second part of his government's plan — the implementation of structural changes in the economy — stalled at the starting gate; the government allowed most of the controls period to go by without working the changes it had insisted were necessary if inflation was not to take up where it had left off.

For a government already weakened by its lacklustre first year of the new mandate, the imposition of controls marked the beginning of real political trouble. On one hand, the government stood to regain some momentum by introducing such a drastic measure, since the action would cast it in the sort of decisive leadership role that the public and the news media had been craving. On the other hand, however, adopting that measure meant completely reversing the most clearly etched position that Trudeau and his government had taken in the campaign only a year earlier. In his announcement of controls and in his subsequent travels across the country to sell the program, Trudeau did not try to confront head-on the issue of his reversal. Instead of making a major effort to explain the difference between the situations in 1974 and 1975, he concentrated simply on the need for controls at the time he had imposed them, and assumed that people would forget how far he had gone in denouncing the measure only a year earlier.

That mistake by the prime minister and his advisors compounded the original campaign error of resorting to over-kill against controls. With the campaign still fresh in their minds, people suspected either that Trudeau had known all along that controls would be necessary and had cynically hidden his intentions, or that he had been irresponsibly wrong a year ago. Coupled with the general disillusionment induced by the contrast between the campaigning Trudeau and the scarcely visible prime minister, this created a new phenomenon: For the first time, people simply stopped believing what Trudeau said.

Neither the prime minister nor his advisors realized how badly his credibility had been damaged until the simmering resentment in the country suddenly exploded in an uproar over some entirely innocent remarks he made in a year-end television interview. In that interview, Trudeau mused vaguely that the economic system wasn't working, that there was a need for a "new society", and that the future might have to hold more rather than less government intervention. He was saying nothing that wasn't obvious and little that he hadn't said before, but his vagueness in that interview was a matter of saying either too much or too little in the prevailing atmosphere of uncertainty. Nerves had been rubbed raw by the shock of controls and the erosion of faith in Trudeau's credibility. Organized labour was angry, business was uneasy; some people suspected that the prime minister was scheming, others feared that he simply didn't know what he was doing. The result was a remarkable outburst of indignation over his remarks — he was accused of everything from fascism to communism by otherwise responsible business and labour leaders — that was only partly assuaged when he quickly arranged a January speech in which he gave explicit assurances that he had no intention of subverting the free-enterprise system.

While the government suffered in the public arena because of the controls decision, it ran into further trouble behind the scenes. Over the summer of 1975, the results — such as they were — of the year-long priorities exercise had finally been polished and condensed, and this material was turned into the outline of a new Throne Speech to be discussed at an all-day cabinet think-in at Meach Lake near Ottawa on September 17. But the week before that gathering, the cabinet was suddenly faced by both Turner's resignation and the finance department's insistence that controls had become unavoidable. At Meach Lake, the cabinet scrapped all discussion of long-range priorities and concentrated solely on the economy.

Once the decision to proceed with controls was reached, the results of the whole priorities exercise instantly became irrelevant.

The government's spending options were rendered virtually non-existent, since controls could only be made credible if the government set an example of financial restraint. All the government's energies were monopolized, moreover, by the huge task of selling and supervising this unprecedented peacetime intervention into the Canadian economy. From that point on, Trudeau and his government found themselves doing exactly what the ill-fated and politically costly priorities exercise had been designed to avoid: they were reduced to stumbling along without a plan, racing to catch up to events, improvising desperately.

Misfortune began to rain upon misfortune. Opposition MPs hammered the government over the Sky Shops affair, in which a prominent Liberal senator and fund-raiser, Louis Giguère, was revealed to have profited handsomely from his involvement in a firm that leased airport concessions from the government. Then Consumer Affairs Minister André Ouellet got himself convicted of contempt of court for publicly questioning the sanity of a judge who had acquitted sugar companies of price-fixing. Next, it came to light that Bud Drury, one of the government's most respected ministers, had improperly telephoned the judge who was about to sentence Ouellet. This revelation led to a brief but colourful little flurry of scandal, at the end of which Trudeau accepted Ouellet's resignation but refused Drury's. This was followed in short order by the government's bungled, on-again, off-again negotiations for a long-range patrol aircraft, and by the clumsily handled air traffic controllers' strike over bilingualism.

This succession of accidents was due partly to the weakness of a cabinet which contained too many ministers whose political reflexes had been dulled, and partly to outside factors. The opposition, weak at criticizing policy, had devoted virtually all its energy since the election to probing for scandal and casting innuendoes. And the press and the public, affected by the spill-over from Watergate, were more suspicious than ever of government and in a particularly unforgiving mood. These problems were compounded by the fact that the government had no momentum to carry it over the hurdles and that few of its ministers made sufficient effort to communicate with the public.

These difficulties quickly spilled over into the area of policy. No citizen is likely to be pleased with everything a government does, but if he is satisfied with the over-all performance he may be expected to overlook the individual irritants. When goodwill has been dissipated and over-all performance is unimpressive, on the other hand, these irritants become a focus for all the discontent. For some, the focus was capital punishment, for others bilingualism, for still others the controls program. But the real problem was not any specific issue, but the general mood. As Keith Davey puts it: "The traditional strength of the Liberal Party has been that we spanned so much of the centre of the stage that we forced the Tories away out on our right and we forced the New Democrats away out on our left, and so this is a party that at one and the same time can contain Ross Thatcher and Walter Gordon; we've managed, to some extent, to make the cities think we are for them and to make the country think we are for them, and even to be the party of labour and big business at the same time — that's been a neat trick. What happened after the '74 election is that the accordion closed, and where everybody had thought we were for them, now everybody thought we were against them."

The period was not entirely devoid of accomplishments. A national petroleum corporation, Petro-Canada, was legislated into existence and established. Capital punishment was abolished. The government succeeded in driving *Time* magazine out of Canada, an accomplishment of dubious merit but one that had been unsuccessfully in the works for years. Trudeau sought and won a vague but potentially valuable link with the European Economic Community, and his trip to Latin America intensified relations with an area long neglected by Canada. The controls program had been introduced, was ratified by the Supreme Court, and was beginning to perceptibly ease inflation. But what was lacking was any clear sense of purpose to illuminate the government's actions. The reduction of inflation is not a sufficient objective for a four-year mandate, but the Trudeau government was not communicating to the public any strong commitment to broader goals.

As his popularity plunged, Trudeau showed signs of losing his political bearings. Although his decline in popularity in those low-

profile months after the 1974 election left little doubt that it was
drift, not excessive change, that had offended the public, Trudeau
believed the opposite. He gave the impression of an unnerved, over-
cautious leader who no longer felt free to say what he thought —
let alone do what he considered desirable — because he had concluded that the public did not want change, the press did not want
to understand him, and the Liberal Party did not want him to rock
the boat. For instance, he had said in a television broadcast in
December 1975: "I will be speaking to you again in the coming
months about the new kind of society we will need to create in
response to the new economic circumstances in which we are living.
. . . I will be speaking to you about the need for new attitudes
toward economic growth and the exploitation of our natural resources . . . toward labour-management relations, social co-operation and the sharing of our wealth." But he and his advisors were
so jolted by the reaction to his year-end TV interview a few weeks
later that he said no more on the subject until the following autumn
— and even then the government's position was stated not in a
prime-ministerial message but in the bureaucratic prose of a document entitled "The Way Ahead". Similarly, when critics complained about the level of government spending, Trudeau didn't
offer a rebuttal or defend his policies. Instead, he gave the complaints additional momentum by meekly admitting that his government had been spending too much and by making economically
insignificant but socially painful cuts that killed or truncated some
of his most creative programs, including Opportunities for Youth,
the Company of Young Canadians, and the Local Initiatives
Program.

He felt and acted increasingly like a prisoner of the electorate he
was supposed to be leading, and the effect of this new pussyfooting
approach was to put into cold storage precisely those qualities
which had made him so attractive — an intellect unrivalled among
Canadian politicians and probably among contemporary world
leaders, a lucid perception of domestic and international needs and
problems, and a refreshing readiness to be his own man and freely
speak his mind. As his political support dwindled, he and his
government slipped into a tailspin that was increasingly difficult

to break out of: The less the government offered decisive leadership, the more its popularity faded; and the less popularity it had,
the more difficult it became to risk taking decisive and potentially
controversial actions. Trudeau himself realized the gravity of his
plight, and he assured his cabinet that he would not try to cling to
the leadership if they reached a point where they wanted him to
leave. At the same time, he warned that he would not tolerate any
plots by small groups of ministers and laid down the procedure to
be followed in the event his leadership was no longer wanted: If
the cabinet as a whole reached a consensus that his resignation was
desirable, it was to send him the message through two ministers,
Marc Lalonde and Donald Macdonald. "He had no illusions," says
a close associate and advisor. "He knew that if the situation in the
polls didn't start improving, the cabinet and the party wouldn't
stand by him out of any sentiment."

As the Liberals languished in the summer of 1976 at the lowest
ebb of their popularity in two decades, Trudeau's aides kept insisting that recovery was just around the corner. "Wait till you see the
cabinet shuffle," they said. "Wait till you see the Throne Speech."
But the political mishaps continued. Trudeau's cabinet shuffle in
September was a major one that brought in seven new faces, but
its attractiveness was marred by the loss of one of his most popular
ministers, Bryce Mackasey; tired and irascible, Mackasey worked
himself into a corner by trying to get Trudeau to beg him to stay,
and he ended up resigning only a few hours before the shuffle was
to be announced. The Throne Speech in mid-October turned out to
be a vague and curiously insubstantial document that gave no real
indication of Liberal policy intentions, attempting instead to soothe
a nerve-jangled nation with a vast outpouring of blandness. The
real policy statement was contained, meanwhile, in a far less conspicuous policy paper, "The Way Ahead".

In this document, Trudeau responded to the growing public
uneasiness about the scope of government intervention with a
simple if obscurely stated message: "You do what's necessary, or
we will." As the document put it, in a continuation of the theme of
individual responsibility that Trudeau had been preaching since
before his entry into politics: "Rather than relent in the pursuit of

social goals, it is both possible and desirable to seek a substantial reduction in the rate of government expenditure and direct government intervention, and to search for alternative strategies — less expenditure-oriented — to serve the legitimate social concerns of government, and in fact to better serve society. . . . If we truly want governments to do less — for us, and to us — we as individuals and in our private institutions will have to do more — for each other." Few Canadians actually heard much about "The Way Ahead", however, because its release was overshadowed in the news media by a day of protest against controls by organized labour and by the noisy though insignificant resignation of Defence Minister James Richardson.

Even though the shuffle and the Throne Speech didn't live up to their advance billing, they revealed sufficient sign of life in the government to contribute to the beginnings of a recovery. Inflation had also diminished perceptibly, and the first glow of novelty was wearing off Joe Clark. The Liberals began inching up in the Gallup Polls from their low of 29 per cent in August to 33 per cent in September and October and 35 per cent in early November, while the Tories slipped from 47 to 44 per cent.

Whether this tentative recovery would have continued until it restored a Liberal lead will never be known, because the Quebec election of November 15 intervened to change everything. The separatist victory forced Canadians to take a more thoughtful look at the leadership alternatives available to them, and Clark increasingly came to be seen as inadequate to the challenge. Trudeau himself, meanwhile, was a man newly galvanized. Ever since the 1972 election, he had suffered a certain lack of direction, uncertain that the public was prepared to share or accept his concerns. But the issues of Quebec's future and national unity were what he cared most about, understood best, and was most confident in handling.

Always at his best when confronted with a crisis, Trudeau was very close to the peak of his form as he began to face this one. While Clark floundered and came off as a shallow young man more interested in scoring partisan points than in providing leadership and NDP leader Ed Broadbent looked earnest but uninspired, Trudeau took to the airwaves in a televised fireside chat in which he spoke with conviction and eloquence of the things Canadians needed and wanted to hear — the deep feelings of Quebecers, the desirability of keeping Canada together, the demands that would be made of everyone in the crucial times ahead. In January, the prime minister went to Quebec City and gave one of the best and best-received speeches of his career, demanding that the Lévesque government's referendum on separation be soon, clear, and reasonably final, and ramming home his theme that "The burden of proof is not on those who want to defend the existence of a country that has belonged to us for three hundred years. . . . The burden of proof is on those who would destroy that reality, a country well advanced on the road to freedom, humanity, even prosperity." In February, he paid a highly successful visit to Washington, establishing a good rapport with the new U.S. President and delivering a frank and elegant speech about Canada's situation to a joint session of Congress.

In politics, nothing succeeds like success, and Trudeau's momentum began to build slowly but inexorably. He made a well-received televised plea for the support and confidence of Western Canada; he successfully wooed one of the Progressive Conservative Party's best-known MPs, Alberta's Jack Horner, over to the Liberal front benches, and then also recruited one of Clark's meagre band of Quebec MPs; he won five out of six by-elections. His volatile relationship with the Canadian public was on another dramatic upswing, and by the summer of 1977 his party's support in the Gallup Polls had soared to more than fifty per cent.

√But the separatist election victory that helped Trudeau recover his popularity and presented him with the greatest challenge of his career also, ironically, exacted a heavy personal price. The man who had so jealously guarded his freedom suddenly found himself, after nine difficult years in power and with his marriage at the crisis point, with his options virtually foreclosed: "In personal terms, it curtails a bit of my freedoms. If the Liberals had won again in the last provincial election, I would have been freer either to leave politics or, alternatively, to sort of say, 'Well, now separatism after three knockouts by Bourassa is really no longer a menace and I can spend much more time on other things.' . . . What I wanted to do hadn't been decided, but the option was open and now it's hardly open. . . . Margaret was very unhappy for the Lévesque victory because she sort of instantly said, 'Now you're never going to be able to get out of politics,' and she saw herself locked into this thing for time indefinite, whereas until then both she and I had sort of kept our options open. And I'm sure she would have supported my decision to stay or leave, or perhaps be pushed out, for all we know, but at least there would have been a freedom to leave which suddenly was much less within reach. . . . So it's a little bit the fates cornering me in the very execution of the task that I got into politics for."

CHAPTER FIFTEEN

Trudeau and Quebec

WHATEVER expectations others attached to him, Trudeau himself has never made it a secret that it was the Quebec issue that led him to enter politics and eventually become prime minister: "Each man has his own reasons, I suppose, as driving forces, but mine were twofold. One was to make sure that Quebec wouldn't leave Canada through separatism, and the other was to make sure that Canada wouldn't shove Quebec out through narrowmindedness."[1]

At the most simplistic level, it is possible to say that a separatist government is now in power in Quebec, the risk of the break-up of Confederation is more immediate than in 1968, and therefore Trudeau has failed to achieve his principal objective. But that would be to reduce the exceedingly complex interplay of historical, social, and political forces to a mindless syllogism. The reality is that some of the elements of Canada's present situation have been produced by forces that existed long before Trudeau's arrival on the scene; others are the result of developments he was powerless to control; and still others can be traced to his own actions, both positive and negative. Trudeau contributed in some ways to the spread of separatist sentiment in Quebec, but he contributed in far more ways to the containment of that sentiment, and there is reason to believe that the situation might have been far worse without the role he played.

At about the time Trudeau entered politics in 1965, Quebec was becoming a society in crisis. The Quiet Revolution had belatedly dragged the province into the twentieth century, but the abruptness of the transition altered and ultimately destroyed the traditional role of the key underpinnings of Quebec society: the Catholic Church, the state, and the family. The first to be undercut was the Church, which had been the principal pillar of authority in Quebec. As its grip was broken by the election of the Lesage government, which refused to play by the rules of the old Church-state alliance, the first beneficiary of secularization was the state itself; Quebecers who had paid relatively little attention to the provincial government suddenly began to make it the principal focus of their confidence and hopes. But Lesage grew increasingly remote and arrogant, and the state too diminished as a pillar of authority under the premiers — Johnson, Bertrand, and Bourassa — who followed him. With modernization, the decline of the Church and the evolution of more free-wheeling life-styles, the role of the family as a source of stability also began to be drastically reduced; this was a phenomenon by no means confined to Quebec, but its impact was greater in that province because the family had played a particularly important role there and because the change was so abrupt.

The result was that the Quebec of the late 1960s and the 1970s increasingly became a society adrift without a rudder. And while the institutions that had previously provided a sense of purpose and direction crumbled, the one force that remained undiminished was Quebec nationalism. Trudeau and his colleagues had hoped that the Quiet Revolution would have the effect of dispelling a nationalist reflex that was born of insecurity and replacing it with a confidently outward-looking willingness to participate in the affairs of Canada and the world. What happened, instead, is that the nationalism itself changed from a defensive form to a more confident, aggressive one: Where Quebec nationalists had previously confined themselves to urging the province to remain turned in upon itself and to reject outside overtures, they now switched their emphasis to demanding greater powers, pursuing an international role for Quebec, and even advocating outright separation from Canada.

At the same time, the new sense of confidence combined with an increased degree of sophistication among Quebecers — the result of accelerating urbanization, a higher level of education, and the impact of the communications explosion — to produce a new sense of grievance toward English Canada and to extend the appeal of extreme nationalism. Where once this nationalism had flourished mainly among a small intellectual élite, it increasingly spread its roots among Quebec's youth and within the province's labour movement. By 1965, an alarmed Royal Commission on Bilingualism and Biculturalism was warning that "Canada, without being fully conscious of the fact, is passing through the greatest crisis in its history. . . . It would appear from what is happening that the state of affairs established in 1867, and never seriously challenged, is now for the first time being rejected by the French Canadians of Quebec."

✓ While other politicians struggled to come to grips with this new reality, Trudeau approached it from the perspective of a man who had made the Quebec problem his central preoccupation for the previous decade and a half. He was — and remains — convinced that the problem resided not in any serious deficiency in the structures of federalism, but in the failure of English and French Canadians to make proper use of those structures. "I am inclined to believe that the authors of the Canadian federation arrived at as wise a compromise and drew up as sensible a constitution as any group of men anywhere could have done.[2] . . . I should be very surprised if real statesmen, given the facts of the problem, arrived at the conclusion that our constitution needs drastic revision."[3]

Trudeau's whole approach is based on a conviction that Canada can survive only if all citizens — French or English — regard every part of the country as their own. To the extent that the French withdraw into Quebec and the anglophones into the other nine provinces, the result must inevitably be the rise of rival nationalisms which will tear the country apart: If French Canada defines itself only as the population of Quebec, then the Quebec government becomes its only exclusive voice; thus confined to a limited territory and endowed with its own government, French Canada must then become increasingly tempted to regard itself not only as a nation in the sociological sense but as an emerging nation-state. On the other hand, if the domain of French Canada — like that of English Canada — extends from coast to coast, then more than one government is its legitimate spokesman and the explosive chemistry of extreme nationalism is largely defused. The constitution of 1867, Trudeau believes, recognized this: "The Canadian constitution created a country where French Canadians could compete on an equal basis with English Canadians; both groups were invited to consider the whole of Canada their country and field of endeavour."[4]

Where the nation went awry, in his view, is in the failure of English and French Canadians alike to play by those rules. "It is wrong to say that Confederation has been a total failure for French Canadians; the truth is rather that they have never really tried to make a success of it. In Quebec, we tended to fall back upon a sterile, negative provincial autonomy; in Ottawa our frequent abstentions encouraged paternalistic centralization."[5] As for English Canada's role, "the rules of the constitutional game were not always upheld. In the matter of education as well as political rights, the safeguards so dear to French Canadians were nearly always disregarded throughout the country, so that they came to believe themselves secure only in Quebec. Worse still, in those areas not specifically covered by the constitution, the English-speaking majority used its size and wealth to impose a set of social rules humiliating to French Canadians. In the federal civil service, for example, and even more so in the Canadian armed forces, a French Canadian started off with an enormous handicap — if indeed he managed to start at all. This was true also in finance, business, and at all levels of industry."[6]

✓ These premises led Trudeau to conclude that the solution to the growing problem did not lie in a major rejigging of the federal arrangement, and his most important contribution in the first period of his political activity was to steer Canada away from its drift toward some sort of special status for Quebec. He perceived, correctly, that special status would not prevent the break-up of Confederation but would make it nearly inevitable in the long run.

To satisfy Quebec nationalists, special status would have to give the province very extensive powers not held by the other nine; Quebec would, in effect, have to be given jurisdiction over all or most of the areas of government activity that Quebecers considered particularly important. The first effect of such a change would be to increase the alienation of Quebec from the rest of the country, making the provincial government "its" government and Ottawa someone else's. Worse, Quebecers of high calibre would have no reason to go as MPs to Ottawa, where their role would be diminished and their sphere of activity limited to matters that their constituents considered to be of secondary importance. But decisions taken by the federal government in those areas where it still had jurisdiction over Quebec — whether in economic matters, foreign policy, or whatever — would still inevitably have an impact on the province; because of geographic proximity and economic interrelationships, so would federal decisions on policy for the rest of Canada. The difference would be that Quebec would now have only weakened, second-rate representation in Ottawa to protect its interests in such matters, and the result would inevitably be unsatisfactory to Quebecers. With so many powers already in the hands of the Quebec government anyway, it would eventually seem only logical to break away from these unsatisfactory federal policies by going the rest of the way to independence.

Instead of accepting a course that would merely aggravate Quebec's tendency to turn in upon itself, Trudeau has pinned his hopes on the opposite policy: trying to give Quebecers a sense of equality in, and proprietary right to, Canada as a whole. "Masters in our own house we must be," he told the Liberal leadership convention in 1968, "but our house is the whole of Canada." His rejection as prime minister of special status and the "two nations" theory was a monumental gamble, and marked a major turning point in the nation's history. But in another sense it wasn't really a gamble at all, because while Trudeau's approach contains a risk of failure, the special-status course carried virtually its guarantee.

The centrepiece of Trudeau's attempted solution to the Quebec problem has been language policy, and it has taken two principal forms: attempted constitutional change, and passage of the federal Official Languages Act. On the constitutional front, Trudeau had preceded the B and B Commission in arguing for the entrenchment in the British North America Act of a charter of human rights that would, among other provisions, guarantee francophones across Canada the same freedom to use their own language in public institutions — including schools and courts — that anglophones had long enjoyed in Quebec; the charter would also, of course, provide the same constitutional protection for those Quebec anglophones. "Once you have done that," he said in 1968, "Quebec cannot say it alone speaks for French Canadians."[7] The French Canadian nation would then stretch from Maillardville in British Columbia to the Acadian community on the Atlantic coast, and "Mr. Robarts will be speaking for French Canadians in Ontario, Mr. Robichaud will be speaking for French Canadians in New Brunswick, Mr. Thatcher will speak for French Canadians in Saskatchewan, and Mr. Pearson will be speaking for all French Canadians. Nobody will be able to say, 'I need more power because I speak for the French Canadian nation'."[8] Though Trudeau has tried, on and off, for a decade to have these language guarantees constitutionally established, they were not yet in place when the Parti Québécois came to power in November 1976, both because no over-all consensus on constitutional amendment had been reached and because provincial premiers balked at committing themselves to the expenditure that implementing the guarantees would require.

The other element of Trudeau's language policy, the Official Languages Act, was within his own power to implement, however, and he brought it before Parliament within months of becoming prime minister. The much-misunderstood legislation — watered down at provincial insistence to omit guaranteed bilingualism in the criminal courts — provides simply that where there is a reasonable demand, every citizen has the right to deal with the federal government, its agencies and Crown corporations in either English or French. This enshrinement of both languages as official and equal in all matters under federal jurisdiction in no way diminishes the rights of any private citizen — on the contrary, it only adds new rights — but this has never been adequately understood in many parts of Canada. At the time of the bill's passage, and in sporadic bursts since then, there has been angry grumbling that Trudeau is "trying to force French down people's throats" or even secretly plotting to make the whole country French-speaking. These misconceptions have been caused partly by Trudeau's failure to persevere in explaining what he was doing, partly by the failure of the news media to dispel confusion about the legislation, and partly by the refusal of many people to listen to reason.

Anyone who takes the trouble to verify the record, however, will see that Trudeau has clearly and consistently stressed the limited scope of the Official Languages Act from the outset. "Bilingualism is not an imposition on the citizens," he told a meeting of the American Society of Newspaper Editors in 1966. "The citizens can go on speaking one language or six languages or no languages if they so choose. Bilingualism is an imposition on the state and not on the citizens." Eight years and many repetitions later, in 1974 he was still speaking in identical terms, telling a panel of Parisian journalists in an interview: "I never expect that the average Quebecer in Sainte-Tite-des-Caps will become perfectly bilingual, nor that the anglophone in Calgary or Moose Jaw must know French. What we want is that the institutions be bilingual. We want the government of all Canadians, the central government, to be able to communicate with the population."

The only instance where the Official Languages Act imposes anything on individuals is in the case of a limited number of federal civil servants, and here, too, no right is infringed in principle. There is no basic right to work for the government or any other employer without having the proper qualifications, and in a country with two principal language groups it is reasonable to require knowledge of both languages for certain government jobs. Even at that, the government has gone to considerable and expensive lengths to avoid injustice to incumbent unilingual employees or to prospective employees willing to learn the second language — and fewer than one-fifth of all federal jobs were classified as bilingual. Although the implementation of public service bilingualism was costly, clumsily handled to an extent that created resentment within the public service, and often wastefully managed, these facts neither justify nor explain the level that public outrage sometimes reached. The total cost of the bilingualism program was estimated in 1976 to be as high as $500 million a year; that is undoubtedly a lot of money, but in the context of total spending that year of some $38 billion, bilingualism's share works out to 1.3 per cent of federal expenditure — hardly extravagant for a program essential to Canada's survival as a nation — and inefficiencies can account for only a very small portion of that 1.3 per cent.

Trudeau has been right in assessing that the hostility toward federal bilingualism is basically irrational, a matter of either ignorance or blind unreasoning prejudice, but he has been politically wrong in stating it repeatedly in those terms. Telling people that they are bigots is unlikely to make them change their ways. Understanding the reasons for their bigoted behaviour, on the other hand, can permit confronting those reasons head-on and working toward improving attitudes. In the case of Westerners, for instance, Trudeau's government has been insensitive to the social and historical factors underlying their suspicion toward a second language. When immigrants poured into the Prairies after the turn of the century, the overwhelming majority was English-speaking — from the United States, England, and Scotland — and Protestant. Their Protestantism was of a very militant variety, moreover, and they closely associated their language with their religion. French, to them, was the language of Catholics. In 1914, when the Saskatchewan government approved the establishment of a course in French at the University of Saskatchewan, the outcry led by the Presbyterian Church was so strong that Premier Walter Scott was forced out of office.

For non-anglophone immigrants to the Prairies — Ukrainians, Germans, Scandinavians, and a variety of others — the identification with English became no less strong, though it stemmed from different reasons. For these newcomers, English was the *lingua franca*, the only common language in a culturally diverse society; to be a "real" Canadian was to be fluent in English. Once English was equated in this way with Canadianism, it was natural for the introduction of any other language into public affairs to be regarded as an intrusion. And, having given up the use of their original language outside the home in favour of English, these newcomers and their descendants had no patience with suggestions that any other language — French included — be given official status: If French, many of them felt, why not German, or Ukrainian, or Swedish?

The attachment to language was passed down through the generations, and nothing prepared Westerners for the appearance of an "alien" language in their midst. Trudeau, blinded by his own rationalism, couldn't understand why a rational explanation didn't suffice at once to eliminate unreasonable hostility to his language law. Instead of patiently cushioning the shock and continuing to explain the law for however long it took for the message to sink in, Trudeau and his government began dismissing critics as racists, thereby making things worse and setting the stage for outbursts of reaction which in turn have offended Quebecers.

It would be over-optimistic to expect that federal language policy — even coupled with entrenched constitutional guarantees — can by itself cause a quick evaporation of Quebec nationalism. The reality is that most Quebecers care relatively little about French Canadian communities in other parts of the country, and there is also no prospect in the foreseeable future of a Quebecer being able to move to, say, Toronto or Vancouver and function entirely in his own language. But if official bilingualism and language equality is not a magic solution to the Quebec problem, it is an absolute prerequisite to keeping the country together, and the absence of the measures Trudeau introduced would have been a guarantee of disaster. If French Canadians had not been assured of even the limited rights guaranteed them by the Official Languages Act and if they had not been given an increased role in the governance of the nation, the battle against separatism would have been fought on grounds which left the federalist forces mortally vulnerable.

Although he sometimes speaks as if he believes that language policy alone can be a full answer to the grievances of Quebec nationalists, Trudeau doesn't really perceive it that way. He believes, rather, that it is a matter of dividing responsibilities: Some of Quebec's problems have been attributable to failures by the federal government and Canadians in other provinces, and the onus is on the federal government to lead in remedying those ills; but other grounds of dissatisfaction are matters that rest in the hands of Quebecers themselves, and Ottawa neither can nor should provide the solution for them.

"I don't think it ends with institutional bilingualism or with accepting the French fact," he says, "but it certainly begins there and that's a precondition. And if that is done, we will still have to fight for a lot of things, we French Canadians, in Canada, because we will always be in a minority. But then the rules of the game would be fair to us, we would be able to fight in our language and at least not have the dice loaded against us. I think that given those conditions, a lot of the responsibility then falls on the individual and the school system and the provincial governments to strive for excellence. . . . This being said, I haven't shown much patience to our successive Quebec governments and Quebec opinion leaders who even now complain about the fact that French Canadians haven't as great a chance in their language as English Canadians. There is a side where the federal government was wrong and it has to correct it, but there is a side where Quebec was the last or the second to last of all the provinces to have a department of education. You know, this is nobody's fault, outside of Quebecers'. . . .

"I still believe that it's in Quebec that the levers exist to make the Quebec people a better people. All I'm trying to do by being in Ottawa is to make sure that the dice are not loaded against Quebecers who want to work in the whole of Canada and that Quebecers be treated fairly in that institutional bilingualism sense. But that's only establishing fair rules of the game. The rest must be done by Quebecers themselves as individuals, as institutions, as members of school boards, as students at universities, as politicians in provincial governments. And most of my life, I suppose, has been to do that, to tell Quebecers that they should be changing in Quebec their ways of governing themselves and their ways of educating themselves and their ways of diverting themselves which would lead French Canadians in Quebec in particular to be a more exciting type of people with a greater future."

Outside the question of language rights, Trudeau's determination to avoid giving Quebec powers which would grant it special status or help it withdraw further from the rest of Canada has led him to take a tough stand on constitutional matters. Though this has given him an image of rigidity, he is in fact rigid only on the matter of Quebec's efforts to be treated unlike other provinces; in other federal-provincial negotiations, he is an exceedingly tough bargainer but he has shown himself flexible enough to eventually move from his original position toward compromise. He has consistently refused to yield as much ground as a succession of Quebec premiers demanded in such areas as social policy, however, and this has undoubtedly driven some nationalists into the separatist camp. Particularly in the area of social policy, he was perhaps more rigid than necessary; had he been willing to yield as much to Daniel Johnson in 1968 as he eventually offered to Bourassa in 1972 — a scheme whereby federal family allowances would be paid according to criteria set by the province — it may be argued, he might have avoided offending some segments of Quebec opinion. But the other side of that argument is that in the earlier years he was pursuing a deliberate strategy of refusing to make piecemeal concessions without knowing what further demands would follow.

"No more of this open-ended negotiation," he said in a television interview in January 1968. "This is the idea of Munich. It may be we need a showdown . . . maybe we have to say, 'Okay, is this your final word, will you live with this . . . be bound by it?' Then we can negotiate." In his negotiations with Johnson and Bertrand, both of whom demanded special status, Trudeau was never close enough to an agreement for a single federal concession to be decisive. By the time of his abortive dealings with Bourassa in 1972, the area of contention had basically been narrowed down to the social policy question and there was reason to believe that a federal concession might serve a useful purpose. It is also worth bearing in mind that the impact of detailed federal-provincial negotiations on the general public is often over-estimated: Government officials, journalists, and certain intellectuals in Quebec may be excited over federal agreement or refusal to yield a certain element of jurisdiction, but the average Quebecer cares less about such constitutional intricacies than many people assume.

While Trudeau held the line against Quebec demands and struggled to advance the cause of bilingualism, other vital developments were taking place within the province that were largely outside his power to control. The Parti Québécois had been formed, with René Lévesque at its head, and was preparing to contest the 1970 election. The Union Nationale, for so many years Quebec's

322   TRUDEAU

governing party, was irretrievably launched on a slow and painful deterioration. And the Liberals were looking for a new leader to replace the spent Jean Lesage.

Though it is generally assumed that Robert Bourassa was Trudeau's personal choice to succeed Lesage, it isn't really quite that simple. Trudeau's first initiative was to dissuade Jean Marchand, who wanted to pursue the Liberal leadership and the premiership of Quebec himself. "Marchand would have liked to have been a candidate himself," Trudeau says. "And if we could rewrite history, I suppose it would have changed the course of history. But we were still pretty weak in Ottawa, our cabinet had less than two years' experience then, and we just couldn't dispense with Marchand. And because of that, we sort of tried to hold him back when the crucial moment might have been for him to do it. Timing was off."

With Marchand out of the running, the real battle for the leadership was between Bourassa and Claude Wagner — and for Trudeau that was a Hobson's choice. He had known Bourassa for a number of years and considered him a competent technocrat, but basically weak. Wagner, on the other hand, had displayed an authoritarian mentality as provincial justice minister in the Lesage government, and Trudeau wasn't enthusiastic about the prospect of a Liberal leader who might give federalism in Quebec a nastily right-wing image. "I'm afraid that in that one, I can't say that I played a very courageous role," Trudeau admits. "I didn't know whom to choose. As between Bourassa and Wagner, I thought both had their pros and their cons or advantages and disadvantages. Some ministers were for Wagner — Bryce Mackasey, for example — and I willingly arranged for me to be meeting Wagner and shaking his hand publicly at that time, and I don't know if they ever used the photos. . . . I guess the role I played there is more or less the role I play in a convention in northern Saskatchewan to choose a candidate for the Liberal Party. I say, 'Look, the democratic process operates and . . .'."

It was Bourassa who ended up with the support of the federal Liberal machine in Quebec, but Trudeau says that decision was made by Marchand as leader of the Quebec caucus. "What you are really saying is that Jean Marchand went behind Bourassa, which he did. And I didn't try to second-guess that one. I didn't try to prevent him, but I didn't try to prevent Mackasey from helping Wagner in every way he could. You know, now that Bourassa is defeated, I am not trying to disassociate myself from him — I think I have done that publicly on enough occasions. But I certainly can't claim any credit for him having been chosen. Or claim any blame, either."

In January 1970, Bourassa won the Quebec Liberal leadership. Four months later, on May 12, he won the provincial election, becoming premier with 45 per cent of the popular vote and 72 of the legislature's 108 seats; René Lévesque's Parti Québécois, fighting its first election, won 7 seats and 24 per cent of the popular vote. Trudeau called it "a victory for Canada", but it took only four months for that federalist triumph to turn sour when the FLQ crisis suddenly exploded on October 5.

Since its beginnings in 1963, the activities of the terrorist Front de Libération du Québec had been slowly mounting in scope and intensity. Its bombings had escalated from the placing of small devices powerful enough to maim or kill an individual or cause limited property damage, to the detonation at the Montreal Stock Exchange in 1969 of an explosion that caused 27 injuries. The bombings had grown in number as well — from some 35 bombs planted between 1963 and 1967 to 50 or 60 between 1968 and 1970. Hold-ups attributed to the FLQ had also been multiplying, from 8 between 1963 and 1967 to some 20 from 1968 to 1970. By the fall of 1970, the activities of successive cells of separatist terrorists had claimed six lives.

When British trade commissioner James Cross was kidnapped on October 5, 1970, Trudeau saw the situation from the outset in the perspective of one of his deepest and most long-standing concerns: the fragility of democracy, particularly in a society as troubled and volatile as Quebec was becoming. His immediate reaction was to insist that there be no surrender to terrorist demands, no sign of weakness which could be construed as a victory for lawlessness. He approved a statement by Sharp — who as external affairs minister was responsible for Cross's safety — rejecting the FLQ's demands but leaving the door open to further negotiation in an attempt to save the diplomat. But Sharp was left with the impression that Cross's fate was not paramount in Trudeau's mind: "At that time, the PM hadn't really concentrated on that part; he was concerned about the FLQ, what we said about it. He was not so concerned about the fact that we had responsibility for Cross. But he was quite happy with the outcome of the discussion, he didn't question the decision."

It was Sharp who took it upon himself, on October 8, to authorize the CBC to comply with one FLQ demand, the broadcasting of its anarchist manifesto, an appallingly shrill document that was personally insulting toward Trudeau and other political and business leaders. "The PM was very angry at me," Sharp recalls. "I said I had taken that responsibility because I thought it helpful to our cause for the exaggerations of the manifesto to be broadcast. It was a means of demonstrating to the public how right we were. The PM's concern was that I had somehow bowed to the requests of the FLQ. My purpose was to have it read so people could see what kind of people these were, but the PM felt I had somehow made a concession."

By Saturday, October 10, the federal government was detecting disquieting signs of weakness in the Bourassa administration. The premier himself had gone to New York on a three-day business trip despite the crisis, leaving Justice Minister Jérôme Choquette to handle the response to an FLQ communiqué in which the kidnappers threatened to kill Cross if imprisoned terrorists were not released by 6 p.m. on Saturday. Says Sharp: "On the day Laporte was kidnapped, just before, Choquette showed signs of weakness. I had decided I would say nothing more. I told Choquette, he agreed. Then he called back, said he had been talking to someone. . . . It was dreadful: He was going to release prisoners, all sorts of nonsense. I thought, it's just possible he's got a deal. I asked him: 'If you make that statement, have you reason to believe Cross will be released?' Choquette said, no. Fortunately, at the last moment, he changed again." Sharp believes Trudeau was encountering similar signs of vacillation in his telephone talks with Bourassa. "I remember having to clear the Choquette situation with the PM, and I said to him that I intended to tell Choquette we would disassociate the federal government from his statement. And he said: 'I'm having the same trouble.' "

At 6.15 p.m., Choquette finally finished broadcasting a statement rejecting the terrorists' demands but pleading for Cross's release and offering the diplomat's captors safe passage out of the country. At almost the same moment, Pierre Laporte, deputy premier of Quebec and minister of labour and immigration, was kidnapped from in front of his suburban home. Laporte was the highest-ranking member of the provincial government after Bourassa himself, and his kidnapping added an entirely different dimension to the crisis: What had initially appeared to be a single crime by a ragtag band of terrorists suddenly began to look like part of a bold and unpredictable escalation by an organization of indeterminate size and resources.

On the day Laporte was kidnapped, Bourassa called Trudeau and raised the question both of calling in the army and of invoking the War Measures Act. As Bourassa later explained: "When Mr. Laporte was abducted, anything could have followed. At that time, I considered it my responsibility to telephone the Prime Minister of Canada, who had jurisdiction over the army and the War Measures Act, and to tell him to take steps to make the army available if I needed it during the next few days or later, or maybe not at all, and similarly that he should be ready to adopt the War Measures Act if the situation called for it."⁹ Trudeau's response was to urge the premier not to formally request either measure unless it became absolutely necessary.

Although he realized that the best strategy was to do nothing but stall for as long as possible while police searched for the kidnappers and their hostages, the whole situation already had Trudeau seething with anger and frustration. He felt this crisis not only intellectually but viscerally, because it was for him a convergence of the two forces he most loathed: separatism and violently anti-democratic action. On Monday, October 12, the federal cabinet summoned armed troops into Ottawa — both to guard potential targets such as cabinet ministers and federal buildings against further terrorist outrages and to underscore that there would be no flinching from fighting as rough as necessary — and Trudeau's anger and determination flashed publicly when a television reporter critically quizzed him the next day about recourse to the army: "There's a lot of bleeding hearts around who just don't like to see people with helmets and guns. All I can say is, go on and bleed, but it is more important to keep law and order in the society than to be worried about weak-kneed people who don't like the looks of an army. . . . I think that society must take every means at its disposal to defend itself against the emergence of a parallel power which defies the elected power in this country, and I think that goes to any distance. So long as there is power here which is challenging the elected representatives of the people, then I think that power must be stopped and I think it's only, I repeat, weak-kneed bleeding hearts who are afraid to take these measures."

On Thursday, the Bourassa government formally requested the federal government to send in the armed forces to assist the police, who were close to exhaustion from working around the clock to search for the kidnappers, guard other potential terrorist targets, and maintain order in an increasingly unsettled situation. Although the distinction has become blurred in many people's memory, the recourse to the armed forces and the invocation of the War Measures Act were two entirely separate and very different developments. In the case of Bourassa's request for military assistance, the federal government technically had no choice in the matter: under the provisions of the National Defence Act, a formal request by a provincial government for military assistance cannot be denied. The War Measures Act, on the other hand, is federal legislation, and only the federal government can decide whether or not to invoke it.

As it happened, Trudeau agreed on the need for troops in Quebec by the time Bourassa made his formal request for their use, so the federal powerlessness to refuse never became a real factor in the situation. But not only were the troops not imposed on Quebec by Ottawa, but their summoning was welcomed even by such staunch Quebec nationalists as Le Devoir editor Claude Ryan, who wrote: "The police forces, which have been kept on the qui vive for almost two weeks, are on the point of exhaustion. . . . The government of Quebec, remembering the experience of recent years, considered that it should ask for the assistance of the armed forces. They were right to do this. They would have been derelict in their duty if they had done otherwise."

The social and political climate in Montreal had been steadily deteriorating, meanwhile, until it reached a state reminiscent of Yeats's evocative lines: "The best lack all conviction, while the worst are full of passionate intensity." Rumours and bomb scares abounded. So much dynamite and weaponry had been stolen in the preceding years that no one knew just what the FLQ had and what it might do with it. In this uncertain atmosphere, a palpable erosion of order and the will to resist began to set in.

On Wednesday night, Robert Lemieux, the radical lawyer the FLQ had chosen as its spokesman and intermediary, addressed an excited rally at the University of Montreal and urged the students to boycott classes. The next day, a campaign to organize a general student strike in support of the FLQ got under way, and students of the U. of M.'s social sciences faculty immediately voted to join the strike; at the largest college, CEGEP Vieux Montréal, there was an all-day teach-in to study the FLQ manifesto; students at the Université de Québec occupied administration offices and demanded that the FLQ's conditions be met. That night, some 1,500 students held a rally in an east-end arena, cheered a reading of the FLQ manifesto, and cheered even louder when Pierre Vallières, one of the founders of the FLQ, told them in an impassioned speech: "The governments claim the FLQ is a small band of criminals. . . . But you are the FLQ, you and all the popular groups that fight for the liberation of Quebec. We must organize the fight for liberation in each district, in each plant, in each office, everywhere."

Given Quebec's history of violent demonstrations in the recent past, there was every reason to believe that this escalation of rebelliousness would soon spill into the streets, with dangerously unpredictable results. The memory of the shooting of four students in the United States at Kent State University only six months earlier was still fresh, and any rioting in the streets of Montreal would have collided with an exhausted police force and nervous troops inexperienced in such situations. In addition, the government didn't know how numerous the FLQ terrorists really were, what supplies of arms and explosives they possessed, and what further escalation they might be planning. It was only weeks later, when the last of the kidnappers and their accomplices had been tracked down, that it became clear that the whole crisis had been produced by only a ragtag, poorly organized handful of self-styled revolutionaries.

Says Trudeau: "I must say I thought they were quite a bit more numerous than they ended up being in the end. . . . Nobody knew how many of these guys there were. There were all kinds of stories going on about the arsenals they had and so on. . . . We had been preparing the RCMP, I suppose — and I am caricaturing, I don't mean to be unkind — but they had been preparing for a generation and a half for a Communist overthrow. But they weren't prepared to deal with terrorists in our midst, children of French Canadian families, some of which were respectable. The whole series of bombings and arsenal raids was made by children of people we knew, classical college students and so on. . . . The police weren't equipped to deal with that."

In addition to the mounting general unrest and the uncertainty about the strength and resources of the FLQ, there was another trend which weighed heavily on federal decision-making: an erosion of will among Quebec's élite of opinion leaders. On October 14, an ad hoc group of sixteen of the province's most prominent figures — including René Lévesque; Confederation of National Trade Unions President Marcel Pépin; Quebec Federation of Labour President Louis Laberge; Le Devoir's Claude Ryan; and Quebec Teachers' Corporation President Yvan Charbonneau — issued a statement which said in part: ". . . we wish to give our complete support to the intention announced Sunday evening by the Bourassa government, which means basically our strongest support for negotiating an exchange of the two hostages for the political prisoners. . . . And we urgently invite all the citizens who share our point of view to make it known publicly as quickly as possible." This statement — and particularly its uncritical acceptance of the FLQ term "political prisoners" for convicts serving sentences for murder, manslaughter, bombings, and armed robbery — struck Trudeau as evidence that the will to resist lawlessness in Quebec was crumbling.

That perception was one of the two pillars of his decision to comply with the Bourassa government's request for invocation of the War Measures Act.

The first pillar, Trudeau says, was a desire to give the police additional tools in the search for the kidnappers and their victims: "The original intention was to give the police the power that they said they needed in order to find out the kidnappers of Laporte and the kidnappers of Cross. They said, 'Look, we have all kinds of names, we think we could find them if we had this power to just go into people's houses and arrest them, and that is what we need to find Cross and Laporte.' And obviously a lot of us reacted that 'just to give you those powers, it's a very big step to invoke the War Measures Act.' But there is no other way in which we could give them these powers. You know, for what they call raking or throwing a net, you have to move instantly on dozens or perhaps hundreds of people at the same time; otherwise, if you take a warrant to go to one house, the people you are hoping to find will have time to move to another house and then you have to get another warrant for that house, and so on. So that was the original intention, nothing more, nothing less."

The second pillar of Trudeau's decision, the one which helped overcome his hesitation about taking such a drastic step, was the deterioration of the political atmosphere as evidenced by the statement by the sixteen opinion-leaders and the response it evoked. To this day, he becomes impassioned and angry when he recalls that episode:

"I had real reason to believe that the inclination of opinion leaders in Quebec to obey their legitimate government was crumbling. In other words, I don't think the government was falling apart from the inside. I think there were some weaknesses and so on, [but] I don't think it was a crumbling of the government which was a factor; I think it was democratic support for a democratically elected government which was crumbling. And the best evidence I can give of that is the statement signed by many dozens — perhaps hundreds, I don't remember — of leading opinion leaders in Quebec. Well known people in different areas, the arts, the law, business, media, they signed this manifesto saying that the Quebec government and the federal government should free the 'political prisoners' and that we should bargain with the FLQ and give in to them. And to the extent that there were perhaps some people in Bourassa's government who were inclined to go in that direction, I was dismayed, but my real fear . . . was so many of these people saying that a democratically elected government of this land should give in to terrorists.

"That worried me no end, and to my dying day I'll think that's where the turning point lay, when I read that. You know, not only we can't go on, we can't give in, but we've got to show that democratically elected governments *are* the governments, they've been elected to govern, and that terrorists will not govern in this land. . . . To me that is, I'd almost say, the dying shame of very eminent people in Quebec, to sign that manifesto."

Though he is unwilling to discuss it publicly — "I'm reluctant to look as if I'm trying to shift some of the blame, because that's one thing that I never lost five minutes' sleep over" — Trudeau and his ministers never expected that the War Measures Act would be used to round up a total of 465 persons. While invocation of the War Measures Act was being contemplated, the police forces involved in the crisis presented the cabinet with a list of fewer than 70 persons they would want to arrest under the emergency powers. The federal government studied that list and ordered several names to be dropped on the grounds that the net was being cast too wide. Then, once the War Measures Act had been invoked, the police not only arrested some of those people whose names had been ordered removed but went on to seize hundreds of others as well. Once that started happening, insiders say, the Trudeau government decided against speaking up, for fear both of demoralizing and antagonizing the hard-pressed police at a crucial time and of adding to the general confusion.

Although much of what happened in the following days, especially after Laporte's death, looked as if the federal and Quebec governments were deliberately countering the terrorist impact with carefully planned political theatre of their own, Trudeau insists that sort of stage-management was never in his mind.

"Even the hint of a theory that I was just waiting for an occasion to sock it to the separatists — you know, the whole Vallières thesis and so on — is completely wrong. There was no glee, there was a great deal of reluctance. As I said, many days lapsed before I finally dropped to cabinet this possibility [the War Measures Act] that had been asked of me. And I guess speaking out of personal feeling and emotion and sentiment, the best example I could give you is to confess that in a sense I couldn't have been producing a drama because I was an actor in it. You know, when I went to Laporte's funeral I said, 'Look, I want to walk from the helicopter to Notre Dame Church, I want the people to see me.' And then we had a meeting, a secret meeting with Drapeau and Bourassa, and I suddenly found myself in a bulletproof car being driven from the Champ de Mars to Notre Dame with cordons of police everywhere. And being whisked into the Hydro-Québec building not by the main door as I always insist — even during demonstrations on Parliament Hill here, I refuse to use back doors — but bringing me into an underground garage and everything else. Montreal, as you know, was seized in a reign of terror."

The most dramatically theatrical event of the crisis, the police-ringed Laporte funeral, was largely a product of police nervousness, Trudeau says. "It was the Quebec ministers [who] decided to hold this funeral. I think the reason for that was not to build a drama, I think it was more in the nature of bravado, saying, 'We are not afraid of any terrorists and we are going to go down there in broad daylight and reassure the people.' That, I think, was the intention, and it's in that spirit that I went there. But obviously it's not the spirit with which the police were acting. They had drawn up these cordons and they had machine-guns everywhere and, I repeat, I was in a sense a victim of this drama. You know, 'We are not reassuring the people, we are frightening them more.' And that certainly wasn't put up by the governments, and to the extent that the police were responsible for it, I think they felt they were doing their duty. They were trying to protect the elected leaders against an unknown menace."

In retrospect, Trudeau says, he has no regrets about his handling of the crisis: "Given the knowledge we had at the time — which was very, very slight — I think we did what we had to do. Given, once again, the fact that the democratic support for the legitimate government was crumbling. I can easily understand how an outside observer, particularly if he is a Quebec nationalist, would sort of suspect that the whole thing was a gigantic drama put together in order to frighten people away from separatism. But I can tell you with all my earnestness that that isn't the way it happened, that it turned out to be a dramatic production but it wasn't designed to be that.

"You know, even the bringing in of the army, the intention wasn't to create psychological terror or impose authority, whatever that meant in terms of reassurance as well as a threat to the wrongdoers. The reason was that the police told us they couldn't do the job. They didn't know how many kidnappings there would be, they knew that they were working around the clock to find the kidnappers that had already acted, and that they just couldn't do the job of protecting the next minister who might be abducted, or the next ambassador. And the army was used as a police, no more, no less. Now, of course, when that police has a machine-gun and a helmet and bayonets and so on, it does create a sense of drama, but that wasn't the intention. I'm sure that I'll disappoint some of the people, who thought that I masterminded something much more dramatic. But I assure you that that's the truth."

Trudeau's recourse to the War Measures Act permanently cost him the support of much of Canada's intellectual and academic community, but history might have judged him far more harshly if he had acted with less firmness. To an extent that could not be perceptible to observers in other provinces, Quebec during the crisis became a society caught in a dizzying vortex of uncertainty and disorder. The government didn't know how many terrorists the FLQ actually comprised and how many other Quebecers might be willing to support or assist them; it didn't know how coherent a strategy the FLQ was following or what its next move might be; it couldn't know where the escalation of events, irresponsible statements, incitements of disorder, and protest meetings in support of the FLQ might lead. All that was clear was that the situation was becoming uglier by the hour and that the possible consequences of inaction were far graver than those of drastic measures that might prove later to have been unnecessary. The government therefore reached for the only tool at its disposal to clamp a lid on the whole situation, reassert the authority of established government, and put an end to the escalation of hysterical rhetoric and incipient disorder.

The suspension of civil liberties is an ugly thing whenever it occurs, but it must be weighed, in a democracy, in the context of a government's over-all responsibilities and of the possible consequences of less drastic action in that particular situation. The individuals detained under the War Measures Act suffered a serious violation of their normal civil rights. But those individuals lost, ultimately, only time and dignity; they were not mistreated or injured, and those who had been unjustly detained later received monetary compensation for their hardship. With the exception of Laporte — whose murder had no clear connection to the War Measures Act — there was no loss of life or even serious injury to anyone during the crisis, and no one suffered more than temporary hardship. If the escalation had continued unchecked, on the other hand, it is entirely possible that there might have been further terrorist actions, however improvised, and that the pro-FLQ rallies would have led to another round of street violence. There might well have been loss of life and incalculable consequences. In the realm of such historical might-have-beens, there can be no more reliable standard for judging an action than a comparison of what *did* happen with what reasonably *might* have happened: By that standard, the Trudeau government's Draconian intervention violated for a period of weeks the right of 465 individuals to physical freedom, but it safeguarded the right of those individuals and Quebec's entire population to continue living in a democratically governed, violence-free society.

As far as long-range political impact is concerned, Trudeau's tough approach to the FLQ crisis undoubtedly hardened the feelings of Quebec's separatists and deeply committed nationalists. In the folklore of Quebec radicalism, it has been conveniently forgotten that both the military presence and the invocation of the War Measures Act were requested by the government of Quebec itself; instead, the midnight knock on the door by heavily armed police has been enshrined as a symbol of federalist repression. But while the importance of such symbols to a militant minority is not to be underestimated, what is far more important is how the federal government's handling of the crisis was perceived by the overwhelming majority of Quebecers.

The answer may be deduced from subsequent election results. If Trudeau's use of the War Measures Act and federal troops had been perceived with enough hostility to turn substantial numbers of Quebecers toward separatism, the first manifestation would undoubtedly have been a marked decline in the next election of support for the prime minister and the party that had resorted to those measures. Instead, in the 1972 federal election, the Liberals won exactly as many Quebec seats as in 1968. While again winning 56 of the province's 74 seats, Trudeau and his party suffered a decline of only some five percentage points in their share of the popular vote — much less than their slippage in the country as a whole and easily attributable to factors other than the 1970 crisis. Moreover, the share of the vote that the Liberals did lose went almost entirely to the right-wing Créditistes, who had consistently urged the government to be ruthless in suppressing terrorism.

While there is no evidence that Trudeau's handling of the FLQ crisis turned any significant number of Quebecers toward separatism, it clearly did turn even the most extreme proponents of separatism away from violence. Before October of 1970, the intensity and scale of terrorist activity had been slowly but steadily escalating; after the crisis, overt terrorist activity ceased altogether. Terrorism is an effective political weapon only if it can extort concessions from the authorities, strike a responsive chord with a substantial segment of the population, or provide a catalyst for escalating disorder. Suddenly and unexpectedly confronted with the awesome power of the state, Quebec's would-be revolutionaries learned a painful lesson: Recourse to violence could only be personally and politically self-defeating, because the federal government, under this prime minister, would fight back with all the formidable resources a society possesses to defend itself. By the end of 1971, Pierre Vallières, the chief FLQ ideologue who had written in *White Niggers of America*, "The sooner we niggers arm ourselves with our courage and our rifles, the sooner our liberation from slavery will make us equal and fraternal men," was publicly announcing the folly of this course: "The FLQ is outmoded," he wrote in a long statement published in *Le Devoir*, "because the situation has changed, and armed agitation is not suited to the present situation. . . . The struggle of the masses in Quebec . . . is on the electoral level, and will remain there as long as the people feel that this is the proper way to attain their main objective — national independence." Before long, he put himself on the federal payroll, working on a Local Initiatives Program project in Mont Laurier.

Though the War Measures Act has been cited by separatists as a metaphor for Trudeau's whole attitude toward Quebec, that argument is transparently false, and even his image as a confrontationist is only half the picture. Far from merely wanting to "put Quebec in its place", he has conducted his battle against separatism on two fronts: In Canada at large, he has fought for Quebecers, seeking for them a greater role in the governance of the nation, acceptance of the French fact, and iron-clad guarantees of freedom to use their language; within Quebec, at the same time, he has fought vigorously against those French Canadians — especially politicians — who seek to withdraw the province more deeply into itself or to trespass on federal powers. In this second aspect of the battle, his role has consciously been that of a polarizer. He has operated throughout his time in politics on the premise that militant Quebec nationalism is a sterile, destructive force that must be fought and vanquished, and that there is nothing to be gained from postponing or sidestepping the clashes.

"The René Lévesque party," he said in 1969, "has become not only official, but it has solved the problem of disunity, at least on the surface, between various separatist tendencies. It has begun to recruit a few people from the better-known outsiders, and so only it is coming down to specifics, it is a polarization of separatist hopes. And, in this sense, you might think things look worse. But I think, on the contrary, this makes things look better because it'll give people a choice. It'll now permit them to know whether they're for or against something, and this is the basis of any action in a free society."[10] In another interview that year, he said: "We want the dialogue to be more clear, so that we may know who are the people who still believe in federalism and who are those who absolutely want to destroy federalism as a form of government. Perhaps it's an appeal for more clarity in thinking, more precision in action."[11]

This stand-up-and-be-counted approach has led him into bruising confrontations with a succession of Quebec premiers. He has been prepared to make a major issue out of virtually every perceived attempt to encroach on federal terrain, and at times he has carried his defence of federal prerogatives too far, giving too much weight to formal considerations and too little to practical realities. Perhaps the most striking example of this was his 1969 clash with Jean-Jacques Bertrand over the location of a new airport for the Montreal area. Though airports are a matter of federal jurisdiction, Bertrand argued that the Ste. Scholastique site favoured by the federal government would benefit Ontario more than Quebec and also conflicted with his government's development priorities for the province; Trudeau, after being pressed repeatedly to accept another site — which, it happened, was in the vicinity of Bertrand's own riding — eventually snapped that the premier was "off his rocker". He later explained: "We have to say that in all areas under federal jurisdiction, the federal government is the spokesman for the Quebec farmer, worker, labourer, intellectual and so on. Therefore, when the government of Quebec, even in areas of federal jurisdiction, tries to tell us what to do because it is the spokesman for Quebec, we must reject that extremely strongly."[12]

Technically, he was right. But in practical terms, the location of a huge new jetport inevitably has such significant impact on the development of a province's economy that it is not unreasonable for the provincial government to want a say in its selection. Trudeau's humiliating rebuff of Bertrand in those circumstances must have stuck many Quebecers as unwarranted federal intransigence.

Since most other Quebec challenges to federal jurisdiction have involved more potentially serious attempts to set a precedent or drive a wedge, it would not be fair to say that Trudeau has established a regular pattern of taking an unreasonably hard line on the province's requests. He has, however, established a pattern of treating a succession of Quebec premiers with open hostility and contempt: with Johnson and Bertrand, he heaped scorn on their pursuit of special status for Quebec; with Bourassa, he made increasingly little effort to hide his contempt for the premier's weakness and indecisiveness.

The problem was that he was devastatingly effective at this. With each premier in turn, he established such an overshadowing presence, so thoroughly rebuffed demands and encroachments, that some Quebecers — if they allowed themselves to forget that Trudeau, too, was a Quebecer and that he controlled his government — may have concluded that their province was being hopelessly thwarted by the federal government. In Bourassa's case in particular, the increasingly evident contempt that Trudeau — whom Quebecers respect if not necessarily like — felt for the premier undoubtedly aggravated Bourassa's image of weakness and may thereby have contributed to his electoral downfall at the hands of the Parti Québécois.

The other side of this argument, however, is that Trudeau filled a vacuum created by the fact that three Quebec premiers in a row were not prepared to make an unequivocal commitment to federalism; even Bourassa, while not making a major pitch for special status, never went beyond defending Confederation on lifeless economic grounds. Says Trudeau: "I guess my greatest disappointment is in my inability to get the provincial Liberal Party, successively in Lesage's day and then in Bourassa's day, to be very strong federalists in the sense that they would recognize that Quebec could be represented every bit as well in Ottawa by its members and ministers as it can by its members and ministers in Quebec City. That has not been a success. There are still . . . too many Liberal leaders that go on the conventional

and intellectual wisdom that somehow 'Quebec City is our government, and Ottawa can only be our government from time to time,
depending on the leaders we have and the particular circumstances.' " In the absence of any other strong indigenous voice
defending federalism and the exercise of federal powers, Trudeau
has stepped into the gap, sometimes dealing harshly with Quebec
premiers but at least making a case that needs to be made. A more
conciliatory leader might have been able to postpone the clash
with separatism by a few years; but at some point there would
have been no more concessions that could be made without im-
perilling federalism anyway, the Quebec nationalists would have
remained unsatisfied, and the confrontation would have come
under circumstances that would not necessarily have been more
favourable to the federalist cause. The electoral evidence also suggests that it would be a mistake to overestimate the extent to
which Trudeau's tough approach alienated Quebecers from him
and the federalism he represents: His electoral support has remained consistently high, and his popularity in the Gallup Polls,
even after the Parti Québécois victory, has matched Lévesque's.

If Trudeau's polarizing approach contributed significantly to the
coming to power of the separatist Parti Québécois, it was in
another, more subtle way that cannot really be assessed in terms
of blame. By the very nature of the new role he sought to create
in federal government for French Canadians, Trudeau began attracting the best federalist talent of a generation to Ottawa. The
best nationalist minds of that generation, meanwhile, gravitated to
the new Parti Québécois, whose policy carried their preoccupation
with the province through to its most complete conclusion. With
Ottawa becoming the outlet for first-rate Quebec federalists and the
PQ attracting the brightest and most committed nationalists, the
Bourassa Liberals were left to function as a government of second-
raters — an impoverishment that played no small role in their
mediocre performance and eventual downfall.

Another sense in which Trudeau contributed somewhat to the
PQ victory was through his failure to spot and quickly defuse the
smouldering resentment in Western Canada toward his language
policy. That resentment found a catalyst in the summer of 1976

in a dispute over bilingual air traffic control services in Quebec and exploded into an ugly outburst of anti-French bigotry, followed by the Trudeau government's acceptance of a compromise which struck many Quebecers as a sell-out. The result was that when Quebecers went to the polls that autumn to elect a provincial government, many of them felt offended by both English Canada and the federal government. Says Trudeau: "I'm disappointed by the inability to do on both sides of the language barrier what was necessary to make Quebecers feel absolutely confident in Ottawa, and I think I've given you repeatedly the example of the air controllers' strike as being the greatest and biggest illustration of that. 'Maybe it's not possible,' was their reaction, 'to get equality of treatment, and therefore perhaps Trudeau is wrong and we do need special status, otherwise we won't be treated as equals.' "

Whatever impact all these factors may have had, however, the reality was that a Parti Québécois victory, sooner or later, started becoming virtually inevitable as early as 1970 — for reasons that had nothing to do with separatism. The basic cause was a realignment of Quebec politics as the Union Nationale that Maurice Duplessis had founded in 1935 slowly but inexorably withered. The UN had begun dying in the mid-1950s, losing popular support even when it was still winning elections: In the 1956 election, it won 51.6 per cent of the vote; in 1960, 46.7 per cent; in 1962, 42.1 per cent; in 1966, 40.8 per cent; and, in 1970, 19.6 per cent.

The reason was simply that Quebec society was changing profoundly and the UN could not find a way to change with it. The party had traditionally been conservative, nationalist, and rural. But the Créditistes began outflanking it on the right, the nationalist vote was wooed away in 1970 by the Parti Québécois, and, most important of all, the traditional UN stronghold of rural Quebec had rapidly been losing its political importance under a strong wave of urbanization. While these changes were taking place, the human resources of the party were superseded as well: The "petite bourgeoisie" which had been the UN's mainstay of support — the small-town mayors and doctors, the notaries, the contractors, and the parish priests — was replaced as Quebec's power élite by the lawyers, economists, engineers, and executives who formed a new class of technocrats.

In the 1973 election, the last remnants of the party's structure crumbled and its share of the popular vote plunged to only five per cent. The Créditistes, decaying after a brief and limited spurt of popularity, also collapsed. That left only the Liberals and the Parti Québécois. The Bourassa Liberals, who took 54 per cent of the vote and 102 of the National Assembly's 110 seats, had by then, as Jérôme Choquette put it on election night, "expropriated" the right wing of Quebec politics; they had taken over the role of functioning as the province's conservative party. The Parti Québécois — which won 30 per cent of the votes and 6 seats and became the official Opposition — had meanwhile added to its basic separatist appeal a package of attractive policies that established it as Quebec's progressive, left-of-centre party; by 1973, opinion polls showed, a substantial proportion of the PQ's support came from voters who did not favour separatism. From 1973 on, unless someone successfully established an entirely new party, only two outcomes were possible: either the Liberals would become a long-governing dynasty like the Ontario Tories, or the PQ Opposition would eventually come to power. Given the deep-rooted turmoil and dissatisfaction of an increasingly rudderless Quebec society and the basic weakness of the Bourassa team, the dynasty hypothesis was most unlikely and a Parti Québécois victory became virtually inevitable. In 1976, with the Bourassa Liberals scandal-ridden and ineffectual, the PQ downplayed the separatism issue, concentrated on a promise of good government, and — to its own surprise — won a majority. But the PQ came to power not because of its commitment to separatism but despite it, and even Lévesque conceded at the time that the vote was by no stretch of the imagination an endorsement of independence.

No federal prime minister could, ultimately, have prevented the sequence of developments that allowed the Parti Québécois to come to power. Trudeau's contribution between 1968 and 1976, however, was to create conditions in which the PQ's victory did not take the form of a mandate for secession and in which the showdown with Quebec separatism can be fought on grounds reasonably favourable to the federalist cause. In the context of Quebec's recent history, what is striking about a succession of opinion polls taken since the PQ victory is not the finding that some thirty per cent of Quebecers would favour sovereignty coupled with economic association with what remained of Canada; what is remarkable, rather, is that an overwhelming majority would not favour leaving Confederation for such an arrangement even if it could be obtained. Sovereignty-association in theory offers any Quebecer dissatisfied with Confederation the best of both worlds: full political independence for the province, along with continuation of the economic advantages of Confederation. Yet at most a third of Quebecers are disgruntled enough with federalism to want that arrangement even if they believed it were possible; and without association, support for independence shrivels to ten or fifteen per cent.

If Canada had not moved beyond the situation of the 1960s — if the top echelons of the government and the public service were still the almost exclusive preserve of anglophones, if French Canadians still had to deal with the federal government and its agencies primarily in English, if Canada still projected an overwhelmingly anglophone presence abroad, and if the prime minister had not been fighting aggressively on behalf of the French fact — the attitude of Quebecers toward Confederation would undoubtedly have been far more sour by the time the PQ came to power.

Trudeau has, as he promised, given French Canadians a more genuine and equal role in the governance of the nation, without thereby taking away anything of substance from English Canada. Under the Official Languages Act, a French Canadian may deal with the federal government and its agencies on the same basis as an anglophone — that is, in his own language. Abroad, Canada is presented at every opportunity as a nation with two official languages; even when Trudeau goes to as unilingual a place as Washington, he often makes a point of opening his press conferences with a few remarks in French.

And perhaps most importantly, he has given French Canadians full and unprecedented participation in Canada's public life. It used to be that cabinet seats were doled out according to an unspoken formula in which only a certain number of portfolios were considered appropriate for French Canadians. Trudeau smashed that system, over the years appointing French Canadians for the first time to such key portfolios as industry, trade and commerce; the treasury board presidency; and finance. When he established the department of regional economic expansion to try to correct regional disparities, it was to another Quebecer, Jean Marchand, that he entrusted the task; when he set out to overhaul the welfare system, he handed the job to Marc Lalonde. Despite the suspicions it aroused in some parts of the country, this new approach did not amount to having francophones "dominate" the government; indeed, the most powerful and influential individuals in cabinet over the years were such English Canadian ministers as Mitchell Sharp, C. M. Drury, John Turner, and Donald Macdonald. Trudeau has also made the top echelons of the public service genuinely open to French Canadians: The Glassco Report described the number of French Canadians in senior positions in 1960 as insignificant; by 1976, 20.4 per cent of public-service officials in the senior executive category had French as their first language.

By the time of the air traffic controllers' flare-up in 1976, when many Quebecers were offended enough to wonder whether they really were accepted in Canada's national life, Trudeau was able to respond: "The Commissioner of the RCMP is a French Canadian; the Speaker of the Senate is a French Canadian; the Governor-General is a French Canadian; the prime minister is a French Canadian; the chairman of the National Film Board is a French Canadian; the chief of the defence staff is a French Canadian. . . ."[13] Progress toward full institutional bilingualism and linguistic equality has been slow, turbulent, and sometimes painful, but no one could reasonably expect an effort fully launched for only a decade to more quickly solve problems that have accumulated over a full century.

What Trudeau has accomplished is to make it possible for federalists to wage the battle with Quebec's separatists over Canada's future without having to be apologetic and without having to resort to desperate measures like special status or an adventure in massive decentralization which could make Canada —

already one of the most decentralized countries in the world — impossible to govern. Instead, federalists can argue, to a Quebec population which still overwhelmingly rejects separation, that progress toward linguistic equality is slow but genuine; that the federal government is not some alien power but their own institution in which they can play a full and powerful role; that their language and culture are protected rather than threatened by Confederation; and that remaining problems require neither separation nor radical constitutional change to resolve.

In the political struggle to make that message prevail over the separatist argument, Trudeau is in a singularly good position to act as the federal standard-bearer. As the prime minister who expanded the role of Quebecers and their language, he can carry his case to them with the credibility of a leader who has already partially delivered on his promises. He has the advantage, too, of a clarity of purpose as firm as that of the advocates of independence: having devoted much of his life to the Quebec issue, he can function from long-elaborated premises about the province and its future without having to improvise answers to questions of basic principle. And, as a French Canadian, he can talk to Quebecers in terms that would be foreclosed to an anglophone, speaking about the dangers of independence and the advantages of Confederation with a brutal frankness that would be perceived as patronizing if it came from an outsider.

Whether he will be entrusted with carrying this challenge through to its conclusion depends on the vagaries of electoral politics. But it is for that challenge — the decisive confrontation between the competing ideologies of federalism and nationalism — that he has been preparing and honing himself, however unconsciously, throughout his adult life, from his world travels to the brave little battles of *Cité Libre* to the prime-ministerial odyssey on which he embarked so reluctantly.

CHAPTER SIXTEEN

A Leader Unfulfilled

CANADA and Trudeau have come a long way together since those euphoric days of 1968 when unrealistic expectations were strewn like a carpet of flowers over the troubled and uncertain land that lay beneath. The nation has changed: the troubles are all on the surface now, unadorned and inescapable, and the simmering uncertainty has boiled over into a crisis that will leave Canada either improved or shattered. Trudeau, too, has changed: he has grown harder, wilier, more cynical, become a better politician and thereby a less open and appealing one. The love-in of 1968 has turned into a love-hate relationship in which the public simultaneously recognizes his skills and his dominance of the political scene and dislikes him for it, and Trudeau — recognizing the public as a potentially hostile force that must be treated carefully — keeps the more attractive aspects of his personality to himself and governs as a wary man behind a shield of remoteness.

Measured against the expectations he helped create in 1968 and 1974, Trudeau has been a disappointment. Despite a creditable over-all performance and a number of significant achievements, he has not accomplished nearly as much as might be expected of a man of his intellect and public appeal. He has repeatedly made the mistake of studying decisions — on general strategy and specific problems alike — so long that time runs out and he must scramble frantically or start from scratch. He has been careless of his political popularity to the point of squandering, not once but twice, majority public support. He has periodically allowed a self-damaging immaturity to creep into his behaviour, permitting himself to be flippant when he should have been solemn, aloof when he should have been concerned, and smart-alecky when he should have been contrite.

He has governed as precisely what he is, and what he is could never have fulfilled the expectations of constantly inspirational leadership that were heaped on him. He is a leader who cares passionately about one issue — national unity and the survival of an open-spirited, bilingual federalism — who is intellectually committed to several others, and who for the rest will accept whatever seems both rational and pragmatically feasible. He is a shy, inner-directed man who never wanted to be a leader and who still shuns the most direct and personal forms of leadership except in exceptional circumstances. And he is a political thinker whose incisive, reform-oriented intellectual perceptions have never been fully translated into action because of a combination of diffidence, caution, and an overly consensual view of the relationship between a leader and the society he heads.

But while Trudeau is a disappointment when measured against the expectations he aroused or against some abstract standard of excellence, neither of those measures is a realistic yardstick. A much more valid test is a comparison of this prime minister with what came before and what is likely to come after: Is Trudeau fundamentally a failure, as many of those who have grown disillusioned with him believe, or do people tend to look for an ideal prime minister who does not — and cannot — exist in today's complex society? Were Canadians really more enchanted with Louis St. Laurent, the bland chairman-of-the-board whose government finally self-destructed in an orgy of Liberal arrogance? How does Trudeau compare with the chaotic and often irrational John Diefenbaker, whose ineptitude so dismayed the nation that the Tories went from landslide victory to ruin in five years? And was the public all that happy with Lester Pearson, who stumbled from crisis to crisis and whom the voters twice denied a majority?

The flaws of political leaders are dimmed in memory when they have left the scene, and hidden in the glow of novelty when they first arrive, but by any objective standard Trudeau is at least the equal of Canada's other three post-war leaders; in most respects, he is by far the most impressive of the lot, and history seems likely to rank him among the most memorable of Canada's first fifteen prime ministers. In international comparisons with his contemporaries, he fares no less well: in foreign capitals, he is respected as an outstanding player on the world stage, and he compares favourably with the likes of Carter, Callaghan, Giscard, or Schmidt.

Trudeau has an intellect unrivalled among Canadian politicians and quite possibly among his foreign counterparts as well. In a world where government is increasingly the management of sudden crises, he is a first-rate crisis manager who has steered Canada resolutely through such shocks as the FLQ eruption of 1970, the Nixon economic measures of 1971, the Arab oil embargo, and the immediate aftermath of the Parti Québécois victory in Quebec. He is a leader who has the persuasive power, when he puts his mind to it, to rally the nation and impose his own reality upon the course of events.

To one of the most important functions of leadership, the analysis of socio-political trends and of the directions in which society must move, he has brought a lucidity of perception that puts him at the forefront of political thought. Long before other political leaders, he was speaking eloquently and persuasively of the need to move from overwhelming emphasis on growth and consumption toward new values based on conservation of scarce resources, greater priority on the quality of life, and a new ethic of sharing; of the need to develop a new and more equitable relationship between the developed and developing countries; of the dangers that face society if people do not moderate their expectations and keep their political and economic demands within reasonable limits; of the need to realize that government cannot do everything for everyone, and to participate in the choice and then the acceptance of priorities.

The tragedy of Trudeau's prime-ministry is that he has never managed to fully translate his personal qualities and his perceptions into action; he has diagnosed where society should be going, but he has never mustered sufficient boldness to try to deliver it there. This failure is made more grave by the particular circumstances of Trudeau's career. There are moments in a nation's existence, very rare and very precious, when it genuinely wants to be led and makes itself malleable to the setting of a new course by a trusted leader. Trudeau has been granted not one but two such moments — in 1968 and again, to a lesser extent, in 1974 — and each time he allowed himself to see only the darker side of the public's confidence, the danger that people might do his bidding for emotional rather than rational reasons. Each time, he deliberately forfeited a unique opportunity to move the country closer to the goals he espoused and to endow it with a clearer sense of purpose. And each time, consequently, the disillusioned public hardened itself into a mood of scepticism that has made it all the more difficult to achieve the sort of consensus that Trudeau values so highly.

Trudeau is a flawed leader, but the reality is that in an imperfect world all leaders are flawed; the only variables are those of type and gravity. Democratic societies choose their leaders from within their ranks and insist that these individuals be not too far removed from the common herd, but once they are installed in office they are suddenly expected to possess impeccable wisdom and a personality free of all defect. Our leaders are routinely hailed as saviours when they arrive, and then despised when they prove to be only human. Not only is the expectation impossible to fulfil, but the matching reality is that a country as diverse as Canada has some problems which allow no perfect solution, nor even a good one; our leaders often face, instead, only a choice of trade-offs which involve helping one interest group at the cost of damaging or displeasing another. In a society conditioned to expect that every problem can be solved if only the right product is used, the proper button is pushed, or enough money is shelled out, this is not an easy reality to accept, and the victims of its non-acceptance are invariably the politicians.

Apart from these general limitations, Trudeau's prime-ministry must also be judged in the particular context of the times in which he has governed. Not only in Canada but around the world, the past decade has been a period of abrupt and often painful transition. We have witnessed the apogee and decline of student radicalism, the birth of the militant feminist movement, the development of "alternative lifestyles" as people seek escape from the competitive pressures of an increasingly complex society. Industrialized societies have been shaken to their foundations by a set of harsh new facts of life: shortages of energy and of vital raw materials, growing realization of the limits that environmental considerations must impose on growth, and the growing militancy of underdeveloped countries in an increasingly volatile and interlocked global economy. It has been a decade, too, in which conventional theories of economic management have suddenly become hopelessly outdated in the face of new phenomena. Instead of alternating as they have in the past, inflation and economic stagnation with resulting unemployment have become concurrent problems, making it virtually impossible to deal with one without aggravating the other. All these developments have made it clear that Canada, like the rest of the industrialized world, is at a major watershed in which the assumptions and techniques of the past no longer suffice. But the changes have been so rapid that there has not been time for governments, here and abroad, to formulate adequate long-term responses to the new global state of affairs. The result has been a period of groping, in which it has been as difficult for the Trudeau government as for its foreign counterparts to pursue decisive long-term strategies.

Partly as a result of the pressures of rapid change, we are in an era of exceptional public confusion and ambivalence, characterized by what Harvard sociologist Daniel Bell has called "the loss of *civitas*, that spontaneous willingness to obey the law, to respect the rights of others, to forego the temptations of private enrichment at the expense of the public weal. . . . Instead, each man goes his own way, pursuing his private vices, which can be indulged only at the expense of public benefits."[1] In this atmosphere, much of the uncertainty and resentment has focussed on the government, as society collectively wills the end without willing the means.

People have reduced their willingness to give to the state without reducing their willingness to take from it. They have come to distrust big government and high levels of government spending; at the same time, they demand government intervention and regulation to protect their particular interests, and they resent any spending reductions that affect a service from which they benefit. Businessmen decry state planning, but they complain bitterly when the government appears to let the economy drift. They expect and require it to stimulate a sluggish economy with expansionary measures or to rein it in when inflation mounts, and they demand subsidies, protective tariffs, and help in securing foreign markets, complaining all the while about the extent of government intervention. Organized labour complains about the power of government, but it wants that same government to provide more cheap housing, control rents, keep energy prices low, curb land speculation, enforce safer working conditions by regulation, find ways of providing full employment, and fulfil a host of other demands. And the general public worries about growing state authority, but it wants that state to do more to prevent pollution, preserve the environment, protect consumers, ensure the availability of jobs, and avoid foreign domination of Canada's economy and culture. Until people decide what they really want, government will be equally damned for acting or for not acting, and no political leader will long be found satisfactory.

Against this background, Trudeau's record has been one of modest accomplishment in a variety of important fields, coupled with relatively unimpressive performance in several others.

The areas of greatest weakness have tended to be those to which Trudeau initially brought little personal interest. Transportation policy, candidly described as "a mess" by Jean Marchand in 1974 when he was transport minister, is still inadequately synchronized to broader national needs and objectives. Energy policy has been erratic, with the government first allowing itself to be convinced that Canada had no worries because of the size of its oil reserves, then scrambling to reverse its position when the estimates were found to be grossly over-optimistic. Agriculture policy has been formulated throughout Trudeau's prime-ministry so far on an uneven, ad hoc basis, instead of being shaped in the context of a broader food-supply strategy that would cover food commodities from the farm through the various stages of processing and distribution that bring them to the consumer or to export markets. Labour relations in the post office have been allowed to deteriorate to the point of reducing Canada's postal services to a state of chaos. The federal prison system has been badly neglected and allowed to operate with outdated, overcrowded penal institutions and with guards who are underpaid, under-qualified, and under-motivated.

Trudeau's management of the economy has been unimpressive, characterized by a constant air of improvisation and excessive changes of course. He has talked like a Galbraithian one day and an advocate of corporatism the next, with each shift in his public musings producing a new wave of confusion and anxiety in the business community. And yet — surprisingly enough in view of the impression he has created — Canada has not fared significantly worse in terms of over-all economic performance during the years Trudeau has been in power than has the United States under its three presidents. Between 1967 and 1976, the U.S. Gross National Product, expressed in constant dollars that take into account the effect of inflation, increased by 26 per cent; Canada's, during the same period, increased by 48 per cent. Between 1969 and 1976, personal disposable income per capita in the United States increased by 75 per cent; in Canada, it increased by 118 per cent. As for fighting inflation, the over-all track records of the two countries between 1967 and 1976 are almost identical: In the United States, the consumer price index rose 70.5 points, and in Canada 72.1. Since it has long been normal for Canada's economy to grow more rapidly than the more mature economy of its southern neighbour, the higher GNP and per capita disposable income growth rates indicate no great triumph of economic management. Coupled with the inflation comparison, however, they suggest that Canada's economy has not been handled significantly worse than that of the United States.

Longer-term economic problems are a different matter. Unemployment has soared above eight per cent and is likely to remain painfully high for years, inflation is again at levels similar to the 1974 situation that preceded the imposition of controls, the prospect is for a relatively slow rate of economic growth in future years, and the value of the Canadian dollar has declined. But while the Trudeau government is by no means blameless for these developments, they are in large part the product of factors — both domestic and international — that would have been extremely difficult for any government to control.

Unemployment is a chronic Canadian problem that has plagued a succession of governments, and now it is at least cushioned by one of the most generous unemployment insurance systems in the world. Comparisons with past levels of joblessness are virtually meaningless, moreover, because the nature of unemployment itself has changed: its main victims are no longer primary family bread-winners laid off from their jobs, but rather young graduates seek-ing their first employment and married women trying to enter a labour market no longer expanding rapidly enough to accommodate all the newcomers. The slowed economic growth which has caused this problem is attributable partly to lack of business confidence in the policies of the Trudeau government, but it is due much more to international economic trends and to deep-seated structural flaws in the Canadian economy. Similarly, much of the inflation which per-sistently plagues Canada is due to problems — higher energy costs and more expensive imports and food supplies — that cannot easily be solved by any government.

To the extent that Trudeau deserves personal blame for Canada's present economic situation, it is primarily for the fact that his government did not manage during nearly ten years in power to develop a coherent strategy for adapting Canada's economy to changed circumstances. When he first came to power, Trudeau spoke of an industrial strategy based on having Canada specialize increasingly on producing a limited number of goods it could manu-facture more efficiently and better than other countries. Then he realized that such specialization would conflict with his goal of regional economic expansion: by encouraging only the most effi-cient and internationally competitive industries, it would undercut the more marginal industries that sustain the economies of dis-advantaged areas like the Maritimes and parts of Quebec. He quickly dropped that approach, but did not replace it with any other comprehensive strategy to remedy structural problems and make Canada more competitive in a changing world economy. While this is a serious failure of leadership, it must also be judged in the context of the times. Any government that attempted major structural change at a time when society was already wary of state interference would do so at its own peril, and during this turbulent

decade there was nothing approaching agreement among businessmen, economists, labour leaders, or politicians on the precise ways
in which Canada's economy should be changed.

On the positive side of the ledger of Trudeau's record, progress
in the field of social policy has been palpable if unspectacular.
When Trudeau came to power, 18.4 per cent of Canada's families
of two or more persons lived below the poverty line; by 1976, that
had been reduced to 11.2 per cent — a 39 per cent reduction in the
proportion of the most direly impoverished families over a decade.
But poverty in Canada is still real and painful, and these figures tell
only part of the story because many individuals living just above
the statistical poverty line still suffer serious hardship.

The attempt to reduce regional disparities through the Department of Regional Economic Expansion has been a modest success.
It has not yet succeeded in breaking the cycle of dependency in
underdeveloped regions, and some of its expenditures have been
questionable, but it has improved individual living standards and
prevented disparities from becoming a great deal worse. Trudeau's
regional development policies have contributed substantially to
halting the erosion of population from the Atlantic provinces.
Between 1955 and 1971, approximately fifteen per cent of the population of those economically depressed provinces migrated to other
regions; in 1973, the outflow was reversed, and since then there
has been an influx of more than 17,000 persons.

In foreign policy, Trudeau has established diplomatic relations
with China, thawed Canada's relationship with the Soviet Union,
forged closer ties with Latin America and the countries of the
Pacific Rim, and obtained a "contractual link" which gives Canada
formal channels of consultation with the European Economic Community and may eventually enhance trade opportunities. He has
been an effective spokesman for Canadian interests in the international arena, and through his personal efforts Canada is now
accepted as a full participant at economic summits of the leading
Western nations. He has also managed, largely through personal
diplomacy, to win the confidence of leaders of the Third World and
to establish for Canada the beginnings of a role as a bridge between
developed and developing countries; his rhetoric on foreign aid and

the need for concessions to developing countries, however, has thus far not been fully matched by his government's actions.

In a succession of relatively little-noted moves that has, in effect, increased the size and resources of the nation, Trudeau's government has also successfully asserted Canadian sovereignty over the Arctic, guaranteed fishing rights in the vast Gulf of St. Lawrence, extended the offshore territorial limit from three to twelve miles, and proclaimed a 200-mile offshore economic and fisheries management zone.

In other areas of government, Trudeau has established new ministries to deal, however tentatively, with urban affairs, communications, the protection of the environment, science and technology, multiculturalism, the problems of small business, and fitness and amateur sport. He has updated Canada's criminal law. He has modernized the federal decision-making machinery. Through some of his major appointments, he has given an important symbolic boost to the principle of equality of opportunity in Canada. Those appointments include: a brilliant, compassionate legal scholar as Canada's first Jewish chief justice of the Supreme Court; the first woman lieutenant-governor of a province; the first native Indian lieutenant-governor; the first native Indian in the federal cabinet; and more women members at a single time — namely, three — than in any previous federal cabinet.

No less important than these specific accomplishments is a much broader one. Through his own actions and personality and his willingness to pronounce himself on virtually every subject, Trudeau has greatly increased the interest of Canadians in their own government; people may admire or despise him, but few can feel toward this prime minister the apathy and sense of remoteness that some of Canada's governing greybeards have inspired in the past — and that's precisely one of the things he set out to accomplish.

Trudeau has not managed to find fundamental solutions to any of Canada's major problems, but he has steered Canada through a turbulent decade of global transition, and he has laid important foundations in such areas as foreign policy, the advancement of language equality, the alleviation of poverty and regional disparity, the settlement of native grievances, and the reduction of dangerously excessive socio-economic expectations. It is unlikely that any other leader, from among those realistically available, would have accomplished much more. Whether Trudeau himself could have accomplished more is another question. If he had matched boldness of leadership more often to his boldness of thought, if he had made more consistent use of the exceptional qualities he brought to politics, he might either have burned out his meteoric career years ago or have crossed the threshold of greatness.

As it is, he has governed intelligently in a difficult time, and his record thus far makes him not a failed prime minister but an unfulfilled one. But the battle that brought him into politics — the struggle to dispel Quebec nationalism and replace it with full acceptance and involvement of French Canadians in Canada's national life — is now entering its most decisive phase, on terrain he himself has prepared. The outcome will determine Canada's fate and Pierre Elliott Trudeau's place in history.

Notes

CHAPTER THREE

1. Réseau TVA television interview, broadcast May 6, 1977.
2. Global TV interview with Peter Desbarats, "In Private Life", May 21, 1976, PMO transcript.
3. *Toronto Star*, profile by R. McKenzie and L. Dempsey, April 8, 1968.
4. *New Yorker*, profile by Edith Iglauer, July 5, 1969, p. 42.
5. TVA interview, May 6, 1977.
6. Ibid.

CHAPTER FOUR

1. Interview with author.
2. TVA interview, May 6, 1977.
3. Ibid.
4. Interview with author.
5. *New Yorker*, Iglauer profile, July 5, 1969, p. 38.
6. Interview with Francine Laurendeau, undated (*circa* 1968), PMO transcript.
7. Ibid.
8. Ibid.
9. Ibid.
10. Ibid.
11. Ibid.
12. Ibid.
13. *Toronto Star*, McKenzie-Dempsey profile, April 8, 1968.
14. Ibid.
15. *New Yorker*, op. cit., p. 39.

16. Ibid.
17. Interview with author.
18. *Toronto Star*, op. cit.
19. Interview with author.
20. *Toronto Star*, op. cit.
21. Ibid.
22. P. E. Trudeau, "The Ascetic in a Canoe", in P. E. Trudeau et al., *Wilderness Canada* (Toronto: Clarke, Irwin, 1970).
23. *Toronto Star*, op. cit.
24. Ibid.
25. Ibid.

CHAPTER FIVE

1. *New Yorker*, Iglauer profile, July 5, 1969.
2. *Toronto Star*, McKenzie-Dempsey profile, April 8, 1968.
3. Martin Sullivan, *Mandate '68* (Toronto: Doubleday, 1968), p. 362.
4. *Toronto Star*, op. cit.
5. *Weekend* Magazine, Sept. 13, 1975, p. 18.
6. *New Yorker*, op. cit., p. 41.
7. Ibid.
8. *Toronto Star*, op. cit.
9. Interview with author.
10. *Toronto Star*, op. cit.
11. Ibid.
12. Trudeau, "The Ascetic in a Canoe", op. cit.
13. *Le Devoir*, May 2, 1949.
14. *Toronto Star*, op. cit.
15. Sullivan, *Mandate '68*, p. 35.
16. *New Yorker*, op. cit., p. 44.
17. P. E. Trudeau, *Réponses* (Montreal: Les Editions du Jour, 1968), p. 20.
18. P. E. Trudeau, *Cité Libre*, June 1950, p. 21.
19. *New Yorker*, op. cit., p. 44.
20. Quoted in P. E. Trudeau, ed., *The Asbestos Strike* (Toronto: James Lewis & Samuel, 1974), p. 9.
21. Quoted in Camille Laurin, "Autorité et personnalité au Canada français", in *Ma Traversée du Québec* (Montreal: Editions du Jour, 1970), p. 21.

22. Quoted in Herbert F. Quinn, *The Union Nationale* (Toronto: University of Toronto Press, 1963), pp. 117-18.
23. Quoted in P. E. Trudeau, *Les Cheminements de la politique* (Montreal: Les Editions du Jour, 1970), p. 57.
24. Trudeau, *Les Cheminements de la politique*, p. 22.
25. Ibid., p. 29.
26. Trudeau, *Cité Libre*, June 1950.
27. Trudeau, *Cité Libre*, December 1952.
28. P. E. Trudeau, *Federalism and the French Canadians* (Toronto: Macmillan of Canada, 1968), p. 120.
29. Trudeau, *Cité Libre*, October 1958.
30. Trudeau, *Cité Libre*, March 1961.
31. Trudeau, *Federalism and the French Canadians*, p. 167.
32. Ibid., p. 170.
33. *New Yorker*, op. cit., pp. 44-5.

CHAPTER SIX
1. Sullivan, *Mandate '68*, p. 275.
2. P. E. Trudeau and Gérard Pelletier, *Cité Libre*, October 1965.
3. Trudeau, *Cité Libre*, April 1963.
4. *The Gazette*, Montreal, Oct. 23, 1965.
5. *Weekend* Magazine, Nov. 13, 1966.
6. Quoted by Peter Newman, *Ottawa Journal*, April 26, 1967.
7. *Ottawa Journal*, June 29, 1967.
8. *Globe and Mail*, Sept. 5, 1967.
9. Quoted in *Globe and Mail*, Feb. 12, 1968.
10. *Globe and Mail*, Feb. 17, 1968.
11. Interview with Patrick Watson, May 25, 1968, PMO transcript.
12. *La Presse*, April 4, 1968.
13. Speech to Kitchener, Ont., Chamber of Commerce, May 21, 1968, PMO transcript.
14. Interview on radio station CKNX, Wingham, Ont., May 21, 1968, PMO transcript.
15. *Globe and Mail*, May 22, 1968.
16. Ottawa *Citizen*, April 24, 1968.
17. Ottawa *Citizen*, June 7, 1968.
18. *Montreal Star*, March 7, 1968.
19. Ibid., May 9, 1968.
20. Ibid.

21. Interview on radio station CKNX, Wingham, Ont., May 21, 1968, PMO transcript.
22. Ibid.
23. *Montreal Star*, Feb. 28, 1968.
24. Ottawa *Citizen*, June 11, 1968.
25. Interview with Patrick Watson, May 25, 1968, PMO transcript.
26. CKNX interview, May 21, 1968, PMO transcript.
27. Trudeau, *Cité Libre*, April 1963.
28. *Montreal Star*, June 18, 1968.
29. *Ottawa Journal*, June 15, 1968.
30. *New York Times*, March 7, 1954, VI, p. 12.

CHAPTER SEVEN

1. Interview with author for *The Gazette*, June 20, 1974, PMO transcript.
2. Speech to Richelieu Club, Montreal, April 2, 1968.
3. Trudeau, *Les Cheminements de la politique*, p. 66.
4. Trudeau, *Federalism and the French Canadians*, p. 209.
5. Ibid., p. 203.
6. Ibid., p. xxi.
7. Remarks in Winnipeg, May 23, 1968, quoted in Brian Shaw, *The Gospel According to Saint Pierre* (Richmond Hill, Ont.: Simon and Schuster Pocket Books, 1969), p. 32.
8. Trudeau, *Les Cheminements de la politique*, p. 28.
9. Ibid., p. 35.
10. Ibid., p. 55.
11. Ibid., p. 35.
12. P. E. Trudeau, *Cité Libre*, February 1951.
13. Ibid.
14. Trudeau, *Les Cheminements de la politique*, pp. 41, 42.
15. Ibid., p. 40.
16. Ibid., p. 120.
17. BBC interview with Robert Mackenzie, Dec. 16, 1968, PMO transcript.
18. CTV interview with Charles Templeton, Dec. 18, 1968, PMO transcript.
19. Interview with James Reston, Dec. 21, 1971, PMO transcript.
20. Trudeau, *Les Cheminements de la politique*, p. 141.

21. CTV interview with Patrick Watson and Gloria Steinem, May 12, 1970, CTV transcript.
22. Interview on New Zealand Broadcast Commission TV program "Gallery", May 14, 1970, PMO transcript.
23. Trudeau, *Les Cheminements de la politique*, p. 141.
24. Ibid., p. 17.
25. Trudeau, *Federalism and the French Canadians*, p. 11.
26. Trudeau, *Les Cheminements de la politique*, p. 119.
27. P. E. Trudeau, "Economic Rights", *McGill Law Review*, Vol. 8, No. 2, June 1962.
28. Trudeau, *Federalism and the French Canadians*, p. 169.
29. Ibid., p. 157.
30. Ibid., p. 161.
31. Ibid.
32. Ibid., p. 163.
33. Ibid., p. 158.
34. Ibid., p. 179.
35. Trudeau, *Cité Libre*, February 1951.
36. Trudeau, *Cité Libre*, June 1950.
37. Trudeau, *Cité Libre*, February 1951.
38. Trudeau, *Federalism and the French Canadians*, p. 35.
39. Trudeau, *Cité Libre*, February 1951.
40. Trudeau, *Federalism and the French Canadians*, p. 35.
41. Trudeau, "Economic Rights", June 1962.
42. Trudeau, *Federalism and the French Canadians*, p. 25.
43. Trudeau, "Economic Rights".
44. Ibid.
45. Trudeau, *Federalism and the French Canadians*, pp. 25-6.
46. Ibid., p. 25.
47. Ibid.
48. Ibid., pp. 28-9.
49. Ibid., p. 29.
50. Ibid., p. xxiii.
51. *Toronto Star*, April 5, 1968.
52. Interview with Alan Grossman, *Time* magazine, Nov. 14, 1968, PMO transcript.
53. Ibid.

54. Interview with J. Walz, *New York Times,* Nov. 22, 1968, PMO transcript.
55. BBC interview with Robert Mackenzie, Dec. 16, 1968, PMO transcript.

CHAPTER EIGHT

1. Interview with Peter Newman, *Toronto Star,* August 7, 1969, PMO transcript.
2. Interview with J. Walz, *New York Times,* Nov. 22, 1968, PMO transcript.
3. Interview with Gerald Clark, *Montreal Star,* Dec. 1, 1969, PMO transcript.
4. CBC-TV interview with Peter Desbarats, "Weekend", Jan. 9, 1972, PMO transcript.

CHAPTER NINE

1. CTV interview, "w5", Dec. 21, 1973, CTV transcript.
2. CTV interview with Charles Templeton, Dec. 18, 1968, PMO transcript.
3. *Toronto Star,* April 27, 1968.
4. CTV interview with Charles Templeton, Dec. 18, 1968, PMO transcript.
5. Interview with J. Walz, *New York Times,* Nov. 22, 1968, PMO transcript.
6. Interview with Gerald Clark, *Montreal Star,* Dec. 1, 1969, PMO transcript.
7. Interview with three European journalists, February 21, 1975, PMO transcript.
8. Interview with Dick Duncan, *Time* magazine, Feb. 20, 1970, PMO transcript.
9. P. E. Trudeau, *Cité Libre,* December 1961.
10. Speech at University of Alberta, Edmonton, May 13, 1968, PMO transcript.

CHAPTER TEN

1. Interview with author for *The Gazette,* June 20, 1974, PMO transcript.

2. Interview with group of foreign journalists, August 9, 1973, PMO transcript.

CHAPTER ELEVEN
1. Trudeau, *Federalism and the French Canadians*, p. xxii.

CHAPTER TWELVE
1. CBC-TV interview, "Twenty Million Questions", Sept. 17, 1968, PMO transcript.
2. CBC-TV interview with Ron Collister and Norman Depoe, Jan. 1, 1969, PMO transcript.
3. Interview with *Chatelaine* magazine, March 13, 1969, PMO transcript.
4. Réseau TVA television interview, broadcast May 6, 1977.
5. CTV interview, Dec. 30, 1969, CTV transcript.
6. Interview with Claude Lemelin of *Le Devoir*, Sept. 21, 1973, PMO transcript.
7. CTV interview, "W5", June 28, 1970, CTV transcript.
8. Walter Stewart, *Shrug: Trudeau in Power* (Toronto: New Press, 1971), pp. 223, 228.
9. Remarks in Ottawa West, Sept. 8, 1972, PMO transcript.
10. Remarks at meeting of Ontario Liberal candidates, Toronto, Sept. 13, 1972, PMO transcript.
11. Remarks at Hopedale Shopping Mall, Oakville, Ont., Oct. 7, 1972, PMO transcript.
12. *Time* Canada, Oct. 30, 1972, p. 5.

CHAPTER THIRTEEN
1. CBC-TV interview with Ron Collister and Norman Depoe, Jan. 1, 1969, PMO transcript.
2. CTV interview with Bruce Phillips and Carole Taylor, Dec. 20, 1972, CTV transcript.
3. *The Gazette*, Nov. 4, 1972.
4. CBC-TV interview with Patrick Watson, "Some Honourable Members", Dec. 18, 1973, CBC transcript.
5. *The Gazette*, April 10, 1973.
6. Interview on CBC-TV, "Weekend", Feb. 11, 1973.

7. Interview with William C. Heine, *London Free Press*, Feb. 5, 1973, PMO transcript.

8. Interview with Claude Lemelin of *Le Devoir*, Sept. 21, 1973, PMO transcript.

9. CBC-TV interview, "Some Honourable Members", Dec. 18, 1973, CBC transcript.

CHAPTER FOURTEEN

1. Interview on CHCH-TV, Hamilton, March 24, 1972, PMO transcript.

2. Remarks on CFRB radio program "Let's Discuss It", Toronto, Oct. 1, 1972, PMO transcript.

3. CFTO-TV interview, Toronto, Dec. 12, 1975, PMO transcript.

CHAPTER FIFTEEN

1. CTV interview, "W5", Dec. 21, 1973, CTV transcript.

2. Trudeau, *Federalism and the French Canadians*, p. 197.

3. Ibid., p. 36.

4. Ibid., p. 47.

5. Ibid., p. 31.

6. Ibid., p. 47.

7. Ottawa *Citizen*, Jan. 24, 1968.

8. Speech at Quebec Liberal Convention, Jan. 28, 1968, reported in Ottawa *Citizen*, Jan. 29, 1968.

9. Press Conference, Nov. 5, 1970, quoted in John Saywell, *Quebec 1970: A Documentary Narrative* (Toronto: University of Toronto Press, 1971), p. 143.

10. CTV interview with Charles Templeton, Dec. 30, 1969, CTV transcript.

11. CBC-TV interview, "Format 30", Oct. 20, 1969, PMO transcript.

12. Interview with Fraser Kelly and Peter Thomson, April 18, 1969, PMO transcript.

13. Radio-Canada interview, July 9, 1976, PMO transcript.

CHAPTER SIXTEEN

1. Daniel Bell, *The Cultural Contradictions of Capitalism* (New York: Basic Books, 1976), p. 245.

Selected Bibliography

BY PIERRE TRUDEAU

Federalism and the French Canadians. Toronto: Macmillan of Canada, 1968.

Les Cheminements de la politique. Montreal: Les Editions du Jour, 1970.

Réponses de Pierre Elliott Trudeau. Montreal: Les Editions du Jour, 1967.

The Asbestos Strike (Trudeau, ed.). Toronto: James Lewis & Samuel, 1974. (Translation of *La Grève de l'amiante*, published in 1956.)

"Economic Rights." *McGill Law Review*, June 1962.

Essays in *Cité Libre*, June 1950 to April-May 1966.

TRUDEAU QUOTATIONS

Conversation with Canadians. Toronto: University of Toronto Press, 1972.

Brian Shaw, ed. *The Gospel According to St. Pierre*. Richmond Hill, Ont.: Simon and Schuster, 1969.

BOOKS ABOUT TRUDEAU

Stewart, Walter, *Shrug: Trudeau in Power*. Toronto: New Press, 1971.

Sullivan, Martin, *Mandate '68*. Toronto: Doubleday, 1968.

Thordarson, Bruce, *Trudeau and Foreign Policy: A Study in Decision-Making*. Toronto: Oxford University Press, 1972.

Westell, Anthony, *Paradox: Trudeau as Prime Minister*. Scarborough, Ont.: Prentice-Hall, 1972.

365

Wilson, W. A., *The Trudeau Question*. Montreal: Montreal Star–PaperJacks, 1972.

Index

Cohen, Maxwell, 8-9
Collège Jean de Brébeuf, 36-7, 53-4, 55, 56-8, 67
Commons, House of, 13-16, 20, 116, 239-41, 242, 243, 270, 274-5, 278, 289. *See also* Parliament
Commonwealth prime ministers' conferences, 242, 280
Company of Young Canadians, 306
Confederation of National Trade Unions, 89, 328
Confédération des Travailleurs Catholiques du Canada (CTCC), 73, 74, 75, 89
conscription, 62-3, 74
Conservative Party, 89, 90, 97, 113, 166, 167, 256, 265, 267, 268, 274, 277, 279, 283, 284, 285, 286, 287, 291, 305, 308, 309, 346. *See also individual leaders*
constitution (Canada), 67, 93-4, 94-5, 100, 179, 180, 313-14, 315, 316, 319, 320, 321, 343
Co-operative Commonwealth Federation (CCF), 82
Coutts, Jim, 5, 6, 7, 9-10, 14, 142, 150, 155, 216, 232, 233
Créditiste party. *See* Ralliement des Créditistes
Criminal Code, 92, 95, 96, 97, 98, 128, 243, 254
Cross, James, 323-5, 329
Cuba, 185

Davey, Jim, 100, 150, 253, 261, 270
Davey, Keith, 6, 223-4, 225, 232-3, 271, 275, 281, 283-4, 305
democracy, 123-8, 132-5, 143
democracy (Quebec), 75, 77-8, 79, 80-1, 88, 146, 323, 325, 329-30, 332, 333
Dempster, Dave, 1
Department of Regional Economic Expansion (DREE), 141, 243, 254, 275, 342, 353
Desbiens, Jean-Paul (Frère Untel), 140
de Tocqueville, 57, 119, 136
Devoir, Le, 63, 73, 227, 228, 326, 328, 335
Diefenbaker, John, 24, 89, 97, 112, 146, 154, 240, 246, 256, 279, 283, 287, 346
Divorce Bill, 92, 95, 96, 97, 98, 128

Douglas, T. C. (Tommy), 25
Drapeau, Jean, 63, 331
Drury, C. M. (Bud), 170, 188, 291, 297, 304, 342
Duplessis, Maurice, 72, 73, 76, 77-8, 79, 80, 81, 83, 263, 339

Economic Council of Canada, 247
Economic Policy committee, 160
economy and economic policy, 14, 15-16, 133-5, 139, 141, 181-2, 183, 184, 185, 247-51, 254, 255, 260, 262, 264, 269, 275, 280, 284-5, 289, 293, 294-304, 305, 306, 349, 350, 351-3, 354, 355
elections, federal: (1958) 287; (1962) 279; (1963) 88-9; (1965) 89-91; (1968) 23, 24, 25, 27, 106-17, 122, 138, 162, 173, 235, 236-7, 239, 241, 252, 260, 261, 262, 265, 271, 278, 286, 288; (1972) 24, 25, 108, 112, 139, 141, 149, 155, 162, 182, 230, 256, 257-65, 267-70, 271, 276, 277, 279, 281, 286, 287, 290, 294-5, 334; (1974) 24, 122, 138, 167, 205, 224, 232, 281, 282-6, 287, 288, 290, 291, 293, 294, 295, 296, 302, 305
Elliott, George, 259
Elliott, Mr. (grandfather), 49-50
Erickson, Arthur, 3
Europe, 32, 54, 66, 67, 68, 69, 70, 162, 184, 243, 292
European Economic Community, 142, 185, 292, 305, 353
Expo 67, 23, 96
External Affairs and Defence committee, 160

Fairbairn, Joyce, 12-13, 17
Family Allowance, 247
Faribault, Marcel, 25
Fascism, 57, 146
Favreau, Guy, 89
federalism, 57, 131-3, 313, 314, 315, 322, 334, 336, 336-8, 341, 342-3, 346
federal-provincial relations, 94, 98, 100, 159, 179, 180, 181, 320, 321
Federal-Provincial Relations committee, 10, 160, 161, 171
Food Prices Review Board, 292
Foreign Investment Review Act, 281
Foreign Investment Review Agency, 185